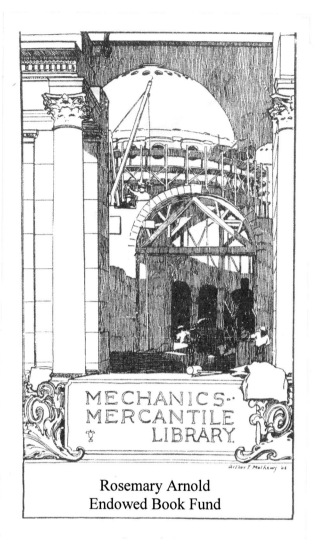

MECHANICS-
MERCANTILE
LIBRARY.

Rosemary Arnold
Endowed Book Fund

D1548819

Keep the Wretches in Order

KEEP THE WRETCHES IN ORDER

America's Biggest Mass Trial, the Rise of the
Justice Department, and the Fall of the IWW

DEAN A. STRANG

Mechanics' Institute Library
57 Post Street
San Francisco, CA 94104
(415) 393-0101
www.milibrary.org

The University of Wisconsin Press

The University of Wisconsin Press
1930 Monroe Street, 3rd Floor
Madison, Wisconsin 53711-2059
uwpress.wisc.edu

Gray's Inn House, 127 Clerkenwell Road
London EC1R 5DB, United Kingdom
eurospanbookstore.com

Copyright © 2019
The Board of Regents of the University of Wisconsin System
All rights reserved. Except in the case of brief quotations embedded in critical articles and reviews, no part of this publication may be reproduced, stored in a retrieval system, transmitted in any format or by any means—digital, electronic, mechanical, photocopying, recording, or otherwise—or conveyed via the Internet or a website without written permission of the University of Wisconsin Press. Rights inquiries should be directed to rights@uwpress.wisc.edu.

Printed in the United States of America

This book may be available in a digital edition.

Library of Congress Cataloging-in-Publication Data

Names: Strang, Dean A., author.
Title: Keep the wretches in order: America's biggest mass trial, the rise of the Justice Department, and the fall of the IWW / Dean A. Strang.
Description: Madison, Wisconsin: The University of Wisconsin Press, [2019]
| Includes bibliographical references and index.
Identifiers: LCCN 2018045778 | ISBN 9780299323301 (cloth: alk. paper)
Subjects: LCSH: Industrial Workers of the World—Trials, litigation, etc.
| United States. Department of Justice—History.
| Trials (Espionage)—Illinois—Chicago.
Classification: LCC KF224.I53 S77 2019 | DDC 345.73/0231—dc23
LC record available at https://lccn.loc.gov/2018045778

"Land of Hope and Dreams" by Bruce Springsteen. Copyright © 2000 Bruce Springsteen (Global Music Rights). Reprinted by permission. International copyright secured. All rights reserved.

345.7302
S816

SEP 0 5 2019

In memory of

Stanley I. Kutler

(August 10, 1934–April 7, 2015)

Contents

Contents

Foreword

Nancy Gertner

You would never have imagined that Dean Strang was a careful scholar of legal history from watching the account of his representation of Steven Avery, whose murder trial was chronicled in the Netflix documentary *Making a Murderer*. Rather, you would have thought that he was an exceptional criminal defense lawyer, zealous, meticulous and creative, in the face of extraordinary odds and pressures. He surely is all that, but as this book reflects, he is much more. Strang takes his advocate's eyes and trains them on the prosecution of members of the Industrial Workers of the World (or IWW) nearly a hundred years ago. The result is not only a compelling and engaging narrative of a trial but (what is more important) a critical analysis of the criminal justice system then and, by extension, today. The story of that prosecution, with its excesses, biases, and unfair and even unconstitutional distortions, like great nonfiction, helps us understand twenty-first-century problems. This book reflects the best of the lawyer as writer, filtering past events through present-day lenses.

I met Dean Strang nearly three years ago at a conference in Kansas City, Missouri. Although I had retired as a federal judge, having served on the U.S. District Court in Massachusetts for seventeen years, I wanted to meet him—just as a fan. I had binge-watched *Making a Murderer* and was intrigued. The documentary gave the viewer a bird's-eye view of Dean's advocacy (and that of his cocounsel, Jerry Buting) at its best, on all levels— in his preparation; in his humane dealings with the client and the family; in his professional interactions with the press, the prosecutor, and the judge; and in his legal trial advocacy. I went up to him, and like a giggling teenager, I said, "You are Dean Strang and I just want to meet you." (I wonder now whether, if I had had a paper and pen, I would have asked for an autograph. I still might.) "I am . . . ," I said, and Dean cut me off. "I know who you are. I have heard so much about you. I wanted to meet you!" After he did his presentation and I did mine, we met in the lobby of the hotel and talked until he was in danger of missing his plane home. That's when I began to understand the layers of the man. When he told me that he was working on a book recounting a historical prosecution, the federal government's prosecution of the IWW, and that he had already written another account of a historical trial, *Worse than the Devil: Anarchists, Clarence Darrow, and Justice in a Time of Terror*, I was not surprised. I was intrigued.

The story of the prosecution of IWW members had a special resonance for me. Before I became a judge, I was a criminal defense and civil rights lawyer. I had represented anti–Vietnam War dissidents who were accused of crimes (from murder to false statements), as well as those who sued the government claiming illegal surveillance or searches. I had been a law clerk for the Seventh Circuit, where the appeal of the IWW convictions had been heard. During my clerkship, 1971–72, the Court decided appeals from those convicted in the Chicago conspiracy case ("the Chicago Eight"). Eight antiwar activists were prosecuted in federal court for their role in violent demonstrations at the August 1968 Democratic National Convention, a case that raised many of the issues in the IWW prosecution fifty years before. And on the bench, I witnessed the extraordinary pressures on prosecutors to bring charges against suspected terrorists after September 11, 2001, using some of the same statutes and theories the prosecutors had used in the case against the IWW.

Like any good storyteller, Strang builds from the story of some of the individuals swept up in the prosecution to the story of the trial. He describes their compelling personal histories, the arc of their politics, and how they came to be active in the IWW. While there was incendiary rhetoric from some of them on occasion, for the most part they were labor activists. Frank Little was the most militant. Edwin Doree was a believer in unions as advocates for working men and women—an idealist, not an ideologue; "Big Bill" Haywood veered from "a firebrand's rancorous rhetoric to a national figure's more tempered talk." Both Doree and Haywood, along with many more, would be prosecuted and imprisoned after their conviction. Frank Little was even less lucky.

The IWW reached greatest prominence just as the United States entered World War I. Animus toward labor in general, and the IWW in particular, crystallized at that time. IWW members were overwhelmingly opposed to the war. They saw only corporate profiteering, stagnant wages, and the wholesale deaths of working-class soldiers. The government and industries supporting the war viewed any strikes, however justified, as treasonous because they undermined the war effort. After the April 2017 declaration of war, the government ostensibly had a solution: under the Espionage Act of 1917, work stoppages, even dissenting views about the war, were arguably no longer just disloyal—they were possibly criminal, or at least that is how the attorney general and his prosecutors saw it.[1] Robust constitutional protections may well be an antidote to an overzealous government pressured in wartime to stifle fair dissent, but in 1917, many of those constitutional structures and doctrine were lacking.

Here Strang weaves in the story of the birth and growth of the U.S. Department of Justice, whose crowning achievement at that time was the prosecution of the IWW. Industry—including those most affected by the IWW's activities—had extraordinary influence over the criminal justice system, largely because of the weakness of an underresourced and underfunded Department of Justice. The transition to a professional centralized corps of lawyers "did not come quickly or evenly."

Still, the DOJ sought to weaponize the federal criminal justice system to eliminate an enemy at the behest of "corporate interests" who expressly petitioned the federal government for help. What is especially compelling in Strang's account is not just *that* it happened, but *how*, and how easily those missteps might be repeated. Just a few examples follow.

The Size of the Case

The 1917 indictment originally named 166 defendants, the largest in the history of civilian trials; by the end of the case it was "down" to 97. An indictment of that size was already a challenge to a system intended to deliver individualized justice. (The largest case I ever tried had thirty defendants in it.) There were only four lawyers representing the entire group: they were in no position to deliver meaningful, let alone conflict-free, advocacy. The prosecution could barely keep track of who was who. While the IWW itself was not on trial, only the individuals named, too often the two were indistinguishable.

The Theory

The indictment was breathtakingly overbroad, charging conspiracy to violate the Espionage Act and sweeping within it operational leaders and board members of the IWW, along with writers, editors, stump speakers, and even poets and songwriters. It included, for example, Ray Fanning of Tennessee, who in the first six months of 1917 had written four letters to IWW officers reflecting his opposition to the war and the draft. One of the "overt acts," defined as the actions designed to carry out the conspiracy's goals, should have been protected speech—the act of mailing *Solidarity*, the IWW newspaper. Conspiracy law at that time (and to a degree this is still true) enabled the prosecution of those whose crime was to plan a crime with others or belong to an organization that did. And where the "crime" was opposition to the draft, or encouraging strikes, the indictment cut a wide swath. As Strang writes, "It would have covered the quiet Quaker in her meeting house, the mother of draft-age sons who were needed on the farm, the aging veteran who, reliving the horrors he had seen, had come to the hard conclusion that spilling blood never in the end is a solution." All were traitors, giving aid to the enemy even if that "aid" was "intangible, unusable, and unknown to the enemy."

The Judge

It would have taken an especially robust criminal justice system to confront these excesses and deliver justice. The system in 1917—and especially the judge—was not remotely up to the task. The judge met with the federal prosecutor, even before the indictment; the government referred to the judge as its "main man," willing to do just about anything it asked. And that bias was carefully disguised during the trial: in Strang's view, "fostering the perception of fairness is the best form of courtroom control a judge ever has," and Judge Landis managed this "adroitly." The problem was "that a perception of fairness" was all there was; the reality was something quite different.

The Tactics

The case began with the execution of search warrants across the country, without probable cause or a particularized description of what the officers were permitted to seize. It was in effect political theater, designed to "dispirit, disorient, and disable the enemy IWW." Strang's description of those searches reflects modern investigative and prosecutorial tactics as well.

> The execution of a search warrant often is tactical and even theatrical: swarms of armed officers arrive at a home before the sun peeks into the eastern sky; doors and jambs are splintered with a loud crash by battering rams; to demonstrate that the target's privacy and sense of security mean nothing, drawers are flung onto floors, mail is torn open, and mattresses are overturned. The terrifying effect is not just intended but intended to last; intended to sap the will to resist by convincing the target that resistance will be futile.

The Defense

It is hard to imagine a more difficult challenge for a defense lawyer than this, as any lawyer representing a political group can attest. The defendants wanted a political trial, raising the broader issues for which the IWW stood. George Vanderveer wanted a "lawyerly" one. He surely had the legal ammunition—challenges to the breadth of the indictment and whether it even charged a crime at all; challenges to the searches; challenges to the evidence, based on the argument that individual defendants had committed no actual crimes but rather had in fact expressed opinions to which they had a perfectly legal right. Even more significant, most of their statements had been made before the statute under which they were indicted, the Espionage Act, had been passed. But would any of this matter?

The Appeal

Perhaps most compelling of all is Strang's portrait of the Seventh Circuit's review of the case. Appellate review, in which a reviewing court consisting of three judges looks at a case afresh, is intended as a means of scrutinizing the record for trial and constitutional errors in a setting that is removed from the pressures of a trial. In theory, it is the system's safety valve, a critical backstop for a defendant wrongly convicted. While many claims were raised in the case, two were key: "How could the government charge and convict the defendants with documents it obtained and held only by violating the Fourth Amendment?" And the second claim raised First Amendment issues: "[W]hat had the defendants done wrong? Specifically, what crimes had they agreed to commit, simply by opposing a war vociferously and crudely?"

Strang's criticism of the Seventh Circuit's decision in the end is acerbic—and fully justified. It was part of a "judicial tradition," he writes, of "dishonesty by fantasy," a court ruling that ignored the real-world context of its decision—who these men were and their objective situation. It suggested that these men would have had the resources to figure out which documents were where, to hire lawyers in each jurisdiction, and to manage all of this in the twenty-three days between the raids and the indictment, when some were in jail. It suggested, in short, that they had the resources of a Rockefeller and the wisdom of Solomon.

Strang trains his criticism of "dishonesty by fantasy" not just on the Seventh Circuit in the IWW case but in explaining that concept, on courts today, and he offers this example. Modern courts will claim that a police interrogation was voluntary, or that the police can ignore with impunity the defendant's request for a lawyer because the defendant just didn't use the right words, by indulging in a fantasy of what a reasonable, articulate adult might well have said. Or better yet, a court might find that the police officer did not understand what the accused meant—when it is clear that he did.

The example resonates particularly with the Steven Avery case, which *Making a Murderer* chronicled. Brendan Dassey, Avery's nephew, was sentenced to life in prison based on his confession to having been an accessory to Avery's crime. Dassey, sixteen years old at the time, with significant intellectual and social limitations, confessed after a lengthy interrogation. Still the state court found that there was no constitutional error; the Seventh Circuit agreed, on technical grounds. To the Seventh Circuit majority, the state court's findings were not unreasonable in the way that they applied the appropriate Supreme Court precedent. The dissent, though it obviously did not use Dean's phrase "dishonesty by fantasy," effectively said the same thing. The majority "turn[ed] a blind eye to [the interrogation's] glaring faults." This interrogation was, to all intents and purposes, a "ghoulish game of '20 Questions' in which Brendan Dassey guessed over and over again before he landed on the story the police wanted."[2]

The Legacy

The DOJ has evolved over the intervening century, but I know firsthand that some of the same political pressures Strang describes remained and still remain today. As Attorney General Robert H. Jackson warned federal prosecutors in 1940, "With the law books filled with a great assortment of crimes, a prosecutor stands a fair chance of finding at least a technical violation of some act on the part of almost anyone. In such a case, it is not a question of discovering the commission of a crime and then looking for the man who has committed it, it is a question of picking the man and then searching the law books . . . to pin some offense on him."

Writer and philosopher George Santayana said it best: "Those who cannot remember the past are condemned to repeat it." This book—and its lawyer-storyteller—goes a long way toward helping us vividly re-create that past and, importantly, try to avoid some of its pitfalls.

———

Nancy Gertner served as a United States District Court Judge in the District of Massachusetts from 1994 until 2011, when she retired to teach at Harvard Law School. She teaches criminal law, procedure, sentencing and law and neuroscience. Her autobiography—detailing her life as a criminal defense and civil rights lawyer before she became a judge—is *In Defense of Women: Memoirs of an Unrepentant Advocate* (2011). A judicial memoir about sentencing in an unjust system, *Incomplete Sentences*, is forthcoming (2019).

Preface

This is the first legal history of the four IWW cases of 1917–19, and of the 1918 Chicago mass trial in particular. But several labor historians have considered these trials in the context of the labor movement's development (or of the IWW's arc specifically) in the early twentieth century. Some dedicate just a few paragraphs to the IWW trials. Others devote several pages or more. To my mind, the fullest and most reliable accounts are Melvyn Dubofsky's *We Shall Be All: A History of the Industrial Workers of the World*, in both original and later abridged forms, and *"Big Bill" Haywood*. Others are valuable also.

Understandably, the labor histories leave a gap for a historical examination from a legal perspective. The Chicago federal trial at the core of this book was by far the largest criminal trial, as measured by the number of defendants, that any American civilian court ever has attempted. That matters, because a trial of about one hundred people inescapably is different in important ways than the typical trial of one or two. Every actor in a trial—from judge to lawyers to courthouse staff to investigating law enforcement officers to the jury—of course is human and shares natural human limitations. For example, twelve jurors together might understand and master one or two days of testimony and ten or twenty exhibits relating to one defendant whose liberty is at stake. But can the same twelve people understand and master three-plus months of testimony and more than six hundred exhibits relating to one hundred defendants? Can they isolate what the prosecution proved against only three scattered defendants, for example, among eight dozen or more? Can they recognize what was *not* proven against another three (or twenty-three) scattered defendants? Almost surely not.

Yet here we see such a trial. The judge had no idea even of the names of most of the men on trial, seated on rows of bleachers before him. The prosecutors did not recognize their faces or know much about them. One small team of defense lawyers represented all of them without any evident regard for the unavoidable conflict of individual interests. We see a trial that well exceeded the human capacities of the people and institutions that, together, claim to operate collaboratively as a system of justice.

And, without getting ahead of the story that follows, we see a trial in which the judge and agents of the U.S. Department of Justice acted in ways that must trouble anyone who would like to presume the good faith, objectivity, and fair-mindedness of judges and prosecutors. We see an appellate court that acted with intellectual dishonesty. Forget about any broader or more complex conception of justice. Here, we see almost no actor who displayed the most basic commitment to rendering justice at an individual level by acknowledging the full humanity of every person accused or, for that matter, of every person who may have been a victim. In all, the Chicago IWW trial, and the two IWW trials that went to verdicts after it, at least arguably reveal as idle vanity the claims of lawyers and judges that they administered justice.

I hope, therefore, that we see much in this past episode in the nation's courts that we agree should not be repeated. We might agree to ask this, too: if it happened yesterday in a trial of one hundred, could it happen today or tomorrow in a trial of just fifty? Of ten? Of one? My own experience convinces me that it can and does. So I have learned. These lessons prompted this book.

A reader may not draw the same lessons from this book. It may be impossible for any book, or for that matter any person, to teach anything. But that leaves the question of learning. My own view is that teaching is impossible; it is only learning that is altogether possible. I admit no paradox in the fact that many of my mentors have been called, in common parlance, teachers. People like Stanley I. Kutler, David A. Martin, Thelma Nehring, Linus Heydon, and others all went by the title professor or teacher. But they taught me nothing. (Indeed, I never took a formal class from Stanley, to whom I dedicate this book.) What they all did was learn well themselves, care deeply about what they learned, and then inspire me and many others to take the opportunity to learn from them.

My hope for this book, then, is that it might offer readers the opportunity and inspiration to learn something about law itself and about the legal institutions that combine and mesh, well or poorly, as a system. If by learning about our past we see our present more clearly, that should help us imagine a future in which we can be better—a future, even, in which we are more just.

Acknowledgments

An author is to blame for a book, but not alone to credit. At least, that is true here. Sara Seo, Brad Snyder, Dennis Conta, and Deborah Conta read the entire manuscript. Their ideas made the book much better.

Many others encouraged me during the five years that I spent on this project, with whatever focus my other work allowed. Chuck Curtis challenged and encouraged me with the heart and head of a historian. Jim Shellow, my most demanding and devoted mentor, urged me on and inspired me in ways only he can. James Boyd White and Sarah Marshall gave freely of their time and intellect, reading and commenting on chapters that caused me anxiety. Lloyd Gardner provided important assurance. Gwen Walker, my editor at the University of Wisconsin Press, is a steady guide and advocate for improvement.

The University of Limerick School of Law gave me the chance to finish the manuscript efficiently, with a visiting fellowship. I am indebted especially to Paul McCutcheon and to Shane Kilcommins, head of the law school, and to the entire vibrant law faculty.

My friend the Dublin barrister Michael Hourigan (still a son of Munster) has coaxed me to broaden and strengthen my grasp of legal history. Anne and Tom Reed have influenced me for more than thirty years in all things. Jerry Buting and I have shared much, and he continues to inspire me, as does the writer Earl Swift.

My sister and her husband, Kristin and Gary Geipel, and their three adult children—Molly, Ethan, and Audrey—remain unfailingly supportive. And my family at work—John, Rachel, and Patrick Bradley—have stretched and helped selflessly when I was absent or distracted.

Baine Alexander, Steve Glynn, Nancy Joseph, Lynn Adelman, and Steve Hurley all offered the support of friendship and spirited, sharp observation. My friends of longest standing, Sheila Reynolds and Bob Chang, I hope understand best how much I rely on them.

I also remember the gentle J. Gordon Hylton, who had this manuscript under review when he died.

In research, I had the frequent help of archivists at the Walter P. Reuther Library at Wayne State University. I also had assistance from the staff at the University of Michigan's Joseph A. Labadie Collection, the Chicago History Museum, the Wisconsin Historical Society archives, and the National Archives.

Throughout, the family of Stanley Kutler, the friend and historian to whose memory I dedicate this book, has been giving and kind in allowing me to attach the name of their late husband and father to this book. Stanley would have done this better.

Last and most, I acknowledge my wife and coconspirator, Jannea Wood. During more than two years of exceptional travel for other reasons, she also tolerated graciously my many research trips and weekends spent writing this book, around the edges of my day job and our lives. Giving another person your time can be an act of love; letting another take essential time away is more, a deep commitment to love for the long run.

So yes, the weaknesses of this book are mine. Whatever strengths it has I owe to these people, who lent theirs.

Part I

Fear is the only force that will keep the wretches in order.

Assistant Attorney General William C. Fitts,
on the IWW in summer 1917

Part I

1

The Railroad Trestle

August 1917 did not begin or end well for Frank H. Little in Montana. June and July had been hard. August, or what there was of it, would be worse.

In April, President Woodrow Wilson had led the nation into the European war upon the declaration of a mostly compliant Congress. Since then, both Congress and the country had hurried to join the fight abroad without hindrance at home. The draft began in early June. Government orders for war matériel were filling corporate in-baskets profitably, as quickly as telegraph wires and post offices could deliver them. For the discordant notes heard above the hum, Congress had a solution, too. Under the Espionage Act, which took effect in mid-June, some dissent no longer was just disloyal: it was criminal.

Like many others in or supportive of the labor movement, Frank Little was a dissenter on the war. Indeed, he was the most vocal dissenter among the members of the General Executive Board of the Industrial Workers of the World, the IWW (also called the One Big Union), and he was among its most inflammatory public speakers. This clean-shaven, plain man with an open face and mouth askew claimed to be "one-half white, one-half Indian, and all IWW." In fact, he probably was all or mostly white. His father, a doctor, had moved the family from Missouri to the Oklahoma Territory when Frank was about fourteen. The young man later followed his older brother into mining, and then into the Western Federation of Miners.

By 1917, Frank Little probably was the best IWW organizer. He certainly was the most militant. His support for direct action to interfere with the draft and the war effort generally put him on the far edge of, and in conflict with, even the General Executive Board.

Men like Edwin Doree, the son of Swedish immigrants and in summer 1917 an earnest, hopeful believer in unions as advocates for working men and women, were more like most IWW organizers. He and his brother-in-law, Walter Nef, were both active East Coast members and IWW organizers who were stalwarts but idealists, not ideologues. They were less concerned with broader political causes than they were with bettering the lives of the men and women around them. Doree especially figures prominently in this story. Fate would deal with him, but not as immediately or as decisively as it would with Frank Little.

As July turned to August, Little lay in his underwear trying to sleep in a boarding house bed, which had been his since he had limped into Butte two weeks earlier. With a broken ankle, either from a beating by company toughs or from a car accident in June, he was uncomfortable almost always. The heat did not help.[1]

But the cheap bed in room 32 on the ground floor of Nora Byrne's lodging house was an improvement over his bitter recent circumstances. A miner by trade, Little had joined the Industrial Workers of the World not later than 1910 in Fresno, California, and had risen rapidly to its General Executive Board. The previous December, he had chaired the IWW's tenth annual convention. Just twelve years old in 1917, the IWW was growing rapidly from coast to coast. Perhaps to stoke fear, the government that year sometimes estimated IWW membership in the hundreds of thousands.[2]

That very July, Frank Little had been in Bisbee, Arizona, organizing copper and lead miners until the Phelps Dodge Corporation, the Anaconda Copper Mining Company, and other mine owners had seen enough of the IWW. Now, with open assistance from the local sheriff and railroads, and the hidden complicity of the U.S. Army, company hirelings herded over 1,200 miners and malcontents onto freight and cattle cars in one-hundred-plus degree heat and summarily "deported" them, with little water and no food, hundreds of miles east into remote New Mexico. Frank Little had left for Butte, Montana, just before the deportation. Others were not so lucky.

After hours, the train simply stopped in the New Mexico desert, then eventually reversed direction and squealed to a halt near an army camp prepared to pen the men in a stockade. The deportees survived because troops provided food and water while holding them for questioning and sorting. Return to Bisbee was unwise: the miners had noticed the new machine guns that sheriff's deputies and the companies' posse had acquired and mounted on cars and trucks to aid the deportation. Some of the kidnapped men decided they would fare better in old Mexico and crossed the border south to find work. Others made their way north.[3]

The gritty, booming mining town of Butte drew Frank Little because miners were striking there and the IWW was seeing real success in its recruiting efforts. Miners, many of them immigrants or native-born itinerants, slowly had grown angry over low wages, spending six days every week in the darkness and choking dust of tight tunnels a mile underground, and the constant danger of fire or collapsing rock. But the Butte mine owners long had succeeded in blocking union drives by limiting the "rustling card" necessary for mining work only to those who rejected all unions. Mine owners were enjoying a war boom. Miners were not.

Yet change was coming. It needed only a spark. On June 8, 1917, fire broke out in the Granite Mountain mine and spread to the adjacent Speculator mine in North Butte. Concrete bulkheads in the tunnels, supposedly designed to prevent trespassing, assured that 164 men would burn to death, or suffocate first if lucky.[4] Their charred bodies lay in piles at the bulkheads, some with fingers bloodied and shredded from trying to scratch through concrete slabs as the flames reached them in great whooshes up the tunnels that had become chimneys. Angry survivors were in a mood to strike. The mine owners would have a harder time blunting a union's appeal now.

But they would try. They would start with Frank Little. The thirty-nine-year-old newcomer was an effective organizer who had risen so swiftly in the IWW for that reason. He also was incendiary. The anti-union *New York Times* reported that, at a mass meeting at the Butte Baseball Park on July 19, Little had stood with his crutches on a podium over home plate and denounced U.S. soldiers as "Pershing's yellow legs" and "Uncle Sam's scabs in uniforms" to three or four thousand miners. In the same speech, he threatened that miners would make it impossible for the federal government to send troops to France if the government took over the mines, as rumored. Frank Little was the loudest antiwar leader of the IWW. Indeed, his militancy had caused a recent rift on the General Executive Board. Little was not just vocal in opposing the war before the United States joined it: he was vocal and unrepentant after. And he moved the miners.[5]

Mine owners, in league with the local officials they had helped to install and with at least tacit support of most western governors, would respond fast and hard. Work stoppage was treason. The owners, sheriff's deputies, private detectives, and informers had no trouble identifying Little as an instigator. With the mines going at capacity, Butte was a big city for Montana in 1917—and for the vast Northwest generally—at about ninety-four thousand residents. But it was not big enough for Frank Little to get lost, especially on only one good leg and crutches.

At 3:05 a.m. on August 1, six masked men arrived at Nora Byrne's boarding house in a black Cadillac. One stood sentinel while the other five went in. They broke into an empty room. Roused from sleep by the crash and clatter, Mrs. Byrne met them in the hallway in her nightclothes. "We are officers," a man barked, "and we want Frank Little." She pointed to room 32. One of the men kicked the door open. The landlady last glimpsed her lodger being half-led, half-carried into the waiting automobile, without his crutches and in his underclothes. He did not cry out. For her part, Nora Byrne was slow to call the police.

Daylight uncovered Frank Little's battered body, hanged from a railroad trestle on the edge of town. There had been time for torture first. Among other brutalities, he had been roped and dragged behind the car by his killers. A scrap of paper written in red crayon and pinned to his right thigh read in part, "Others Take Notice. First and Last Warning, 3-7-77." The last numbers were not a date. They were the dimensions of a grave.[6]

Although William D. Haywood, head of the IWW, later referred to the men who killed Little only as "thugs," many inside and outside the IWW suspected that Anaconda Copper Mining Company gunmen, law enforcement officers, or both were among those who tortured and killed Little. They had not much actual evidence. But the lethargy of local police in investigating the crime fed circumstantial suspicion.[7]

Indeed, neither federal nor state officials even feigned much concern about Little's death. Burton K. Wheeler, then the U.S. district attorney for Montana and later a progressive U.S. senator, commented tepidly, "It is the most unwise thing that has happened in Butte. The men who perpetrated the affair should be brought to justice." Although Wheeler probably was the federal official most genuinely appalled at the lynching, he did not expend much effort to bring anyone to justice. (In fairness, the lynching alone did not violate any federal law.) The local county attorney sounded more outraged. He named it "a cold-blooded murder." "Every effort," he promised, "will be used to apprehend the men who did it. If they are caught they will be prosecuted to the full extent of the law." That lasted a day. They were not caught.[8]

In truth, they were not much sought. A proposed reward of $3,000 went unclaimed.[9]

In Washington, DC, at the highest levels of the federal government, the response was even greater indifference. No less than the vice president of the United States, Thomas Riley Marshall, thought the lynching hilarious. "[A] Little hanging goes a long way" toward labor peace, he quipped.[10]

What the federal government did, rather than seek Little's murderers, was send hundreds of federal troops to patrol Butte less than two weeks after Little's death. Butte remained under army occupation for more than three years.[11]

For its part, the IWW recognized an opportunity to show and strengthen its support. Rather than send Little's body home to Oklahoma, it buried him in Butte. The funeral was the largest ever in Butte, with more than 3,500 marching in the funeral procession and another 10,000 or more lining the streets of the four-mile route to the cemetery.[12]

So began August 1917 for the country, and so it ended for Frank Little.

In a way, his death marked another ending as well. Little had been tortured and murdered, brazenly. No top leader of the IWW had been targeted that way before. Either industry or law enforcement, or both, may have been involved directly in this extralegal execution. They both certainly were complicit in diverting any real investigation into the crime. At the very least, this was unseemly violence that was likely to foster sympathy for the IWW and labor radicals generally. The U.S. Army was patrolling Butte, Montana. Something had to change, and it soon would.

The federal government was on the verge of a sweeping new effort to quell radical organizations, particularly among laborers and most urgently west of the Mississippi River. Until then, combat with radical unions had been left to industrialists, with such active or passive assistance of state and local officials beholden to them as they could garner. This necessarily meant an uneven, patchwork response. If a sheriff was in the thrall of local businessmen, he might agree to make company gunmen "special deputies" who then could dispense vigilante violence under color of law. A compliant governor might call out the militia. But in cities or counties just dozens or hundreds of miles away, a more populist sheriff or mayor or governor, or even one just imbued of law's niceties, might refuse the same aid to private corporate efforts. The companies relied on private detectives, anti-union workers, and hired local muscle, deputized or not, to break strikes. In state and local hands, the campaigns of capital to harass, intimidate, or arrest radical labor elements were situational, disjointed, and mixed in effect.

Where the federal government had taken some active part, that role had been military or quasi-military in nature before August 1917. The army lent spies and its intelligence apparatus to state and municipal governments, to infiltrate labor meetings and local unions. It sometimes provided arms to local sheriffs and businesses when asked. On occasion, it provided broader logistical support, as after the Bisbee deportations earlier that summer.[13]

This domestic military intervention was awkward and could have become more so, had the public noticed or the commercial press cared. Moreover, the armed forces had a war to fight in Europe. Substantial resources could not be diverted to labor skirmishes at home.

A markedly different strategy was about to replace these ad hoc responses. That strategy would be controlled centrally. It would be federal. It would be active, not reactive. And it would be legal, not quasi-military. The government's strategy would be legal in the sense that it would embrace the federal courts as places in which radicals and radical groups, and perhaps radical ideologies themselves, might be examined and destroyed, or at least weakened, systematically. Officialdom's new warriors would be lawyers, not strikebreakers, vigilantes, sheriff's deputies, or militiamen. Courtrooms, not streets or docks or lumber camps, would become the fields of battle. The U.S. Department of Justice would claim a role in a federal offensive to assert power and control that only the War Department ever had claimed before. Every part of this strategy was fundamentally new, untested in American life. Until this time, the role of courts in labor disputes generally had been limited to issuing injunctions against strikes and the occasional contempt prosecution when strike leaders ignored an injunction.

As July ended, neither Frank Little nor his fellow members of the IWW General Executive Board could have anticipated this exactly, even had they lain awake sweating in the dark, conjuring what they might meet next. But had Little survived just another five weeks, he would have seen coordinated federal raids on IWW offices across the country that swept up almost every accounting ledger, pamphlet, membership roster, letter or onionskin copy, button, flyer, and book that the organization had. He would have witnessed the prelude to the largest mass trial any American civilian court ever had attempted from the founding of the republic to that day—a trial that remains, by a factor of maybe two or three, the largest ever attempted still to our day. That trial itself would have been but the opening act for three more choreographed, huge federal criminal cases that would follow.

Not ninety days after deputies in Butte cut his body from the rope on the railroad trestle, Little's name would find the most prominent place in the first and largest mass indictment, in Chicago. He was the government's *bête noire*: the unindicted coconspirator around whom the entire indictment was drafted and a frequent reference point and speaker from the grave at the Chicago trial that would follow. He would become the central specter in that case. In 1918, the trial would play out in the shadow of a corpse dangling from a trestle.

Several men with a future would gather at that Chicago trial. A forty-year-old poet and journalist, later to become Abraham Lincoln's most famous biographer and partly responsible for the iconic Lincoln who holds the public imagination still, would be in the packed courtroom. Across a sea of heads, he could watch intently the future first commissioner of major league baseball, who went on to serve long and imperiously in that post, an animated man with a great tuft of white hair. A vigorous corporate lawyer at the prosecution table in Chicago two decades later would lose a case before the U.S. Supreme Court that produced the court's most famous footnote.[14] Not all there who would attain fame had a long future ahead. A younger but noted bohemian journalist, late for the trial because he was freshly back from Russia and the Bolshevik revolution, would be entombed at the Kremlin Wall just over two years later.

For now, the looming indictment and mass trial would not seek justice for Frank Little. On the contrary, the Justice Department would seek to kill the One Big Union, for which he had lived and died.

Buried in the same rubbly western earth he had mined, in Butte's Mountain View Cemetery, Frank Little would see and suffer none of it. From afar, his murderers, whoever they were, might have enjoyed all of it.[15]

2

One Big, and Different, Union

―――――――――――――――――――――――――――――――――

Twelve years earlier, in 1905, a small group of leaders of the Western Federation of Miners (WFM), other union organizers, and the socialists had gathered in Chicago to implement a big idea. They saw a vast nation of American workers, and indeed workers in all nations, with much less influence than their numbers should have allowed. Divided into craft or skill groups since its start in the mid-nineteenth century, the labor movement lacked broader unity. More, the racial separation that was the rule meant that white workers usually excluded black workers from their unions. Women, too, often were unwelcome or just unconsidered. The same was true of the foreign born. Many unions, notably those allied with the American Federation of Labor, focused narrowly on wages and working conditions, leaving more general political issues to members' consciences. Samuel Gompers (1850–1924), the first and longest-tenured president of the American Federation of Labor (AFL), had been a cigar maker as a boy and then a leader in the New York local of the cigar makers' union by age twenty-five. He helped found the forerunner of the AFL in his early thirties. He was a tiny man but a titan in labor history. Still, his rigid wariness of political radicals and his conventional belief in organizing by craft or trade assured him many detractors in the labor movement for the nearly forty years he ran the AFL.

By contrast, the small group of unionists and socialists in Chicago instead saw militarism, nationalism, economic freedom, and all the important inequities of life as inseparable from the capitalist system that made "wage slaves" of millions. They saw political action as inseparable from economic action. They saw workers divided by craft or skill, but ready to be amassed and called to unity by industry as a whole instead. And worker collectives in one industry would be natural allies of workers in every other industry.

What, then, if they could create one big union—an industrial union, not a craft union—that would unite all wage workers, regardless of trade or skill, race, sex, or nation? A union that would forge workers into a potent political force that could hasten the fall of capitalism and deliver ownership and control of the means of production—and then of government— into workers' hands? An aggressive union that would flex the muscles of millwrights, farm hands, lumberjacks, longshoremen, seamstresses, miners, and millions of other workers every day? That would eschew labor contracts altogether, agreeing to work on Tuesday only if wages and conditions had been satisfactory on Monday, with no promise that employment terms would suffice when the sun rose on Wednesday? That would lay down tools and idle machines within minutes, any time owners and bosses failed to heed workers' voices?

Those were the dreams, or at least the spoken aspirations, of twenty-two tough men and one tough woman, Mary Harris "Mother" Jones, who gathered in icy Chicago just after New Year's Day, on January 2, 1905. Their meeting was secret. After three days, the conferees agreed on an Industrial Union Manifesto—and on meeting again in Chicago in late June. Before scattering, the group elected William D. "Big Bill" Haywood of the Western Federation of Miners its permanent chair.

Back in Chicago that June, wary allies in the streams of the labor and socialism movements gathered to quell rivalries and disagreements for a time, and to act on their new year's manifesto. Many of the biggest names on the American left were there. They were a diverse group. Eugene V. Debs, the gentle socialist from Terre Haute, Indiana, whose experience leading the American Railway Union in the 1890s (and going to jail for his efforts) had made him as straight in his socialist ideology as a length of rail, was among the most widely known delegates. He had gotten 400,000 votes as the Socialist candidate for president the year before, his second presidential campaign, and would run three more times through 1920. From the Western Federation of Miners, Frank Little came with others, including of course Big Bill Haywood. Mother Jones, the Irish immigrant and former dressmaker, was back; at age sixty-eight, she was the oldest and among the most famous labor organizers in the group. The charismatic Vincent St. John was there; he was a likeable Colorado miner and organizer who had become president of the Western Federation of Miners at just twenty-four. There too was the divisive, self-absorbed Daniel DeLeon, a socialist hardliner who, in spite of a "very mild" character and his history as a law professor, had a remarkable gift for infuriating his supporters as readily as his opponents.[1]

Some 203 delegates in all from forty-three organizations gathered at the intersection of present-day North Clark Street and W. Ontario Street in Brand's Hall on June 27, when Haywood opened the conference, declaring, "This is the Continental Congress of the working class. We are here to confederate the workers of this country into a working class movement that shall have for its purpose the emancipation of the working class from the slave bondage of capitalism." It was, on the whole, a gathering of the left edge of the American left: centrist socialists like Milwaukee's Victor Berger refused to participate, and almost all the delegates shared broad hostility to Gompers and the compliant socioeconomic views and patriotism of his AFL. Not a few anarchists and incipient anarchists were present in the ranks of the IWW, both in summer 1905 and in the years to come. Socialists were present in large numbers, although they were split among the DeLeon and Debs factions and along other lines as well.

One important figure in what would become the IWW was not there in Chicago. She was fourteen years old, after all. But Elizabeth Gurley Flynn, whom the IWW bard Joe Hill later dubbed affectionately the "rebel girl," would be a delegate by the time of the third annual convention, in 1907. Not yet seventeen at that third convention, by the age of twenty-seven she would be an ambiguous figure in the trial to come. But before ambiguity arose in her relationship with the IWW, she would become one of its most effective and popular polemicists and organizers, especially among east coast textile workers. She would play a major role in the 1912 "bread and roses" strike against textile mills in Lawrence, Massachusetts, and in the silk workers strike in Paterson, New Jersey, the following year. In 1916, before a sharp political disagreement with Haywood and others, she would pen and the IWW would publish a pamphlet, *Sabotage: The Conscious Withdrawal of the Workers' Industrial Efficiency*, which eventually would draw the Justice Department's attention.

By the time they scattered on July 8, 1905, the founding delegates had erected the spindly framework of something very different. Delegates overwhelmingly had approved a constitution and a grand name, the Industrial Workers of the World. They had elected a president and a secretary-treasurer. Haywood and other westerners, interestingly, had no formal position. Most of all, they had given structure to an idea: one big union.[2]

That idea was the core of an even bigger idea. The preamble they wrote began and ended, "The working class and the employing class have nothing in common. . . . By organizing industrially we are forming the structure of the new society within the shell of the old."[3]

In fact, the founding efforts had begun about a year earlier, if spotting any origin point is possible. Inspired by Debs, his pamphlets and speeches, the board of the WFM had resolved at its May and June 1904 annual conference in Salt Lake City to do what it could to form a new and vast industrial union. The WFM had arisen in Butte, Montana, in 1893, some twenty-four years before Frank Little was tortured and murdered there. Big Bill Haywood was the WFM's secretary-treasurer by 1904, leader of a triumvirate that also included Charles Moyer and Vincent St. John. June 1905 found all three in Chicago, enthusiastically bringing the IWW into being. More than any other existing organization, the WFM spawned the IWW.

No longer would miners struggle alone against well-organized and collusive owners. The mine owners' interlocking boards of directors at the top and close communication at the street level assured that owners would not compete over wages and that a union advocate fired by one mine would find no work in any other mine in the area. If the capitalists could have their trusts and employers' associations, now at least one union would seek to link all workers in every industry together in a common cause.

The ideals were sweeping. Longshoremen would ally with lumberjacks. Migrant farmhands bringing in the wheat in Kansas or South Dakota would ally with millwrights in the biggest cities. Within one industry, copper miners in sunbaked Arizona would join efforts with iron ore miners snowbound on the Mesabi Range in northern Minnesota. More, white workers theoretically would stand with black workers, side by side in union halls. Immigrants from every nation would find the same place in the union as the native-born. Women would be as welcome as men. And all would aim not just at living wages, shorter hours, or a fair shake from capital: they would aim to abolish the capitalist system and to replace it with "industrial democracy," a term perhaps deliberately undeveloped but suggesting direct democratic control of industry by workers' majority votes. In sum, those who produced the nation's wealth would control it for the first time.[4]

The preamble to the IWW constitution that the Chicago convention adopted proclaimed these purposes in stark, unmistakable terms:

The working class and the employing class have nothing in common. There can be no peace so long as hunger and want are found among millions of the working people and the few, who make up the employing class, have all the good things of life.

Between these two classes a struggle must go on until the workers of the world organize as a class, take possession of the means of production, abolish the wage system, and live in harmony with the Earth.

We find that the centering of the management of industries into fewer and fewer hands makes the trade unions unable to cope with the ever growing power of the employing class. The trade unions foster a state of affairs which allows one set of workers to be pitted against another set of workers in the same industry, thereby helping defeat one another in wage wars. Moreover, the trade unions aid the employing class to mislead the workers into the belief that the working class have interests in common with their employers.

These conditions can be changed and the interest of the working class upheld only by an organization formed in such a way that all its members in any one industry, or in all industries if necessary, cease work whenever a strike or lockout is on in any department thereof, thus making an injury to one an injury to all.

Instead of the conservative motto, "A fair day's wage for a fair day's work," we must inscribe on our banner the revolutionary watchword, "Abolition of the wage system."

It is the historic mission of the working class to do away with capitalism. The army of production must be organized, not only for everyday struggle with capitalists, but also to carry on production when capitalism shall have been overthrown. By organizing industrially we are forming the structure of the new society within the shell of the old.

Membership, then, would consist only of wage earners, although in any field. The salaried man, the employer, and the owner would be unwelcome, regardless of sympathies. Employers of just a single worker would be barred from IWW membership.

In time, a certain pragmatism would take hold as to those sympathies. The IWW would come to need friends among the wealthy and the comfortable. It would need liberal scions of great fortunes who would post bail for workers, speak to politicians whom they knew well, and lard the union's coffers. At the outset, though, the lines were drawn rigidly and the class conflict was pure. Vincent St. John's role with the union eventually would put a human face on the compromises that reality would require, for the sake of finances and influence.

For now, the IWW set about reshaping the labor movement. This would mean persuading hundreds of thousands of skilled workers to see that their destinies were inseparable from the unskilled millions. The proud native-born, whose American roots might be two, three, or more generations deep, would have to come to view the newly arrived, with little or no English, as their comrades. White workers would have to accept black colleagues as sharing their plight, and deserving the same gains—this at a time when the law drew clear racial lines across much of the United States. Whites who until then had not shared bathrooms or drinking fountains with black coworkers, let alone neighborhoods, in theory now would share a union card, a union hall, and a sense of unity.

Progress came slowly at first, unsurprisingly. By the third national convention, in 1907, the IWW had about 6,000 members. That was the first year that Elizabeth Gurley Flynn served as one of the twenty-six delegates. Five years later in this experiment, the IWW's 1912 membership in the United States stood at probably 25,000. But by 1915, at its tenth anniversary, membership had fallen back to about 15,000.[5]

The European war would reverse the decline. Although estimates of the IWW's membership are slippery, given the ulterior motives of both the federal government and the union in offering those numbers, by September 1917 the government would claim that IWW membership stood at 200,000. A prosecutor months later backed off that estimate, although he still guessed that membership was three or four times the 1915 numbers: 40,000 to 60,000. Melvyn Dubofsky, a preeminent labor historian with deep knowledge of the IWW, suggested that membership may have reached 100,000 at one point in 1917. In fact, with membership rapidly transitory because many miners, farmhands, and lumberjacks led migratory lives (and because from the outset, the IWW sought to recognize all other union cards, too), some 1 million American laborers may have kept an IWW membership card tucked into a sweaty pocket at some point.[6]

Whatever the actual rolls, the IWW clearly grew considerably after war broke out in Europe. Looking back, the war would be the peak of the IWW's membership and influence. The reasons were related.

American industrialists enjoyed large profit margins on government contracts when the Wilson administration began preparing for, and then led the country into, war. But little of this wartime prosperity reached workers. Businesses vital to war—mining, logging, farming, textiles, munitions, shipbuilding, livestock production, and more—enjoyed a double boon. Federal government contracts calling for massive quantities or quick delivery provided generous prices, while the government and the commercial press were quick to condemn any threat of work stoppage over wage demands as unpatriotic because the nation was scrambling to prepare for and then to wage war. For that matter, many workers and their allies, whether on farms or in factories, had a growing sense that the European war at bottom was but a commercial conflict, fought to protect the immediate interests of international bankers and industrialists, and the fortunes of decaying monarchies. As working-class soldiers in European countries began to die in trenches by the hundreds of thousands, their American (and Canadian) counterparts became more and more suspicious that the many were dying grotesquely for the financial advantage of the few—and for nothing more.[7]

With wages stagnant, corporate profits soaring, and suspicions of war motives high, IWW organizers exuded a renewed sense of urgency. And they started drawing large audiences and new recruits. That recruiting effort, and the swelling audiences at rallies, would put the IWW and its leaders on a course pointed directly into the bayonets, clubs, and truck-mounted machine guns of large employers and the sheriffs, governors, and Loyalty League citizens they controlled in many places.[8]

But none of that is what made the IWW such a different union in the end. What made the IWW different is that it tried, at least fitfully, to unite men and women of different races and languages; that was radical at the time, and it would be for decades more (but the IWW's efforts were inconstant, as the open and common racism of the time appeared in IWW ranks and among its leaders, too). It printed its pamphlets, newspapers, and flyers in as many as fourteen languages; that was new, if not radical, for the labor movement then. It eschewed collective bargaining agreements or labor contracts, preferring instead to return to work tomorrow only if wages and hours satisfied its members today; that was radical and would be radical still for a union today. It saw the shared plight of workers everywhere and developed locals in England, New Zealand, Ireland, Finland, and elsewhere. No other labor union yet was doing that as broadly and systematically.

Soon the IWW picked up a nickname. Members became the "Wobblies." Individually, each member was referred to as a Wobbly or Wob. The origin of this name is obscure. A common tale attributed it to an immigrant

Chinese restaurant owner in Alberta, Canada, who was sympathetic to the cause but struggled to pronounce the English "W" in "I-W-W." Whatever the origin, the Wobblies embraced the romance of the nickname. It made them different from other union members.[9]

Whimsical name aside, the union was radical in the strict sense. It meant to effect change, actively. Its publications often sounded a strident, even fiery, tone about the evils of capitalism and the need for an "industrial democracy," in which producers would replace owners of capital in controlling their destinies. To that end, the IWW distributed books and pamphlets that advocated work slowdowns and jobsite vandalism or other mischief, as a form of sabotage when employers would not meet union demands. It printed and widely distributed the philosophical anarchist Emile Pouget's popular booklet *Sabotage* (1912) and Elizabeth Gurley Flynn's 1916 pamphlet of the same name.

As with the term "industrial democracy," the exact meaning of "sabotage" to the IWW was unclear, and this ambiguity may have been deliberate. For their part, employers and the commercial press accused IWW members of driving spikes into logs to destroy the teeth of lumber mill saws in the Northwest; of dropping bolts into wheat threshers to ruin them or setting the threshers on fire; and of putting lye or acid in the boots of lumberjacks who refused to join. But IWW leadership stoutly insisted that "sabotage" meant exactly what the subtitle of Gurley Flynn's pamphlet specified: "The Conscious Withdrawal of the Workers' Industrial Efficiency." By their account, it did not mean destruction of property.[10]

Whatever meaning the IWW intended, sabotage undeniably played a role in the correspondence and rhetoric of both its rank-and-file and leaders. One symbol was the wooden shoe: the "sabot," in French. IWW internal correspondence, from one "Fellow Worker" to another, included frequent references to using the wooden shoe, and stickers and posters sometimes included that image. Another prominent if more abstract symbol of sabotage in the IWW's refinement of it was the black cat (possibly an allusion to "wildcat" strikes). The IWW banner came to include the black cat as a mascot: a hissing black cat, with teeth and claws bared, back arched, and tail on bushy alert. Letters and printed pieces—notably by the IWW's poetic writer and editor, Ralph Chaplin—referred commonly to the sab-cat or the sabo-tabby, to having kittens, and so forth.

This was, in short, a union that favored "direct action," another term that it shrouded deliberately under a rhetorical tarp when officialdom ventured close. Strikes, either planned or of the impromptu wildcat variety, intentional slowdowns, and more were fair game in the eyes of those hastening the arrival of industrial democracy and the workers' victory in a great class war. The IWW was not alone in the labor movement in touting these tactics. But it set the radical edge, with Samuel Gompers's AFL at the opposing, conventional edge.

The IWW's leaders were working men, too, or at least had been. They were not far removed from their members; they had not led, and did not lead, coddled lives. In 1917, four members of the General Executive Board—the IWW's governing body—had but one good eye. Big Bill Haywood, Frank Little, Richard Brazier, and Charles Lambert all had lost sight in an eye somewhere along the way. Workers could see readily the interests, and travails, they shared with IWW leaders.[11]

In the end, maybe what made the IWW most distinct, at least to casual observers, was the singing. This union sang. Husky, soiled working men joined their voices and sang exuberantly—at the end of a long day in a lousy logging camp, in the boxcars that served as public transport for many itinerant members as the sun disappeared behind miles of swaying wheat, on streets outside factories with stacks raining soot down on the peeling clapboard and blackened brick of city slums. Everywhere, they sang.

The songs collected in the small, stapled red songbook of the IWW were set to folk tunes or religious standards that working men and women knew by heart. Their lyrics, though, were the work of Ralph Chaplin, eventually the leading writer at IWW headquarters in Chicago, or other working stiffs inspired to scratch out rhyming stanzas with a pencil stub. Perhaps most of all, the lyrics came from the legendary Swedish immigrant whose shortened name sounded like that of an iconic American everyman, Joe Hill. He gained immortality not just by the voices that have given air to his lyrics, and still do, but also by a martyr's death before a Utah firing squad in 1915 on a shaky murder conviction. As he faced execution, Hill's jailhouse telegram was both his epitaph and, eventually, his One Big Union's battle cry: "Don't waste any time mourning. Organize!"[12]

3

Big Bill

That right eye was ruined, but the left eye worked fine. And he rarely covered the right one with a patch. William Dudley Haywood Jr. could appraise or stare down a crowd of hundreds or thousands with the left one. Still, Bill Haywood had vanity enough that he insisted photographers capture him only in profile, from his left side.

The accident that took Haywood's right eye occurred when he was eight years old, probably in 1877. He was carving a slingshot in the mining camp Ophir Canyon, Utah, where he lived with his mother and stepfather after they wandered from Bill's birthplace, Salt Lake City, in search of work. While Bill was slicing away at a piece of scrub oak, the knife slipped and jabbed his eye. Doctors in Salt Lake City could not save it.

Before he lost that one eye, a three- or four-year-old Bill Haywood had seen the fresh grave of his father with both. The elder Haywood, all of about twenty-seven years old, had died of pneumonia in a mining camp before his wife could get there with the boy. "When we visited his grave," Haywood recounted at the other end of his life, "I remember digging down as far as my arm could reach." Other than fragments of his third birthday, this failed effort to feel his father was Haywood's only memory of the man.

At seven, the boy had watched Mannie Mills fall facedown, dead, in the dirt street of the mining camp when Slippery Dick proved the better shot in a gunfight Mills had started. He saw three men sprawled dead, two from one family, after another "shooting scrape" the same year. But these shootings made a lesser impression on him than when his schoolmates Willie Duke and Pete Bethel played with a gun they had found in a livery barn. Bill watched the blood drain out of Willie's head. It had been an accidental killing, but Haywood never forgot that "Little Pete Bethel was scared speechless." At the age of seven, Bill had already taken in all of this death with two eyes.

The carving accident that took away his eye was the next year, the year before he first entered the mines. Out of school because of the injury, young Bill worked in the half-light near the mouth of the mineshaft, a one-eyed nine-year-old plucking unwanted rock from the conveyor that whisked away the valuable rubble streaked with ore. When he went back to school intermittently among the Mormons—he seemed generally to like school, if not Mormons—he fought almost weekly with any boy brazen enough to call him "Squint-eye" or "Dick Dead-eye." "I used to like to fight."[1]

By Haywood's teen years, he had grown big. The family also had returned to Salt Lake City when the mine at Ophir was worked out. A series of odd jobs, starting when he was twelve, followed. That first year, while working as a messenger, he watched a gruesome mob lynching of a black man. That moment and another event not long after, when he sat next to a black man who was attacked in a speech by a racist U.S. senator from South Carolina, were turning points. As he later wrote about sitting next to the man under attack, "[it] caused me forever to feel that he and his kind were the same as myself and other people. I saw him suffering the same resentment and anger that I should have suffered in his place; I saw him helpless to express this resentment and anger." In spite of this awakening, Haywood's speech continued all his life to reflect in moments the casual racism of his day.[2]

By age fifteen, after fleeing his mother and the abusive farmer to whom she and an uncle had indentured him, Haywood returned to the mines. Initially, he joined his stepfather in hard-rock mining in Nevada. He spent the next sixteen years working underground.[3] Whatever one can say about him, indisputably Haywood came to the labor movement from the inside and made his way from the bottom up. He was the opposite of the stereotypical college-educated idealist drawn in later decades to union organizing.

Haywood came to that movement at about age sixteen. A fellow miner introduced him to the basics of class struggle and trade unionism, but he took little interest initially. Then came the Haymarket Square tragedy in May 1886 and the hangings of four radicals that followed. Bill Haywood, a seventeen-year-old western miner at the time, later remembered those events as "a turning point" in his life. They had the same meaning for another seventeen-year-old: a Russian émigré seamstress in a Rochester, New York, sweatshop named Emma Goldman.[4]

But it would be almost ten years later, after he had heard WFM president Ed Boyce speak in 1896, that Haywood committed to unionism. By then, he had wandered the West, from mine to mine, occasionally taking up other hard work; entered into a strained marriage with his "sweetheart, Nevada Jane Minor"; fathered one stillborn son and one living daughter, soon followed by another; and come to his longest pause, in Silver City, Idaho. Boyce led the WFM, then only three years old and struggling with its relationship to the AFL. Haywood found in Boyce a man whose "features were good, but his teeth were prominent. This was due to salivation, contracted while working with quicksilver in a quartz mill." "But," Haywood added, "I was greatly interested in what Boyce had to say." Haywood became a charter member of Local 66 of the WFM, serving immediately on the finance committee and later at various times filling "the different offices of the union."[5]

His fellow miners perhaps were greatly interested in what Haywood had to say, too, for he rose quickly in WFM leadership. His local sent him as a delegate to the 1898 WFM convention. In 1900, they elected him president of Local 66. The same year, national delegates elected him to the General Executive Board. Just one year after that, in 1901, Haywood became secretary-treasurer of the General Executive Board. He had reached the top.[6]

Haywood moved his wife and two daughters to Denver, Colorado, headquarters of the WFM. He made frequent forays from there to the mining camps and towns on the frontlines of the clash between working men and children on one side, and employers, their associations and retainers, politicians, and troops on the other. In places like the Coeur d'Alenes, Telluride, Colorado City, and Cripple Creek, he helped press the fight for an eight-hour day and for cohesion among miners. Arrests, trials, the threat of violence, martial law—all of these found Haywood and his fellows. Not infrequently there was blood, sometimes lots of it.

Yet the WFM survived and even thrived. And Haywood, now rubbing shoulders with the likes of Debs, Daniel DeLeon, Mother Jones, and other national leaders in both labor and overlapping socialist circles, began thinking more broadly of a coalition of all workers, across industries. In no small measure, by the early 1900s anger at Samuel Gompers specifically, and at the AFL generally, animated him.[7] All of that led him to Chicago and the founding of the IWW.

The Haywood whose head supposedly rose several inches above the other hats and heads at labor conventions certainly was unbent by years of labor in the mines. Photographs taken throughout his life show a man who knew, by his posture, how to make the best of his physical stature. As if posing for a granite statue, he stood rigidly erect (and again ever in profile, right eye obscured by the bridge of his nose) when a photographer asked him to pose. He learned how to wear a suit well. He learned how to keep prostitutes quiet afterward. And he grew comfortable in the lobbies of big-city hotels. As to his actual stature, there appears to have been more myth than measurement at work. A 1919 physical examination claimed to find a man less than six feet tall (a mite over five feet eleven), overweight, and with maladies common to many who for four or five decades had lived hard, drunk much, and eaten badly.[8]

Although Haywood left the Chicago convention in July 1905 with no formal title or role, allowing two easterners to appear as the leaders of a new union whose strength resided initially in the West, he was and would remain the most important figure in the IWW. The easterners, Charles O. Sherman and William E. Trautmann, were incompetent managers. Under attack from Samuel Gompers and his AFL from the start; riven with squabbles among its socialist factions; struggling to keep the essential WFM faction, with its ideological fissures; and left to Sherman and Trautmann's inept management, the IWW was on the verge of collapse in its first two years. By the time the 1907 convention all but dissolved in parliamentary bickering, the IWW was more at war with itself than with capital.[9]

The willingness Eugene Debs and others had shown in the founding convention two years earlier to bridge ideological divides disappeared in the 1906 and 1907 conventions. By the time the September 1906 convention ended, not only were Sherman and Trautmann out, but Sherman's managerial incompetence and self-dealing in particular had discredited the very name of the office he held. Never again would the IWW have another president. Going forward, it would have only its General Executive Board, with a secretary-treasurer as first among equals.

Haywood, leader of the WFM, still the largest bloc of the IWW, would have been the logical choice for that top position. But he was seriously indisposed in 1906 and through much of the summer of 1907: he was in jail in Idaho, awaiting and then standing trial on a murder charge that threatened to end in his hanging. In late December 1905, Harry Orchard had rigged a bomb on the front gate of former governor Frank Steunenberg's home in Caldwell, Idaho. Steunenberg died in the snow a few paces from his own hearth. Idaho authorities brought in a Pinkerton manager, James McParland, who had made his reputation in the Pennsylvania prosecution of the Molly Maguires years earlier. McParland inveigled, threatened, cajoled, bribed, and lied to Orchard for weeks, meeting with him in jail. Orchard took the hint, eventually, and named Bill Haywood, Charles Moyer, and George Pettibone—all WFM leaders—as his coconspirators. Idaho charged them, too, with capital murder.

Throughout May and June 1907, at age fifty, the famed labor and criminal defense lawyer Clarence S. Darrow (1857–1938) strove to save Haywood (who was tried first). There, Darrow arguably reached the zenith of his career—certainly in defending prominent members of the labor movement. But during the two-month trial in Boise, Haywood and the other two languished in jail.

When the Idaho jurymen acquitted him on June 28, 1907, Haywood left the Ada County Jail and received a hero's reception from workers and labor's supporters everywhere. Thousands met his train when it arrived back in Denver. By his count, within days the telegrams were in the hundreds. "I replied to them all," Haywood insisted. In Chicago, 60,000 paid to see him at Riverside Park. In smaller Milwaukee, he drew 37,000.[10]

Acclaim did not trump intrigue, though, or at least not for long. In Chicago in early spring 1908, Haywood seemed surprised to read a short notice published in *Miners' Magazine*: the WFM had "decided to terminate the services of William D. Haywood as a representative of the Western Federation of Miners in the field, the same to take effect on the eighth day of April, 1908." The WFM, now under Charles Moyer's control, was moving strategically to the right and had withdrawn from the IWW. The relationship between Haywood and Moyer had been icy while they both awaited trial. After Haywood's acquittal, he noted an omen: Moyer did not even rise from his seat as Haywood left the jail, bidding his colleague farewell only with, "That's good." After his own release—the state dropped the charge against Moyer when Pettibone's trial also ended in acquittal—Moyer now broke with Haywood altogether. "If to be conservative meant to stay out of prison," Moyer explained, "I am going to be conservative."[11]

By contrast, Haywood was moving left, although not consistently. He joined the National Executive Committee of the Socialist Party. He traveled both the country and the world for over three years, lecturing and haranguing for the causes of labor and socialism. But over time, a confusing pattern emerged. Maybe it was because Haywood spoke extemporaneously most of the time, and would get carried away with his own emotions and the crowd's reaction. Maybe it was more calculated. Maybe it was a product of his unusual trajectory, from conventional roots and even a conservative approach to labor unity to an ever more radical view of the world—a trajectory likely altered by the time in an Idaho jail. Or maybe it was just that he was adjusting to life on a lecture circuit. Whatever the reason, Haywood veered sharply and unpredictably from a firebrand's rancorous rhetoric to a national figure's more tempered talk.

Two appearances at New York City's famous Cooper Union provide a good example. Four days before Christmas 1911, he fairly spit fire. Haywood scorned parliamentary and political process, and urged "direct action." That meant "a little sabotage in the right place at the proper time." Warming to both cheers and jeers from the crowd now, he roared, "Do you blame me when I say I despise the law? I am not a law-abiding citizen, and more than that, no socialist can be a law-abiding citizen." Then for good measure, he added, "We are the revolution!"

A little more than three weeks later, back at Cooper Union for a debate in mid-January 1912 with the socialist lawyer Morris Hillquit, an incrementalist who labored within the law's bounds, Haywood sounded a much more conventional and less incendiary tone. Socialism competed within the political system and sought to persuade members of existing labor and political institutions not to destroy those institutions, Haywood argued; it did not seek to destroy the political system itself. Soothingly, even diplomatically, Haywood argued that industrial unionism was just "Socialism with its working clothes on."[12]

So it went during those years after the Boise acquittal: Haywood bounced between the radical edge and the midranges of liberal and socialist ideology, flirting one day with the rhetoric of revolution and anarchy but seeking the next day to broaden his appeal and expand the IWW's institutional presence. Five or six years later, clever corporate lawyers, enjoying temporarily the perquisites and power of public office, would retrace that zigzag trail to his peril.

But for now, it was Haywood's heyday. When later in January 1912 he joined Elizabeth Gurley Flynn, Joseph Ettor, Arturo Giovannitti, and other IWW leaders in Lawrence, Massachusetts, to support the woolen mills strike there, Haywood drew massive attention to both the strike and the IWW. After all the lectures and open-air meetings, he had learned how to speak to working people, including those who spoke almost no English. "We did have interpreters in these forty-five different languages," Gurley Flynn remembered fifty years later. "But half the time we didn't know whether the interpreters were telling them to stay out on strike or go back to work. So you have to have other interpreters to watch the interpreters and it got pretty complicated. So Bill Haywood decided that we had to speak English so these people could understand it. And I will never forget the lesson he gave to us. I was very young at that time, I was 22, and he said, now listen here, you speak to these workers, these miners [*sic*] in the same kind of English that their children who are in the primary school would speak to them and they would understand that. Well, that's not easy—to speak to them in primary school English." Haywood did, though. The textile workers flocked to him and stayed on the picket lines. They won the strike—temporarily, for there were setbacks to come the next year. At the moment, though, the IWW had won new relevance and credibility among workers.[13]

The mill owners and their compliant local authorities fought back, jailing Ettor and Giovannitti. At yet another Cooper Union meeting in May 1912, which was part celebration of the victorious strike and part rally to support the two jailed leaders, Haywood demonstrated just how simple and powerful his oratory could be. He also did not hide the link between his experience and his cause, reminding the audience of his legitimacy as a working man at risk. "The capitalist class are feeling your strength. They see the tremendous growth of socialism; they are going to stop that growth if they possibly can. They are going to stop the growth of unionism. It will require your every effort. And let me appeal to you tonight, comrades, one and all to stand shoulder to shoulder, hand in hand, heart to heart and mind to mind."

The applause was deafening.[14]

This was the Bill Haywood whom old colleagues like Gurley Flynn would remember decades later as "a tower of strength," whatever their differences with him in the day. Even some sympathetic outside observers recalled a "rugged intellectual, with his facility of phrasing, his marvelous memory, and his singularly clear and apt method of illustration," as did Frank P. Walsh, a liberal Democrat and chairman of Woodrow Wilson's Commission on Industrial Relations.[15]

In September 1912, the reinvigorated IWW embraced Haywood as its general organizer. To the outsider, the IWW belonged to the now-famous Haywood, and he to it. His rise to general organizer completed the transition. Or it nearly did: maybe it was Haywood's expulsion from the National Executive Committee of the Socialist Party of America in February 1913 that finished his transition. Eventually, he would leave Denver for the IWW's headquarters in Chicago. He became secretary-treasurer, functionally the leader of the General Executive Board, in 1914. Over time this inconsistent, charismatic man was moving ideologically from right to left, geographically from west to east, and organizationally from labor to socialism and then to his own mixed brand of the two. He would have to straddle factions within the IWW, though. As the outbreak of war in Europe in 1914 began to affect politics and public attitudes in the United States, he increasingly would have to collar or cajole those on his left in IWW leadership, especially Frank Little.[16]

4

Ed

By 1916, then, the IWW bore the stamp of Haywood and one or two others on the General Executive Board. The fiery Frank Little was the most important other living face of the IWW in the minds of employers and politicians. But Haywood and Little never did and never could define its actual membership, the One Big Union as a whole. It was convenient but not accurate for those in power to paint the whole with the face of Little or Haywood.[1]

Were it possible instead to compress and meld all the genes, experience, and accidents that make a human being from the collective tens or hundreds of thousands who once carried a Wobbly card, that composite embodiment would be closer to Edwin Doree. A red-headed son of Swedish Lutheran immigrants with a French surname, he married an older Jewish woman and worshipped her; left regular education at thirteen but "read widely and deeply in literature" and could "discuss complex subject matter with perception and precision"; lost two fingers in an industrial accident in his teens; still played baseball semi-professionally; lived itinerantly in Skagway, Alaska, in deep south Louisiana, and in many places in between; organized desperate workers like an idealist; avoided scraps when he could like a pragmatist; and provided for his family like a realist. This was Ed Doree.[2]

Edwin Frederick Doree—"*Ed*-vin," as his Swedish mother still called him late in life—was born in Philadelphia in 1889, the first of six children. The family soon moved west to the Pacific Coast, and Ed's father, Frederick, continued working as a carpenter constructing rail cars for railroads. With the discovery of gold in the Klondike, Frederick moved north to Alaska and eventually sent for his family. Although he would pick up two years of night school later, young Ed's ordinary schooling ended there at age thirteen. He went to work on a truck farm and, later, on the railroad for which his father worked. When he was sixteen, a saw accident at work took two fingers on his right hand. The railroad reacted instantly to that maiming by firing him—because he could not work for a few days with the injury— and threatening to fire his father if Ed made a stir.

He did not make a stir. Instead, Ed left town. But Ed's daughter speculated almost one hundred years later that perhaps the company's mercenary disinterest in its workers stirred something in him. "This object lesson in corporate ruthlessness and labor powerlessness must have marked the beginning of a radical," she guessed.[3]

For the next three years or so, the eight-fingered, lanky teenager played semi-pro baseball, mined, and logged in Idaho and western Washington, where he lived with a bachelor uncle. "Skag" Doree's ball-playing days were in the Northwestern League, and he dreamed of the major leagues. He recalled later, perhaps gauzily, that he "was good at the game and was rapidly going up." Ed also joined the new IWW briefly in 1906 but dropped out after a few months.

In 1908, his horse stepped into a post hole, tumbled, and fell on top of Ed Doree. It "crushed" his leg, sending Ed to the hospital for eleven months. By family lore, he narrowly escaped amputation. Skag Doree's baseball days were over.[4]

But his days of organizing workers were just beginning. In January 1910, he rejoined the IWW a few weeks before he turned twenty-one. Soon he was recruiting. An early photograph showed a young Ed Doree speaking outside in the Northwest. The sign near him read, "Lumberjacks and Roustabouts, Organize."

By his own account, Doree spent nine months of 1912 in the softwood lumber and turpentine camps of southern Louisiana and Texas. There he found two kinds of small towns: free towns and mill towns. Neither sort of town had any real rule of law: "I didn't see any law the whole time I was there," Doree reminisced. The mill towns, owned by a company, consisted of a sawmill surrounded by shacks for ordinary workers and somewhat roomier homes for foremen. There were business houses, too. But the difference from free towns was that the whole mill town then was encircled by a fence, eight to twelve feet high with either barbed wire or a live electric wire strung at the very top. A guard house sat at the only road into the town. Company gunmen patrolled, often as sheriff's deputies: free town or mill town, "the sheriffs and deputy sheriffs, they belong to the mill company." Gunmen would meet each train if the tracks ran through the mill town to a small depot there. Anyone trying to step off the train would be met with an armed man's gruff inquiry: Union organizer? Unfamiliar face? Just not the right sort? The stranger would be shoved back aboard the train with a warning not to return.

The workers' shacks were divided into three classes. The best were for the white foremen, with as many as six interior rooms—although these shacks were made from the same unpainted cull lumber as all the rest, consisting of rejected pine boards hammered together haphazardly with no effort to seal gaps. The next class of shack went to the so-called hillbillies, or "poor white trash"; they usually had two full rooms, one for the family to sleep in and one for everything else. The "negroes" got the lowest class of house, the "gun-barrel shacks." They had a high slant roof, with separate quarters on each side of the spine of the roof. They had either one room "or a room and an apology for a room, which is used as a kitchen." Doree recalled with sardonic wit, "You can go inside of the house and you can study the directions in any way and you can study astronomy at night through the roof." The black men got from 85 cents to $1.35 a day. For being white, a hillbilly worker got a premium of 15 cents a day above that.

Mill towns had three effective ways to keep workers there. The most direct was to control departures from the towns, just as they did arrivals. A man who wanted to leave could, in the more relaxed mill towns, get a numbered brass check at night, which he would return to the guardhouse when he came home from a neighboring free town. But only the most backward of the mill towns allowed workers to carry any package or food back in with them; the most modern of the mill towns forbade that sort of cheating the company stores. And at the company stores, prices were anywhere from 10 percent to 200 percent higher than in the free towns. "Often," Doree explained, "the gunmen go out of the mill town, where it lays close to a small free town," to remind the free town of the company's force.

Of the two less direct strategies to keep workers from leaving the mill, one was to issue company scrip rather than pay wages in U.S. currency. Only a company clerk could change scrip to ordinary currency, at a hefty discount. And the scrip, of course, was useless anywhere but in the mill town, at the company stores.

The second indirect strategy was to keep workers constantly in debt to the company. Because prices were so high for food, clothing, and other necessaries at the company stores or commissaries, workers often put purchases on a tab, against their wages for that month. The black workers especially never were shown any documentation supporting the accounting of their debt. For those workers, as Doree describes it, "[One] will come in this month and he will say, 'Well, how does I stand around these parts?' 'Well, Sam, you are just $11 in debt this month.' 'Yes, seh, I kind of think I was getting out of debt last month. I went pretty close.'" But the black worker would not try to argue with the timekeeper or the commissary clerk over his proper wages or the tab to the commissary. "If he argues too much, well they have got a funeral, that's all, and he knows it. It costs $7 to kill a negro in Louisiana." If another mill needed black labor, it would buy the worker's debt from the first mill—at a substantial discount—and the worker would begin his job at the new mill with the face value of the debt already on his tab.

Organizing black and white workers alike, and side by side, in those mill towns, Doree and his fellow IWW emissaries had several scrapes. More than once in a mill town, Doree had to turn around immediately and reboard a train either at gunpoint or with a threat to crack his head open.[5]

Even in the free towns, the companies' sheriff's deputies or Burns detectives were a frequent menace. Doree once went to a Louisiana town that had the entire executive board of a lumber workers union in jail. He wanted to visit them, but on the first day, the sheriff told him to come back tomorrow. When Doree returned the next day, the sheriff brushed him aside and left him sitting for half an hour. When Doree saw him again and asked to visit the prisoners, this time the sheriff said, "No. No, I don't think I will let you in at all any more. I have had too damn much trouble with you anyway." Doree protested to no avail. As he trudged out of the building, a Burns detective, probably in the employ of the Southern Lumber Operators Association, accosted him.

"Your name is Doree, ain't it?"

"Yes."

"I am just here to tell you to lay off of the Burns detectives."

"All right. That is jake with me."

"Now, you lay off of them."

"All right," Doree said again, as the men stopped at the top of a staircase.

The detective kept at it. Over and again, he grunted the same warning.

"You have told me that about a half a dozen times. Now, that is all, that is enough. All right."

"You be damn sure it is all right," the Burns man growled, stepping in front of Doree.

Doree slammed the man, who tumbled down the stairs. Loping down the steps himself, Doree ran straight to the office of the lawyer for the jailed union men. There was nothing they could do, the lawyer told Doree with a matter-of-fact tone. Doree fretted, "I don't know what he is likely to do."

The southern lawyer paused. "I don't know," he agreed. "After he does it, we have got plenty of law to handle it."

That left Doree not at all reassured. "That don't sound good to me," he announced as he left the lawyer's office.

But the Burns man, now "kind of belligerent," as Doree put it, met him leaving the office. With a stream of profanity, the detective resumed his earlier harangue, without much creative advance. "You will have to lay off these Burns detectives or there is going to be trouble around here!"

Doree assented yet again. But the detective persisted, "I want to see you back up at the courthouse."

"I am not going back over to the courthouse." At that bit of defiance, the detective took his gun out of his pocket and put it up under Doree's coat, against his back. "Now, I reckon we will go. I want to talk to you," the detective sneered. "You lay off the Burns detectives."

"That is about the fourteenth time I have heard that. I am willing to do anything now that you say. You have got a gun and that settles the argument."

The detective marched him toward the courthouse and the sheriff's office again. "You be damn sure of it!" he added for emphasis.

"If I have said anything or done anything that you don't like, here we are right in the court house," Doree responded reasonably as they approached the courthouse steps. "Here is the sheriff. Get me pinched."

"I wouldn't pinch you for a thousand dollars."

"Why?" Doree wondered.

"Too damn much fun shooting people like you."[6]

Doree, in a pragmatic mood, not long after decided to leave Louisiana altogether, in part for a persuasive reason: he saw posters in which local lumber companies offered $1,000 for his body, dead or alive, and for the bodies of three fellow IWW organizers. It was time to go.[7] He beat it on a freight train, as Wobblies did.

The following year he joined with Frank Little to go to the other end of the continental United States, organizing iron ore handlers on Minnesota's

Mesabi Range. There, in the foreshadows of Butte, local businessmen arranged Little's kidnaping in Duluth. Reporters rescued Little—that time. During this sojourn above Lake Superior's north shore, Doree and Little came to think of each other as "pals."[8]

From there, it was off to rally rubber workers to the IWW in Akron, Ohio. A local union there that seemed promising was not growing or prospering for reasons unclear. Eventually, Doree and other IWW organizers learned that every elected official of the local was a secret agent of the owners. The local disbanded.[9] Doree moved on in search of members elsewhere.

In September 1914, Doree spoke to garment workers in Rochester, New York. There at the rally, he and a tiny, chestnut-haired woman five years his senior caught each other's eye. The itinerant IWW organizer and the seamstress did not waste time. Just three days later, Doree and Ida Salinger married. By every available account, that shaky, accelerated courtship between two very different people (he was buoyant and active while she was reflective, domestic, and "irredeemably sad") became an unshakeable marriage. He called her "Chiky" (pronounced like the English word for a baby chicken), likely because he could not pronounce her Yiddish nickname, Chaika.[10]

By January 1915, Doree was off to organize again and to seek paying work himself. He went to Kansas in bitter cold weather, traveling in unheated boxcars, with another IWW stalwart to whom he eventually would be related: Walter T. Nef, who married Chiky's sister, Feige, in early 1917. The trip to Kansas was to organize agricultural workers. Other organizing campaigns followed, in other places and with workers in other industries, including textile workers in Baltimore and dockworkers in Philadelphia.[11]

How and why Doree rose from the ranks of members in the IWW to the small group of organizers so quickly remains unclear. But it may have been no more than a combination of idealism, native intelligence, willingness and ability to speak publicly, and a sunny personality. Talent could rise quickly in the fluid and relatively flat (meaning nonhierarchical) organization that was the IWW in the years just before the United States joined the European war.

Doree personally opposed the war, too, which aligned him with the views of most IWW leaders. Speaking of the war in 1918, while it still raged in Europe, Doree displayed his blend of the idealistic and the pragmatic. "I don't hardly think it's cowardice," he protested of his objection to war. "I am opposed to war in the same spirit that I am opposed to strikes. . . . I do not like them. If there is any way of avoiding any kind of fighting, blood-shed, murder, it is desirable. However, as I stated a while ago, there comes a time when you have got a strike; there comes a time when you have got a war, and there you have got issues, real issues; they are no longer theories. Whether I am sentimentally for war or sentimentally against war, it exists; I cannot stop it; therefore I am swept up in the maelstrom and when there comes a war or strike, I have to get on one side or the other, but I do not like them."[12]

In addition to his other talents, Doree also read. That did not slow his rise. Among the books and pamphlets he read were some IWW standards: the French anarcho-communist Emile Pouget's book *Sabotage* and the tracts by Elizabeth Gurley Flynn and Walker C. Smith on the same subject.

During the three years before America joined the war in 1917, Doree remained loyal to Chiky and got home when he could. Unlike so many roaming IWW workers and organizers who lived tough, untethered lives of migrants or hoboes and often answered that they had no home, Ed Doree viewed himself always as having a home. It was wherever Chiky was. And she preferred to stay put for as long as their meager income and Ed's travels allowed.[13]

In 1916, Doree traveled home to Chiky frequently, to Baltimore and then Philadelphia. Their first child, a boy, was born on February 18, 1917, about seven weeks before Congress declared war. They named him Fred-erick Lee Doree, but to his exuberant father, he was "Bucky." Ed's letters home almost always included playful messages and kisses for "little Bucky" long before the toddler could read. Ed Doree had work that mattered to him, a wife he loved, and now a son on whom he doted.[14]

Life was good, if not easy. But that soon changed. Ed Doree left an unusually rich record, maybe second only to Bill Haywood's or Ralph Chaplin's, of the changes he would see. Of the men's accounts, Doree's arguably was more accurate and contemporary, less revised and calculated, than Haywood's.

But a looming confrontation with the U.S. Department of Justice would shape considerably the record that all three men left. And the Justice Department's own record started almost a half century earlier.

5

Qui Pro Domina Justitia Sequitur?

W hen William Haywood's mother delivered the bawling baby who would become Big Bill in 1869, the republic of the United States of America was celebrating its eightieth anniversary of a functioning federal government with an executive branch. The Articles of Confederation that preceded the U.S. Constitution conceived of no independent executive branch. After the 1788 ratification of the Constitution, with its Article II executive branch for a new federal government, the Electoral College elected George Washington the first president on February 4, 1789. That was eighty years to the day before Haywood's birth. Haywood in turn preceded the birth of the U.S. Department of Justice by more than one year.

The DOJ came to be in 1870—on July 1, to be exact.[1] In a sense, Congress had answered the question, or asserted the claim, that soon became and remains the motto on the Justice Department's official seal: *Qui Pro Domina Justitia Sequitur*. It means, roughly, *Who for the Lady follows (pursues) justice*, or, in context, *Who prosecutes on behalf of justice*. Who indeed? The attorney general and the Department of Justice, that's who.

Before the congressional act that finally created a department under the attorney general, and for decades after, federal law enforcement and prosecution were a largely insignificant overlay on the nation's legal landscape. Not even a patchwork quilt blanketing the nation incompletely, the federal legal presence looked more like a flimsy, embroidered doily. Criminal prosecution always has been principally the province of the states, and it still is. The federal government, at least structurally, has no general police power, unlike the states. Federal functions in theory are limited to what the Constitution extends to the federal government explicitly, with the only room for expansion lying in doing what also is "necessary and proper" to carry out its affirmative duties.[2] So even today, perhaps 99.5 percent of all criminal prosecutions arise in state courts under state law. Federal criminal violations make up less than 1 percent of the total, and federal prisoners about 10 percent of all people in American prisons. One hundred years ago and more, the role of states in criminal law enforcement was, if possible, even more lopsided.[3]

Why? The first Congress established the office of attorney general, in the Judiciary Act of 1789. But that office had no broad, national responsibilities. Initially, the attorney general's duties were just two: represent the United States in the Supreme Court, and give advice and opinions on legal questions to the president and heads of federal agencies. In the late eighteenth century, this was a part-time position for one man. He had no assistants, let alone a department. In 1831, forty-two years after Congress created the attorney general's position, it first appropriated money for office expenses and one "boy to attend to menial duties."[4]

Prosecution of such few federal crimes as there were, and representing the United States in civil cases in the federal courts, instead were the tasks of U.S. district attorneys. The same section of the Judiciary Act of 1789 created that office, too. And the Judiciary Act gave the attorney general no supervisory authority at all over the district attorneys. The district attorneys were presidential appointees, upon advice and consent of the U.S. Senate. Every judicial district—the unit of jurisdiction of federal trial courts—had one. That meant the president could appoint at least one district attorney in every state and territory and, in populous states divided into more than one district, two or more.

Congress did not fund the district attorneys directly, either. Compensation for the district attorneys came from fees taxed by the federal trial courts on the cases filed, both criminal and civil, in the given district. In other words, the district attorney had a direct stake in assuring a busy court docket: the more cases filed, the more take-home money. Not until more than one hundred years later, in 1896, did Congress provide a fixed salary for the job of U.S. district attorney. In other words, federal prosecutors moved from bounty hunters to salaried public servants hardly more than twenty years before the Chicago trial.[5]

Even after generous fixed salaries came, though, these were glorious patronage jobs. They were as good as—or better than—the job of postmaster. With no one overseeing them in their fiefdoms, other than a distant president who was unlikely ever to notice the day-to-day work of federal trial courts, district attorneys could prosecute their way to prosperity if they chose to work hard. The more people they prosecuted and convicted (for mail theft, theft of government property, or, in later days, harboring fugitive slaves), the more they might make. Or, they could coast along lazily, even with utter indolence. Private civil suits, most of which would require little of them, would line their pockets at least modestly with a share of the fees and costs the courts assessed. From the president's perspective, he could reward a local lawyer who was a party loyalist or an early supporter without ever thinking of the man again or worrying that he might cause some national embarrassment in his outpost. The job of U.S. district attorney was an ideal spot for a political hack.

Between the paucity of federal criminal laws and the low wattage of many federal prosecutors that the structure of the U.S. district attorney position and patronage produced, the federal role for lawyers and courts in law enforcement was modest by modern lights. On the rare occasion when something dramatic begged a federal response, throughout the nineteenth century that response usually was military or quasi-military in nature rather than judicial or legal. The president either called out federal troops from the U.S. Army proper, or called up state militia units that were subject to presidential control in times of insurrection or imminent invasion, under the Militia Act of 1792 and its successors.[6]

There were a few relatively early and spotty examples of the new Justice Department addressing ideological violence in court. In the south, some U.S. district attorneys prosecuted members of the early Ku Klux Klan here and there for attacks on black citizens. But these were isolated examples of a legalist and federal response to a widespread threat of violence.[7]

Consider an extreme, but early and defining, example of the more typical federal role throughout the nineteenth century. When for the first time an assassin struck down a president of the United States, Abraham Lincoln in April 1865, there was no federal statute in play, and no federal law enforcement officers responded. Other than the U.S. marshals, yet another creation of the Judiciary Act of 1789, there simply were no federal law enforcement agencies. (Congress created the Secret Service, within the Treasury Department, in response to Lincoln's assassination, and it became the first federal law enforcement agency with a policing mission.) The ragtag group that aided John Wilkes Booth either before or after he shot Lincoln ordinarily would have faced only state-court prosecution for state crimes; they would have died on state gallows or lived in state penitentiaries.

36

These events were not ordinary, though, and Booth's accomplices in fact did not live or die in state custody. But the federal government's response was military, not judicial or legal. U.S. Army troops, not law enforcement agents, pursued John Wilkes Booth and his confederates. An invented military commission of hazy legality, not a civilian court, tried all but one of the surviving accomplices—some with attenuated moral culpability—and sentenced four to hang and another four to serve prison terms. Only the ninth, who evaded capture initially, was tried (and convicted) in a civilian court. The four who received death sentences died on the gallows in a federal military camp.[8]

Again, the first assassination of an American president is an extreme example. But it is not a misleading one. The radical ideology, disruption of commerce, and threat of violence perceived as attending labor strikes generally brought a response that was military or quasi-military, not legalist in the sense of oriented to the use of courts and judicial process to tamp down radical ideology and action. The military or quasi-military responses also were local and ad hoc: they depended on the accidents of the ideology or sympathies of a local sheriff, say, and his willingness or reluctance to deputize company strikebreakers or private operatives of the Pinkerton or Burns detective agencies. Or they might depend on how responsive a governor or a mayor was to pressure from local businessmen. A governor beholden to big business might accede quickly to the demands of factory or mine owners to call up the state militia. But a governor more sympathetic to labor or socialists might be very slow—or altogether unwilling—to call out the militia.

Not long after the Civil War, capitalists and their lawyers did adopt the tactic of going to state or federal courts to seek injunctions against work stoppages or strikes, on the theory that these restrained local or interstate commerce or interfered with the movement of the U.S. mail. Courts often complied readily in issuing such injunctions. But even so, it fell to sheriff's deputies—their ranks perhaps swelled by deputized company hirelings— or to the militia or, less frequently, to regular army troops called out by the president to enforce those injunctions and to take supplemental steps to break a strike or quell radical action.

Examples abound. When the Molly Maguires began assassinations and other violent actions in the Pennsylvania anthracite coal region in the 1860s and 1870s, the official response was quasi-military in the main, led by Pinkertons hired by the mine owners and limited to the state and local levels. Instances of governors calling out the state militia to stop a strike, or at least to discourage union members (if not company toughs) from violence, are too numerous to count. The Bisbee deportations of July 1917 were an example of company gunmen and toughs deputized by a compliant local sheriff, who then coordinated with vigilantes in a Loyalty League chapter and with the U.S. Army, which operated a military camp near where the freight cars stopped (by no coincidence) in the New Mexico desert.[9]

Prosecutions sometimes followed, of course, but in a sense they were a cleanup or collateral strategy. Eugene Debs went to the Woodstock, Illinois, jail for contempt of court, following two trials, when his American Railway Union did not comply with court injunctions meant to stop the 1894 strike against the Pullman Company and railroads that entrained Pullman cars. Alleged leaders of the Molly Maguires eventually were prosecuted in Pennsylvania state courts, and some of them were hanged. But these were back-end and limited legal tactics, employed only when the radical action or strike already had been quelled. In Oshkosh, Wisconsin, the local district attorney charged three leaders of a woodworkers' strike in 1898, but only after workers had returned to the job. And the charges related to the death of a striker, not to the strike itself. Legalism often was an afterthought in addressing union action and the effects of other agitation by those outside mainstream political ideology. Bayonets, guns, and a show of state or police power were the first response.

That Oshkosh case—in which the jury promptly acquitted—shared another element quite common when radicals found themselves hauled into court. The local district attorney, although nominally in charge of the prosecution, in fact turned his office and its powers over to a private lawyer hired by the sawmill owners aggrieved by the strike. That private lawyer, paid by the city's largest mill owners, led the prosecution at trial. All of the state's powers, including the power to imprison, passed to moneyed private interests in a public prosecution. Theoretically, wealthy private industrialists should have had only civil remedies available to them directly.[10]

This was a familiar partnership, even the norm, when capital and its servient politicians sought to put down radical disruption. Federal courts were no exception. Enjoying a sleepy patronage job, some U.S. district attorneys had neither the skill nor the energy and ambition to take on the prosecution of labor leaders and radical agitators. Resources also were a meaningful problem as federal law enforcement agencies were practically nonexistent and a federal district attorney's office budget would not necessarily cover a prosecution with far-flung witnesses. So they would hand off the case to lawyers retained and paid by the industrialists eager for the prosecution.[11]

Eventually, the unseemly appearance both of using military or quasi-military force (militias, special deputies, federal marshals) to quell actions by radical reformers, and of garbing private industrial interests with the full sovereign powers of the U.S. government, led to pressure for change. As to using military troops domestically, there was the statutory awkwardness of the Posse Comitatus Act. Passed in 1878, the basic purpose of the act was to prevent (or at least limit) the use of federal troops to impose Reconstruction policies in states of the former confederacy or to police southern elections. But more generally, it forbade use of the army or navy to enforce or execute local and state laws, except as federal law expressly allowed. That made it legally tricky for the president to call out federal regulars to quell local labor disturbances or to aid local law enforcement. While the president and his high-level subordinates were at no real risk of prosecution, the Posse Comitatus Act at least gave their political opponents a trenchant argument against federal overreach when federal troops showed up to supplement local sheriff's departments in capital's skirmishes with labor or radical agitators.[12]

And as to empowering private lawyers retained by corporations or businessmen to act as public prosecutors, Congress had acted to rein in that practice modestly in 1870. In the same act that gave the attorney general supervisory authority over U.S. district attorneys, Congress provided that no public payments would be allowed to lawyers other than federal district attorneys and their regular assistants "unless hereafter authorized by law, and then only on the certificate of the Attorney-General that such services were actually rendered, and that the same could not be performed by the Attorney-General, or solicitor-general, or the officers of the department of justice, or by the [federal] district attorneys." Further, the act stated that every specially appointed lawyer "shall take the oath required by law to be taken by the district attorneys, and shall be subject to all the liabilities imposed upon such officers by law."

In other words, the attorney general had to commit in writing to the need for a special prosecutor, and that outside lawyer had to take an oath of fidelity to the Constitution and federal law, accepting whatever liabilities the law imposed on public prosecutors. A mining or railroad lawyer well paid by millionaires could not take up a public servant's role without the attorney general's affirmative statement of reasons and without assuming

39

the public servant's duties. The statute proposed to "protect the Treasury from the expense incident to the employment of special counsel where the government did not have the assurance of the head of the Department of Justice, in the form of a certificate, that the services to be rendered were actually rendered, and could not be performed either by himself or by the Solicitor General or by some officer of that department or by the proper district attorney."[13]

Seventy years after Congress imposed this modest limitation on private interests crowning their eager lawyers with sovereign powers of search, arrest, criminal prosecution, and urging imprisonment upon conviction, the Justice Department convened just the second annual conference of chief federal prosecutors. As they sat gathered in the Great Hall of the U.S. Department of Justice in Washington, DC, Attorney General Robert H. Jackson warned these presidential appointees, "With the law books filled with a great assortment of crimes, a prosecutor stands a fair chance of finding at least a technical violation of some act on the part of almost anyone. In such a case, it is not a question of discovering the commission of a crime and then looking for the man who has committed it, it is a question of picking the man and then searching the law books, or putting investigators to work, to pin some offense on him."[14]

Jackson's words were not prescient. Instead, they may have reflected in part awareness of the course his department set twenty-three years earlier, as summer 1917 turned into autumn and then the last winter of the Great War. They certainly reflected awareness of decades of American experience preceding that. The transition from local, ad hoc, and military or quasi-military responses to labor unrest and radical ideas, to a national, more uniform, and legalistic or judicial response to the same forces in American life, did not come quickly or evenly. The transformation of federal prosecution from isolated patronage outposts operating essentially on a bounty system, often tendered to private mouthpieces when capitalists howled, into a professional corps under central authority of a high federal official running a department ambitiously named "Justice," did not come quickly or evenly, either. Jackson knew that by 1940.

But the IWW—and its leaders in thought, word, and administration— were only about to learn it. They could not know, and might not have cared, that their experience would mark an important point in that process of transition and transformation. All the same, in 1917 and 1918, the motto of the Department of Justice remained as much a question as an assertion.

6

Something Must Be Done

Although Woodrow Wilson won a second term in 1916 on a platform of keeping the United States out of the European war, staying out also was as much a question as an assertion when his second term started. President Wilson and his cabinet spoke euphemistically of preparedness in 1916. Their preparedness campaign was both a product and a producer of war anxiety.

Labor historians and labor economists—for example, Philip Taft, Melvyn Dubofsky, Philip S. Foner, William Preston Jr., and Eric Thomas Chester—have traced methodically the sequences of cables, commissions, letters, meetings, and maneuvers by which corporate interests petitioned the federal government for help in quelling the IWW specifically, and radical action among workers generally, in 1917. Broadly speaking, that collective effort, that wave, began in the West and moved east toward Washington, DC. Mine owners, shipbuilders, lumber barons, and their commercial associations did not ignore local and state governments; indeed, they co-opted many of those and swept them up in the swell. Congressmen and senators also wrote the president and several of his cabinet members: the secretaries of war, the interior, and labor. Most frequently, perhaps, they sought to influence the attorney general and his Justice Department.[1]

The files of the Justice Department were stuffed with correspondence from these business interests and local, state, and federal politicians writing at the behest of businessmen or their industrial associations, all urging that the federal government take action against the IWW. The department organized this correspondence with a separate file for each state. Some of the

41

state files were thin, just five or ten pages. Others, especially for western states or large eastern ones like New York, were fat, with hundreds of pages. Together, just the correspondence to, from, and within the Justice Department about the IWW in the summer of 1917—a smaller fraction of it written years later, but all of it about 1917—fills most of six boxes at the National Archives.

Some writers wanted deportations of IWW aliens. Some wanted summary detentions of any or all IWW activists, without charge or trial; it was wartime, they reasoned. Some wanted the federal government to give more support to state prosecutions. Some wanted federal prosecutions or stiffer sentences when federal courts acted. A few, such as one W. G. Miller, took a very direct approach. He sent a telegram to Woodrow Wilson on August 7, from Berkeley, California. It read simply, if ungrammatically: "The lives of our relatives, friends and possibly our own which is important are endangered by the delays caused by Senators, I.W.W.'s, Congressmen, draft rioters, wooden politicians and other pests. I can shoot quickly and straight. Can I do anything for you? I would rather begin in Washington."[2]

Few spoke that bluntly. But almost all of them wanted *federal* action; their letters and telegrams shared a theme that local and state efforts were insufficient to curb the IWW danger to the war effort. The wave they created bore down on the federal government.

That was fundamentally new. What still bears comment after the work of these labor historians and labor economists is a legal perspective on the historical import of that new, broad support for federal action.

War anxiety took many forms. For draft-age young men, most obviously, the unprecedented carnage in Europe created a specter of grim and early death if America joined the war (the specter became reality: in just more than a year and a half between declaration of war and the Armistice, almost 88,000 members of the American Expeditionary Force died in fighting. Over 37,000 more died of illness, often influenza, at home). For working people more generally, especially in the West and on farms, the coming war also threatened loss of needed hands in the field and barns. That home labor shortage was not only theoretical. Canada had been in the war since 1914, supporting the commonwealth, and resentment that young men were absent from family farms was real and high; American farmers anticipated the same. Young families, for that matter, would struggle with loss of wages if husbands and fathers went to war, regardless of their trade.[3]

For employers and industrialists, there were mixed anxieties. Many enterprises wondered whether strikes would cripple or crush their ability to fill wartime contracts. Surely there was some strain of patriotism and public spirit in that concern. But some of the anxiety also was craven. Setting aside the critiques of WWI as a purely capitalist war, government contracts and purchase orders (both foreign and domestic) were and would be very lucrative if—and only if—companies could fill them. Strikes, or even the prospect of them, presented a real risk to profits. So did shortening the working day, providing clean bedding and water in logging camps, improving safety measures in mines, or meeting labor's other demands.

Not just radicals leveled charges of corporate greed. Demand was sending commodities prices higher, large government contracts with tight delivery dates paid well, and employers simultaneously resisted wage increases and improved working conditions in part by questioning publicly the patriotism of unions and workers who sought a greater share of rising gross revenues. None of this was a secret.

With cloaked motives, even the federal government acknowledged it. In September 1917, after Samuel Gompers and others urged him to act, President Wilson appointed a Presidential Mediation Commission, with Labor Secretary William B. Wilson as its chair and four others as commissioners. William Wilson chose a young Felix Frankfurter as his secretary, the Mediation Commission's most important staffer. The commission's unstated but widely understood purpose was to aid the federal effort to destroy the IWW, in part by bolstering Gompers and his AFL as an acceptably mainstream labor organization. Six months into its hearings and investigation, the Mediation Commission concluded in the first of its seven recommendations, "The elimination to the utmost practical extent of all profiteering during the period of the war is a prerequisite to the best morale in industry."[4]

Consumers and the public generally were aware, of course, that profits and prices were rising but wages were not. As AFL membership increases suggested, support for organized labor—within patriotic limits—was growing. This was the Progressive Era, too: middle-class values and an interest both in improving the condition of the working poor and crimping the excesses of the rich were widely shared. Speaking generally of a forty-year period ending in about 1917, the labor historian Melvyn Dubofsky wrote, "Many Americans, especially workers, thus began to question the humanity and the social efficiency of the new industrial order." Not surprisingly, then, "Regardless of which union initiated conflicts, the strikers asserted that if Americans could wage war abroad to spread democracy, they could also struggle at home to win the industrial democracy so long denied them by capitalist 'autocrats.'"[5]

Whatever their mix of motives, with American soldiers shipping out by the thousands to France and elsewhere in Europe, western employers especially sought new ways to block or destroy the IWW in the summer of 1917. The Bisbee, Arizona, deportations were one novel effort at corporate self-help, in coordination with the local sheriff and the U.S. Army. Through employers' associations, capital also leaned on mayors, state legislators, and governors for aid.

But the necessary help was not just local or state aid. At the local level, some measures created more problems than they solved. For example, the Bisbee deportations of striking miners and their supporters led to resentment in New Mexico that Arizona had shipped its problems there. The AFL and Gompers also reacted badly to Bisbee, in part because a number of AFL members got swept up in the indiscriminate herding onto cattle cars and in part because the employers' action was so blatantly unlawful that Gompers could not remain both silent and credible among workers.[6]

More importantly, the radical IWW had members from coast to coast and in every major industry necessary to war preparedness or war itself: farming, lumber, mining (of copper, lead, and iron—everything essential to munitions and war matériel), textiles, and shipping. Many IWW members were migrants, "beating" their way on freight trains that they could hop without paying a fare and living in "jungles," or hobo camps, near the tracks or outside towns. They could pick up and go when local efforts to quell a strike succeeded and then show up to make trouble in another town. The breadth and transitory nature of IWW's membership threatened to defeat purely local efforts to contain the radical threat that western businessmen and politicians perceived.

So, the real help that business sought from local and state government officials in the summer of 1917 was intervening with the federal government. Three principal points of confluence emerged. First, in Minnesota, former governor John Lind led a newly created Commission on Public Safety that industry and loyalist groups had persuaded the Minnesota legislature to create. It had broad wartime powers, including to remove elected public officials it considered disloyal. As one of the commission's seven members, Lind began a secret investigation that he hoped would prove the IWW's reliance on German money to finance it. He planned to feed that evidence to the Department of Justice, once he found it. More, he devised a legal strategy that would draw attention.

Second, further west, the California Commission on Immigration and Housing became the active agent of, eventually, eight western governors who were under pressure from, and responsive to, businessmen and their associations. That commission dated to the August 3, 1913, Wheatland incident, in which a fight between frustrated migrant workers, picking hops in deplorable conditions at the remote Durst ranch, and undisciplined sheriff's deputies left the county district attorney, a sheriff's deputy, and two workers dead. Following a marred trial that convicted an IWW organizer, "Blackie" Ford, and a learning-disabled IWW migrant worker, Herman Suhr (who was imprisoned for life), the California governor had appointed the Commission on Immigration and Housing to vent labor tension and to investigate working conditions in the state's vast agriculture industry. George Bell, the commission's chairman in 1917, ardently opposed the IWW. As a spokesman for western industry, he played a very active role in Washington, DC, as the summer went on.[7]

Third, the Wilson administration took federal control of state militia units in some western states and therefore could direct troops in suppressing strikes and maintaining order on streets at the call of mayors, governors, and industry. This effectively established martial law in parts of the West.

Lind was a useful messenger for capital because the Swedish immigrant was a progressive populist in the public eye. A Republican when he became the first Swedish American in Congress in the late 1880s, he was a Democrat by the time he served as Woodrow Wilson's envoy to Mexico in 1913–14. But liberal ideals notwithstanding, Lind was close to Minnesota's mining, lumber, and wheat farming leaders. Mining and lumber companies were large and few; farmers were small and many. In some ways, then, fighting the IWW in the agricultural sector was hardest—although grain elevator companies and commodities traders, including Cargill most prominently, were major players in Minnesota. Lind's commission hired dozens of Pinkerton detectives to snoop on the IWW.

In late July, he met with Hinton Clabaugh, head of the Chicago office of the Department of Justice's Bureau of Investigation (eventually to become the semi-autonomous FBI) to present his files and a plan. His idea?

The Justice Department should prosecute IWW leaders for conspiracy to violate the new Espionage Act of 1917. Although Lind was not acting directly for businesses outside Minnesota, and was the most local actor in that sense, his idea would stick. He underscored the Clabaugh meeting with a telegram to Attorney General Thomas Watt Gregory warning, "If IWW organize agricultural workers, crops will be wasted and lost, lumber industry paralyzed." But Gregory, writing tersely in reply, remained leery of federal jurisdiction. "Is interstate commerce or movement of mails being threatened and how," he inquired. "If situation beyond State control have Governor of State telegraph President and United States Attorney telegraph me."[8]

The thrust of this effort in midwestern and western states always was roughly the same: the federal government should step in and step on the IWW. Importantly, Lind, like many others that summer, proposed to the federal government a legal strategy, not a military one.

George Bell's California Commission on Immigration and Housing was even more aggressive than Lind's commission in pushing a federal legal strategy. Bell demonstrated, too, that not everything legal, in the sense of making procedural use of the law's tools, is substantively lawful: his recommendation in the end was incommunicado detention of suspected IWW radicals without charges. Costumed plausibly in moderation, the California commission spoke of improving working conditions and wages in agriculture, canning, and lumber and implicitly recognized a role for loyalist labor organizations such as the AFL. That gave it license to attack industry's principal nemesis, the IWW.

And attack Bell did. Consulting with politicians and undercover agents planted in the IWW, Bell proposed four points that would require and strengthen federal coordination, both agency with agency and federal government with state governments. First, the federal government would seek voluntary self-censorship by the commercial press, and impose censorship if necessary, to stop coverage of the IWW. The press provided the IWW oxygen with the public. He would pinch that off. Second, the federal government would address bad working conditions that made labor agitation easy. Third, the federal and state governments would increase dramatically the infiltration of the IWW with covert agents, to improve intelligence on IWW plans and allow disruption. Finally, the federal government quietly would arrest, detain, and intern troublesome IWW members—without charge or trial and without a peep from stifled newspapers about this unlawful action. Eventually, Bell and others appended a fifth point, convening a conference of western governors to the end of adopting a uniform state policy to supplement the federal.[9]

Lind had proposed using an overbroad new wartime statute, the Espionage Act (which punished spoken or written opposition to the draft and anything close to sedition), and expanding and blurring its scope with the help of conspiracy law. Even a fuzzy agreement to do something the Espionage Act forbade would become criminal, regardless of whether the forbidden act happened or whether most conspirators took any step beyond talk. But Bell one-upped him. He did not need charges, trials, or even the appearance of legality. Internment incommunicado would do the trick. A war was on.[10]

Bell worked hard to sell the plan. When President Wilson diverted him to the departments, Bell met with the secretaries of labor, justice, and the interior. Most importantly, he got an audience with Wilson's Council of National Defense on July 18. He made his pitch for preventive action against the IWW, admitting that the IWW had not yet done anything decisive as an organization to thwart the war effort but urging the federal government not to wait until the One Big Union did. When the federal government did not leap immediately, Bell set loose an onslaught by western governors and industrialists. As Dubofsky put it, "the governors flooded the White House with telegrams demanding immediate repression of the IWW and full censorship of all news dealing with labor affairs. Throughout July and August the President, the Labor Department, and the Justice Department came under increasing pressures from Western businessmen and politicians." Bell had reach. By the end of August, the reactionary Arizona senator Henry F. Ashurst, who had already come up with "Imperial Wilhelm's Warriors" for the IWW, giving the false rumor of German financing some heft, warbled to Wilson, "Unless prompt and courageous action looking toward the efficiency and firmness of the Government is taken, no man can foretell what may occur."[11]

Just as some of Bell's plan was unlawful, so too was it a hybrid: partly new and legal in form, and partly old and military. Internment would have required sheriffs' departments at least, and maybe some troops. The overarching idea was federal, but its implementation would have been only partly a legalist strategy.

Finally, vestiges of local military responses to labor unrest led indirectly to a federal legal strategy that summer. The reason is that the 1917 military or quasi-military strategy no longer was under immediate state authority. It concerned specific western militia units that the president had declared under his control, just as Article II, Section 2, and Article IV, Section 4, of the U.S. Constitution together allow him to do. Although these units were state militias, then, the power to direct them now was federal.

The Wilson administration had taken federal control of a state militia in New Mexico in 1916, after Pancho Villa's raids there. Indeed, Villa's March 1916 raid on Columbus, New Mexico, was part of the reason an army camp remained there to feed the Bisbee deportees more than one year later. After Wilson assigned General John Pershing to chase Villa, he took federal control of other militia units. Then, after America joined World War I, the War Department used both regular federal troops and state militia units under federal control, ostensibly to guard western railroads, bridges, and telegraph lines against possible German action. But in fact, the use of militia units and federal troops was most common well away from the Mexico border and away from any pockets of German sympathy. It was common in the Pacific Northwest and in mining country.

There, the actual use of troops and militia units was to break or prevent labor strikes and to raid IWW halls. They intervened in strikes in Eureka, Montana; in Globe, Arizona; elsewhere across the mines, lumber camps, and railroad towns of the Northwest; and most notably in Butte, Montana. Butte had been under martial law periodically beginning in 1914, not just after the Speculator fire and the lynching of Frank Little in summer 1917, and troops remained there through 1920. In all, the War Department bragged that soldiers had broken up twenty-nine "revolts," generally a euphemism for IWW strikes. It was a "massive program of strike-breaking, including raids on IWW headquarters, breaking up meetings, arresting and detaining hundreds of strikers under military authority," according to political scientist Robert Goldstein.[12]

For the Wilson administration, this commitment of troops—and exercise of federal control over state militia units—presented problems both political and practical. The appearances were not good: troops were siding with industry against working people at the very time when the federal government needed young working men to register patriotically for the draft and face death willingly in Europe. There also was the Posse Comitatus Act to acknowledge (or appear to acknowledge), which again generally forbids federal troops from enforcing state law or policing. True, the U.S. Constitution explicitly allows the federal government to protect the states from "domestic Violence." But the line between protecting a state from violence and protecting its richest businessmen from labor demands might at any time prove hard for a restive public to discern.[13]

Writing in late August 1917, an assistant attorney general who would play a large role in events to come, William C. Fitts, recognized exactly the legal problems with calling out federal troops. He sought to explain them to Senator Miles Poindexter, a progressive Republican from the state of Washington. In closing, he assured Poindexter, "The Department is now vigorously endeavoring to punish and stamp out the lawlessness of members of the I.W.W. and similar organizations wherever the same can by any means be properly brought within the jurisdiction of the Federal courts."[14]

There were other good reasons for both the Justice Department and the Labor Department to fill gaps that state law enforcement had left. Practically, the War Department needed troops in France more urgently than it needed them in Spokane, Butte, or dusty western mining boomtowns. A federal military response to the IWW and radical labor elements just seemed less and less appealing. Prosecutors, on the other hand, use only courtrooms, not cannons. The Justice Department could play the domestic role more comfortably than the War Department.

So, federal legalism, not federal militarism, seemed the answer in the summer of 1917. Western businessmen and politicians, whether local, state, or federal, grasped that. In addition to the three main areas of confluence in seeking a federal response—Lind's public safety commission, Bell's California commission, and federal military deployment—hundreds or thousands of western businessmen, mayors, governors, and state legislators were calling on and writing to their local U.S. district attorneys as soon as Congress declared war, if not before. They wanted federal action, and they wanted it coordinated across states. In the South, by contrast, even fifty-two years after the end of the Civil War, there remained deep bitterness about coordinated federal intervention during Reconstruction. But that was residual, cultural; after four or five decades, it was nearly beyond direct living memory. And those seeking broad federal help now were westerners, anyway. They had not shared the Reconstruction experience.[15]

The Wobblies faced a wave. The fact that they saw it coming did not mean they could outrun it.

7

The Color of Law

Of course, the wave had to hit Washington, DC, before it could hit the Wobblies. As late as midsummer 1917, the federal government was not yet uniformly and consistently arrayed against the IWW, or at least not against all of its goals. Most prominently, Secretary of Labor William B. Wilson once had been a member of the United Mine Workers and personally retained sympathy for labor even at its unruly edges. For a time, his Labor Department took a comparatively restrained and balanced approach to the struggle between labor and industry.

But the Department of Justice and the Post Office Department would not strike the same balance. The Post Office had only one important tool to use against radicals and the spread of their ideas—but it was an effective one. The postmaster general could deny a second-class postage permit to newspapers or publications that violated any provision of the new Espionage Act of June 15, 1917. Violators included anyone who "attempt[ed] to cause, insubordination, disloyalty, mutiny or refusal of duty" in the armed forces "or who shall willfully obstruct the recruiting and enlistment service of the United States." As newspapers were by definition "mailable matter" falling within the second of four such classes, denial of a second-class mailing permit made a newspaper "nonmailable matter." It could not pass in the U.S. mails, period.

As a practical matter, what you could not mail in 1917, you could not disseminate widely at all, for private couriers, like Wells Fargo or American Express, were expensive. So a newspaper that printed antiwar editorials or articles that might dissuade young men from registering for the draft or serving loyally was a newspaper that could move only so far from the printing press as its publishers and readers could carry it themselves, on the Post Office's say-so. That section of the Espionage Act was a useful way to silence dissent, on the prospective decision of one government official that a future edition of the newspaper probably would contain opinions that made it nonmailable. In a case that began in the fall of 1917, involving Victor Berger's *Milwaukee Leader*, the Supreme Court upheld exactly that power more than two years after the war ended, over the strong dissents of Justices Louis D. Brandeis and Oliver Wendell Holmes.[1]

Although the Justice Department lacked this powerful censor's tool, it had many more tools than the Post Office in the end. Among them were its role running prisons and its growing Bureau of Investigation. By late July, many in the Justice Department were ready to use those prisons to hold IWW leaders. They already were using the Bureau of Investigation's special agents to dog the IWW, in coordination with the citizens' American Protective League and, often, in competition with the Treasury Department's Secret Service.[2]

Top Justice Department officials mostly were lawyers who had served railroad magnates, mine owners, or other large corporate interests as a career. They were comfortable company men. On the whole, they did not share Labor Secretary William Wilson's reservations about repressing labor radicals.

At the Justice Department, Attorney General Thomas Watt Gregory in some ways was the least beholden to capital—and perhaps the most politically aware of the risks of unstable public support if the government appeared too eager to coddle capital and lash labor. The son of a Confederate Army captain killed in battle shortly after his birth, he had been an Austin, Texas, lawyer with some experience prosecuting trusts on behalf of the state of Texas. Gregory left no great mark as a lawyer, other than as an important supporter of the University of Texas. Better at serving his ambitions than at lawyering, he was a Democratic Party activist. As a delegate to nominating conventions, he made connections nationally and locally. Loosely, he fashioned himself as siding with the progressive wing of the party.[3]

Gregory also was soaked in the Democratic Party's southern populism of the late nineteenth and early twentieth centuries. In July 1906, seven years before he took his first political appointment at the Justice Department, he addressed a joint meeting of the Texas and Arkansas Bar Associations. Speaking forty years after the fact, he defended the rise and role of the original Ku Klux Klan as a necessary response to the "nightmare of

Reconstruction." The speech evinced the open racism common then. ("The most remarkable characteristics of the negro race at the present day are their vivid imagination and universal superstition"; he peppered the talk, too, with references to "insolence" as an offense.) Gregory also divided southern society into "whites of the lower classes" and the "better elements of society" or "the intelligent class" from whom the original KKK drew its members, in his view. Apart from those social layers, in fact not in the slice of cake at all, were those he termed "scalawags," "carpetbaggers," and "negroes." The last he seemed to blame more than once for their inability to read or write; he called some drunken and, repeatedly, insolent. In a later written version of the speech, he summed up his message fairly. "Did the end aimed at and accomplished by the Ku Klux Klan justify the movement?" he asked with a flourish. "The opinion of the writer is that the movement was fully justified, though he of course does not approve of crimes and excesses incident to it."[4]

Even so, in the context of summer 1917, Gregory would remain a comparatively moderate voice. He leaned toward the rule of law when others such as George Bell advocated mass detentions and worse. But by July 11, 1917, he believed, on no evidence at all and in league with men like Senator Henry Ashurst, that the IWW must be financed by German gold—or by "some hostile organization," as he put it more diplomatically.[5]

Gregory delegated most specific decisions and operational control, as an attorney general even then had to do. His principal subordinates were assistant attorneys general in the days before Congress created the office of the deputy attorney general. Some of those assistants headed divisions of the Department of Justice: Public Lands, Court of Claims, or Antitrust. Four of the seven assistant attorneys general led no division, though. In the summer of 1917, Gregory turned to two of those with undefined portfolios, Charles Warren and William C. Fitts. Each had left a lucrative private practice and now was taking home a government salary of $7,500 annually, not at all a pittance then but probably a cut in pay for both.[6]

Warren eventually would become a famous historian of the U.S. Supreme Court, winning a Pulitzer Prize in 1923 for his three-volume *The Supreme Court in United States History*. But he always was a prosperous practicing lawyer and never held an academic post. A lifelong Democrat from a family of Democrats in the heavily Republican Massachusetts of his day, a young Warren had cofounded an anti-immigrant group, the Immigration Restriction League, in 1894 and also opposed women's suffrage, his own party's argument against the gold standard, and imperialism.

Approaching fifty in the summer of 1917, he now thought of himself as a progressive—a term distinguishable from liberal in his day. Indeed, at home in Massachusetts, Warren had demonstrated a long commitment to civil service systems and to reforming patronage and machine politics at the local level, which was classic progressive work. But his suspicion, or worse, of immigrants persisted: he was an important drafter of the 1917 Espionage Act.[7]

Fitts was an Alabaman and also a practicing lawyer for most of his life. The son of an Episcopalian minister, he was born in Tuscaloosa just after the Civil War. He practiced law just eight years before Alabama voters elected him state attorney general at age twenty-eight. He served for four years. Then he resumed practice in successively larger cities: first Mobile and then Birmingham. In 1914, Fitts came to Washington as a special assistant to the attorney general. Three years later, Gregory elevated him to assistant attorney general. With General Enoch Crowder, Fitts wrote the 1917 draft law. After government service, Fitts would move to a larger city still— New York—where he served ten years as general counsel to the Postal Telegraph & Cable Company, the main competitor of Western Union until the larger company bought it in 1943.

For now, though, Fitts had exactly the sharp edge that his boss, Gregory, did not when it came to the IWW. "Fear is the only force," he snarled, "that will keep the wretches in order."[8]

Both Warren and Fitts occupied offices in one of a succession of temporary homes for the Justice Department in its first sixty-five years. That itinerant existence lasted until 1934, when the Classic Revival building between 9th and 10th Streets and Constitution and Pennsylvania Avenues that today still serves as "Main Justice" opened. Throughout the summer of 1917, the two men showed their resolve to quell the IWW, playing important roles as surrogates for the attorney general as hundreds of western businessmen and politicians beseeched the Wilson administration to take action. Even the preceding winter and spring, it would have been hard to write the Espionage Act (Warren) or the new conscription law (Fitts) without thinking how to curb opponents of the war in general and many in the IWW specifically.

But while they agreed on the same end for the IWW, Warren and Fitts did not agree entirely on means to that end. Warren generally was inclined to go the farthest. On July 17, with Gregory's approval, he sent instructions to all U.S. district attorneys and to the offices of the Bureau of Investigation. They were to make extraordinary efforts to gather intelligence on the IWW and its future plans and feed that back to the Justice Department in Washington. More, Warren suggested arresting and detaining noncitizen German members of the IWW without charge. He leaned toward George Bell's views, favoring trial of civilians by military commission for violations of the Espionage Act. This was too much for Gregory, who remained the moderating voice.[9]

Fitts either took a more moderate view, too, or knew that Gregory did. He inclined to former governor Lind's basic approach: criminal charges in civilian court, taking advantage of the new Espionage Act's breadth and using its conspiracy provisions to expand its reach yet farther. But as late as July 28, Fitts told the U.S. district attorney in Oregon that the IWW was "for the States themselves to control under such laws as they deem proper to enact and to enforce." Even then, though, he hinted at possible federal action. His response evinced no sympathy for the IWW or labor radicals. This corporate lawyer had none. Fitts just seemed to understand that wholesale extralegal detentions, internment, or military trials for domestic activity would not win a consensus in the Justice Department or gain approval of the president and his cabinet as a whole.

By the end of July or the first days in August, Gregory and his Department of Justice had settled on a basic plan. The federal government would step in decisively. It would implement a coordinated strategy against the IWW from coast to coast. The fledgling Bureau of Investigation within the Justice Department, just over eight years old and employing something more than 425 special agents (but growing rapidly), would have its first national role. The strategy would be legalist: it would display the forms of law and, in the end, entail a trial in the federal courts under the ordinary rules of evidence and procedure. Thanks to Attorney General Gregory's comparative moderation in judgment, perhaps in part a reaction to the unease of Labor Secretary William Wilson and the president's own political and esthetic sensibilities, this legal strategy would look lawful.[10]

But it would rest on a stunningly broad statute, the new Espionage Act, and would stretch even that breadth through clever use of the act's conspiracy provisions. The government would not hold itself to proving that the IWW defendants committed any completed crimes: it would allege only that they committed crimes by agreeing that someday, some of them would commit substantive crimes.

The government's strategy, then, was to follow Lind's plan without much change. The head of the Chicago office of the Bureau of Investigation,

Hinton G. Clabaugh—the very man with whom Lind had met—would win a leading role. Lind's Minnesota Commission on Public Safety would share the inside information its private detectives had gathered from within the IWW, where they posed as members. The Justice Department would take it from there.[11]

This national, coordinated, federal legal strategy to take on a whole radical structure, to destroy an organization or a movement at pen point and finger point rather than bayonet point, truly was new. Leaders in the DOJ sensed it. On August 30, 1917, Fitts wrote to Senator Albert Fall of New Mexico to reassure him. "I may say to you that under the direction of the attorney general something quite effective is under way with respect to the I.W.W. situation," Fitts hinted. "This is as far as it would be prudent to go at present, and even this much which is revealed to you you will please treat in confidence. I do not think you or any of your western friends will be disappointed if the results which we hope to obtain are achieved."[12]

As August came, with Frank Little's funeral procession in Butte, back east in Washington, DC, the wave had arrived. Now it was washing back westward. IWW leaders only could watch it swelling toward them.

8

Five Tons

It's not that Big Bill Haywood did not try, or did not make a show of trying, to avoid the deluge. Rather than stand in front of it, he tried to surf it. By mid-August, President Wilson had appointed a judge in Washington, DC, J. Harry Covington II, to conduct a visible investigation into the IWW. Haywood welcomed that investigation publicly. Also for public consumption, he invited Covington to visit IWW offices and simply ask for what he wanted. The Wobblies would turn over any and all documents on his mere request.[1]

No takers. Covington ignored Haywood's gambit.

His response would not have mattered. As it played out, Covington was but a figurehead anyway. The real work had happened and was happening in the Bureau of Investigation and among the Justice Department's lawyers and outside counsel, under Fitts's supervision. The department had much more than the information that Lind's private detectives had gathered. It had reports from dozens or hundreds of undercover Bureau of Investigation agents, plainclothes sheriff's deputies, and employers' private detectives, all of whom had blended into IWW ranks for years. (A Toledo, Ohio, local had expelled an undercover private detective, working for an employer, as early as August 1914, for example.) That August, the private detectives and undercover agents were so thick and bold that Haywood watched them out the windows of the new IWW national headquarters at 1001 W. Madison Street in Chicago. He learned to tolerate them trailing behind when he walked out for lunch. Presumably, they wanted to be seen: that carried a message that the government was closing in.[2]

Outwardly, Haywood kept on as before. One of his traits was organization. With the help of two secretaries, Hilda Seery and Elizabeth Serviss, Haywood kept meticulous files of correspondence. Every letter he received went into a file bearing the writer's name. An onionskin carbon copy of his typed reply went into the same file. Some of the files were years old and bulging; others were new and thin. Account books of dues payments and expenditures were good, too. A new member's $2 initiation fee went only to the specific industrial union local he or she joined. But after that, 15 cents of the 50-cent monthly dues from each member went to Chicago headquarters. The account books were a trove of members' names. National headquarters also charged a bit more than cost for pamphlets, buttons, stickerettes, and the slim books that IWW local unions could order for members and recruiting. The national office kept records of what went where and when.[3]

Soon, the government would find all of this useful. The file marked "Frank Little," for example, held a sheaf of letters that Little and Haywood had exchanged that summer. Again, Little stridently favored the organization taking an anticonscription stance. He was implacable on that point and had some allies. Throughout their correspondence, Haywood deflected and stalled, but when forced on the issue, opposed Little's demands. On July 24, 1917, Little wrote a telegram to Haywood, prodding, "When will Board's statement be out?" Haywood cabled back, referring to an article in the IWW newspaper, *Solidarity*: "Editorial covers the essential points of Board statements; so useless to print it." He saw danger to the institution in Little's uncompromising approach. Haywood's tack was to argue that a shooting war was peripheral to, and more transitory than, the long war for industrial democracy and economic parity that the IWW was waging. In Europe, one alliance of capitalists was using the working poor to fight another alliance of capitalists hiding behind their own working poor, in his opinion.

The IWW, by comparison, was fighting capitalism everywhere. Yes, he hated the war. But the board should leave participation in the draft or the army to the individual conscience of each member, in Haywood's tactical view. Just ten days after Congress declared war in April, Haywood had answered another Frank Little letter urging that the IWW General Executive Board take a public stand against enlistment. Haywood's telegram then said, "Keep cool head; not talk. Good many feel as you do, but world war is of small importance when compared to great class war."

That view prevailed; Little's did not. But the exchange of correspondence, and the craftiness of Haywood's politicking, eventually would serve the government's interest all the same.[4]

Back in Washington, with Covington playing a public role perhaps as a diversionary tactic, Gregory, Fitts, and other top Justice Department lawyers were working out of public sight. On Friday, August 10, they made significant, unseen moves. That was the day they first approached a corporate lawyer in Salt Lake City, a man favored by western mining and railroad companies, about a role as lead prosecutor. It also was the day that provided the first written record of a more ominous overture: the Justice Department already had sought out a specific federal judge in Chicago for a case not yet begun.

Something ephemeral—maybe a telephone call, a personal visit, a telegram that through someone's discretion did not make its way into Justice Department files—must have occurred before August 10, with the attorney general himself proposing a meeting between Judge Kenesaw Mountain Landis and William Fitts. The first document in Justice Department files is a cryptic 1:20 p.m. telegram from Landis back to "Hon. T. W. Gregory" that Friday: "Am obliged to hold court at LaCrosse [Wisconsin] Monday can Mr. Fitts be here Sunday morning. Landis, District Judge." Gregory replied later Friday afternoon. "Please meet Assistant Attorney General Fitts Congress Hotel, Sunday morning, eleven o'clock. Answer." Other than the sender's name, "T. W. Gregory," that was all it said.

Bright and early on Saturday morning, at 7:34 a.m., Landis replied to Gregory. "Will meet Mr. Fitts Cinpen Hotel eleven oclock Sunday. Landis, District Judge." That caused confusion back in Washington, where Fitts and others were at work that Saturday morning. What was the Cinpen Hotel? Fitts sent a telegram to the U.S. district attorney in Chicago, Charles F. Clyne, who obviously was in the know and on duty that Saturday morning, too. "I want to meet Judge Landis and you in Chicago tomorrow Sunday morning. Have telegram from the Judge in which he says I shall come to the Cinpen Hotel. Not knowing of any such hotel please meet me Congress Hotel promptly at ten o'clock tomorrow morning in the meantime making arrangements so that I will not miss the Judge."

Some confusion seems to have continued. Later that morning, Fitts wired the chief of the Bureau of Investigation office in Chicago, directing him with some urgency, "Meet me tomorrow Sunday morning nine-thirty o'clock Congress Hotel. Have your automobile so that I can find Judge Landis." The agent replied promptly. "Telegram received will meet you with automobile as instructed. Judge Landis informs me already had engagement meet you eleven oclock Congress Hotel. Please advise whether prefer see him anywhere else at any other time and will make appointment accordingly."[5]

There the paper trail ends, abruptly. Given the commitment that Landis and both Gregory and Fitts showed to arranging a weekend meeting, one reasonably can assume that the meeting happened that Sunday morning, August 12, in the large Congress Hotel at the corner of Congress Parkway and South Michigan Avenue, facing Grant Park's Buckingham Fountain. It was urgent enough to warrant an assistant attorney general taking an overnight train from Washington, DC, to meet the judge. For his part, Landis presumably had to catch his own train at some point that Sunday, to be in La Crosse, Wisconsin, for court the next day. This meeting was sufficiently important to warrant some real inconvenience on both sides.

Whatever they discussed, no one seems to have committed anything to writing after the meeting. In any event, there is no further record in Justice Department files or in Landis's papers.

Assuming again that the meeting happened, it raises questions. Ethically, it may not have been improper in itself: there was no pending case, so the usual bar on a judge meeting with lawyers from only one side of a case (setting aside rare exceptions) would not apply here, strictly speaking. There is nothing improper about lawyers or federal agents talking to federal judges socially, for example, if they are not discussing a pending case in the absence of their adversaries. But at the same time, the risk of approaching or crossing ethical lines in the haze was high. This surely was not a purely social meeting: Fitts had business to discuss with the judge, and under the circumstances that business had to concern an anticipated prosecution of IWW members. Logically, this almost surely was a planning meeting. Participating in prosecutorial planning sessions for criminal cases was not and is not the work of federal judges.

Moreover, this further question is inescapable: why pick this federal judge? Chicago had two sitting district judges at the time, Kenesaw Mountain Landis and George Albert Carpenter. The unbroken federal court tradition was and is that no litigant, not even the United States, gets to pick the judge if more than one judge sits in a jurisdiction. Rather, after—and only after—a case is filed, the clerk of court assigns it to a judge by some random method: at the time, often by pulling a slip with a judge's name from a tumbler. In many places, to this day the process for assigning a judge may be referred to as "the wheel," a reference to bygone mechanical means of assuring random selection. So, in theory, Landis had only a 50 percent chance of becoming the assigned judge once the government filed an indictment. Yet no one seems to have sought to include Judge Carpenter in the Sunday morning hotel meeting.

An available inference, then, is that Landis was able, and perhaps willing, to override the clerk of court's random assignment process and pick his own case. That is not the only possibility. But it may be the most likely.

Then there was the issue of search warrants that would precede an indictment. For obvious reasons, government agents always have approached federal judges ex parte—without the other side, or the target of the search warrant—to make the showing of probable cause for a warrant. But that is not what the Justice Department was doing that Sunday morning, and it hardly would have sent a top official from Washington just to apply for a search warrant. Then and now, seeking search warrants is a routine mission often left just to law enforcement agents without any prosecutor present.

Whatever happened on Sunday morning at the Congress Hotel, by the end of August, Fitts and the Justice Department were ready to move against the IWW in court. They would launch the assault with a large number of search warrants, to be executed simultaneously across the country. That would lead to seized documents and other evidence. Culling through all of that would produce admissible evidence for trial, and also would clarify which IWW members and supporters could be charged with what. Indictments and arrests then could follow, and finally trials.

But that first step—obtaining and executing search warrants—would be the essential opening salvo: it would dispirit, disorient, and disable the enemy IWW. The judicial system is at its most physical, muscular, and fearsome when approving execution of search or arrest warrants. The execution of a search warrant often is tactical and even theatrical: swarms of armed officers arrive at a home before the sun peeks into the eastern sky; doors and jambs are splintered with a loud crash by battering rams; to demonstrate that the target's privacy and sense of security mean nothing, drawers are flung onto floors, mail is torn open, and mattresses are overturned. The terrifying effect is not just intended but intended to last; intended to sap the will to resist by convincing the target that resistance will be futile. Moreover, executing search warrants can lead to publicity, as searches often are very visible—whether intended that way or not. The Justice Department recognized that reality. On August 30, Gregory wired prosecutors in Chicago, "If all of you are agreed that you have progressed to point where publicity will not be harmful, proceed with warrants."

Indeed, once the prosecutors were ready, the publicity would help in deflating the IWW and its supporters.[6]

Under the Fourth Amendment, which the states ratified with nine other amendments in 1791, a federal search warrant must meet two main requirements through an application under oath: probable cause and particularity. Probable cause means a showing of reasonable possibility; an objective display of good reason for the search or seizure, with facts allowing a neutral magistrate to draw that conclusion. Particularity means that the warrant must direct and limit government actors to specific things or people they reasonably may clasp. The warrant is not a broad license just to rummage around until they find something or someone, as British general warrants and writs of assistance in the colonies had been. All the requirements serve the Fourth Amendment's central goal: that the federal government search or seize—intrude upon person or private places and things—reasonably or not at all.[7]

Absent probable cause and particularity in a warrant, in other words, the search itself is unreasonable unless it has some legal footing without a warrant. Just more than twenty years before 1917, Justice Joseph P. Bradley had explained why, in terms almost poetic for a man not remembered for poetry. "It is not the breaking of his doors and rummaging of his drawers that constitutes the essence of the offence," Bradley wrote of officials searching a person's effects in *Boyd v. United States* (1896), "but it is the invasion of his indefeasible right of personal security, personal liberty, and private property, where that right has never been forfeited by his conviction of some public offence."[8]

In 1917, federal courts still understood the Fourth Amendment as imposing another limit on government seizures. A search warrant could not permit seizure of "mere evidence." Even a subpoena could not compel the production of a "man's private papers" as evidence if the purpose was to forfeit his property. Letters or financial records, for example, that simply might be useful later in court to support a criminal charge should not be taken by warrant, or even demanded by subpoena. Only the actual fruits or instruments of crime—stolen goods, burglary tools, the murder weapon—were fair game. If the bank book in Smith's house was stolen from Jones's house, the police could seize it with a warrant. But if it was Smith's own bank book they could not, even if it recorded deposits of stolen money. In effect, when the government was considering how to attack the IWW that summer, a warrant usually allowed only seizure of contraband, not things that were innocent in and of themselves.[9]

But earlier that summer, Congress arguably had given federal law enforcers something new. The Espionage Act had included the first general statutory procedure for seeking search warrants. The long formal name of that June 15, 1917, act ended with the words "and better to enforce the criminal laws of the United States." True to that end, the act expanded the items that a search warrant might target to include "property, or any paper, . . . possessed, controlled, or used" by those acting "in aid of any foreign Government." This opened to the Justice Department a path around the mere evidence rule. If the IWW was acting in aid of a foreign government, Germany's, then the papers it possessed were fair game for seizure—all of them.[10]

Justice Department lawyers set to work. They drafted one application for use with every search warrant they would seek. Local U.S. district attorneys only had to copy the application verbatim, and to insert the name of a Bureau of Investigation agent who would swear to it under oath. But what of the fact that the U.S. government had no evidence at all that the IWW or any of its members actually were giving aid to the German government? Prosecutors and Bureau of Investigation agents had the general antiwar attitude of the IWW's newspapers, like *Solidarity*, and the stump speeches of some of its organizers and leaders. Still, the idea that anyone opposed to a war for any reason necessarily was aiding the other side in that war, in a legally culpable sense, was breathtakingly broad and incoherent. It would have covered the quiet Quaker in her meeting house, the mother of draft-age sons who were needed on the farm, the aging veteran who, reliving the horrors he had seen, had come to the hard conclusion that spilling blood never in the end is a solution. All of them would have been seen as giving aid to a foreign enemy—even if that "aid" was intangible, unusable, and unknown to the enemy.

If the danger of this proposition, that antiwar sentiment equaled illegal aid to a foreign government, gave anyone in the Justice Department pause, the lawyers overcame their doubts quickly. Their warrant application simply would assert, as a flat conclusion, that the IWW was aiding the "Imperial German Government." It would assert as well that the IWW was "willfully causing and attempting to cause insubordination, disloyalty, mutiny, and refusal of duty in the military and naval forces of the United States" and "willfully obstructing the recruiting and enlistment services of the United States," thus interfering in the government's efforts to fight the "Imperial German Government." On what facts were these assumptions based? On none, it seems: using a favorite lawyerly phrase, they were based solely "on information and belief." At that moment, this meant hearsay, innuendo, and supposition. The application would offer no facts from which a neutral judge might draw his own conclusion that the government had shown probable cause for the search. Instead, it simply would feed the judge a conclusion based on undisclosed "information" and on the affiant's own untested "belief," then rely on the judge's shared suspicions about radical labor's motives and hidden actions. In short, the search warrant applications made no showing of probable cause by any measure. The government later admitted as much but shrugged it off.[11]

The search warrants themselves also had almost no limitations. The Justice Department left some discretion to local U.S. district attorneys on how to describe the objects for seizure. For example, the Pittsburgh warrant for the IWW office there directed law enforcement officers to take:

1. Lists and memoranda of names and address of officers, agents, employees and members of the Industrial Workers of the World.
2. Text books, pamphlets and prints explaining and advocating the principles of the association, union or society of persons calling themselves "Industrial Workers of the World" commonly known as the I.W.W.'s.
3. Account books, letters, carbon copies of letters, telegrams, express receipt books, freight receipt books, parcel receipt and record books, ledgers, journals, cash books, day books, memorandum books, bank books, check books, receipt books, code books, sketches, drawings, photographs, letters and invoices.
4. Constitution, charter, by-laws and credentials for organizers of the association, union or society of persons calling themselves the "Industrial Workers of the World" commonly known as the I.W.W.'s.

There was nothing more specific than that. Anything that might explain or advocate the "principles" of an organization was fair game. Three years later, a federal appeals court would admit, "The affidavits, on which the search warrants issued, failed to describe the property to be taken except by reference to its general character, and failed to state any facts from which the magistrates could determine the existence of probable cause."[12]

For now, though, the Bureau of Investigation had forty-eight nearly identical search warrants for IWW offices around the country. The plan, as the prosecution team in Chicago conceived it, was to execute them all more or less simultaneously. That coordinated effort would tax the Justice Department even today: executing four dozen related search warrants at the same moment would be possible now, but rare.[13]

In 1917, it all was unprecedented. Dozens if not hundreds of local police officers and sheriff's deputies would have to help in executing the warrants, supplementing the few Bureau of Investigation agents sprinkled around the country outside the nation's capital. Coordinating these local law enforcement officers with a skeleton federal staff would prove a remarkable logistical achievement, by some measures, in a day when the telegraph was the surest means of long-distance communication (the telephone remaining unreliable for great distances just three years after the first transcontinental telephone lines were connected).[14]

But at 2:00 p.m. on September 5, 1917, across the country, that is exactly what hundreds of officers did. A Bureau of Investigation agent or two led the search parties, but most of the searchers came from the ranks of deputy U.S. marshals, sheriff's deputies, and local policemen.

With authority as broad and vague as the search warrants gave them, searchers acted with varying degrees of zeal. In Philadelphia, in addition to all the records and correspondence, agents took three typewriters, an adding machine, all unopened mail, blank report sheets, and postage stamps. In Great Falls, Montana, agents decided that a rip saw, blank typewriter paper, and blank envelopes all had sufficient evidentiary value to warrant taking. In Butte, agents grabbed "about 3000 more or less" photographs of Frank Little, and the office's Remington Typewriter No. 10. The Omaha, Nebraska, office saw two boxes of cigars, its two copies of Victor Hugo's *Les Miserables*, and one copy each of Shakespeare's *Julius Caesar*, Frederic W. Farrar's *The Life of Christ* (1874), Oliver Wendell Holmes Jr.'s *The Common Law* (1881), and even the *Holy Bible* hauled off, presumably as bearing on the principles and advocacy of the IWW. The Chicago headquarters were emptied, essentially, with even furniture seized; from there, the greatest bulk came. By contrast, in Minneapolis, Dan Buckley, secretary of one of the locals there, reported to Haywood that the six-hour search by five officers "was conducted *courteously*." C. W. Anderson added in his report to Haywood that searching agents cooperated well enough that the office's business could continue during the search. In the end, the search party took nothing at all, even though the warrant instructed seizure of "all records and effects of the union." Anderson quoted the lead searcher, Bureau of Investigation Special Agent Campbell, as saying that he "could not in the world see why they had ever been ordered to raid the offices."

Soon, apparently, the reluctant Minnesota office of the Bureau of Investigation would get a scolding from Washington. On November 2, agents were back in the Minneapolis IWW offices with an identical warrant, and this time they took much. Then on November 19, they returned a third time, again with an identical warrant, and announced that they "had come to take everything." They did.[15]

The forty-eight warrants on September 5, 1917, were just the beginning. Depending on the city, other searches followed on November 13, November 22, December 19, and December 26. In the end, the federal government seized more than five tons of IWW documents, furniture, and miscellany. With financial records, membership records, cash, plates for printing presses, and all correspondence gone—even in offices in which the government left typewriters and other office equipment—the entire union was disabled for the time. That was the idea.[16]

Local and federal officers then trucked everything, from all corners of the country, to the federal courthouse in Chicago. A freight elevator took it to the eighth floor. There it filled two rooms and Bureau of Investigation agents began the laborious task of reviewing and cataloging all of it. Two dogged agents, Chicago agent-in-charge Hinton G. Clabaugh and George N. Murdock, took the lead in that task. They paper-clipped notes to documents of special interest. They scribbled catalog information on some documents with blue pencil. In the end, they cross-indexed all the correspondence by both senders and recipients. The government eventually would offer some fifteen thousand pages of correspondence, articles, and pamphlets in court, which was just a tiny fraction of the documents seized.[17]

For now, agents burrowed into the five-ton mound furiously. Hardly more than three weeks after the September 5 searches, the Justice Department would have something tangible to show for its efforts.

9

The Copper Trust Lawyer

With truckloads, literally, of documents to review and assemble into usable trial evidence, the Bureau of Investigation's agents only could carry the process so far. The Justice Department would need capable trial lawyers in Chicago. Lawyers would have to steer the agents. They also would have to make a plausible showing to a federal grand jury to secure an indictment, for a trial could not proceed otherwise. Since 1791, the Fifth Amendment to the U.S. Constitution had required that all contested felony cases in federal courts proceed on indictment, which only a grand jury can issue. Then they would have to shepherd the case through pretrial proceedings: arrests, bail hearings, likely challenges to the seized evidence and perhaps to the indictment itself, and eventually a protracted trial. A later appeal, assuming convictions, also was an immediate tactical consideration, as the government would want to avoid the embarrassment of an appellate court disapproving the whole effort. Finally, there was the reality that the nationwide IWW problem could not be addressed adequately in one trial, or in one city; there likely would be other trials, too.

No one, absolutely no one, seems to have imagined that the U.S. district attorney in Chicago was up to the task. Charles F. Clyne, Woodrow Wilson's appointee in the Northern District of Illinois, with Chicago as the court's main seat, was like most U.S. district attorneys then. At forty years old, he was a political patronage appointee, entrusted with routine local federal prosecutions and nothing more, and assisted only by a small staff of assistant U.S. district attorneys. His University of Michigan Law School classmates considered him someone with a "felicitous manner," good as a toastmaster. But this also was a man who later would beam to newspaper reporters during jury selection that he owned two pairs of pants and mistakenly had climbed into the wrong pair that morning, so in addition to a mismatched suit he had no dime in his pocket for the shoeshine boy on his way to court. He made the boy shine his shoes anyway.[1]

William Fitts, of course, was vitally interested in the prosecution and in charge of it. He probably had trial experience during his days practicing in Alabama. But Fitts now had an important position in Washington as an assistant attorney general with overall control of the new legal attack on the IWW. He would not undertake the mundane, time-consuming tasks of putting together and trying a large case, and probably could not spend months in Chicago without neglecting his broader role. Other assistants to the attorney general, notably Oliver E. Pagan, would help substantially. But they, too, could not be assigned to Chicago for the entire trial without impairing the Justice Department's work in Washington, DC.

So, the Justice Department would look to outside talent to lead the Chicago effort. Although it soon would be fifty years since Congress had tried half-heartedly to rein in appointments of lawyers for wealthy industrialists to act as "special attorneys" for the Justice Department in the public name, the practice hardly had died. Top Justice Department officials still came, usually, from lucrative corporate practices and were responsive in the main to the wishes of moneyed businessmen. Fitts, who had exactly that background after leaving the Alabama attorney general's office, began by early August to look for an outside corporate lawyer in the same mold. As the department was arranging the secret meeting with Judge Landis, he had found his first choice.

How exactly Fitts selected Franklin Knowlton Nebeker is not clear. Maybe he thought it useful to seek a western corporate lawyer, given the IWW's origins and strength in western mining country. But that is a guess. In any event, on August 10, Attorney General Gregory sent a telegram to "Honorable Frank K. Nebeker, Salt Lake City, Utah." He was even more succinct than telegrams required. "Government needs your professional services prosecuting disloyal offenders operating from Chicago. Will you meet Assistant Attorney General Fitts Chicago when called? He will disclose plan and discuss compensation. Answer."

Nebeker must have assented verbally before August 15, for on that day Gregory instructed Frank Dailey (another outside lawyer), Clyne, Pagan, and the head of the Chicago office of the department's Bureau of Investigation, Clabaugh, to confer with Nebeker on the proposed indictment. But not until August 21 did Nebeker confirm by telegram to the attorney general that he had "arranged to take up Government prosecutions" and would leave for Chicago soon. "Am now familiarizing myself with federal statutes and decisions. Letter concerning compensation follows," Nebeker added.

In response the same day, the attorney general instructed Nebeker that it was "very important that nothing be published in regard to matter discussed with you. See that nothing gets out about employment." Nebeker's role, and perhaps his form of compensation, was to be kept secret for the time. He arrived in Chicago on August 28, 1917.[2]

Once the government obtained and executed the search warrants across the country, secrecy would be impossible, as senior Justice Department officials understood. At that point, the role of the outside corporate lawyers could be revealed. With a dateline just two days after the September 5 searches, the *New York Times* reported that Clyne "is to be assisted by Frank C. Dailey of Indianapolis and Frank K. Nebeker of Salt Lake City, and the investigation will be under the personal supervision of William C. Fitts, Assistant Attorney General, under whose direction the seizure of I.W.W. documents was made. Mr. Fitts will make daily reports to Attorney General Gregory." The investigation, the *Times* added, "would probably be prolonged." Dailey soon dropped into invisibility. But Nebeker remained the visible leader of the prosecution team.[3]

Nebeker came from a sprawling and well-known Utah family. He was a distant and younger cousin of Aquila Nebeker, former president of the Utah State Senate and a member of the 1895 convention that wrote the state's constitution. Aquila became a wealthy rancher and miner and a "straight silver" Democrat—a populist in the William Jennings Bryan faction of the 1890s. This elder Nebeker cousin served as U.S. marshal for Utah, another patronage post, during the Wilson administration. A still earlier ancestor, John Nebeker, had been the first "public complainer" in Salt Lake City, a sort of city prosecutor working for the High Council of the Church of Latter Day Saints. In a late 1840s case, the soft-hearted John had quailed at administering ten lashes in a public whipping, as the High Council had ordered. Eventually he did it. By the 1890s, the largely prosperous extended family included lawyers and doctors.[4]

Frank K. Nebeker (he dropped "Franklin" and went by "Frank" most of his life) was the son of Ira and Delia Lane Nebeker, born in 1870 in Laketown, Utah. His childhood is obscure. At barely twenty, he married Elizabeth Lillian Martineau in Logan and graduated in 1891 from Brigham

Young College. From there, the young couple left for Cornell University, where Frank was one of sixteen law graduates in 1895. Nebeker won recognition at graduation for his "Thesis of Distinguished Excellence" on "Interstate Extradition." He moved promptly back to Utah and became first county attorney and then district attorney in Cache County, with its seat at Logan, eighty-plus miles north of Salt Lake City. He then went back into private practice in a partnership with his younger brother (whom their Democratic parents had named after the antislavery Whig and then Republican journalist Horace Greeley) in Logan and eventually joined a more established firm in Salt Lake City. There in the state's largest and most important city, he represented business interests, especially the Oregon Short Line Railroad Company, and became a member of the Salt Lake Commercial Club and the Salt Lake Transportation Club, where he could rub elbows with current and prospective clients. Together he and Lillian, as she called herself, had six children, two boys and four girls, whom they raised in comfort.[5]

Nebeker also became increasingly active in Democratic politics. By 1908, he had a plum role on the Speakers Committee for the Democratic National Convention. He was a prominent corporate lawyer at home and a rising figure in the national Democratic Party. Although Nebeker now lived and worked in Salt Lake City, the place of Big Bill Haywood's birth, the two had very little in common. Nebeker served profitably the sort of men who owned the mines and mining camps in which Haywood's father had chipped out a living and died at age twenty-seven. Haywood himself had gone to work in those mines at age nine.[6]

After the Democratic Party came back to power nationally with Woodrow Wilson's election in 1912, following sixteen years of Republicans in the White House, Nebeker was in a good position to get tapped for a federal role. His chance came in late summer 1917. In a sense, he never really would go back to Utah. He later would become the assistant attorney general for the Public Lands Division, a nice assignment for a westerner who might placate mining and ranching interests in dealing with rights to use the federal government's vast land holdings in the West. From there, Wilson moved him briefly to the Antitrust Division, policing the very class of corporations he had represented. Nebeker swiveled in and out of government service for much of the rest of his working life. As late as May 1935, at age sixty-five, Nebeker still had a special appointment to the Justice Department. It paid well. Other than the attorney general, he was one of only seven men in the department earning $10,000. That was more than the assistant attorneys general and the director of the FBI, J. Edgar Hoover, made: all of them took home $9,000 salaries.

A lucrative corporate practice in Washington, DC, thrived in between Nebeker's stints in government service. He represented not just large companies but also, for example, the Cherokee Nation.[7]

In the years after 1918, Nebeker's family settled into District of Columbia society. They had a lovely home on Woodley Road in the city's leafy, genteel Northwest section, directly across from the National Cathedral's grounds. His younger daughter's and granddaughters' weddings would make the *New York Times* society pages, and that newspaper in later years added the honorific "judge" before his name, although there is no record that he ever held such an office.[8]

For now, though, the Wobblies nicknamed the western newcomer "the Copper Trust lawyer," or used an even more sarcastic variation, such as "the legal luminary of the Copper Trust." The specific accuracy of that derisive label is uncertain. Utah was a copper mining area, like Nevada to the west and Arizona to the south, and Salt Lake City was a regional center including for the legal profession. So Nebeker almost surely had represented mine owners, probably copper mining companies among them. His membership in the city's Commercial Club and its Transportation Club supports an inference of close business relations with mining companies and railroads, among other businesses. But short biographies mention only his role representing the Oregon Short Line Railroad Company, not his role for any mining company or consortium.[9]

He was forty-seven in the fall of 1917. Trim and erect, Nebeker cut a lawyerly figure. As a younger man, he had a pompadour of thick black hair, which now became wavy but still thick as his hair grayed. In some photographs, he wore small wireless, oval eyeglasses; in other photographs, he had no glasses at all. His cheekbones were high and his features generally sharp, with the exception of a wide and slightly flattened nose; the sort of nose that hinted it might have been broken once or more than once and not set. His suits were sharp. No bumbling Charles Clyne was he. From outside the Justice Department altogether at that point, this special prosecutor who served private corporate interests would enjoy public powers.

With those powers, Nebeker quickly revealed a thin-skinned sense of his importance. After the search warrants and publicity about them, Nebeker did not like what he read in his hometown newspapers. On September 10, he sent a frosty telegram to Fitts. "In Washington despatches appearing in my home papers," Nebeker sniffed, "I am referred to as investigator and assistant to Clyne. You will understand that this is most humiliating to me. I feel sure you will have the erroneous impression corrected." Fitts did. The very next day, no less than the acting attorney general, in Gregory's brief absence, sent a telegram back to Nebeker. "It is desire of Department for you to have full credit. Proper statement has been furnished newspapers."[10]

Nebeker's principal helpmate at trial would be another outside lawyer, Claude R. Porter of Iowa. But Porter was not a corporate lawyer; he fundamentally was a politician, a Democrat in heavily Republican Iowa. Porter was serving in 1917 as the U.S. district attorney in Des Moines, for the Southern District of Iowa. He had been President Wilson's appointee since 1914. Just two years younger than Nebeker, Porter was born a lawyer's son and raised in small towns in far south-central Iowa. A strikingly handsome man, every bit of six feet tall with a slightly sad expression almost perpetually, Porter had served in the Spanish-American war and joined the Iowa House of Representatives at just twenty-three. From there, he moved to the Iowa Senate for four years, becoming the youngest member there as he had been in the House. His style was straightforward. "He is a dangerous antagonist in debate. His talk is of the sledge-hammer sort. He does not talk unless he has something to say, and seldom tells a story," an admirer wrote. "He never effects sarcasm or causticity," the admirer added. "He simply strikes and strikes hard." Porter's later performance at trial would bear out only some of that.

Porter did not like radicals or the unpatriotic. But he was not an enemy of labor generally. In the legislature, "He was specially interested in the adoption of laws ameliorating the condition of the miners. He was the author of a law that perfected the frequent payment of miners' wages and prohibited the operators from holding back earned wages."[11]

From the state legislature, though, his elective career stalled. A popular young man personally, he drew substantial crossover Republican votes in runs for governor and U.S. senator, but never enough to carry this progressive-wing Democrat in a Republican state. Three times he would run for governor and lose; five times he lost races for the U.S. Senate. Indeed, he was on the brink of a run for Iowa governor when he accepted the call from Fitts and the Justice Department to serve as Nebeker's principal assistant in Chicago.[12]

William Fitts now had his team in place for trial. A trial could not come, though, until an indictment did. The five-ton mound of IWW papers would be sifted not just to secure the indictment but to support that indictment later at trial. Meanwhile, something would have to be presented to a grand jury, such as summary testimony. The grand jury would indict. Arrests would have to follow across the country. Arraignment and pretrial hearings would come next. Hundreds of anticipated trial exhibits would have to be identified, marked, and linked to witnesses who could introduce them. The war added urgency to all this. Fitts, Nebeker, Porter, Justice Department lawyers back in Washington, Murdock and Clabaugh and their colleagues in the Bureau of Investigation, and yes, even Clyne all had work to do.

10

True Bill

All considered, the indictment came very quickly. On Friday, September 28, just twenty-three days after the raids, a grand jury in Chicago's federal courthouse handed up an indictment. At that point, IWW offices still were trying to reconstruct membership rolls, finances, and basic ongoing operations. The IWW was starting essentially from scratch, in some offices without even a typewriter.[1]

Although the lapse of barely more than three weeks between searches and indictment might suggest that the government had worked very quickly, in fact the seized materials had little to do with the indictment directly. The indictment had been planned and drafted, in outline, weeks before in Washington, as a legal strategy emerged in the Justice Department over the course of the summer now ending. Of course, by the time a trial started, the mass of documents seized would have to be culled to support the indictment. But agents and prosecutors really did not have to examine them closely to *obtain* the indictment. Yes, they would have to read and sort through the documents closely to *sustain* the indictment at trial. But trial was months away.[2]

And a grand jury, which returns an indictment, was not then and is not now a petit jury, which decides a case at trial. The grand jury does not decide guilt; it decides only whether the government has shown "probable cause" that the proposed defendants committed a crime. It decides "maybe," in other words. When it approves an indictment, the grand jury returns a "true bill." In the very rare instance when a grand jury declines an indictment, it returns a "no bill."[3]

Unlike trial juries of twelve, a grand jury need not be unanimous: a bare majority of the full grand jury will do to hand up the indictment. Most importantly, perhaps, the grand jury did not then and does not now hear from the defense. Indeed, it does not even hear from a judge. The only lawyers in the room with the grand jurors are one or more prosecutors. There are no cross-examinations of witnesses to test their recall, truthfulness, or motives; no objections to questionable exhibits or claims from the witness stand; no competing opening statements or closing arguments; no defense witnesses or exhibits; no instructions on the law from a judge. The prosecutor has his way, guided by little more than his sense of fairness and an ethical obligation to share with grand jurors evidence plainly suggesting that the prospective accused may be innocent. That prosecutor may offer hearsay without limitation and may give the grand jury even illegally seized evidence that will not be admissible at trial. The rules of evidence simply do not apply in the grand jury room, privileged statements aside. Finally, the whole proceeding is conducted in secret and is beyond defense challenges later to the sufficiency of the evidence presented to the grand jury.[4]

The Chicago federal grand jury sitting in September obediently returned this indictment, exactly as Justice Department lawyers had drafted it in Washington, DC, weeks before. The indictment was, and is, the only of its kind in some respects.

First, the indictment named 166 defendants, all charged together in each count. For all that research discloses, never before and never since has one case in the civilian courts of the United States charged so many. No other civilian case even has come close, and few military cases have. In 1862, a hastily convened military commission summarily "tried" some 393 Dakota Sioux Indians following the six-week Dakota Conflict. But the commission actually conducted individual trials, such as they were, many of them lasting only minutes. On the last day the commission sat, for example, it tried nearly forty cases. Of the 393 defendants, 303 got death sentences and mass hangings followed. This was an irregular military commission of doubtful legality at best. The "trials" occurred altogether outside the civilian courts of any state or the federal government. Then, in 1917 and 1918, a total of 118 black soldiers from the 24th Infantry in Camp Logan (one unit of the famed "Buffalo Soldiers") stood trial in three loose, hurried proceedings for a riot in Houston, Texas. The first and largest group was 63 defendants. In the end, 19 were hanged and 63 given life sentences. Again, however shamefully flawed, these were courts-martial, not civilian proceedings in the ordinary courts.[5]

For cases within the civilian court system, this indictment and the ensuing trial were America's largest mass trial. In 1944, the U.S. government prosecuted sixty-three *Nisei*, or Japanese Americans who were born in the United States to immigrant parents, in a Cheyenne, Wyoming, federal district court for resisting the draft. The hypocrisy of the government, and the irony of the prosecution, were stunning: the resisters were internees at the Heart Mountain Relocation Center, functionally imprisoned without charge on suspicion of disloyalty, whom the government then decided to draft into the army. All were convicted after a brief trial. They received prison terms. But that still was more than one hundred fewer than the Chicago IWW indictment named, and just over half of the number who would start trial on the Chicago indictment.[6]

Quite accurately, the lead prosecutor, Nebeker, later crowed that his was "America's biggest criminal case." And that was without considering the fact that the Chicago case eventually was just one of four in the federal government's nationwide strategy to break the IWW. Coordinated indictments against many more IWW members, with substantially identical conspiracy charges, followed in Sacramento, Wichita, and Omaha. There was some overlap in names, but more than five dozen were indicted in Sacramento; almost three dozen in Wichita; and dozens in Omaha. In all, then, about three hundred IWW members faced federal conspiracy charges following directly from the September 5 raids.[7]

The Chicago case undeniably crowned them all in stature of the defendants and size of the indicted crowd. Most criminal cases have only one defendant. For multiple-defendant cases, two probably is the most common number. As the quite rare case involving many defendants arises, practical difficulties become important. Although U.S. marshals were the first federal law enforcement officers, and always have been in charge of housing federal defendants before and during trial if they are not released on bail, U.S. marshals' offices never have owned or operated any lockup. They must rent beds for pretrial detainees from willing county jails or, today, from urban correctional or detention centers that the U.S. Bureau of Prisons operates. So a sudden influx of many detainees in one case can strain the marshal's resources greatly, both for housing and for transport under guard to and from court.

In the courthouses themselves, courtrooms were and are not equipped to seat large numbers of defendants: ten or more would require makeshift arrangements in almost any courtroom. Those temporary arrangements themselves might make sightlines difficult or impossible for jurors and accused alike, might imperil courtroom safety (at least from the viewpoint of deputy marshals and bailiffs), and might gobble up public seating—creating tension with the Sixth Amendment's public trial guaranty.

And jurors, or for that matter judges, are only human: at some point, human beings cannot keep track of what evidence supports (or undermines) a case against one defendant as opposed to other defendants. Every person accused is entitled to a jury's decision on his or her own guilt, so when numbers of defendants climb to a half dozen or more, the risk of guilt by association might exceed human capacity to sort individually. That difficulty would multiply if there also were many charges. Ten defendants facing one charge would mean ten separate guilt determinations by a jury or judge, but ten defendants facing four charges each would mean forty separate determinations.

Relatedly, trials of many defendants together become long trials. Long trials exacerbate the strain on capacities of intellect and memory for jurors and the judge: what they might remember of the evidence after a two-day trial is different from what they would remember after a two-month trial. Extended trials also mean greater cost for everyone: jail housing for detained defendants for which the marshal must pay, a courtroom and judge unavailable for other business for a protracted time, prosecutors tied up, and higher lawyers' fees for the accused.

The really big trials in the history of the U.S. courts, then, tend to top out at around two dozen defendants. The noted "pizza connection" case against Mafia figures in federal court in Manhattan, for example, may be the largest trial in modern memory. Nineteen defendants remained after seventeen months of trial in that case: twenty-two had started, but two pled guilty midtrial and one was murdered. By the end, too, only eleven jurors remained to decide the case. And that trial occurred in a busy federal district with greater resources than most.

The pizza connection case was the kind that made careers. One prosecutor went on to become a federal judge and then director of the FBI. Another later led a notable terrorism prosecution after the 1993 World Trade Center bombing and then became a columnist for the *National Review*. The lead prosecutor by title, although not by courtroom role, Rudolph Giuliani, eventually became mayor of New York City and in time a presidential candidate. Yet the Chicago IWW indictment started with nearly eight times as many defendants as the pizza connection case, and ended with fully five times the number still on trial.[8]

Who were these 166 defendants? They were the IWW's operational leaders: General Executive Board members, local union secretaries, and national organizers. And they were its intellectual and spiritual leaders: writers, editors, stump speakers, poets, and songwriters. They were native-born and, in about equal numbers, immigrants. Some of the immigrants from Italy, Ireland, England, Sweden, Finland, Poland, Russia, Mexico, and elsewhere were naturalized citizens; some were not. Most of the accused were in their twenties and thirties. But a few were gray. They included one black man: Ben Fletcher, head of Philadelphia's Marine Transport Workers Local 8. They included one and only one woman: Elizabeth Gurley Flynn. They also included, of course, the prize, Big Bill Haywood. His name was first on the caption of the indictment, the marquee defendant. Down the list, they included organizers and local union secretaries such as Ed Doree. And perhaps most improbably, they included a nineteen-year-old Harvard student, Ray Fanning of Chattanooga, Tennessee. The only evidence against him was that in the first six months of 1917, he had written four letters to IWW officers such as Walter Nef, asserting opposition to the war and the draft. Only one of the letters came after Congress declared war.[9]

None of the remaining defendants had Fanning's prospects in life, and the reasons for indicting most of them were as obscure and accidental as the reasons for indicting him. Many of their names merely appeared in correspondence files containing letters with one or more comments the government viewed as disloyal or contrary to the war effort.

But the most prominent name in the body of the indictment, a recurrent reference point, was not a defendant. It was a dead man. The government wove Frank Little into every count, using him as a spectral image of all that was un-American, dangerous, and radical about the IWW. He became an evil caricature in the indictment, and in the trial to follow, who could not possibly make himself human or nuanced because he would not be there to explain or defend himself. He would speak only from the grave, in intemperate letters and speeches that the government could introduce in well-chosen fragments. He was a safe, and arguably brilliant, choice by the Justice Department to serve as the unseen black beast, casting his shadow over the living men on trial.

The charges in the indictment were unusually complex and airy. They were conspiracy, and conspiracy only; five counts claiming five separate conspiracies. A conspiracy is an incomplete (or "inchoate") crime of *agreement* to go forth and commit some substantive crime or crimes, and it long has been a common charge in federal prosecutions. The Chicago IWW case did not start the government's pursuit of thought or handshake crimes rather than completed crimes, but it marked an early and especially aggressive use of conspiracy charges. Today, the typical federal case against several defendants will lead with a conspiracy count, and then back that with one or more (often many) counts alleging completed, substantive crimes. The first count, conspiracy, ties the defendants together and tells a summary story of their criminal efforts. The remaining counts allege the finished crimes they committed.

The IWW indictment was different. It alleged no completed crimes. The five conspiracy counts alleged tens of thousands of "overt acts"— specific actions designed to advance a conspiracy's goals, although the overt acts may or may not have been crimes themselves. The overt acts that the government alleged were in service of a variety of criminal goals or objectives (in formal legal jargon, "objects") of each conspiracy. Since one conspiracy, one criminal agreement, may entail any number of illegal objectives, the indictment might have explained why the division of these objectives (and the overt acts furthering them) into five separate criminal agreements made sense: why not just one conspiracy embracing all the illegal purposes? But the indictment did not explain that, and the prosecution never faced that question from the defense or the judge.

At the outset, then, the government arguably contrived to take five bites at the same apple. That way, the government immediately had the advantage of any later jury compromise: if the jury were to reach unanimity only by striking a deal to acquit the defendants on some counts and convict them on one or more others, the government might obtain the total sentences it actually sought on any one of the counts.

The Chicago conspiracy charges themselves fell roughly into two groups: "industrial counts," as the parties soon called them, and "war counts." Counts One, Two, and Five were industrial: the defendants allegedly conspired to block the flow of wartime goods to the government in violation of several laws, including appropriations and acquisition provisions, the war declaration itself, and the new Espionage Act, specifically by using "force to prevent, hinder, or delay the execution of any law of the United States" (Count One) and to burden or obstruct the rights of employers to complete contracts with the government—a "right or privilege secured" to employers "by the Constitution and laws of the United States" (Count Two). Count Five contended that the 166 defendants conspired to defraud employers who hired IWW members and acted on that conspiracy by mailing *Solidarity*, the IWW's newspaper, and stickers that urged sabotage, strikes, or action contrary to the employer's interest.

Count Three, the first "war count," rested on the new Selective Service Act, establishing a draft to supply troops for the war. It alleged that the defendants conspired to commit the offenses against the United States of urging 10,000 eligible men to refuse to register for the draft and another 5,000 to desert military service. The allegation of these 15,000 separate offenses, objects of the conspiracy, was uncluttered with the names of anyone whom the defendants sought to influence, either to refuse registration or to desert once conscripted, or with the places or times where such efforts occurred. The remaining "war count," Count Four, charged a similar conspiracy to cause insubordination in the army and navy, but here by obstructing the recruitment and enlistment provisions of the Espionage Act, which forbade public solicitation, speeches, pamphlets, and articles "urging insubordination, disloyalty and refusal of duty" in the military. In short, speaking or writing publicly in opposition to the draft was a crime; so was making an agreement with someone else that such advocacy should happen.[10]

On the topic of its structure and counts, drafting the indictment presented an unusual, although probably not unique, legal problem for the government. The Selective Service Act, which was the basis for Count Three, became law only in May 1917. That restricted the possible duration of an illegal conspiracy: the government hardly could claim that someone committed a crime by plotting to violate a law not yet enacted. The Espionage Act, to which all five counts referred and on which Count Four rested entirely, exacerbated the problem, for that was not enacted until June 1917. Justice Department leaders had a solution. They would assert that the five conspiracies began only "on the sixth day of April, 1917," the day Congress declared war, and continued to the date of the indictment—a period of less than six months. But even there, that span embraced weeks before anyone could have violated the Selective Service Act and two months before the Espionage Act sprang into existence.[11]

Effectively, then, the conspiracies could have operated only during a short sequence of months: the summer just past, roughly. Would this mean that the government's evidence of conspiracy also would have to date just to those few months? A reasonable person in some field other than law might think so. But by the time they drafted the indictment, the government's lawyers had a plan to work around that expectation.

Altogether, the indictment ran to forty-three single-spaced, typed pages. Its formal language was dense, deadening, and for those reasons, confusing.

Even on a close reading, it was difficult to distill into a satisfying, plain explanation of what the accused did wrong and why it was a crime.[12]

The formal charges each contended that the 166 named defendants "unlawfully and feloniously have conspired, combined, confederated and agreed together, and with one Frank H. Little, now deceased." There he was, five times over, the hobgoblin haunting the indictment.[13]

No sooner had the grand jurors returned the indictment in the Chicago federal courthouse than a small army of federal agents and local police officers blitzed the city and IWW halls elsewhere. Some twenty detectives and agents barged into the Chicago headquarters at 1001 W. Madison Street alone. There, they arrested Big Bill Haywood and eight others. Dozens more would be arrested in other cities that day, the next day, and then in a trickle during the following weeks. The Chicago group offered no resistance. "I expected it," Haywood muttered, "and I don't care to talk about it."

Cash bail was steep. In a day when the average American adult male worker took home around $700 a year, the federal court set cash bonds of $10,000 to $25,000 for each of the defendants. None could post those sums. The U.S. marshal transferred them to the massive Cook County Jail, which would become home for months.[14]

In all, more than 115 of the 166 indicted defendants eventually either surrendered or were apprehended. Haywood urged indicted IWW members to surrender, reasoning that submitting to justice would send a political message that Wobblies had done nothing wrong and had nothing to fear. Not all accepted that reasoning. Some dozens escaped arrest and never faced the charges. At a time when law enforcement coordination and sharing of information across state lines, or even across municipal lines, was rudimentary and difficult; when arrestees or convicts were not routinely fingerprinted or even photographed; and when border controls were loose or nonexistent, the relatively low apprehension rate was unsurprising. Just adopting a different name could thwart apprehension. And many of those indicted were immigrants from other lands. Some simply may have decided that it was a good time to return home, or to travel elsewhere.[15]

Importantly, though, it is not clear that the holes in the government's net even were a great concern. The point of indicting this massive group, after all, was not really to punish most of those indicted as individuals. It was to break up, disrupt, and disable the IWW as an organization. The U.S. government was trying to prosecute a war effectively; prosecuting individuals criminally through the Department of Justice was a subordinate aspect of that bigger goal. When the trial began, Justice Department prosecutors were notably indifferent about the missing defendants and would prove to be casual about releasing even some of those who were in custody. For example, when one defendant, A. C. Christ, later appeared for jury selection in his U.S. Army uniform, that was enough to cause the prosecution to drop the case against him on the spot and send him on his way. As a matter of public perception, the Justice Department was not about to have a soldier sitting on trial.[16]

By early December, the government had succeeded in arresting 103 of the defendants. It was time for the case to begin in earnest. Given the August 12 meeting at the Congress Hotel, the assigned judge was no surprise: the Honorable Kenesaw Mountain Landis. He would preside at the first formal court appearance, the arraignment, set quite unusually for a Saturday morning, December 15.

A telegram earlier that week also was unusual. Two days before the arraignment, Gregory himself wired Clyne, Nebeker, and Porter with an oblique but unmistakable and stunning reference to Landis: "Have Clyne acquaint main man with state of your preparation, indicating when you will be ready for trial so that when you move in open court for the setting desired it will be granted. Prepare everything so that there will be no appearance of defendants having victory on motion to set the case or on any other point."[17]

That was a tacit confession. A federal judge was the prosecution's "main man" here, and scheduling would be rigged with him in advance, so that a motion in open court would be but play-acting. The implications of the Sunday meeting in the Congress Hotel four months earlier became darker still. Now, if in fact the prosecutors acted on Gregory's direction, they and Landis stepped well over an ethical line.

Saturday came. The December 15 date was the appearance at which the accused entered a formal plea to the charges. As at most arraignments, it seemed pretty dry, procedural stuff, with one exception. The lead defense lawyer, George Vanderveer of Seattle, came to court with a gun in his hip pocket. "Certainly, I have a gun," he barked at the bailiff and announced his name. "I'm one of the attorneys for the defense." The bailiff was unimpressed. Vanderveer spent a few minutes in custody until he explained the gun—an odd tale about unpacking too hastily—and local lawyers vouched for him.

Only a few of the arrested defendants were out on bail by December 15. One of them was Elizabeth Gurley Flynn. Now the first fissures among the defendants, and indeed among the ranks of the IWW, had begun to appear visibly.

Gurley Flynn and her lover, Carlo Tresca, had been fired by Haywood and the General Executive Board in late 1916 in a strategic spat over the end of a strike on the Mesabi Range in Minnesota, and related guilty pleas. They remained generally aligned with, but no longer members of, the IWW.[18]

Thrown together again in court a year later, Gurley Flynn urged a legalistic strategy. To her mind, everyone should file a motion to have his case severed from all others, which in effect could result in over one hundred trials and certainly a great practical benefit to the defense. This would frustrate the government's effort to prove guilt by association, too, she contended. But the other defendants saw strength in solidarity. Gurley Flynn convinced only the small New York contingent—all her allies—among the defendants. She, Tresca, Arturo Giovannitti, and Joe Ettor alone pursued severance of their cases.

The prosecution team in fact was worried that it could not prove conspiracies beginning in April 1917 against defendants expelled from the IWW in 1916. Seven weeks before the arraignment, Nebeker had opined to Attorney General Gregory that membership in the IWW "at some time during the period" alleged in the indictment (that is, after declaration of war) was enough. As to Gurley Flynn and three others, then, he fretted. "These defendants are among the most obnoxious agitators and organizers of the I.W.W., but so far as investigation now discloses they have not been members at any time during the period covered by the charges in the indictment."[19]

That was a problem. As his telegram two days before the arraignment demonstrated, Gregory and other top Justice Department officials were eager from the outset not to allow even the appearance that the defendants might win on any point, no matter how trivial.

The government's concern that the public not perceive the IWW defendants as winning anything gave an opportunity to Gurley Flynn's skillful New York lawyer, George W. Whiteside, for severance. Gregory instructed the same three prosecutors the very next day, the eve of the arraignment, to "examine carefully" the case against the four who sought severance. If they found the case wanting, then "gain the advantage of doing voluntarily what Government would have to do at trial [concede insufficiency of the evidence and invite dismissal]."

After arraignment, Whiteside and Gurley Flynn played their hand well. On January 10, 1918, Gurley Flynn sent a handwritten letter to President

Wilson's personal secretary, enclosing a typed, five-page letter to the president. The personal secretary had suggested that she send such a letter.

To the president, she described herself as a "humble and obscure citizen" who merely struggled for democracy. Referring to her poverty and her effort to support her own child, two sisters, and a brother "who is now eligible to the draft," Gurley Flynn went on to explain why it would be unfair to try her with the greater number of defendants who remained members of the IWW after the president had declared war. The letter stressed the unfairness of the case to her individually. She made only one direct mention of the other 165 defendants, and it was ambiguous: "I know some of my co-defendants and their unselfish devotion to labor is unquestionable. Others I do not know and some have possibly acted most foolishly." She sought, implausibly, to explain away her pamphlet, *Sabotage*, as intended only for the trial defense after the Paterson, New Jersey, silk strike. If severed and allowed to make her defense separately, Gurley Flynn promised diplomatically "to suspend judgment in these days of world upheaval, to watch the silent progress of events, to hope that the world may be purged of tyranny and greed and that the best we have all dreamed of, may emerge triumphant." In other words, tacitly, she would stand down in opposing the war if granted severance.

It worked. On February 6, Fitts told her lawyer that, if he would withdraw his opposition to the indictment itself and instead ask for severance, "This application for severance will not be resisted on the part of the Government." There was more. The cases against these defendants would be held in abeyance with the understanding that they would not be "brought to trial under the indictment." Fitts closed by hoping pointedly that Whiteside would "cooperate with these persons represented by you in order to influence them toward a patriotic course," and specifically hoped that they would not give aid to the IWW.

Nine days later, it was done. Nebeker sent a letter to Fitts advising him that Landis had granted severance that morning. On March 25, Nebeker wrote again to Fitts that the government also had agreed to sever Ettor and Giovannitti.[20]

Not only had the notables from New York secured bail, then; they also had found an early escape on technical grounds from the rigors of trial and whatever awaited after that. The others, loyally displaying IWW solidarity, were not so lucky. Speaking more than forty years later, near the end of her life, Gurley Flynn would omit her brief role in the case but reminisce glowingly of the IWW and its loyalists.[21]

Meanwhile, the remaining defendants pled not guilty at the arraignment, reserving the right to enter a demurrer to one or more counts later. A demurrer, now almost extinct in the United States, is an old common law plea positing that, even if the facts are as an accusation alleges, still as a matter of law there is no basis to proceed.

The defendants entered that demurrer, through counsel, shortly after the new year. Judge Landis, though, was not much interested in technical legal arguments in this case. He overruled the demurrers with little discussion.[22]

A later defense challenge to the use of documents seized under the September 5 search warrants led to more serious discussion. The basic problems were that the search warrant applications neither demonstrated probable cause for the searches, nor guided agents specifically on what they could seize. Again, both a showing of facts supporting probable cause, so that the issuing judge can assess that independently, and particularity in naming what officers can seize are textual requirements of the Fourth Amendment. Initially, all but two of the defendants moved to quash the indictment, on the theory that the government obtained it by presenting unconstitutionally seized documents to the grand jury. Then, on February 1, some ninety-two of the defendants petitioned for return of the property as not lawfully in the government's possession, given the unconstitutional seizures. The government responded with an opposing request that the court allow it to impound for use at trial all the property seized.

That government response relied heavily upon the Espionage Act. Recall that for the first time, Congress relaxed there, by statute, the judicial rule that search warrants could not be used to seize "mere evidence" of crimes. Search warrants had been only for the actual fruits of crime—recovering stolen goods, say—and the discovery of any evidence merely proving a case against the perpetrator had to be incidental. Section 2 of the Espionage Act expressly allowed search warrants aimed at seizing items used in commission of the crime of aiding a foreign government. The act also provided, in sections 15 and 16, a procedure by which a person could challenge a search warrant.

This allowed a clever government argument. The defendants had not gone to the judges or commissioners around the country who actually issued the forty-eight disputed search warrants. Rather, they had waited to challenge the seizures in a trial court, before a judge who had issued no warrants at all. This, the government posited, was an improper "collateral" attack on the warrants.

Moreover, the government continued, it had submitted with its impoundment request an affidavit from a key agent, Murdock, that showed the individual defendants did not own the papers seized; the IWW as an organization did. Since Person A cannot complain of a Fourth Amendment violation that only Person B suffered, the defendants were out of luck: the IWW should have sought return of its property, but it was not a party to the case as an organization, so no harm, no foul.

Landis tried to lure the defendants into joining the factual dispute that the Murdock affidavit created. If the defendants would testify to establish their personal ownership of various documents, he would reassess after the fact whether there was probable cause to issue the warrants and seize those documents. This of course would negate the Fourth Amendment in large part: if the government could prove later, based on what it seized, that it got lucky and happened to uncover evidence of a crime in an unlawful search, then the requirements that it show probable cause *before* the search, and name particularly what it wanted to seize, would offer citizens no real protection at all.

Defense counsel stood their ground and refused. Judge Landis then conceded—at least for sake of argument, and seemingly on the merits—that the search warrant applications were invalid and violated the Fourth Amendment. Still, he held, the government would keep and could use the evidence. The defendants had gone to the wrong court and at the wrong time with their objections that the warrants were bad. They should have gone before indictment to the separate judges across the country. Further, the wrong people were bringing the challenge now: the IWW, not the individuals, would have been the right party, but the organization was not a defendant and therefore could not be heard. The motion for return of property to the defendants was denied.[23]

If the government's argument and the court's ruling were lovely artifices of law, they were ugly edifices of life. In the real world, could individual working people, IWW members, who had no way to know exactly what government agents had seized from where, have gone to forty-eight federal courts around the country with legal challenges in the twenty-three days between the raids and the grand jury's indictment? Of course not, as a practical matter. Even setting aside the fact that many were in jail during most or all of that three-week period, they had not the information, the money, the lawyers, or the time to mount four dozen legal challenges from coast to coast. Even had they undertaken that task, in an imaginary world, what if some or most or all of the forty-eight judges who issued the warrants had refused to order return of property? Could the individuals then have pursued appeals in all the appropriate federal appellate courts, still within the twenty-three-day period they had? This all would have been impossible, as a practical matter. The government and Judge Landis made law mock life.

With that ruling, the preliminary legal issues receded. Trial loomed for the largest group ever to fill an American courtroom. By now, ten more of the indicted defendants either had surrendered or been arrested. At the start of trial, there would be 112. Without a hint of irony, Landis set jury selection to begin on April 1, 1918. That was no surprise: it was the date the government wanted.[24]

Part II

Ah? What caution must men use
With those who look not at the deed alone,
But spy into the thoughts with subtle skill.

Dante Alighieri,
Inferno, Canto XVI, lines 114–16,
Henry F. Cary, trans.

11

Twelve Good Men and True

With no one in immediate need of hanging, the corner of the "big tank" in the Cook County Jail served as the place for Sunday church services. An old piano stood on the gallows platform where the noose or nooses sometimes would dangle. It had been a cold Easter Sunday, which came early that year and brought with it a heavy rain. In place of a choir and organ, bearded and stubble-faced men sang hymns by heart to the plinking of the piano in the bare corner. Slowly, unevenly, a Chicago winter was yielding to a raw spring. The next day, trial would start as did April.[1]

On this last day of March 1918, fifty-eight members of the IWW remained in this main part of the old jail. They had the company of hundreds of other inmates who either were awaiting trial or serving short sentences for all sorts of crimes. Another forty-eight IWW members, whom the sheriff viewed as harder cases, resided apart from other inmates in the "wing" section of the old jail. In all, 106 IWW leaders and stalwarts now had spent months in the gloomy, damp jail, minus a very few in the DuPage County Jail one county to the west. The Cook County Jail was imposing. With the adjacent Cook County Criminal Courts building, the sooty walls circumscribed a square city block west of Navy Pier and just north of the loop that the Chicago River made around the nest of ten-, even twenty-story skyscrapers jutting through twinings of elevated train tracks in the city's commercial center.[2]

When jury selection began the next morning, these 106 men in jail would not be quite all of the defendants in the trial. Of the 166 originally indicted, 39 never were apprehended. At least one more got a dismissal the hard way: a Russian immigrant had been carried out of the jail, spitting blood, just in time to die at the hospital. Haywood described him, perhaps for effect on his readers, as "in rugged health" before the months in the Cook County Jail. And of course, Elizabeth Gurley Flynn, Carlo Tresca, Joe Ettor, and Arturo Giovannitti, separately represented, all had secured a separate trial; practically, the chance that they ever would face trial was very remote.[3]

A half dozen more had won release on bail by the time Big Bill Haywood took a head count just before April 1. Judge Landis would continue to release others on bail in a steady trickle through jury selection and the trial itself. By the end of the trial only eight would remain in custody. All would continue dutifully to appear for trial every day—with one exception, late in trial, when one Wobbly arrived thirty minutes late to court. But for now, the police and deputy U.S. marshals would escort 106 men from the Cook County Jail, one-half block west on Hubbard and then eleven blocks south on Clark Street to the Chicago federal building. For some time, they made the journey in handcuffs, two-by-two, on foot and closely watched. In all, 113 defendants gathered for the beginning of jury selection that Monday morning, but another one in poor health soon would be gone. For practical purposes, 112 would start trial.[4]

Not two months earlier, Vanderveer had made one last attempt to avoid the trial altogether. He had enlisted Roger Baldwin of the fledgling National Civil Liberties Bureau—to be renamed the American Civil Liberties Union in 1920—and had secured meetings with both Secretary of War Newton Baker and, maybe better, President Wilson's personal secretary (the same one to whom Gurley Flynn had written in her personal plea for severance). Politely, the personal secretary had offered to convey to the president any message Vanderveer might want to put in writing. Notably, Vanderveer made no mention of even discussing the case with the Justice Department.

On February 11, 1918, Vanderveer took the president's secretary up on his offer. He submitted a nine-page letter to "His Excellency Woodrow Wilson, President of the United States," on letterhead with his temporary Chicago office address. The letter was hyperbolic and indirect. Implausibly, after explaining that he had been "conducting the more important cases for the I.W.W." for over a year, Vanderveer claimed, "I am not writing this letter on behalf of the organization nor in any sense as its advocate." Rather, he argued, he was writing as someone who understood the current attitude of "unorganized, unskilled workers" especially. From that vantage point, "As a citizen . . . interested in the extermination of German autocracy, I cannot help wondering what the effect of this [Chicago] trial will be upon our own industrial efficiency."

He argued that the Chicago trial and others might cause the very disruption of production that the government feared; as to the Justice Department's tactic of prosecuting, he wrote, "What stupidity!" Because of the heavy-handed tactics of the department, which he listed, "A verdict of 'Guilty' would make martyrs of these men, and a verdict of 'Not guilty' prove the vindication which they have been so long denied."

Vanderveer's closing request was as indirect and expansive as the letter. "I am not even asking for justice, although no one should ever be ashamed to do that; but I am merely trying to convince you that the Department of Justice, into whose hands, for some reason or no reason, the solution of the labor problem seems illogically to have fallen, is adopting the most stupid possible method of dealing with it; and my hope in doing this is to avert industrial troubles which I believe would just now amount to a national calamity."[5]

In all, the letter was a mixture of bluster, rumination, veiled threats, frustration, and insults. It did not have its desired effect. The president seems to have taken no action to divert the case to some resolution short of a verdict. The trial would go ahead.

The scene in court the first morning of jury selection was chaotic. The defendants were there, visibly excited to see proceedings finally under way. Abuzz, they shook hands and at least two of the more expressive foreign-born defendants kissed on the cheek. Chicago's largest and most reactionary newspaper, the *Chicago Tribune*, sneered that the defendants were freshly shaven, with unkempt beards gone, and in their "best clothes." Rows of bleachers had been set before the judge's bench for the defendants and they might sit where they pleased. One of the accused, young A. C. Christ, raised the ante. He stood out in his new U.S. Army uniform. Inducted after arraignment and released on bail, Christ secured a one-week furlough to appear at his trial. The prosecution, intent on portraying the IWW generally and these men specifically as rabidly antiwar, was not about to have a smartly uniformed defendant. Prosecutors and Landis promptly released Christ with his case vaguely "held in abeyance." It was all over for him before it began.

In addition to milling around and chatting, the defendants wanted to enjoy a good chaw. But spittoons were few. Both judge and bailiffs had overlooked that little detail in preparing a courtroom that usually held a few plaintiffs or defendants and lawyers at most. By the next morning, Judge Landis ordered sixty new spittoons, placed at intervals among the bleachers, and Landis specifically allowed the defendants to chew tobacco—to "aid their health," he added.

Of course, more than nine dozen defendants were just one group in the courtroom. There was a larger one crowding in. The panel of two hundred prospective jurors had to find room on spectators' benches or along the courtroom's walls. Dozens of police officers and twenty deputy marshals stood by to keep order and to screen visitors and lawyers.[6]

Those lawyers were plentiful. The prosecution table included Nebeker, Porter, Clyne, and almost certainly one or more junior lawyers from Clyne's office and possibly from the Department of Justice's main office. At the defense table, Vanderveer presided. But Fred H. Moore, Caroline Lowe, William B. Cleary, and Chicago's own Otto Christensen all sat with him.[7]

Wherever standing room remained, newspaper men and magazine writers crowded in. Finally, whether curious members of the general public or courthouse buffs also tried to squeeze in, none of the contemporary accounts mention. But there likely were some such spectators.

Over this assembled throng, numbering well over three hundred, wiry Judge Landis presided. Restless and animated, as always in a plain business suit rather than a judicial robe, he alternately stood over the bench or flitted around as he sought to get jury selection under way.[8]

Court began after 11:00 a.m. (Landis was handling the rest of his calendar between 9:00 and 11:00 a.m. during the early days; later, as proceedings dragged on, he would devote the whole day to the trial.) The first order of business was a long roll call of the defendants. How else could he know whether they all were there? When Landis's clerk came to his name, the colorful J. T. "Red" Doran "thundered in a stentorian voice, 'On the job!'"[9]

Soon enough, though, a very practical problem in trying 112 men at once arose in the hubbub. One of the defendants failed to answer the roll call. Landis inquired and learned that the missing man was too sick to come from jail. Never overly concerned with legal technicalities, even Judge Landis understood that the Sixth Amendment guaranteed the accused the right to be present at his own trial. All was for naught that day. Proceedings would have to be postponed until Tuesday, with the defendants in custody all trooping back to the jail under guard.

The next day, the scene repeated itself, leading to the same abrupt conclusion in a few minutes. Someone else was sick.[10]

So, with most of the men now showing some effects of the months in the crowded, unsanitary Cook County Jail, Judge Landis had some decisions to make. If he could not try them, he could not sentence them. Practicality prevailed. This is when Landis started reducing bail for the men who seemed compliant, so that they could gain their release. He would continue that for weeks.

And for all defendants, he undertook to improve their diets. Borrowing Judge Evan A. Evans's courtroom across the hall, he dubbed it "the chuckhouse" and arranged noon meals there for the defendants. Over the lunch hour on Wednesday, Landis hurried over, toured the room, and tried the food and coffee himself.

He found both up to snuff. So did the IWW men. After months of rotten meat and fish at the Cook County Jail, and at least once a large cockroach baked into the crust of a loaf of bread, all agreed that the food the federal court provided was far superior. The judge was gaining credit from the defendants with this simple appeal to their stomachs.[11]

Landis already had made one other clever gesture that morning, too. He had allowed four-year-old Sam Perry to snuggle in court with his father, defendant Grover H. Perry. Little Sam had not seen his dad in five months. With everyone present, fed, and plied with coffee—to say nothing of the new spittoons and the calculated flash of humanity shown Perry and his boy—jury selection at last was under way.[12]

But within a day or two, the prosecutors were grumbling. Their concern was not that two hundred men made up the jury pool. Women would not win nationwide eligibility to serve on federal juries for nearly another forty years. Neither had the prosecutors any concern that daily wage earners—laborers—were all but excluded from this and most jury pools in favor of the more affluent. The country had a long tradition of "excusing" laborers from jury duty on the rationale that they would lose their jobs, or at least lose pay intolerably, if pressed into jury service; that was at once the truth and a handy means of perpetuating their status as a distrusted underclass. It would be another twenty-eight years before the Supreme Court began to take aim at that tool of social and economic discrimination.[13]

For now, juries mostly were the province of salaried men and business owners. Watching firsthand after the government formally severed the case against him, Arturo Giovannitti reported early during jury selection, "The prosecuting attorney was chiefly concerned about their loyalty, their family tree and their pocketbook." Indeed, "it seemed from what he asked that the prerequisite of the ideal juryman," Giovannitti continued, "is to be a substantial citizen, a shrewd investor, and an arrant ignoramus of the great social problems of today."

What vexed the prosecution team now, though, was "loyalty," as the *Chicago Tribune* also put it darkly. Many of the prospective jurors had German surnames; given the mood of the time, that alone put their loyalty and patriotism in doubt. Indeed, the weekend before the trial started, an American with German parents in Collinsville, Illinois, had been lynched by a mob of 350 after he supposedly made "disloyal" comments in a speech to miners. Of more direct concern to the men on trial was an incident on February 12 in Staunton, Illinois, downstate midway and northeast of St. Louis. An angry mob had beaten John L. Metzen, an IWW lawyer, and an IWW member with clubs and stones, eventually stripping them naked, pouring a bucket of molten tar over their heads, and chasing them out of town and into the February night. Before jury selection would finish, another German American in Oklahoma narrowly would escape lynching after he disobeyed local Council of Defense demands to fly the American flag in the front window of his house every day until the war ended.[14]

Aside from their ethnic heritage, a number of the venire men were giving answers that seemed to the prosecutors dangerously close to open-minded about the IWW members' guilt. The prosecution had accepted only two potential jurors after the first full day of questioning the panel. With the prosecutors unhappy, jury selection moved at a glacial pace. And defense lawyers would not even start their questioning until the prosecution was done.

Matters reached a head two or three days later when a member of the venire admitted under prosecution questioning that the preceding week he had received a telephone call asking whether he planned to vote the Socialist ticket in the April 2 election. This was intolerable. Surely the defendants, or their supporters, must have been behind the telephone call. The conclusion, it seemed obvious to the prosecutors, was that an anonymous inquiry plumbing political views on behalf of Socialists meant an effort at jury tampering. Clyne and Porter wanted the whole panel dismissed and another large panel assembled. They wanted to start over.

On Saturday, the fourth day of jury selection, Landis obliged. He dismissed the entire panel of two hundred prospective jurors. Starting over would require the clerk of court to assemble another similar group. Yet somehow that would take only seven to ten days. That was much less notice than the original jury venire would have had. What sort of citizens would be able to drop everything for a trial expected to last months, on one week's notice at most? Men of means, disproportionately—those who either would not lose income if absent from their daily duties for weeks or months, or who could sustain the loss of income. Still, the men on trial were glad to see the first panel of two hundred go. It contained almost no workingmen, and the jury box had "looked like a meeting of the Employers' Association," one of the accused grumbled.[15]

True to Landis's order, two hundred new panel members filled the courtroom when jury selection resumed nine days later, on Monday, April 15. Now Nebeker took charge of questioning the new prospective jurors. He did not beat around the bush. "Are you a member of or affiliated with any organization connected with the defense in this trial?" he demanded of each. The *Chicago Tribune* understood: socialists would not win a seat on the jury. Nebeker also questioned each man "upon his Americanism, whether he read radical literature, and if he was in full accord with President Wilson's policies on the war." He liked what he heard. On that first day, the prosecution accepted six men.[16]

Nebeker sought to speed the pace in other ways, too. Landis obliged. The defendants would stop wandering in and out of court at will, as apparently the judge had allowed up until then. And the deputy U.S. marshals would count the defendants in the morning and after breaks, which would avoid lengthy roll calls every time court reconvened.[17]

Landis took advantage of the increased pace of jury selection to handle at least one other case on his docket that Monday. The IWW members could have seen an omen, if they learned of the case later. One Hendricks, "whose anti-American activities have kept him in trouble for months," the *Tribune* scolded, apparently had pulled down an American flag and made other recent poor choices in wartime. Landis gave him five years in prison. Reminded by detail-minded lawyers that the maximum sentence was only four years, Landis relented and shaved a year off.[18]

In the IWW case, jury selection continued the next day at great speed with Nebeker leading the effort. By Wednesday afternoon, after just three days, the prosecution had seated twelve jurors it liked. Now the defense would question them. As strikes for cause or peremptory challenges, which required no reason but were limited in number, thinned out the jury box, new venire members would fill the vacated seats. Vanderveer slowed the pace. Once the defense had accepted twelve, the process would repeat itself: the prosecutors then could question the newly seated men; more would be substituted as strikes replaced an ever-narrowing number; and the process would shift back and forth until each side had accepted the same twelve.

Come Saturday, April 20, Landis was growing impatient. He kept everyone late that day and announced that, beginning on Monday, court would convene at 9:00 a.m. rather than the 11:00 a.m. that had been his custom as he heard other cases on his calendar before returning to the IWW. Illness struck again twice; two more days were lost. When the following Saturday arrived, strikes for cause and peremptory challenges had exhausted the venire again. The jury selection process ground to a halt until the clerk could summon still more candidates for the jury. The *Chicago Tribune* fumed.[19]

With a final mad push, the last day of April ended with eleven accepted jurors at 11:30 p.m. Landis had wanted to finish that day but gave in, exhausted.

The next day, May Day, saw jury selection end quietly. At 2:45 p.m., a twelfth juror took his seat. It was over—but not before one IWW sympathizer had been indicted in connection with the polling call that led to the dismissal of the first jury pool.

Opening statements and evidence would begin the following day, Thursday, May 2, at 11:00 a.m. The twelve men on the jury included a plumbing contractor, a fifty-five-year-old president of a manufacturing corporation, two farmers (one retired), a city plumbing inspector, the secretary of a medical sanatorium, and four men who were wage earners in skilled or unskilled trades. They ranged from twenty-eight to sixty-five years of age, and only five of the twelve lived in Chicago, with the rest scattered in smaller towns as far away as eighty miles or more. They were a rough cross-section of white, American men of that day and location—tilting slightly toward the prosperous but not as lopsidedly as did many juries. And all had been vetted carefully for their "Americanism."[20]

By now, the number on trial probably was 111. In addition to the dismissed soldier, A. C. Christ, another missing man was A. D. Kimball, an Arizona miner who had been deported at Bisbee. Landis had released him on bail when he was near death, "spitting up his lungs" and a "physical wreck." But there also was Henry Meyers, whom Giovannitti reported as having gone insane in the Cook County Jail. "He is now in the madhouse at Kankakee," Giovannitti explained. "His reason has fled." Pietro Nigra had been in and out of the hospital, too, because of another's mental illness. An "insane" inmate had attacked and beaten him seriously in a federal lock-up in Springfield, Illinois, before he arrived at the Cook County Jail.[21]

Back to jail the remaining men went. The opening act was over. The next day would bring the main show.

Mechanics' Institute Library
57 Post Street
San Francisco, CA 94104
(415) 393-0101
www.milibrary.org

12

Van and the Squire

———————◆————————◆————————

At the long, polished wood table for defense counsel sat George Vanderveer, an impresario of that main show. None of the other defense
lawyers had the stature to compete with him for the leading role, even assuming they had wanted to do that. He would lead, handing out research,
writing, investigative, and menial tasks to the others; assigning witnesses
for cross-examination (and later, in the defense case, direct examination);
handling the most important witnesses himself; giving the opening statement; making final strategic decisions; and rising to his feet as the principal
advocate for the defense in arguments with the prosecutors and the judge,
in or out of the jury's earshot.

At forty-two years of age when the trial started, George Francis
Vanderveer—"Van," to his friends and clients—already was an accomplished lawyer and an extraordinarily skillful one, the most notable lawyer
not just in Seattle but throughout the Northwest. He also was a complicated, even contradictory, man. For those inclined to attach labels to lawyers, any number might have applied in his case: hero, scoundrel, idealist,
cynic, prosecutor, defender, drunkard, brilliant tactician, loyalist, oppor-
tunist, philanderer, devotee, optimist, pessimist, radical, traditionalist, and
patriot. He was the sort of defense lawyer who not only had a gun in the
hip pocket of his suit pants but also forgot it was there. In short, at latest
by the time his hair grayed before the Chicago IWW trial, he was a criminal
defense lawyer in full.

As his biographers said thirty-five years later, Vanderveer was "[p]erhaps
the most colorful and certainly the most controversial legal figure of the
Pacific Northwest during its most dramatic era," the late nineteenth and

early twentieth centuries. Colorful: still a favorite label that the courteous but wary apply to noted trial lawyers.[1]

Any observer of the day, though, reasonably might have asked why Vanderveer led this defense at all. This was not Seattle or the Northwest. It was Chicago, Clarence Darrow's town. Indisputably the most famous trial lawyer in America, Darrow had risen to fame defending labor and the criminal accused. There was much overlap between those groups at the time, for capital and government often treated the acts of labor organizers as criminal. Indeed, Darrow already once had defended Big Bill Haywood and the two other Western Federation of Miners leaders on the Idaho murder charges. He had beaten a seemingly strong prosecution case and saved the men's lives. So why wasn't Darrow heading the defense team?[2]

The IWW likely did seek out Darrow initially. Accounts for his absence vary, but they come down generally to Darrow being too busy. Darrow and others would have had reasons not to give entirely full or candid explanations, but the following points certainly are true.[3]

First, Darrow's standing with organized labor had fallen after he saved the lives of John J. and James B. McNamara by pleading them guilty to the *Los Angeles Times* bombing in 1911. The labor movement had embraced the McNamara brothers, believing in their innocence, and working people all over the country had sent small donations to fund their defense, often with money they hardly could spare. The guilty pleas seemed a betrayal from afar—a betrayal by Darrow, who had been labor's hero until then, ever since he had defended Eugene Debs in the 1894 American Railway Union strike. Plus, Darrow himself had been charged with jury bribery after the McNamara brothers' guilty plea and had endured two trials in Los Angeles. By the time he returned to Chicago a free man in 1913, he had won one trial and escaped with a mistrial in the other, exhausting his savings and the goodwill of some of his friends and creditors in the process. Organized labor certainly had fallen out of love with Darrow.

Second, Darrow supported America's entry into World War I. He took an active role, stumping for Liberty Bonds and for the Wilson administration's war policy generally in speeches around the country, until the war ended. Most of Darrow's friends were on the political left, and his war posture cost him with them, too.

For both of these reasons, Darrow's relations with labor, some liberals, and many radicals were strained when the government brought the Chicago indictment. They remained that way when the case went to trial that spring of 1918. With at least some, Darrow still was in bad odor altogether. But of course, he also was the most famous defender in the country and, along with Earl Rogers in Los Angeles and George Vanderveer in Seattle, among the most successful.

Third, Darrow was rebuilding his law practice in 1917–18 and still needed to rebuild his bank account. By then his law practice was busier than, say, in 1914, but he was not yet financially flush. Possibly, but only possibly, the prospect of a financial loss after a long, difficult trial was part of the explanation for Darrow's absence from the defense team. Darrow did offer some help behind the scenes, though. Later, too, he posted $1,000 to help secure Haywood's bond.[4]

In any event, for now the defense was Vanderveer's, whose very existence was improbable from the beginning. His father, David Vanderveer, was a successful grain broker in Grinnell, Iowa, with grown children when his first wife died. David soon remarried Mary Atwood Francis, seventeen years his junior and perhaps younger than his daughter. He was over forty-five when Mary bore him a son, George Francis Vanderveer, in 1875. Neighbors clucked. Little George would be David and Mary's only child, and the only one in the house.

The boy was short-tempered but very close to his mother, in part because David's business occupied him. Then, when George was eight, Mary died suddenly. David did his best to raise George alone. A blacksmith before he turned to speculating on grain markets as a broker, David had made the transition from using brawn to brains for his livelihood. He understood the difference in prospects and wanted George to go to college. For his part, George liked boxing (or maybe just fighting) but wanted to play football.[5]

The elder Vanderveer settled on relatively new Stanford University for his son and moved to California with George to keep an eye on him. There, George's friends were from the Northwest, Washington mostly, and they played football. Not George, though. David made him promise not to play football because he thought it too brutal. In the senior Vanderveer's view, football threatened permanent injury to its players and should be abolished as a college sport. He had no objection to boxing.

George obeyed. But as he graduated, he took a life lesson from that acquiescence to his father's wishes. Talking to his friend, a football player, as they walked across campus in the waning days of his senior year, Vanderveer regretted not having played football. "And it's too late now to change it. That's the part that gets you—realizing that it's all over, and that your last chance is gone. I can imagine that's what it's like when you get old and you're about ready to die, and you look back over your life and realized that you never did the things you really wanted to do . . . and there's not a thing in the world you can do about it."

His friend told him he was making a big deal over nothing.

"You big dumb ox!" Vanderveer moaned. "You don't even know what I'm talking about, do you? It's not playing football that's important—it's the satisfaction of knowing that you did what you wanted to do, while you had the chance! Or it's that damn empty feeling in the pit of your stomach when you realize that you've let your last chance slip past, and now it's too late to change it. It's the—aw, hell. You wouldn't understand!"[6]

From Stanford, George Vanderveer and his friends went off to Columbia University Law School in New York. After law school, big firm practice excited none of them at the turn of the century. Even then, getting into court was hard as a young lawyer at a New York City corporate firm. His friends decamped back to the Pacific Northwest and the growing city of Seattle. After some hesitation, George followed. A college friend now was the chief prosecutor in Seattle and offered George a job as an assistant prosecutor. He was going to do what he wanted to do while he could.

Van thrived as a prosecutor, especially in cross-examination. He liked winning. He loved slumming in the cheap bars, where the people he prosecuted also did their drinking and brawling. At age thirty, he also liked seventeen-year-old Ellinor Hausman, who with her mother and sisters lived in the same boarding hotel that George shared with his buddies. Behind his back, Ellinor and her sisters called him "Grumpy Gus," an allusion to a comic strip character of the day, apparently because of Van's contentedness sitting by himself in the hotel dining room. One Christmas Eve changed that, and Ellinor and Van married in 1907. He flipped the nickname she and her sisters had used for him and called her "Gus" ever after. Van was almost thirty-two; Gus was about nineteen. After a lovely honeymoon, she quickly found a house on a wooded lot near Lake Washington where they could settle down. But Van nixed it and instead moved her to an apartment close enough for him to walk to work.[7]

That all was ten years before the Chicago indictment. He had been five feet nine and 160 pounds in college. Now, booze and beef thickened him. He won a nasty race for King County Prosecuting Attorney as a Republican in 1908. For two years he fought crime with zeal and little attention to ethical niceties. In a narrow sense, he was an idealist determined to root out crime and corruption. He cared little how. Quickly wearing out his welcome with county officials, the police, and the public alike, he did not run again in 1910. He relinquished the Republican nomination, but not without a parting shot at his nemesis, the local Democratic Party boss: "You frizzle-headed old bastard! I'll still be here when you're dead and gone—and I'll go out and puke on your grave!" With that farewell, Van's crime-fighting ended.[8]

He then went into private practice with his old Stanford friend Bud Cummings, defending criminal cases. It was a switch that bewildered Ellinor, but he explained his decision: "It may seem a little odd at first, but it's like a baseball player who gets traded in the middle of the season. First thing he knows, he's playing against the team he used to play for, but he just gets in and plays the best he can and doesn't let it bother him. It's the game that's important, Gus—not which team you're on."[9]

For a time, after Washington enacted prohibition at the state level by ballot initiative, effective at the start of 1916, Vanderveer was flush with money. Many of his smaller clients were affluent and had gotten into trouble for offering a drink. More significantly, he also became counsel, at great profit, for a successful bootlegger. During this time, worried about his client's rivals, Vanderveer began to carry two pistols, each in a shoulder holster under his suit coat, with police permission. Maybe this was a man who could forget he had a pistol in his pocket after all.[10]

Other than during the Prohibition boon, though, the fighter often seemed a lousy businessman in private practice. He was in high demand but neglectful about fees, more out of indifference or lack of discipline than out of generosity or kindness. Too often he took fees in barter. Once, he got an automobile as a fee but promptly gave it to Cummings—who already had a car, while the Vanderveers did not. He snapped at Ellinor's incredulous expression with the reply, "Why, Gus, you know we don't have a garage." Private practice was a wild ride of profligate extravagance when the money rolled in and stacks of unpaid bills and icy confrontations with Ellinor when it rolled out.[11]

Early 1917 brought Vanderveer his first IWW case. In Everett, Washington, deputies and vigilantes with violence in mind had met a boat carrying IWW members. Shooting erupted. The dead included five Wobblies and two policemen. Eventually, seventy-five Wobblies faced potential first-degree murder charges in the deaths of the two officers. The local Snohomish County prosecutor elected to try just one man first, Thomas H. Tracy. A Los Angeles lawyer who had represented the Wobblies in several of their free speech battles, Fred H. Moore, would defend. But Moore needed local cocounsel in Everett, so he asked a Seattle judge for advice. The judge offered only one lawyer with the necessary courage and capability: George

Vanderveer. In response to Ellinor's alarm, Van responded with a smile, "You can't be a criminal attorney and have nothing but Sunday School teachers for clients, Gus." He was in.

The Everett Wobblies wanted a political trial. Vanderveer stoutly insisted on a lawyerly approach instead. "Political, hell! It's just a bunch of men in jail who are going to be charged with first degree murder. Actually, it's nothing more and nothing less than another murder trial. That's all it is, and you can't make anything else out of it!"

After nine weeks of trial, during which Congress declared war at President Wilson's prodding, the jury acquitted Tracy on May 4, 1917. Until then, Van and the Wobblies had eyed each other with mutual distrust or unease. They doubted his commitment to their cause, given his insistence on a purely legal approach. And they were right: he did not endorse their cause, although his sympathy for them personally was growing. For his part, he had wondered indelicately "how in hell the I.W.W. ever expected to run American industry when it couldn't even handle its own [financial] affairs with any slight resemblance to intelligent operation."

But the acquittal changed both Van and the Wobblies. He disappeared for two days after. When he stumbled home, his clothes were filthy and his face bruised. He stank of stale alcohol. "Don't ask questions, Gus. Just forget it." The next morning he said, "Don't ask me where I've been because I don't even know. I've never been that drunk before in my life, and I hope I never am again." He would be.

For now, though, after days of brooding at home while playing solitaire following the Tracy acquittal, Van suddenly announced to Ellinor that he was joining the army. Even though they had a child, five-year-old Barbara, he thought it was the right thing to do. He took it hard when the army refused him, at forty-one, as physically unfit.

By 1917, too, Vanderveer was much better at defending clients than preserving his marriage. In his biography, Ellinor appears as an afterthought to him. During these ten years, Van had given Gus exactly one Christmas present: a heavy wool sweater. He never had given her a birthday present. "George Vanderveer," his biographers noted, "was not a sentimental man."

Instead of joining the army, he would heed the call to Chicago that fall. In Everett, Fred Moore had led him in the defense. Now, as a sign of the IWW's gauge of his skill, their roles would flip: he would lead Moore.

Vanderveer's experience in Everett reinforced his belief that he could win even the politically freighted battles of the IWW with a lawyer's approach and that the system would work as it claimed to work. As he saw it, practice would reflect theory, reality would mirror ideals, if only lawyers were skilled enough. This deeply human lawyer, a complicated man of contradictions, expected criminal justice institutions as an assemblage to exceed the failings of their human labor force. He expected the system to operate without contradiction if he worked hard, if he fought.[12]

Frank Nebeker, his nominal chief adversary, approached the practice of law in much the same uncritical way. But the adversary system is not a rope with opponents tugging from each end. Rather, the rope encircles its combatants, who usually number three, not two: the judge and the two opposing lawyers. Trial is a triangular contest, with each corner straining against and within the law's rope. Often in a criminal case, the judge essentially pulls with the prosecution; in rare cases, the judge may pull with the defense. Mostly, the accused is an observer, left to hope that the same rope is not looped into a noose at the end.

The judge in Chicago might have used a noose on occasion if he could. Earlier in the summer of 1917, the Honorable Kenesaw Mountain Landis had sentenced 121 "slackers" who had not registered for the draft and had been picked up in a June 6 riot in Rockford, Illinois. All but four he sentenced to one year and a day at hard labor, sneering that they were "whining and belly-aching puppies." Recall, too, that during jury selection in this case, Landis sentenced the man who had pulled down an American flag. Landis had given him five years in prison—until sheepish lawyers on both sides reminded him that the statutory maximum was only four. A few months after the IWW trial, Landis would preside over the trial of a U.S. congressman and socialist newspaper publisher, Victor L. Berger of Milwaukee, also under the Espionage Act. Upon conviction, Landis sent Berger to prison for two decades. He remonstrated later, in a speech to an American Legion convention, "It was my great disappointment to give Berger only 20 years in Leavenworth . . . I believe the law should have enabled me to have him lined up against the wall and shot." And that was after the war.[13]

But then, war in a sense had shaped Landis from birth. His father, a country doctor who enlisted as a physician in the Union Army, had been wounded at the Battle of Kenesaw Mountain in Georgia. When Abraham Hoch Landis returned home to Millville, Ohio, he and Mary Landis soon had their sixth child, and fourth son. They named the boy after the battle that nearly had cost Dr. Landis his left leg below the knee. Kenesaw Mountain Landis was born on November 20, 1866.

By the time "Kennie," as the family called him for a time, was nine, Abraham and Mary had moved them—now with a seventh child, Frederick—to Logansport, Indiana. There they stayed. On Abraham's side, the family had been Swiss Mennonite for generations. In Logansport, they attended the Presbyterian Church. But Kennie was a religious skeptic from youth.[14]

The boy seemed to have no exceptional qualities. He was slight: never more than five feet six and even in adulthood, about 130 pounds. He had enough athletic ability to play semi-pro baseball in a small town in the 1880s, improbably (given his short stature) at first base. He took up bicycling when that became popular. But he could boast no great athletic achievement. In school, he was adequate until he met algebra. That caused him to quit school altogether, at age fifteen. His late teen years and early adulthood then saw uninspiring stints as a grocery store clerk, a railroad office errand boy, and a county court reporter after he took a course in shorthand.[15]

Two distinctive qualities emerged, though. First, he had a sense of the theatrical that outstripped his intellectual and professional talents. He played a larger part than he actually held or should have held, given his merits. "No one ever accused Kenesaw Mountain Landis of being shy. Most saw him as a hopeless ham, whose flair for the dramatic often outshone his legal or judicial acumen," a biographer, David Pietrusza, explained. "There was just *something* about him, a lord-of-the-manor air; a bearing that marked him as, well, different." A more academic student of Landis, John Henderson, added, "He demonstrated an aptitude for leadership and an inclination toward bluster and showmanship." This quality prompted his family to call him the "Squire," a nickname that stuck for a lifetime.[16]

Second, Landis had a knack for finding, and attaching himself to, patrons. The first was a friend, Charles F. Griffin, whom Landis supported in his run for Indiana secretary of state. When Griffin won, Landis got a nice patronage appointment in the department at age twenty-two. That job enabled him to use a provision of Indiana law allowing his automatic admission to the bar. The young man who had abandoned school at fifteen over algebra and had come no closer to studying or reading law than as a court reporter now was a lawyer.[17]

His next and more important patron was his father's acquaintance Walter Q. Gresham. A populist Republican, Gresham's personal grudges against other Republicans (especially fellow Hoosier Benjamin Harrison) led him to support Grover Cleveland, the Democratic candidate for president, in 1892. Victorious, Cleveland was grateful and appointed Gresham secretary of state. The personal secretary Gresham brought to Washington was twenty-six-year-old Kenesaw Landis, who by then at least had completed law school to catch up with his status as an attorney by statute. Landis was loyal to Gresham—and to President Cleveland. He called Gresham "the best friend I ever had." The president, who had regarded Landis with caution initially, offered to appoint him ambassador to Venezuela after Gresham died. Landis declined. But he had improved his position dramatically by taking patronage jobs and serving loyally.

After serving in the State Department, in 1895 Landis returned to Chicago, where he had completed his law studies. He practiced corporate law with two other veterans of the Cleveland administration, a former undersecretary of state and a former assistant postmaster general. Landis also returned to Republican politics. The same year, he married Winifred Reed, whom he had met through yet another patron. Landis now had ties to both political parties, contacts, a wife, and a lucrative practice.[18]

Additionally, the Squire shared a family trait: political ambition. By 1903, two Landis brothers were serving in the U.S. House of Representatives. Older brother Charles had been elected in 1896; younger brother Frederick, in 1902. The two represented adjoining Indiana districts. Another brother, Walter, favored patronage posts as Kenesaw did. He secured a spot as postmaster general of Puerto Rico. For his part, Kenesaw managed the unsuccessful Illinois gubernatorial bid of a Chicago lawyer friend in 1904. He also worked assiduously behind the scenes during his ten years practicing in Chicago to secure an appointment as a federal judge. In at least one way, he made no secret of his wish to become a judge: he developed the hobby of collecting judicial gavels. Back in the Republican fold, he cultivated his image as a member of the party's progressive wing. With Theodore Roosevelt in the White House since President McKinley's assassination in 1901, that progressive posture was expedient.

In 1905, his chance came. Congress created an additional federal judgeship in Chicago, the seat of the Northern District of Illinois. It was a judgeship for which Landis had lobbied hard over several years, in the expectation that he might get it once it was created. After his brothers and the unsuccessful candidate for governor whose campaign he had managed all spoke to Roosevelt about him, at Landis's urging, Roosevelt appointed him and Landis got his commission in March 1905. He was thirty-eight years old when he moved into the grand, two-story courtroom on the sixth floor, done in mahogany, marble, and brass.[19]

When his mother, now a widow, learned of his confirmation, she sent her second youngest son a telegram. "Always be a just judge," she implored him simply.[20] For Landis, though, the notion of justice—however defined— never would have much connection to judicial impartiality.

The new judge quickly established his progressive *bona fides*, even if his decisions were erratic. As he had while serving in the State Department, Landis eschewed formal attire, adopting a folksy appearance with his sense of show. He did not wear a robe on the bench but favored instead a plain, dark business suit: this gave him a common touch and made him seem approachable. In an early case, he imposed the maximum fine, $4,000, on the Allis-Chalmers Corporation for importing foreign workers illegally. Another judge might have recused himself, as one of Landis's patrons and mentors sat on the Allis-Chalmers board. But the maximum fine undercut any claim that he played favorites.

And that fine was nothing compared to the sentence in his most famous case, *United States v. Standard Oil Co. of Indiana*. Upon conviction for 1,462 antitrust violations, Landis fined John D. Rockefeller's company a stunning $29.24 million—after forcing Rockefeller's personal appearance in court earlier, and playing the press masterfully as U.S. marshals sought to serve Rockefeller a subpoena. It was the largest criminal fine in U.S. history. In 2018 dollars, it would be over $728,666,000.

It also did not stand. The U.S. Circuit Court of Appeals for the Seventh Circuit, in Chicago, overturned both the fine and the conviction in 1908, in a stinging rebuke written by a former friend of Landis. A different judge acquitted Standard Oil on retrial. But Landis had burnished his progressive image.[21]

Vanderveer and his IWW clients would have done well not to make too much of the Squire's folksy ways and showy progressive posture in relation to trusts and American business generally. They could have seen Landis's sentence of Hendricks, the man who pulled down the flag, during the weeks of their jury selection. They could have read of his earlier treatment of the 121 "slackers."

They probably would not have known, though, of his handling of a federal habeas petition for a German serial murderer of wives, Johann Hoch, twelve years earlier. Hoch's lawyers filed a writ of habeas corpus and the case came to Landis on the very day of the scheduled execution. The claim was that extradition to Illinois from New York on bigamy charges, after which Illinois tried him instead for murder, violated the constitution. Landis conceded that the lawyers might be right—but ruled that the death sentence would stand all the same. The brief habeas proceeding apparently did not even delay Hoch's hanging.[22]

And the hundred-plus men, many of them immigrants, now facing trial before Landis certainly knew nothing of the graduation speech he had given before his law school classmates in June 1891. Landis titled his oration "The Conservative Man" and in it extolled conservatives for defending society against the impatience of "radical men, extremists, agitators." Then, just before praising the modern United States for "less bigotry, less ignorance, less superstition, less prejudice" than ever in the past, he inveighed against "the danger that threatens from the wholesale importation of the ignorant and vicious Hun and the cowardly and revengeful Sicilian." Nothing in his speech betrayed any sense of the tension, even contradiction, in it. The Squire, too, was complicated.[23]

Finally, there is no reason to think that the men on trial, or their lawyers, knew anything about Landis's Sunday meeting in the hotel with prosecutors back in August 1917. Surely, too, they were unaware that the attorney general of the United States considered Judge Landis the department's "main man."

The nation now was in its greatest war since the one that left this main man's father limping, the memory of which past war Landis's very name honored. This new war was against the "ignorant and vicious Hun." The defendants were the men seen as the war's great resisters. Vanderveer, as their advocate, and the Squire, for his causes, joined their own battle across the well of the courtroom.

13

A Gathering

That splendid courtroom in mahogany and marble that Landis occupied
on the sixth floor of Chicago's federal courthouse bore only a number on the double doors, in government fashion. It was Room 627. Now,
with the successive groups of two hundred prospective jurors pared to the
twelve who would serve, space opened for the long trial itself. The month
of jury selection had spanned springtime's arrival. Although Chicago would
be pleasant now in early May, with crabapple trees abloom, much of the
trial would play out in summer's heat. Given the crowd in the courtroom,
just beginning with the men on trial, soon Landis and his bailiffs would
have to resort to the only means of cooling the two-story courtroom they
had: opening the large windows to the din of downtown streets and elevated
trains below, in the gut of the Loop.[1]

American courtrooms do not separate a defendant from his lawyer as
many English-speaking countries do; there is no "dock" for the prisoner,
let alone a cage or other seclusion in which the accused sits in some countries. Defendants sit next to their lawyers. In a typical criminal case, with
one or maybe two defendants, long tables ahead of the rail, facing the
bench either side by side or one behind the other, suffice to seat both prosecutors and a law enforcement agent or two at their table, and client and
defense lawyer at their table. Counsel tables, as they are called, generally
accommodate three or four chairs on one side so that all can face the judge.

This case was not typical, though. No courtroom could hold enough
tables to seat one hundred defendants. Landis had arranged the rows of
benches for the IWW men to occupy behind and next to the defense table,
with the new spittoons dotting this bleacher section so bored working men

could have a chew while testimony droned on. As the weeks and months passed, the men fidgeted, slouched, and even sprawled and slept on the hard benches. When the weather warmed, they stripped to shirtsleeves. They could chat quietly among themselves without disturbing much or read newspapers. They rustled and spat. They looked around the room, nodding to friends or relatives, appraising the jury, or just passing time staring at the stately surroundings. The trial transcript offers nothing to suggest that Landis was rigid about where they sat on a given day or what they did. Witnesses surveying the bleachers almost invariably could not pick out one man from the others when asked to identify a given defendant in the crowd, but Vanderveer always signaled strategically his view that the men had done nothing criminal by directing the defendant at issue to stand and be seen. The man did.[2]

The roster of lawyers remained essentially the same as during jury selection. At the front counsel table, nearest the bench, the prosecution team was Frank Nebeker, Claude Porter, U.S. District Attorney Charles Clyne (as a matter of courtesy), and now the lead Bureau of Investigation agent, George Murdock. Nebeker and Porter would handle all witnesses and legal arguments in court after jury selection.

Immediately behind the prosecution table, the defense table still included Vanderveer in the first chair, with Fred Moore and Caroline Lowe next to him, and Chicago lawyer Otto Christensen, now in a rising role. William B. Cleary completed the defense team. The idea that one set of lawyers would represent more than one hundred codefendants, with the inevitably divided loyalties that would entail, went wholly unchallenged in 1918 and for years after. Multiple representation in big cases was the rule, not the exception, before the U.S. Supreme Court held that the poor have a right to counsel at public expense. That shift in interpretation of the Sixth Amendment would not be completed even in felony cases for another forty-five years. Absent really unusual circumstances, in 1918, the accused could have lawyers if and only if they or their families or friends could hire lawyers. For these men, then, it was a matter of shared lawyers or no lawyers.

Vanderveer and Christensen would handle witnesses and the speaking roles in court. Lowe would corral witnesses out of court, do legal research, and handle essential details: files, exhibits, notes on testimony to aid evidentiary objections later or closing arguments, midtrial correspondence with supporters and potential witnesses, accounts of fees and expenses, lists of possible trial errors if an appeal should prove necessary, and so on. Cleary's exact role in court is unclear today, although he gave at least one

Sunday speech out of court to rally support and solicit money. Moore seems to have been absent frequently, whether because he also was working on the other IWW indictments or for other reasons.[3]

There would be personal tension between the opposing lawyers from the start. Vanderveer seemed not to care for the prideful Nebeker, or at least made frequent efforts to unnerve the lead prosecutor. For his part, Nebeker certainly did not trust or respect Vanderveer. Back in early December 1917, Nebeker had written to Attorney General Thomas W. Gregory with a warning, when he knew that Vanderveer was planning a trip to Washington, DC, to make an informal appeal to government brass to dispose of the case favorably. "We are advised by the United States District Attorney in the State of Washington that Mr. Vanderveer is not at all reliable," Nebeker wrote, "and that it is advisable to watch him at every turn."[4]

To the side of counsel, the jury box ran perpendicularly with twelve chairs in two rows of six. Five deputy U.S. marshals sat nearby to protect the jurors. Time and again during the testimony to come, jurors at the end farthest from the witness seat would complain they could not hear, or lawyers and Judge Landis would implore a witness to speak loudly enough for the last juror to hear. As summer came, street noise only added to the problem.[5]

On the bench, above more white marble and brass, sat Landis. No one had to rise when he entered the courtroom after recesses. In his rumpled dark business suit, and without even a jacket or vest once summer came, the judge would spring around, standing to get a better look at something or craning to hear a mumbling witness or even perching at the corner of the jury box. This affected informality resulted in the men on trial becoming less guarded about the judge; it made him seem more human. Generally, the Wobblies' writings and comments credited Judge Landis during the trial for giving them a relatively fair shake, although they remained deeply skeptical of the role of any judge in maintaining an unfair social order.[6]

Fostering the perception of fairness is the best form of courtroom control a judge ever has. Landis managed it adroitly. But of course, his August meeting with Fitts at the Congress Hotel and the attorney general's later reference to Landis as the department's "main man" suggest that a perception of fairness perhaps is all that Landis sought to foster.

So far as the trial transcript reveals, though, he did present a general appearance of impartiality, at least when he was listening. The transcript reveals time and again that Landis, when a lawyer objected to some question that his adversary posed, had browned out, hearing neither the question nor the preceding minutes of testimony that set its context. His lapses, and the lawyers' awkward efforts to explain the state of proceedings without embarrassing the judge utterly, give a nearly comic undertone to the long trial transcript as a whole.

Landis did pay attention when acquaintances of his dropped by the courtroom, and consistent with his show of unorthodoxy, from time to time he invited a special guest to join him on the bench to watch the trial. The famous evangelist and former major league ballplayer Billy Sunday had that honor. So did the actor Louis Mann and Senator William S. Kenyon of Iowa. A privileged few, then, enjoyed Imperial box seats at the Colosseum to watch part of a day's entertainment.[7]

Just in case his personal charm and calculated generosity did not keep the IWW men in order, Landis also had twenty deputy U.S. marshals in the courtroom. Most of them would have been seated ahead of the rail separating the public viewing pews from the well of the courtroom, again with five looking after the jury specifically. Some likely stood along the walls and at the back, to survey the entire room.[8]

The press took up seats at a long table near the rail. Among the reporters watching the trial was a young journalist with the *Chicago Daily News*, a socialist but quiet enough about his own views to keep employment with a commercial newspaper. He was Carl J. Sandburg. One of the very few mainstream press reporters with any sympathy for the Wobblies, Sandburg won an interview with Bill Haywood in jail well before the trial started. Showing some of the lean beauty of language that marked his later work as a poet and Lincoln biographer, Sandburg noted that Haywood "discusses the alleged 10,000 crimes [in the indictment] with the massive leisure of Hippo Vaughn pitching a shut-out." Sandburg would be in and out of the trial, from beginning to end.[9]

Only much later in the trial would another more radical journalist, a much more familiar name than Sandburg at that time, appear to follow the proceedings. He was John Reed, an eager proponent of the Russian revolution who later would write *Ten Days That Shook the World*. He returned from Russia only in August. But once back in the United States, he promptly went to Chicago to cover the end of the trial for radical-minded readers. Reed, whose writing skill was indisputable, turned perhaps the most famous phrase of the trial. He described Judge Landis as "a wasted man with untidy white hair, an emaciated face in which two burning eyes are set like jewels, parchment-like skin split by a crack for a mouth." His face, Reed wrote, was that of "Andrew Jackson three years dead."[10]

Although she seems not to have gone to Chicago, Helen Keller also weighed in on behalf of the Wobblies and their cause. "Despite their errors, their blunders and the ignominy heaped upon them," she wrote, "I sympathize with the 'I.W.W.'s.' Their cause is my cause. While they are threatened and imprisoned, I am manacled. If they are denied a living wage, I, too, am defrauded. While they are industrial slaves, I cannot be free."[11]

Rarities like Sandburg and Reed apart, most of the reporters were hacks reliably piling up column inches for the *Chicago* (then *Daily*) *Tribune* and other mainstream newspapers with accounts that scorned or mocked the defendants. They made little or no pretense of objectivity. Efforts at factual accuracy were little better. Even basic facts like the number of men on trial were not consistent, often seeming rounded off or approximated.

Behind the reporters and the rail sat the general public. Many of these were friends or supporters of the men on trial. For whatever reason, the mainstream press took special notice of the women who came to support the defendants. Maybe part of the reason was that women were less common visitors to court generally in the first decades of the twentieth century, for courtrooms still were not considered suitable environs for them. Courtrooms of the day sometimes had special "ladies' galleries," elevated above the courtroom floor in two-story courtrooms. Women could not yet serve on juries in most states, although Utah allowed them in 1898 and territorial Wyoming had experimented with female jurors as early as 1870.

Whatever the reason, though, the commercial press reported sneeringly about the women in attendance but commented not at all on the male spectators unless they were prominent. When former Senator R. E. Pettigrew of South Dakota stopped by to support his "old friends" Bill Haywood and George Vanderveer, for instance, the *Tribune* took comparatively respectful note.[12]

A final important figure remained behind the scenes; he made no public appearance at the trial. This was Samuel Gompers of the AFL. For months, the Justice Department had been sharing information and collaborating with him quietly. Gompers got copies of the seventy thousand-plus IWW membership cards, for example, that Bureau of Investigation agents had extracted and logged from seized files. Gompers could have cross-checked those against AFL members. Then, when prosecutors noticed that the IWW was fundraising for the defense with claims that the government meant to quash the right to strike, Nebeker suggested to the attorney general "that this false impression be corrected and the fraud denounced at the Buffalo meeting of the American Federation of Labor." And Fitts referred at least one inquiring congressman to Gompers for information that would distinguish the IWW from other organized labor. No one more than Gompers, Fitts assured the congressman, "understands the distinction better or states it more forcibly."[13]

So, with Gompers unseen but celebrities wandering in and out of the courtroom doors, flies making their own entrances and exits through the open windows, and the din of the street drowning out testimony and the muttering of spectators and defendants alike, the trial was on. Frank Nebeker soon would lift his lanky frame from a chair, smooth his crisply ironed suit, and stand before the jury. But first, a deputy marshal would call the crowd to order: *Hear ye, hear ye. The United States District Court for the Northern District of Illinois is in session. The Honorable Kenesaw Mountain Landis, presiding. All having business before this honorable court draw near, for the court is now sitting. God save this honorable court and these United States.*

14

This Un-American Institution

Nebeker took it from there. Many judges speak convivially to a jury in the morning, inquiring how the panel is doing or making banal small talk to ease anxiety—or resentment—about being in court. Some judges may be chatty at the lunch break or the end of the day. They also may take these moments at the beginning or end of a session to remind jurors that they must not discuss the case until the evidence is closed, that they should keep an open mind, and so on.

Landis was not one of those judges. For all the transcript reveals, he paid no more attention to the jurors than a train engineer might pay to passengers in the last second-class coach.

So, within a few seconds after court convened on Thursday morning, May 2, 1918, Frank Nebeker had the floor. On paper, he sounded as crisp as the pleat of his pants and as stiff as his collar.

"You gentlemen," Nebeker began. Skillfully, he made a concession to the jurors at the outset that sounded as if it conceded nothing. "I might say at this time, as it occurs to me now, that a large part of the evidence which the Government expects to introduce in this case consists of the pamphlets, newspaper articles, circulars, bulletins, and letters between the members and between officers of the organization and a great majority of those papers . . . were taken from the various headquarters of the organization known as the I.W.W." That is, if the jurors were expecting lively testimony and dramatic finger-pointing from the witness chair, they should reconsider. Another concession he smoothly slipped in early, too: Nebeker himself was not sure, as he stood there, exactly how many men were on trial. "About 113," he told the jury, explaining that some of those indicted never had been found. "Still others," he murmured, "were found upon a more complete investigation, not to have been active in the furtherance of the criminal conspiracies charged here during the period of the war." The government, in other words, had taken a "fire, ready, aim" approach to indicting people in the heady days after the September 5 seizures. And it had not advanced beyond approximations as trial opened.[1]

Nebeker also soon had to confront the issue of IWW membership and the role of the organization itself. Technically, as the government would remind Landis time and again when it suited prosecutorial purposes at the moment, the organization was not on trial; it was not named in the indictment, certainly. But was membership in the organization sufficient to prove individual guilt on the five charged conspiracies? If sufficient, was it also essential? Or could one be a member of one or more of the conspiracies, without also being a member of the organization?

The questions were central. Nebeker told the jury that his case would feature evidence in just three categories: (1) proof showing "the external features of this organization; that is, its outward features"; (2) proof of "practices and its tenets"; and (3) proof of its organizational "tactics." The government's entire case revolved around the organization. Nebeker admitted midway through his opening statement that one defendant, Stanley J. Clark, had not been an IWW member. He also admitted "some little doubt" about whether a founder of the IWW, Vincent St. John, remained a member during the period of the indictment. Then he gave his answer. Both Clark and St. John had been members of the conspiracy, even if not of the organization at the right time. With those two exceptions, "the defendants are charged here as being members of the I.W.W.—members and officers." So, membership was sufficient but not essential.[2]

With that stretch of legal rapids navigated, Nebeker laid out the government's theme. He read from the Preamble to the IWW Constitution, which closed with the thirteen-year-old aspiration that "by organizing industrially we are forming the structure of the new society within the shell of the old." Then he pounced:

> I pause right now on that last sentence long enough to say that that is the conception these people have of the function that they are to perform in society. They treat themselves, and regard themselves, or at any rate part of them do—and that seems to be the scheme that they are a government within the government; an *imperio in imperium*. That is what they think they are. The highest officer in the organization [Haywood] regards himself as being at the head of that government. That is, he has his functionaries.

He has his cabinet, so to speak. He has his bureau of propaganda. He has his emissaries, and his minions, while he sits enthroned as an uncrowned king, in a swivel chair, at 1001 West Madison Street in this city and gives his orders with unlimited power to the dupes and members of the organization throughout its entire reach.[3]

The image of a "swivel chair king" was, in addition to being a persuasive rhetorical flourish on its own, an effective invocation of another term then current: swivel-chair soldier or swivel-chair officer, the derisive label for wealthier or well-placed men who were volunteering for military service if assured desk jobs far away from the hazards of the trenches and the front. Nebeker at once pulled a lawyerly double trick, then. He cast the one-eyed, hardscrabble former miner, Bill Haywood, as a lazy, indolent emperor, living luxuriously, and by tacit comparison as a coward at that. Haywood's secretary and bookkeeper, Elizabeth Serviss, made $18 a week; Haywood himself, $22.50 a week. That was the actual pay gap in the IWW, from bottom to top. But Nebeker had created an image of a privileged elitist, duping honest but naïve workers into doing his bidding.[4]

Haywood, Nebeker expanded, "is the man above all men, as the evidence will show in this case, who is responsible for this un-American institution that has been brought to the attention of the American people at this time on account of the war, although it existed prior to that time." However disingenuously, from his opening statement through the entire trial, the copper trust lawyer would assuage whatever guilt jurors or prosecutors might have felt about appearing to attack laborers and their unions by portraying the men on trial, starting with Haywood, as members of an elite; officeholders manipulating those beneath them.

> You will notice in the letters that will be introduced that they always address each other as "Fellow-worker. Fellow-worker." Men who have not worked during the period or life of the oldest inhabitant refers to himself [sic] and to other men of the same kind as "fellow-workers." These men sit in their offices here in Chicago and in Minneapolis, Salt Lake, Spokane, Seattle, Philadelphia and other places where these branches are, and are being supported by these members—these what I will refer to as the honest members of the organization that are out there toiling for a daily wage.[5]

Of the men on trial, Nebeker noted that thirty-seven were secretaries of local branches of the IWW, seventeen were officers known as delegates, and four were members of the General Executive Board: Haywood, Charles Lambert, Richard Brazier, and Francis Miller. And of course, there always was the fifth General Executive Board member, "one Frank H. Little, now deceased," who "as you remember was hanged by a mob last year in Butte, Montana." Yes, he was referring to Frank Little, the man whose torture and murder had so tickled the vice president of the United States.

The rest of the defendants consisted of "quite a number of people who are associated with the organization as writers; contributors to newspapers and writers of pamphlets and things of that kind." Ralph Chaplin was one example. "The evidence will show that Ralph H. Chaplin is a man of considerable talents, but like the rest of them, with a twist in his mind that gets him off on this line of work."[6]

Nebeker's next challenge was to prepare the jury for the niceties of the time frame of the indictment. It covered only the months between the declaration of war, April 6, 1917, and the date of the indictment itself, September 28, 1917. "That is the period covered by the indictment," Nebeker conceded squarely enough. Even that was fudging a bit, though. The actual laws these men allegedly conspired to break did not yet exist on April 6, 1917. The draft the IWW supposedly wished to obstruct was not established until May 18, and the all-important Espionage Act not until May 16. Functionally, then, if one cannot conspire to violate a statute as yet not passed, the period of the indictment was barely more than four months.[7]

Did the writings that Nebeker promised as evidence fall within that period, then? For the most part, no. In fact, the government would offer, over the next six or seven weeks as it presented its case, very few letters, editorials, or other writings during even the broader period of the indictment. Some stump speeches, overheard by undercover detectives, occurred during the summer months that the indictment covered fairly. But most of the men on trial would hear no evidence at all that they said, wrote, or did anything during the period that the indictment covered.

Nebeker had reassurance for the jurors. "There will be evidence offered here by the Government covering a period anterior to" April 6, 1917, he explained. "But only for the purpose of explaining and rendering intelligible to you, evidence that will be introduced relating specifically to the time covered by the indictment."[8]

Prior to the declaration of war, Nebeker supposed, "there might not have been any Federal law . . . that they had directly violated; and by these same principles that they had adopted as the fundamental principles of their organization, they created the instrumentality that was just like making a large caliber cannon and pointing it directly at the Government as soon as we got into war." Moreover, the IWW was "a criminal organization from its inception." It flourished most just before and just after the declaration of war, Nebeker insisted (although he admitted that the indictment's 200,000 membership number was wrong; it probably was more like 40–60,000 because membership is "fluctuating, ambulatory"). "These people began their active anti-war propaganda, and it appealed to the people who did not want to perform their duty as American citizens."[9]

The tactics that the IWW proposed for thwarting the government's war effort were not armed force, Nebeker conceded strategically. Rather, the tactics were industrial sabotage: the wooden shoe or the black cat, in IWW parlance. Nebeker gave examples of acts of sabotage that he contended the government would prove, from putting foreign substances into food, to driving spikes into logs so that sawmill blades would break, to removing nuts from farm machinery, to putting phosphorus in lumberjacks' boots while they slept, and more.[10]

In all, the government's written exhibits would show that the IWW proposed, by its tactics, "to destroy the wage system." Now Nebeker warmed to his task. Destroying the wage system meant "to destroy it in such a way that no man in this country can hire a man or a set of men to carry on any line of employment." "Every employer," he told this jury of employers, "is a bad man by virtue of the fact alone that he is an employer."

Nebeker's peroration had him in full throat. "Now they propose to run the country. They propose to substitute our political institutions with this sort of thing some day, when they get strong enough, and our political institutions will vanish into thin air, and Haywood and his cohorts will establish their industrial organization in its place. Now that is the grand work gentlemen—that is what the evidence will show, stated very generally and imperfectly—this organization stands for; what it was created for, what it is and what it has been."[11]

Retrenching just a bit after catching his breath, yet pushing the IWW further from other unions, he explained, "An I.W.W. strike is an altogether different thing from any strike that any legitimate organization ever conducted. We will show from the evidence introduced here that they are against such a strike as the American Federation of Labor stands for, and as other legitimate labor organizations stand for."[12]

Nebeker had one last surprise for the jury. "Now, gentlemen, realizing that this is a conspiracy case,—that is to say these men are charged with having conspired to do these various things, — with having actually done those particular things, — let me say to you that with that in view the government will perhaps from time to time, introduce evidence showing or tending to show the actually completed events, but it will only be for the purpose of illustrating the general proposition of the aims and purposes of the organization; in other words for the purpose of showing the conspiracy."[13]

Perhaps no prosecutor has understood better the advantages of conspiracy statutes. The government need not prove crimes; it is a crime merely to plan crimes with others. You need not do anything. You need only agree that you will, or belong to an organization that agrees.

With that, Nebeker sat. Haywood thought him "a smooth individual, a slimy creature, even more foxy than he tried to prove me to be."[14]

Now it was Vanderveer's turn to give an opening statement. He did not: rather, he reserved his opening until the conclusion of the government's case and the beginning of the defense case—as is the defendant's option in an American criminal trial.

That decision, for reasons Vanderveer did not explain, meant forfeiting the chance to meet the government's narrative immediately; to offer the jurors a competing overview of right and wrong, innocence and guilt. Vanderveer's decision meant that it would be weeks before the jury heard any coherent explanation from the defense of why the government was wrong, why nine dozen men were innocent. Jurors would hear from the defense only on cross-examination until then. Thursday ended with only the prosecution version of fact ringing in jurors' ears.

That initial silence from the defense was not the only problem for the men on trial. From the afternoon of May 2 through June 19, when the government rested its case, the two contending sides were trying different cases. The defense contended that individual defendants committed no actual crimes; they may have held and expressed opinions, even rash ones, but they had a right to do so and had taken no illegal action. But they were not defending the claims that the U.S. government actually was making. The government's case instead was that the men belonged to, or agreed generally with, an organization that consistently opposed the war and urged workers to do the same; an organization that threatened by its words to inspire others to refuse the draft or to slow essential industrial production by strike or spite.

Always, the prosecution had the foil of Frank Little, the dead man who could not speak now but had left a legacy of incendiary letters and speeches.

120

Nebeker sought over and again to tie living defendants to Little's views, as the defendants could not call upon him now to provide a response or even context. Vanderveer and his clients quite understandably viewed a corpse nearly one year buried as not rightly on trial. Nebeker viewed Little as the hub or touchstone of the prosecution's case, the one man who never could answer an accusation or defend a fellow worker as someone less radical than he.

In a fundamental way, neither side was addressing the other. Vanderveer and his clients saw no proof from the government of actual crimes. Nebeker and Porter saw no need for that proof.[15]

For his part, by and large Landis coolly let both sides try their cases. If the defense was tilting at charges never made, why should he care?

On one point, the prosecution would be unable to make part of the case it had hoped to make. Nebeker, Porter, and Clyne had sought help from the U.S. Army in finding witnesses who would testify to IWW disruption within the ranks of soldiers. On January 21, 1918, the Chicago depot quartermaster, a colonel, had written that "this Depot has had no trouble whatever that would in any way indicate a connection with the representatives of the I.W.W., and the writer is unable to give any facts respecting the manipulations of the I.W.W. in regard to the Army." A noticeably peeved Fitts had written to the three prosecutors that this response was "very disappointing." He suggested that they get in touch with the army "and see if better assistance cannot be obtained with respect to securing evidence with which to make out the case."[16]

Nothing better came from the army. All the same, the prosecution case began on Friday, May 3. Slowly, grindingly, the two prosecutors put in the evidence for the charges the government did make. Vanderveer was lawyerly, entering a continuing objection to the government's use of any documents seized by search warrant and also formally moving, again, for return of all property. Landis and Nebeker both understood that Vanderveer was "making a record" for a possible appeal, should the jury convict, and they too were courteous and businesslike. But Landis would not budge.[17]

Early government witnesses, Hilda Seery and Elizabeth Serviss, were assistants in the Chicago IWW headquarters. While palpably unhappy to be under government subpoena, they were polite and forthright under Nebeker's questioning. Objections were few. Both Nebeker and Vanderveer adopted, for the time, a civil tone with one another. But Landis's mind already was wandering. In response to a technical objection by Vanderveer, Landis replied, "What is this question? For a moment my attention was distracted; what is the question, Mr. Stenographer?"

And for their part, many of the defendants could not hear the witnesses at all. Vanderveer suggested moving the witness chair closer to the jury box, as the defendants could not hear anyway. Claude Porter, Nebeker's ambitious second who often ran for office in Iowa, knew who he wanted to hear the testimony: the newspaper reporters at their tables behind counsel and immediately in front of the rail. He spoke up for them early when they had trouble hearing the witness. Porter hardly was the first, or last, lawyer to curry favor with newspaper reporters. It did not help his electoral ambitions in the end.[18]

At the moment, though, a long, strange trial was under way.

15

Polly-Foxing

The trial soon settled into a consistent pattern. Weekdays, court would begin promptly at 10:00 a.m. (or, after Landis thought it all was moving too slowly, at 9:30 a.m.) and go to 1:00 p.m. with a short morning break at 11:00 a.m. Lunch was limited to one hour. At 2:00 p.m., Landis would settle informally on the bench, robeless as always, and call everyone to order. Testimony would continue unbroken until either 4:00 p.m. or an abruptly announced stopping point near that hour that was convenient to Landis. On Saturdays, the session was from 9:00 a.m. until 1:00 p.m. with a short break midway. Timing had a clipped, military precision, with Landis still offering the jurors not a moment of chitchat.[1]

A pattern developed eventually with government witnesses, too. In the early days of the government case, Nebeker or, more often, Porter called witnesses who either could identify individual defendants by sight or identify documents as theirs, whether by signature and handwriting or by virtue of the witness's role as keeper of documents. Often, Vanderveer entered lawyerly objections to relevance: yes, a certain defendant might have written a given letter, but what was its relevance as personal opinion—especially if dated before the period of the indictment—unless some other evidence tied him to the conspiracy? Landis did what cagey judges often do. He overruled these objections and admitted the document "conditionally," on the predicate that the defense could move again to strike the document if in the end the prosecution failed to link the writer to the conspiracy charges. With dozens upon dozens, even hundreds, of such letters and weeks to go before the prosecution case ended, Landis was playing the odds that the defense would lose track of its objections, conclude that they were too trivial to repeat, or simply forget. The limits of human attention and determination play a role in any trial, especially a long one. Landis placed a good bet.[2]

He also tired of the charade of conditional admissibility, though; Landis was, if nothing else, an impatient and direct man. During the testimony of Justice Department special agent Phillip James Barry, who oversaw the third raid of the Chicago IWW headquarters on December 28, 1917, jurors heard that searching agents took fifty-seven large packing crates containing some 250,000 documents over the course of twelve days (all without a new search warrant; they apparently relied still on the September 5 warrant). Vanderveer made his usual foundation and relevance objections. He also complained that many of the documents never were distributed publicly. Landis let them all in: every page.

"The evidence is against you on that proposition," he told Vanderveer, "on the question of the admissibility of unpublished documents. The indictment in this case is a charge of conspiracy to accomplish certain things by certain processes, certain means. Assuming both of these to have never been edited—never have been given publicity, or to have been in the headquarters or in the store room or in the Printing Bureau, they are admissible on this theory: If an indictment—I will illustrate the theory by what I am now going to say. If the indictment was a conspiracy to accomplish a result by the use of explosives and there was found on the premises of a defendant or defendants or persons of defendants whom the indictment charges as conspirators, as in this case, dynamite—or, if there was found on the premises of said persons preparations for the manufacture of explosives not used, evidence of the fact would be admissible. I say, it would be admissible—it is my opinion that it would be admissible. The objection is overruled." Words of protest, even if never spoken publicly, now were equated with explosives.[3]

Nebeker won himself even greater leeway in admission of documents with a witness, Marie Coppens, who had been the stenographer and translator for the defendant John Avilla, a paid organizer among Italians. She wrote and signed most of his letters, which she identified. Landis sustained Nebeker's objection when Vanderveer sought, on cross-examination of this friendly witness, to establish that she knew of no instance when Avilla or anyone in the office advocated the destruction of property or the commission of violence; after all the documents that the government had shoveled in through Coppens, Landis agreed that this specific inquiry was in some way "improper, immaterial and irrelevant."

Emboldened, Nebeker then went further as to a peculiar letter in red ink not written or signed by Avilla or the witness, and indeed of unknown authorship altogether. "Well, I just want to suggest that in the first place I think it is true that there is no evidence there that would be competent showing that this emanated from Mr. Avilla," Nebeker admitted. "But there is abundance of evidence that makes it admissible. We cannot always make the offer,—cannot state exactly what it is admissible for, but clearly this would be admissible. It comes from the Chicago files."

Landis bought it. He let the document in. Arguably, that ruling cast the die for the trial. Any document, no matter how anonymous, was relevant to conspiracy and admissible if found in an IWW office. But admissible against which defendant or defendants? Landis did not say.[4]

Vanderveer got hot about this for a time. "We are trying men here," he sniped at Landis, not trying an organization. In what became "the general rule," however, Landis explained only that writings admitted this way would have "not any greater effect as against him [the particular defendant otherwise being discussed at the moment] than as against all the other defendants." In short, many of the trial exhibits were admissible against no one in specific, but against everyone in general. Nothing against anyone became something against everyone. To this general rule, Vanderveer would have to content himself with "the regular objection."[5]

The transcript suggests he knew that the IWW cause had been hurt. Days later, Vanderveer complained again about conditional admissibility rulings. A particular admitted document showed only that "these people disliked pork and beans," something they had a perfect right to do. Landis responded, "You cannot prove the whole lawsuit in one afternoon." Vanderveer's riposte was immediate. "I understand, but sometimes the whole lawsuit is never proved at all, and yet things go to the jury." Still, Landis stood his ground.[6]

In the early weeks, the prosecution also called several undercover detectives or deputies who claimed to hear inflammatory speeches from one or another of the defendants—or more often from Frank Little—while mixing with the crowd, pretending to be IWW supporters. A few witnesses also described incidents of real or suspected sabotage on job sites, which they sometimes attributed, more or less speculatively, to unknown IWW members. These moments dotted the prosecution case. Especially after Landis tired of sorting through the relevance and linkage to a specific defendant of any one letter or editorial, and admitted seized documents wholesale, much of the prosecution case consisted of either Porter or Nebeker standing up and reading most or all of a document to the jury. In the course of nearly seven weeks of prosecution evidence, the voices of the prosecutors themselves reading letters to the jury may have exceeded in time the voices of actual witnesses. On occasion, snoring could be heard from the defendants' benches, as someone stretched out and napped.[7]

As in any long trial, the lawyers began to get on one another's nerves. Moreover, all of them began to annoy the Squire. At the prosecution table, Nebeker and Porter plainly were jockeying for playing time and control. Porter was doing most of the direct examinations—the questioning of the government's own witnesses—and capably enough (his cross-examinations later were another story: most prosecutors get little opportunity to cross-examine, and in Porter's case it showed). But Nebeker, who seemed to have a good sense of Landis's moods, was not above interrupting Porter's unwise objections, to say curtly that the government had no objection. Nebeker also referred derisively to Porter as his "associate" at one point, after interrupting Porter yet again.[8]

Vanderveer and Nebeker became especially antagonistic. While Nebeker usually was icy calm, Vanderveer seemed to enjoy needling or even provoking him. And Vanderveer was a master of legalistic discursion, probably for the sake of talk. He did give away, on occasion, his fear that the trial would end in conviction, worrying explicitly how something would look on the paper transcript as part of an appellate record.[9]

But he also was capable of sheer filibuster, and of trying to unnerve Nebeker for sport. One day, Nebeker was offering into evidence Gurley Flynn's pamphlet, *Sabotage*. As if unsure of the answer (and possibly he was), Vanderveer chimed in, "Has the case been dismissed against her, or a severance granted?"

Calling his bluff, Nebeker responded with deliberate ambiguity, "Yes."

Porter, oblivious to the swordplay but happy to even the score and interrupt Nebeker, interjected, "A severance."

"The same thing," Vanderveer shot back.[10]

Several days later, Porter wanted the court, for almost no reason, to admit a box of stamps bearing defendant Albert Prashner's signature in different sizes. "I do not see as they are material," parleyed Vanderveer as to this Exhibit 294. "We have admitted Mr. Prashner's signature, which takes that out of the case."

"The only thought I had in mind was whether or not the admission would carry with it the stamp signatures; that was the main thing I had in mind in offering these."

"The introduction of these would not prove the stamp signatures," Vanderveer replied, for mere gamesmanship.

"It would help to prove it," Nebeker interrupted Porter yet again.

"It might help to prove it," Porter added lamely.

"Well, it is in gentlemen," Landis steamed. "Let us go on to something else." On another occasion, after more sniping between Nebeker and Vanderveer, Landis snapped, "Gentlemen of the jury, you will disregard the talk between the lawyers across the table. I have mentioned it before, but I seem powerless to stop it. You won't pay any attention to it. The only result of it is to waste time. It is not instructive. It is certainly not even interesting. Overruled."[11]

Mostly, Landis let the lawyers try their cases—two separate and seemingly unrelated cases though they were. He placed few categorical restrictions on cross-examination, although his individual rulings on objections were erratic. Likewise, he was liberal in allowing redirect examination, including beyond the classic limit of confining it to new information adduced during cross-examination. Indeed, Landis generally allowed the cycle of redirect, recross, further redirect, and so on to repeat itself until the lawyers had exhausted themselves or the witness. From time to time, though, he would have his fill. Just five days into the prosecution case, he broke in during a long volley between the lawyers and a witness. "Well, I do not want to waste any more time on this kind of polly-foxing. Call another witness." The government did.[12]

On the whole, Landis made a show of enjoying the intellectual jousting of legal arguments over evidentiary rules. He often posed hypothetical questions to one lawyer or another, sometimes clearly for the rhetorical purpose of underscoring Landis's set view but sometimes apparently out of curiosity. For all the record shows, these exchanges with the lawyers, often lengthy and detailed, seem to have occurred in the jury's earshot. Both Vanderveer and Nebeker clearly were up to this sort of lawyerly debate, often over abstractions. Porter seemed left behind. And at the defense table, Otto Christensen, who proved himself both a capable cross-examiner and direct examiner and played a quite active role in court, mostly deferred to Vanderveer on legal arguments for whatever reason.

Landis's willingness to engage in these theatrical debates over fine points of law may have been calculated in part to reassure the defendants that he had an even hand. Vanderveer won roughly as many of these debates as Nebeker, or seemed to; Landis was capable both of spreading a deliberate fog in his rulings and of quietly and quickly changing his mind later and adopting a position contrary to the one he had seemed to stake out. And if Nebeker was winning most of the major battles, as he did, and Vanderveer prevailing on minor skirmishes only, the defendants well may not have known the difference. For example, when Landis reversed his earlier view and held that Vanderveer could inquire, after all, of a Cook County jailer whether signatures on jail cards really are voluntary—winning a grudging concession that they are not—the men on the bleachers may have thought they had notched a win.[13]

Nebeker won a much more significant victory, though, on the subject of reading only excerpts of the letters and writings of the defendants—and, always, of Frank Little. An old (and current) evidentiary rule, the doctrine of completeness, requires that a full document go to the jury where fairness requires that, or at least all portions that place it accurately in context. Advocates ought not to create a false impression by offering only a snippet out of context. This was Vanderveer's gripe more than once about the prosecution's frequent reading of exhibits to the jurors.

He was in good form one morning.

"Your Honor, where part of an article is read, I am going to ask permission to read the rest of the article. I do not want to break in upon counsel's plan of presenting his case, but part of an article does not give a fair idea of what the writer intends, and in honesty and fairness to the writer and to the defendant, I think it is my duty to ask this privilege. Where counsel reads extracts from a book, I won't make the same objection." A strategic show of reasonableness.

Nebeker was having none of it. He had moved the whole into evidence; the jury could see it, and Vanderveer could read what he wanted when it was his turn.

Landis agreed with Nebeker.

Unwilling to drop a good objection, Vanderveer persisted. "Well, a false impression only will have been created. It will have been lodged in the mind of this jury for a month or two or three months, and we will perhaps by that time have forgotten this, or at that time it may not seem important enough, and probably won't be, to justify reading it." He understood the problem with rulings of conditional admissibility and the rigors of long trials generally.

"How much of this article is there?" Landis asked.

"Well, this is a short article. But what is the context? What is the writer referring to? Upon that depends the significance of all he said."

Nebeker pushed back. "There is not a qualification in the article. The proposition that I am laying down here is the proposition that this organization expected to become stronger than the state, and to open the jail doors and let people out that have been guilty of violation of criminal laws."

"You will find things in the Bible which isolated in part sound blasphemous and vulgar," Vanderveer objected. "It is not a fair way to present anything."

Landis again sided with Nebeker. As he went on to read part of the article, under a heading *Slaying the Dragon*, Vanderveer tried to draw the sting. "That will be admitted without controversy, so you need not waste any time proving it. We propose to socialize industries."

"That is amusing," Nebeker sneered.[14]

In all, the prosecution scored a significant win. The jury would be left with only the juiciest excerpts from defendants' writings, unless and until the defense chose to revisit these prosecution exhibits weeks later in its own case. Rehashing an opponent's case in one's own case rarely is a good idea: it sounds at best defensive and quibbling.

Aside from his mostly good-natured banter with the lawyers on legal issues, though, Landis privately took the case very seriously. Sometime in April or early May 1917, he had written to the White House offering to accept a commission in the U.S. Army at the improbable age of fifty if his services were needed. President Wilson must have received enough such pro forma offers from prominent men that the White House had engraved notes to send back in response: "The President deeply appreciates your very generous and patriotic proffer of your services, and wishes in this informal way to express his grateful thanks."[15]

Although Landis would not serve, his son did. Reed Landis was in Europe during the trial, serving as an aviator. Initially, he flew with the British flying corps and then in the new—and statistically risky—Army Air Corps. Reed would turn twenty-two that summer. He notched twelve air victories between May and August 1918, right during the middle of the trial in Chicago. Landis's correspondence with his son was constant, and no small number of his letters to others reflected intense fatherly concern over harm that might befall the young man—and some efforts to intervene. The junior Landis won both a British Distinguished Flying Cross and an American Distinguished Service Cross.[16]

By day, then, Landis was presiding over an interminable trial of wartime dissenters and malcontents in the heat of summer. By night, he was worrying whether his only son might perish in the war. Landis never said a word during trial about any of it.

He was not interested in levity in the courtroom, though. One day, Vanderveer made a side comment while a Bureau of Investigation agent was testifying that the Justice Department has broken down doors many times. Porter predictably took the bait and howled. Many in the courtroom, probably the defendants and their friends, began to laugh. Landis would not have it.

"Now I do not want any more laughter or anything more systematically pulled off here, one way or the other, during the trial of this case. There is nothing here to excite anybody's laughter. Proceed."[17]

Jurors seemed attentive as the government slogged through weeks of reading pamphlet excerpts, routine correspondence, and accounting records of expense reimbursements. They frequently urged witnesses to speak up, the street noise and rustling of well over one hundred people in the courtroom remaining constant problems. Out of the blue, too, on a Saturday morning, jurors asked Nebeker to read the full version of the articles from the *Industrial Worker* that he was excerpting—raising the possibility that Nebeker had been too clever by half, perhaps squandering some credibility, in winning his fight on completeness.[18]

And in fact, the prosecution did back off its win on that point. When Porter was reading a portion of defendant Joseph Graber's article in *Solidarity*, for example, Vanderveer asked him to read all of the article.

Porter balked. "It will take a good deal of time."

Vanderveer had a ready answer. "Time is of less importance than justice."

Porter read the whole article.[19]

While jurors struggled to remain attentive, the mainstream press found it all pretty tiresome. Very quickly, newspaper articles became short or disappeared altogether. When there was an article, it often focused on which of the defendants were sick and unable to attend court. Illness happened with some frequency, given conditions in the Cook County Jail. Perhaps in part to boost attendance, Landis quietly granted bail to almost all the defendants who remained in jail during the course of the prosecution case.[20]

At least one of the defendants, Salvatore Zumpano, was dismissed altogether as the government's case wore on. He accepted deportation and the government dropped the case against him.[21]

Landis all but abdicated part of his role as the prosecution case continued. Two weeks in, it became clear that the clerk of court was not performing the basic task of keeping admitted exhibits. Landis deferred to the government to do that, which meant that in the end, the court would have to rely on prosecution recordkeeping if jurors wished to see some or all admitted exhibits.[22]

He did not abdicate entirely, though. When the *Chicago Tribune* ran an especially slanted article titled "Reign of Terror Caused by the I.W.W. Shown at Trial," and the defendants wrote a letter to Landis complaining, the judge quit ten minutes early for the day. He blasted a *Tribune* reporter and grilled him on the source of his information. The reporter exonerated the government lawyers but fingered two recently released government witnesses.

Slowly, tediously, the prosecution case moved through each of the defendants in no apparent order. On a given man's day, one or more witnesses would identify him briefly, usually with the man standing at Vanderveer's prompting, and then folders of his letters or editorial comments would be read to the jury. On it went. Nebeker himself did not recognize most of the men on trial. Landis, though, several times did not recognize a witness who had been testifying at the end of the previous day, or even a witness recalled after just ten minutes. But he did become more fastidious about not allowing the government to offer evidence about speeches by the defendants, if they had not been disclosed to the defense in a "bill of particulars," which elaborates government evidence if necessary to assure notice and a fair opportunity to respond.[23]

As the government's presentation progressed, Nebeker expressed the view that three letters written by one defendant, Alexander Cournos, which the government conceded never were mailed, still were admissible against all the other defendants, as proof of their conspiratorial views. He also demanded that Joe Foley, the author of still other letters, stand up and identify himself. Told that no such man was indicted, on trial, or in the courtroom, Nebeker made light. "Well, he can sit down then."[24]

While Nebeker was enjoying himself, the trial had become agony for jurors and the defendants lolling on their benches while the prosecution read aloud long excerpts of letters, editorials, or pamphlets. One Saturday session opened with Nebeker announcing, "I will continue to read the *Agricultural Workers Bulletins*." After an hour of more of reading aloud, Nebeker proposed to "suspend the reading at this time and put on a witness

I have here and continue later on with the reading." No doubt the jurors hardly could wait.[25]

All good things must end, though, and the prosecution case did stop rather abruptly on Wednesday, June 19. The court adjourned and convened the next day without the jurors for motions, now that the government's case was in.

That case included 693 admitted exhibits, almost all of them letters and writings of various defendants. Few of those writings were dated during the period in the indictment. The greater share of the government's case consisted of private opinions, intemperate breast-beating, and heated political broadsides before the United States declared war. It had been in a real sense a two-dimensional case: a case measured in the width and length of pieces of paper, read monotonously to the jury by two prosecutors who seemed not to like each other.

Nebeker was unworried. By now, he took the confident view that any active participation in IWW activities after June 15, 1917, "*per se* makes them guilty." But even with that low bar, he conceded that the government had not offered enough evidence to support a guilty verdict against nine of the remaining men. Landis dismissed them on the government's motion. But Landis also denied Vanderveer's motions to strike evidence and motions for a directed verdict as to all other defendants and all counts. The Squire was taking all his cues from Nebeker at this point. If Nebeker thought that he could defend convictions on appeal, Landis would let him go to the jury against any man he chose.[26]

Fittingly, in a sense, the arguments after the prosecution rested came to a close with a long fight, probably thirty minutes or more, over the admissibility of Frank Little's many speeches and writings, with which the government had peppered its case. That fight consumes fourteen pages of transcript, with Vanderveer, Nebeker, and Landis all actively engaged—and intelligently. In the end, Landis went with Nebeker; he had been leaning that way all along. His final ruling forecast much about how he would rule in the defense case to come, and how he would instruct the jury in the end. Landis explained, "But the trouble is with your position, as I take it, and it is fundamental here,—the trouble with the situation is that they continued the advocacy,—to persist in that advocacy, after we got into it [the war]. That is the trouble with it." Once the United States joined the war, Landis elaborated, "Thereafter there was a persistence in that attitude, and that is the vice of the situation if there be any."[27]

This was fundamental to Landis. What a person might say before war he no longer could say during war. It would be the principle of Courtroom No. 627.

Perhaps because two of the defendants, Prashner and Pietro Nigra, were too sick to come to court again that Thursday after the government rested, Landis adjourned until Monday. Vanderveer had a long weekend to prepare his opening statement, now seven weeks after the jurors had heard Nebeker's opening. Given the sheer number of documents with anti-war sentiments, admitted against no one in specific but everyone in general, the similar speeches overheard and recounted, the insinuations of sabotage by nameless Wobblies, and the long delay in offering a coherent claim of innocence by the defense, Vanderveer's opening statement would have to be good. Back to the Hotel Washington he went.[28]

16

If Christ Came to Chicago

Vanderveer was tired, though. He had handled most of the cross-examinations during the prosecution case himself. Otto Christensen had taken some, capably but without Van's panache, and William Cleary one or two, incompetently. But mostly, when the defense was on its feet as early May turned into late June, it was in the person of George F. Vanderveer. He remained just as colorful, was in his prime as a trial lawyer at age forty-two, and had undeniable lawyerly skill and flourishes. But seven weeks in trial, a long way from home and living in a hotel, with many weeks to go, would drain anyone.[1]

There were other problems. Vanderveer was not being paid what he had expected. He had been promised $10,000, plus expenses, which would have been a reasonable fee then, even for a long trial. Nothing close to that had come in, though. Now, with a months-long commitment like this trial, and no new business because he was in Chicago, it was becoming a crisis for Van and Ellinor, his "Gus." At home, Gus was frantic: creditors were threatening to repossess the furniture. She had hung up the phone on a long-distance call with him, sobbing, after he had nothing to offer but advice to buck up or go live with her mother. She sold the diamond ring he had given her to hold the creditors at bay.[2]

And Ellinor was at home, not in Chicago. There were other women in Chicago, and one in particular. Whether he was on the prowl or she was, by this stage of the trial Van was in the midst of an affair with Kitty Beck. A wealthy young liberal from Portland, Oregon, she was head of the IWW defense committee there and had come to watch the trial in Chicago. So, he had that diversion after hours in court, and hours more preparing for the next day in court and hearing what other members of the trial team had accomplished outside court that day. There were about a hundred clients who wanted his ear, too. At some point, he had to eat. That left only spare moments for guilt over the fact that a lonely and despairing wife in Seattle was selling her diamond ring to slow the approach of creditors. What else might he add to the mix? Booze. Vanderveer was a drinker. He also had taken to rolling his own cigarettes, like many of his clients, and was beginning to neglect his business attire.[3]

Prepared or not, sharp or shabby, though, he was ready for court at 9:30 a.m. on Monday. He spoke with clarity, all considered:

> In name, it is the case of the United States against William Haywood, James P. Thompson, John Foss and some other men, about whom, —most of whom at least, you never heard of before, —charged with a conspiracy, or five different conspiracies. In fact, however, it is not a case against any one of these, but it is a case against an organization which, for the moment, is representative in our American thought of a certain social ideal.
>
> Without presuming now to question the quality of the motives underlying this prosecution, I want to make it plain to you in the beginning, that the real purpose of this prosecution is to utterly shatter and destroy the ideal for which this organization stands.[4]

Vanderveer continued with a worried quip that the prosecution got all of "the decent weather" and the defense evidence would come "while you are sweltering here in the hot weather of the summer." But then he launched gamely into the heart of the defense: the inequity of the current social structure. Vanderveer used the 1915 report of President Wilson's own Industrial Relations Commission, whose chair was the progressive Frank P. Walsh. By summer 1918, Walsh had gone on to cochair, with former President William Howard Taft, the National War Labor Board. Vanderveer began a barrage of stony statistics: just 2 percent of people in the United States owned two-thirds of all its wealth; the bottom 65 percent owned less than 5 percent of the wealth of the country. One man, John D. Rockefeller, "reputed to be worth a billion dollars," owned more wealth than 2.5 million of the poorest American families combined. Fully 100 percent of railroad employees work for corporations; 90 percent of mining employees; and 75 percent of workers in all industries.[5]

Nebeker unfolded to his feet. "Mr. Vanderveer, I did not want to interrupt you. Are you through now stating your general position on the report of the Industrial Relations Committee?" If so, Nebeker did not want to acquiesce; he wanted to raise an objection on behalf of the government. Interrupting an opponent's opening statement or closing argument is dicey for a trial lawyer: jurors very easily can see it as rude and not fair play, since these are advocates' speeches, not the back-and-forth of testimony in which evidentiary concerns understandably might arise. Nebeker did it delicately and skillfully.[6]

What followed turned from a discussion of the propriety of general social and economic figures and trends, like those the Industrial Relations Commission had reported, and the possibility that the defense wanted to try the entire societal structure of the United States, into something even more important for the practical course of the defense case. Landis predictably agreed that the defense could not put on trial the system of capitalism; the Industrial Relations Commission report would be out. But the Squire had more trouble with a related question. Would he permit the defendants to offer testimony on their states of mind in doing acts that looked illegal at face value? Vanderveer's basic point was that the defense ought not to be limited just to denying that the men's intentions were as the government claimed—to obstruct the war, for instance. The defense ought to be allowed to prove what the men's intentions instead actually were, Vanderveer argued persuasively.

"And, therefore," an unconvinced Landis quizzed him, "if it appeared here that in that contest the defendants here have in fact done the things charged in this indictment, they are not guilty?"

"Why, not at all," Vanderveer countered. "As to some of these things, sabotage, disloyalty, and what-not, our answer is a denial absolutely, but as to other things, the purpose to overthrow the government, our answer is more than a denial; it is a denial plus an explanation of what we were doing, and why we were doing it." Vanderveer, speaking always to audiences beyond Judge Landis, customarily was careful to include himself with "we" rather than to stand apart from his clients with "they."

For the time, Vanderveer fought to a draw here. While Landis excluded the Industrial Relations Commission report as "immaterial," as for that matter was "the general industrial condition of the United States," he avoided ruling on the issue of the defendants testifying as to their intentions. Nebeker cleverly laid down a marker, though, that Landis had given him the Thursday before, in part to cement the judge's view. An otherwise lawful strike, Nebeker proposed, becomes unlawful simply because it is wartime, and the strike could affect the war effort. Vanderveer appreciated immediately what Nebeker was doing, and responded adroitly. Landis again was unready to rule. But Nebeker had made good use of the judge's view that what one might say in peacetime could become unlawful in wartime.[7]

Deprived of his argument about the unfair conditions of capitalism, Vanderveer devoted most of the rest of his opening statement to a roughly chronological discussion of the abuse that workers generally, and the IWW in specific, faced through the summer of 1917: children working at age twelve, prostitution, and among other horrors the Speculator mine fire, the Bisbee deportation, and the Little lynching. He argued the need for political action. But he also noted that maybe one-third of the defendants held Liberty Bonds, and that "hundreds" of Wobblies, including some on trial, were registered for the draft.[8]

As he came to his finish, Vanderveer took on the issue of patriotism squarely:

> The government says that the I.W.W. is not patriotic. Before considering the facts, I think perhaps it is well to consider what is meant by "patriotism." If counsel means that the I.W.W. is not patriotic in the sense—the chauvinistic sense that it does not get up on the housetops and yell about its patriotism, and then go out and profiteer, then I consider most frankly that the I.W.W. is not patriotic, because the I.W.W. has not done that.
>
> Patriotism may be the inspiration of many a heroic deed, but it is often used as a cloak by many a scoundrel as well, and you cannot always judge a man by the amount of noise,—patriotic noise he makes, and I do not want you to judge the I.W.W. that way.
>
> If patriotism means that one must believe in war as the best way of settling things, that one must believe that the wholesale slaughter of innocent people is right, then again I say the I.W.W. for years, has been in that sense unpatriotic, because the I.W.W. has not believed and does not believe in war.[9]

Finally, Vanderveer proposed that, in deciding "whether or not they have been guilty of crime," the test is "the test of their manhood and you are going to see them here under cross-examination, by the most astute counsel the government could enlist in its service, and if they do not measure up by that standard of manhood by which you would like to have your own son judged," well, "then, my friends, you may condemn them." Vanderveer was promising testimony from defendants, then—something

137

no defendant in any criminal case in English-speaking countries ever is required to offer. But he wisely did not bind any individual among his one-hundred-plus clients to take the stand; he named no one.

"I want you to consider what Christ," Vanderveer implored with his last words, "if he came to Chicago and looked down upon these men and the things they have done, and the motives that have moved them, would say,—whether he would condemn, or whether he would approve, and when you have answered that, I want you to write the answer in your verdict."[10]

"Call Mr. Thompson," Vanderveer said after just a momentary pause to let Christ settle in among His Chicagoans. The garrulous James P. Thompson, prominent among the defendants, would be the first witness.

It was a good opening move. Thompson, in addition to being likeable and articulate, was an American farm boy, born in Grand Rapids, Michigan. He looked the part. Handsome and square-jawed, Thompson had a broad, handlebar mustache and stood a head taller than most of the other working men on trial.

Vanderveer seems to have anticipated the constant thrust of cross-examinations by Nebeker and Porter that would follow: invariably, if a defense witness was not an American citizen and had not admitted his alien status, that would be the prosecutors' first question. With their opening questions, they also would force more than one defendant, beginning with Charles Ashleigh, to admit his "racial stock": his Jewish lineage. The government's appeal to xenophobia and racism was overt and systematic. The prosecutors also favored cross-examination on past arrests that had not resulted in convictions, which Landis allowed liberally.[11]

For now, though, the American-born Thompson told a compelling story of his life. By age sixteen, he was working on the Great Lakes as a fireman and deckhand. Because he was big for his age, he got a man's wages. He then had turned to work as a longshoreman, which he had done in Chicago since 1899. He had taken part in the founding convention of the IWW in 1905. Was Chicago his home? "Well, to tell you the truth I do not say I ever had a home."[12]

His story may have seemed too compelling to Nebeker, who objected. What possible relevance to conspiracy charges limited to five months in 1917 could work and labor organizing years or even decades earlier have, asked the same prosecutor who had offered speeches, letters, and editorials from defendants years before the period of the indictment. Vanderveer made a lawyerly argument, but on this one, he had won over Landis before he spoke. Nebeker had stirred some deep notion of fair play in the Squire. "This is the rule, Mr. Nebeker," Landis spoke emphatically. "A defendant on trial may tell, as the expression of the man on the street goes, he may tell the story of his life."[13]

That ruling stuck. Vanderveer and the Wobblies would have almost unlimited room, throughout the remaining weeks of the defense case, to tell the jury the stories of their lives. If nothing else, those who testified were heard; they got to say their piece.

Thompson even succeeded, on Vanderveer's persistent questioning, in reading portions of the Industrial Relations Commission report that Thompson himself had quoted in his speeches. Now, the report was offered not for the truth of the facts it asserted but only as evidence of what the witness had said in his lecture. By this artifice, Vanderveer got the report admitted (Defense Exhibit 22) and much of its content before the jury after all.[14]

Thompson had an earthy, accessible way to express concepts like economic "value." He was given to vivid but not pretentious speech. "I saw so much misery as I went around" lecturing for the IWW, Thompson commented, "to tell you about it would be like kicking your heart around as a football."[15]

He also explained practically why workers should organize by entire industry, not by craft. "When the Longshoremen would be on strike they would get scabs to load the boats," he began. "Then the union crews would go to sea with the scab cargo; then they would get scabs to unload the boats and union teamsters would haul the scab freight away from the docks, so from that we got the idea that all Marine Transport Workers, the Longshoremen, Seamen, cooks, engineers, firemen, everybody who came under the head of Marine Transport Workers, just as they worked together, so they should organize together."[16]

Thompson spent three days on the witness stand. He seemed a success.

A still more charismatic Wobbly, John T. "Red" Doran, followed Thompson. He was the man who had boomed cheerily, on the first day of jury selection, that he was "on the job." Barrel-chested, round-faced, jocular, born in New York City but of close Irish ancestry, Red Doran had a shock of red hair sticking out from under his hat that explained his nickname—although the government and mainstream press took it to explain his politics, too. Doran was a skilled and popular IWW lecturer and recruiter, and Nebeker's cross-examination suggested that Doran could speak Irish as well as English. An electrician by trade, Doran worked at any job he could during the day, spoke for the IWW in the evenings (mostly without pay), and sent money home to his wife, whom he described as "crippled." He supported America's role in the war, as he had two brothers serving, one in France and both officers.[17]

In his seven years of soap box oratory, Red Doran used a flip chart or chalk board to aid his talks on "economic determinism" and how the worker might get more of what the boss had. For a remarkable several hours, beginning at about 9:40 a.m. on Thursday, June 27, and continuing through that day and for another forty-five minutes or so on Friday afternoon, June 28, Doran stood at a chalk board in the courtroom and gave, by memory, his talk. Otto Christensen, handling Doran's direct examination, never put a question to him during those hours. And Nebeker never objected. Doran undeniably was a gifted public speaker: earthy, pithy, modest, informed, and good-humored. When he spoke of vermin in bunkhouses at lumber camps, or of the practical blacklist that the "rustling card" system allowed western mine owners to enforce, or of the life of migrant workers bringing in the crops during harvest on the great plains, his audiences well might have felt as if this itinerant electrician had set out his bedroll next to theirs some night not long past.[18]

Doran held the courtroom, too. An enthralled juror asked Doran to move at one point so that the juror could see the chalk board. Even Landis got engaged enough to get down from the bench and wander near the jury to get a better vantage point on the chalk talk. Earlier that morning, Landis had scolded one of the assistant prosecutors for being late to court.[19]

As he closed his performance, Doran explained, "Now then, usually we have questions and literature for sale, and collections and things of that kind but coming back to the present, I think we can dispense with that part of it." Many in the courtroom, Landis likely included, laughed aloud.[20]

Nebeker's cross-examination was sarcastic and snarling; not necessarily effective on a witness who probably had charmed almost everyone not at the prosecution table. Sarcasm was not what Nebeker did best, ever: the elegant corporate lawyer was at his best when he displayed icy clarity in an appeal to conventionality. Nebeker asked Doran if he ever had sold patent medicine (no), or whether he at least thought that he could, and whether he was a gambler (yes). Then came the arrests:

Q: How many times have you been arrested?
A: I have been persecuted and arrested a number of times, never tried.

Q: Answer my question; how many times have you been arrested?

A: In Los Angeles they arrested me four or five times a week for months, and never let me see a judge.

Q: How many times have you been arrested?

A: I don't know, hundreds of times on that kind of charge; I was never convicted of a felony in my life.

Q: Have you been arrested a dozen times?

A: Yes, several dozen times.

Q: In every case you were in the right and they were in the wrong, I suppose?

A: They never tried me.[21]

The IWW General Defense Committee thought Doran's turn on the witness stand sufficiently good news for the organization that it published his entire testimony in pamphlet form, for 15 cents.[22]

In all, the defense was off to a fine start, exhausted, philandering lawyer with a drinking problem and declining wardrobe or no. At least so it seemed to those sympathetic to the Wobblies and their cause.

17

Lives

———————◆——————◆——————◆———————

Whatever flush of hope those early days of the defense case brought the Wobblies and their friends, near and far, an act of faith was on display in the sixth-floor courtroom. A secular passion play of sorts, the trial, suffering, and possible death of a very different labor union, was on stage in an American courthouse. More, this first and largest group of IWW members on trial was participating wholeheartedly: they were in court daily, behaving as the judge asked, and taking their turns on the witness stand. They were trying to claim roles as players themselves. While they remained wary of the judge and the institutions he represented and served, they seemed to display some residual faith, or at least hope, that their fellow citizens on the jury would believe them, accept them, and see the justice in their cause.

The Chicago trial was striking for many reasons, but one in particular stands out. In the biggest trial the country ever has mounted, those accused of being criminal conspirators still hoped for justice as they faced charges based almost entirely on their opinions rather than their actions. They seemed to believe that a mass trial could deliver mass justice.

One after another, the accused continued to take the witness stand. Vanderveer in time was able to stretch courtroom decorum, referring to Charles Ashleigh as "Charlie" during his direct examination and others by their first names, too. How that sort of familiarity sat with jurors is unclear; Landis allowed it in any event. Ashleigh was the first of many who flashed a Selective Service registration card or testified to registering.[1]

Nebeker continued to affect a mocking tone and demeanor in court. He and Vanderveer escalated their snide remarks to one another, as when

Vanderveer challenged the lead prosecutor for seeming to find a serious stretch of one defendant's story humorous (Nebeker denied smiling, unconvincingly). Landis comported himself judicially, though, and almost wistfully at moments.

THE COURT: Objection sustained.

MR. VANDERVEER: Exception.

THE COURT: In keeping out this kind of material, I am enforcing what I understand to be the rules of evidence that are binding on me in this trial of this case, as they are binding on any court in the trial of any kind of a case.

MR. VANDERVEER: All of which illustrates, your Honor, that as human beings, we cannot all agree.

THE COURT: Certainly.

MR. VANDERVEER: One of the difficulties we are having in this lawsuit is we cannot agree.

THE COURT: The unfortunate thing about it is that ultimately I have to say yes or no.

MR. VANDERVEER: Surely. Quite right, of course.

THE COURT: And in that connection it may not be improper to add that there are a lot of courts that have recorded permanently in their records, their disagreement with me.[2]

At times, Landis let himself display a dry sense of humor, too.

Q: What happened to the Socialist mayor elected in 1913?

MR. NEBEKER: This seems to me rather immaterial. I object to it.

THE COURT: Well, I don't know whether it is or not. Is it material?

MR. VANDERVEER: I believe it is. It is, according to my notion.

THE COURT: According to my misguided rulings in the case?

Two days later, Landis again evidently was feeling fine:

MR. NEBEKER: This is objected to as immaterial and irrelevant.

MR. VANDERVEER: I would like to brand this disloyalty charge right on the nose, where anybody can see what is behind it.

THE COURT: Well, I am not averse to seeing most anything hit on the nose, but I don't want to spend any time seeing something hit on the nose whose nose I don't care anything about right now.[3]

In the main, though, the defense weeks were given to rich, three-dimensional stories of hard lives. Vanderveer organized his witnesses loosely along ethnic lines, calling groups such as Finns, Italians, and Hungarians in succession. He had led with the Irish.

Much of the testimony was as rough as the men themselves, and Vanderveer occasionally lost control of witnesses who did inadvertent damage to themselves, their codefendants, and their cause, or just seemed awkwardly out of place—as of course they were. A veteran of the Speculator mine explained that it was so hot underground "that no white man would work in the place where I was, and they had probably eight or ten Mexicans and they were working with every stitch of clothing off except their shoes." A fifty-five-year-old mining machinist who was born in Germany met Nebeker's wrath on cross-examination, as did every other defense witness of German or suspected German heritage. A sixty-four-year-old Wobbly, James J. Keenan, had a son fighting in France but had been arrested in December 1917 and held until June 1 on charges unclear. A lumberjack described how the federal government hired IWW members specifically as firefighters in the summer because they were loyal and courageous. One defendant, Charles McWhirt, chewed gum while testifying.

Vanderveer had particular trouble with the defendant G. J. Bourg on direct examination. Bourg was excitable. "Let us not get excited now," Vanderveer urged. "Let us just tell it ordinary." He was fighting a losing battle with Bourg. As the witness described a raid on an IWW office by drunken members of the Third Missouri National Guard, he quoted the sergeant as saying, "Live up there, you cock-suckers!" An upset Vanderveer barked, "Bourg, will you listen to me?!" Nebeker, at his best again for the moment, exploited the moment, objecting to Landis, "I suggest, if the Court please, that the witness ought to be able to tell it in his own way without any suggestion from counsel." Bourg soon quoted the sergeant again as calling him a "son-of-a-bitch." A defeated Vanderveer begged, "Whenever he swore, you may just mention the fact without repeating it."

A crying defendant, Siegfried Stenberg, made Vanderveer just as uncomfortable. A Swede who had come to the United States six years earlier, Stenberg broke down describing his wife and baby girl. Arthur Boose described life on the Mesabi Range in northern Minnesota just as plainly and a series of false arrests and jailings without charges. He admitted writing an editorial that labeled Woodrow Wilson a "czar," but he had registered for the draft all the same. A strike on the range ended not because the IWW settled: workers resumed mining "with the recognition that they were beaten."[4]

Not all defense witnesses were friendly to the IWW. Some were deputy sheriffs, or members of other unions. Asked on direct examination what he thought of the IWW, for example, William F. Dunn, an electrician from Butte, replied, "I think more of their hearts than I do of their heads, if that is sufficient."[5]

As trial wore on, both Christensen and Cleary began to handle more defense witnesses. Vanderveer remained the most common questioner, though, and made almost all the legal arguments.

Later in the defense case, out of the blue, Landis intervened. The defendant Harry Trotter had no sooner told the jury his name and that it was his forty-second birthday than Landis interrupted. Giving no reason, he announced that the case against Trotter was dismissed. In fact, Trotter may have been much older and having difficulty either comprehending the questions or testifying lucidly. In any event, Trotter left the stand, the courtroom, and, if he was smart, the city. A week later, the government invited dismissal of Peter Kirkanen, for insanity. Landis sent him home, too. Landis's interventions did not always favor the defense. The Squire revoked Charles Ashleigh's bond on August 16 and remanded him to jail when Ashleigh arrived half an hour late that morning.[6]

Nebeker and Porter continued to split the load about evenly, with the other members of the prosecution team invisible on the transcript. Throughout, the two prosecutors gave no quarter. Their projected attitude was consistent with the prosecution theme: these simply were very bad men. The prosecutors did not spare any base appeal in suggesting that. They attacked German-born witnesses especially. But any noncitizen came in for suspicion. Over and again, they made Jews identify themselves that way. They pressed the homeless and divorced or unmarried men (perhaps with an insinuation that they were gay) to admit to their status.[7]

In other ways, Porter and Nebeker revealed their own ignorance on cross-examination more than once, as when Porter plainly did not understand that "Mexican" and Spanish were the same language. The prosecutors also made the mistake of confusing lack of formal education with lack of knowledge and intelligence. On cross-examination of the defendant C. H. Rice, Nebeker asked condescendingly if the IWW library had any books written by Wobblies themselves. Rice mused, "I don't know whether Victor Hugo was a IWW or not; I have never seen him around the hall there."

"Oh, you have not?" Nebeker responded sarcastically. "No; Karl Marx might have been." Nebeker quit.

Six days later, before Nebeker even got his chance, the defendant John J. Walsh edited his direct testimony to avoid "Hearsay, as Fellow Worker Nebeker would call it." Porter did not intimidate him, either. The prosecutor thought he drew blood with his accusation on cross-examination that Walsh had been a Wobbly since the founding. "Yes sir," Walsh shot back. "Never has been a scab in my family. I would drown them if there were."[8]

On August 1, all the defendants came to court wearing small red and black silk ribbons beneath a button with Frank Little's picture. It was the first anniversary of the lynching in Butte. Although the buttons caused a stir among deputy marshals and other officers, Landis apparently allowed the men to wear them.[9]

The government fought the case not just in the courtroom. As early as October 22, 1917, less than one month after the indictment, Nebeker had written to Attorney General Gregory, "It has occurred to me that some steps should be taken for the purpose of preventing the [IWW] organization from using the mails as a means of distributing pamphlets advocating sabotage and other unlawful practices." In closing, he said that he was "convinced that a large portion of the literature of the I.W.W. is for the purpose of carrying out a fraudulent scheme." The accusation of fraud would allow the government to invoke statutory authority to refuse to carry or deliver the organization's mail at all.

Eight days later, Nebeker put it more bluntly in a letter to Fitts. "In my view, the organization *per se* is a scheme to defraud. . . . It seems to me that the mail should be closed to all I.W.W. literature." "Of course," he added piously, "no one would attempt to prevent the defendants from obtaining funds for their defense, but under the circumstances they should content themselves with the accomplishment of this purpose without attempting to advance the welfare of the organization itself in the same circulars in which they are asking for contributions." The inference, at least from the second letter, that Nebeker already had seen intercepted IWW mail, or that the government had an active informant inside the union, was strong. How else could he have described the substance of the General Defense Committee's appeals?

Someone, presumably in the Justice Department, did prevail on the Post Office to withhold outgoing and incoming mail for the General Defense Committee and the defense lawyers. That meant defense letters asking witnesses to appear never arrived, and donations to the defense costs never reached the IWW treasury. Jointly, the Justice Department and the Post Office also pressed private interests into service. At their request, the American Protective League followed IWW trucks from Chicago headquarters to note where they were depositing outgoing mail.

Again at the Justice Department's directions, private couriers held and even opened and read parcels from or to the IWW. According to Fitts, writing to the solicitor of the Post Office Department, "the various express companies throughout the United States" had agreed to refuse to accept IWW materials as to which the government had revoked second-class mailing permits. Wells Fargo sought directions from the Justice Department on what to do with parcels it held after opening and reading the contents. Similarly, American Express refused to deliver private courier packages for the defense, "on account of orders issued by the government."

By July 1918, though, during the defense case, Fitts and maybe others were wary about the government going too far. In an early July meeting with Post Office officials, the Justice Department expressed concern that blocking all mail to and from the IWW "would jeopardize the Government's case against the defendants now on trial at Chicago." On July 25, Fitts formally rejected the Post Office Department solicitor's proposal to invoke the statutory power Nebeker had cited the previous October to deny the IWW all use of the U.S. mail. Fitts wrote, "I have given careful consideration to the matter, and have felt compelled to reach the conclusion that it would be a grave mistake at this time to put into force the proposed order. Seems to me it would be better simply to exclude such publications and particular letters as are found to be violative of Federal law, and for that reason should not be transported through the mails." In other words, the government would continue to intercept, open, and read IWW mail— but some of it eventually would make its way to the intended recipients. Justice Department files contain at least one explicit admission of the interception and reading of IWW mail. In early April 1918, Haywood sent a letter to the Mexican Workers' League (Liga de Trabajadores). Post Office censors opened it, read it, and prepared a memorandum of its contents that by April 22 they passed along to the Justice Department's Bureau of Investigation.[10]

The Justice Department rejected Nebeker's extreme position, then. The concern that excluding the IWW from use of the mail altogether might hurt the prosecution effort may have had two specific aspects, or some combination of the two. The government may have worried that, when the IWW and its lawyers started to complain loudly about a complete exclusion from sending or receiving mail, either the judge or the public (or both) might view the government as ceding the moral high ground to the defendants. Or, the government may have been unwilling to give up the information it was gleaning from opening and reading IWW mail: if the IWW knew that it could not use the mail at all, it would stop trying to send material, and there would be nothing for the government to intercept. How the government weighed these two drawbacks to a total bar from the mails, or whether it had other considerations in mind, the Justice Department's files do not disclose.

Apart from interference with mail and private courier deliveries, two active-duty soldiers who were IWW members but not defendants were arrested by Bureau of Investigation agents in the courthouse after testifying. They were held on the fifth floor, apparently until the government agents were satisfied that the two had approved furloughs.

Hundreds more IWW members—Haywood estimated one thousand—had been arrested around the country and held without charge, functionally closing IWW offices so that dues and defense contributions again could not be collected. At least three other civilian defense witnesses, Charles Krattiger, Elias Castellano, and Frank Crego, were arrested and harassed after testifying, too. Government agents may have intimidated at least one other witness, a hotel detective, as well. Although Nebeker objected repeatedly and strenuously to testimony from Haywood, Ed Doree, and defense lawyers about these lawless government actions, he denied none of the claims.

Landis showed scant interest in intervening, although he did question police officers, a Bureau of Investigation agent, and the hotel detective himself after the arrests of the three civilian witnesses. Although the witnesses supported the defense claims, in the end, Landis did nothing.[11]

Viewed more than one hundred years later, one defense tactical decision remains a particular mystery. Vanderveer called Bill Haywood neither at the beginning of his case nor at the end. Haywood took the stand as the defense case wound down, but he was nowhere near the final defense witness. Big Bill drew by far the most attention in the government's case. Much of the correspondence that prosecutors read to the jury consisted of letters to or from Haywood. Although Frank Little got frequent prosecution comment, Haywood got even more. At one point, Vanderveer felt enough pressure about the absence from the witness chair of the most notable and discussed of the defendants that he promised in the jury's presence to call Haywood eventually.[12]

He did. Haywood took the stand on Friday, August 9, shortly before the lunch break. He, too, told the story of his life, beginning with "twisting drill, carrying steel and water; blowing the bellows" in the mines at age nine. In a blatantly racist appeal to jurors, he claimed to have seen black soldiers raping the wives of jailed white miners in front of them, outside the bullpen, at Coeur d'Alene. But jurors could not hear him any better than they could many other witnesses, and on the whole his testimony was careful and guarded. Vanderveer's questions often were longer than Haywood's answers on direct examination. Vanderveer read from many of Haywood's letters, which often were more diplomatic than, say, Little's or many other Wobblies' writings. With the same diplomacy, Haywood complimented Nebeker, on direct examination, for the imagery Nebeker had used in his opening statement of Haywood as a swivel-chair king at the center of sixteen industrial unions.

On cross-examination, Haywood maintained his discipline. Answers were tight, responsive, and polite. Vanderveer had to remind a subdued Haywood again to speak up on cross-examination. In all, there were very few fireworks—and also very few real high points—during Haywood's more than three days in the witness chair. Haywood did hit one high near the end of Vanderveer's redirect examination. He drew a nice comparison between the IWW's supposed illegal "direct action" against employers and the government's own "direct action" interfering with the defense during the course of trial. That stung the prosecution.[13]

In all, some eighty of the defendants testified, with Haywood the seventy-second. The defense called another ninety-nine witnesses as well, including the lead special agent, Murdock, and prosecutor Claude Porter, by surprise. Porter admitted that he had been asking every soldier who testified for the defense his company, regiment, and location after the man testified. But he denied ordering five copies of the transcript of each soldier's testimony. How many more witnesses the government's refusal to deliver mail and outright intimidation prevented the defense from calling is unknowable.[14]

In striking contrast to the government's two-dimensional, paper case, those who did testify presented gritty depictions of their lives: often rootless, sad, gutsy, desperate, or poignant lives—but nonetheless full. They were orphans (practically or actually), loyal sons, lost husbands, immigrants, proud native-born citizens, brawlers, dreamers, illiterates, poets, cads, gentlemen, boys, stooped and sinewy men, active-duty soldiers, war resisters, the melancholy, the jovial. They had cut the forests' thickest trees, harvested the prairies' wheat, loaded eastern ships, unloaded western ore at the mouths of mine shafts, shoved tons of orange-glowing steel under showers of cinders, and spent months or years in bars, rooming houses, freight cars, hobo jungles, sweltering army bullpens, jails, and now courtrooms. Many had seen the span of the country, on foot or beating it by rail, but only a few had seen the span of a formal primary education. One exception stood out, and one only: the stray Harvard student, Ray Fanning.

Throughout, this three-dimensional, scratchy, unshaven defense case did not meet the two-dimensional, smooth, paper-white case that the government tried. Landis oversaw one courtroom where two separate trials were proceeding side by side, moving in opposite directions but never meeting.

If the defense had any indirect effect on the government case, it was to rebut effectively Nebeker's ploy in his opening statement of portraying the IWW defendants as pampered occupiers of office chairs who manipulated "honest" working men and women in the ranks. That prosecution stratagem had been a clever idea that might have blunted suspicion that the government case was an attack on union members generally. But it failed. Still, the failure hardly was fatal to the prosecution case.

The defense case had been bumpy and uneven. If Vanderveer hoped to show that none of the men really meant to obstruct the war or engage in industrial sabotage, he had failed, too. But now the accused had been heard. That mattered, as it always does, to the perception among those on trial that the process was fair.

On Saturday morning, August 17, the defense rested. The government's rebuttal case was insignificant and took just a few minutes. In a sense, it was fitting: it was just letters that the prosecutors offered to counter a minor issue on malicious damage to threshing machines. Nebeker did not even bother to read them aloud. With that, the evidence in a four-and-a-half-month trial closed quietly.[15]

By that time, though, Vanderveer and Nebeker long since had reached the point of accusing each other flatly and loudly of lying about defense access to government exhibits. Landis was sick of it all, too. "I will not spend any more time on this kind of a cat fight," he declared. Vanderveer, intentionally or not, had gotten entirely under Nebeker's skin. While Vanderveer was examining Murdock, Nebeker hissed a warning not to come so close to him.[16]

Now, with the evidence closed, the quarreling lawyers would have their last words, and the judge his. Then the defendants' last hope, twelve jurors who shared not much more with them than wearing pants and hats and spending most of five months in the same courtroom, would have the final say.

Two days earlier, close listeners would have heard an ominous rumble from the bench. It came on August 15 while Vanderveer was advancing a point. "You may assume that, in your argument of that proposition," Landis warned, "you may assume that the Court is of the opinion [that the President of the United States] is the Commander in Chief in time of war, not merely of the army and navy, but of the one hundred million civilians. That is my conception of his power."[17]

George Vanderveer gave no indication that he caught the import of that remark.

18

Argument

At least as early as Friday, August 16, Vanderveer had goaded Frank Nebeker to forego closing arguments altogether. Perhaps Vanderveer really was dead serious about that: after all, he had forfeited his chance to make an opening statement at the outset in early May, right after Nebeker's, and waited until the government rested in June. But Vanderveer also may have been playing a game, trying both to unnerve Nebeker as the case drew rapidly to a close and to learn the prosecution's plan for closing arguments.[1]

That plan would have mattered to Vanderveer because in a federal criminal trial, in closing arguments the prosecution gets both the first and last chance. The prosecution gives its principal summation. Then the defense has a chance to make its closing arguments. Finally, the prosecution gets rebuttal. The ostensible reason for this lopsided arrangement is that the government bears the burden of persuasion in a criminal case, and the highest burden at that: proof of guilt beyond a reasonable doubt. Practically, though, with both the first and last argument, the prosecution has an incentive to give a relatively anodyne initial summation, a dutiful traipse through the evidence, but a blistering and emotive rebuttal once the defense is silenced and unable to reply. Tough prosecutors often save their best for last.

There was the added factor here that the government had two prosecutors who had been jostling all along for control and visibility. Vanderveer may have hoped that he could provoke Nebeker to drop some hint of how he and Porter would divide responsibilities in closing arguments.

One of the Wobblies on trial, Harrison George, gave a nearly contemporaneous account that could explain some of what happened next. Claude Porter had distributed copies of his intended rebuttal argument to the Iowa papers in advance, according to George. So Nebeker would give the principal summation, but Porter had snagged the grand finale. It might win him the governor's office. If Harrison George knew this—and he did not explain how he knew it—then likely Vanderveer knew, too.[2]

As court opened Saturday morning, Nebeker asked how long the last defense witnesses would take. He noted that he and Vanderveer had struck an agreement: each side would have two hours in total for closing arguments. "There will be no trouble about accomplishing all that we want in that respect," Vanderveer assured the court and Nebeker. Both sides hoped to submit the case to the jury by the end of Saturday. Vanderveer seemed in a convulsion of collegiality.[3]

Each lawyer was placing a bet here; both could be wrong, but at most one of them could be right. They had agreed, tactically, that they wanted a tired jury to get the case late on a Saturday—on the sixth straight day of court, at the end of the longest Saturday session yet, and after more than four months confined daily in the courtroom. Each was betting, in other words, that deliberations would be quick and that his side would benefit from tired, impatient jurors who wanted to get home and be done. Again, both could be wrong: sensible jurors might elect a foreman late Saturday afternoon, decide nothing more, and then tell the judge that they wanted to resume on Monday morning, fresh.

It was a high-stakes gamble. Whether right or wrong in their calculations of which side would gain from a quick verdict, both lawyers seem to have expected and preferred one.

With the agreed schedule in mind, Landis wanted Nebeker to give his closing statement immediately after the government finished its brief rebuttal case. The judge warned the jurors that lunch would be late, so that Nebeker's argument could go uninterrupted. Implicitly, lunch would follow the prosecution's initial summation. Vanderveer then would have his two hours. Porter would give the government rebuttal with what remained of the prosecution's two hours. Landis then would give final jury instructions, assuming enough time remained.[4]

Nebeker rose and gave a comparatively restrained closing argument, just as Vanderveer might have expected. His remarks cover only twenty-seven pages of transcript, without interruption by the defense; perhaps thirty-five or forty-five minutes of spoken word. He started by impressing upon the jurors the importance of the case: it was much greater, he contended, than any ordinary criminal case, even for murder, because "if the government's contention is true, the welfare of our country is involved." Indeed, Nebeker waxed, "The welfare of the country demands that the evidence that has been introduced here shall be carefully weighed, both the evidence of the prosecution and the evidence that has been introduced by the defense, so that when the verdict is rendered in this case, it will be a verdict, gentlemen, which you, in the future will not only be proud of, but your children, and your children's children will be proud of the fact that you sat on the jury in one of the greatest history making trials that it has fallen to the lot of any jury in this or any other country to try."[5]

He never did get to a discussion of the evidence and how it proved any count of the indictment. For this Nebeker offered an apology, whether sincere or not: "Now I must close, gentlemen. I regret that I am not able in the time allotted, to take you over the counts of the indictment with a view of showing you the conception that the Government has of the place that the evidence bears, or of the relation that the evidence bears to the particular charges of the indictment. I did that somewhat completely, I think, in my opening statement. The first count, as you will remember, is a count that these men conspired, and these are all conspiracy charges; the Government is not called upon to prove the actual commission of a single offense."[6]

Nebeker's closing did have a coherent theme, though. It was simply that the defendants, by their written and spoken words before trial and to a large extent at trial, had convicted themselves. "I want to say to you gentlemen of the jury," Nebeker confided, "and I say it in all sincerity, if there was not a bit of evidence in this case other than what has been produced by the defendants themselves in their case, in the defense here, it would be your bounded duty to convict them under every charge of the indictment."[7]

Why? Because the defendants were not patriots. He returned to the idea that the government had no quarrel with "the interests of honest workingmen, of men who want to associate themselves together in any kind of lawful organization that they may select." And Nebeker now pushed hard on the "Americanism" about which he had questioned prospective jurors so carefully back in April.

"Take this same organization, put it in the hands of honest, patriotic American citizens," Nebeker implored. "Let them do away with their criminal practices, let them do away with sabotage, whereby the working man is deprived of all honor, and a workingman or any other man that is deprived of honor is as bad as a woman without same,—slough that off, and then let them, if you please, be patriotic, work for their country, love their country, revere their flag, not desecrate it, not revile it, not go out to undermine the institutions of the country that it has taken thousands [*sic*] of years to build up, because the struggle for liberty did not begin one hundred years ago. Let them square themselves with American institutions, and then neither the Government nor you or anybody else will interfere with them."[8]

Honest workingmen, in other words, "are men, not with soft hands and hard faces like these defendants, but men who work in the industries." These men on trial, with "soft hands and hard faces"—a nice line in the abstract but not a persuasive one here after weeks of defense testimony— instead believed that workers have no duty to anything or anyone but other workers everywhere. From the first convention of the organization, they had "struck a blow at patriotism." Many were not citizens and, if they reached other noncitizens with their ideas, they would undermine the entire republic.[9]

Nebeker acknowledged the nation's unfortunate disparities in wealth, the impropriety of war profiteering, and even the unlawfulness of some of the treatment of the Wobblies. All of that was unfortunate and regrettable. But these were side issues "not involved" in the case, for concerns like those gave the defendants no license to act as they did; democratic institutions alone provide the legitimate means of addressing bad laws and bad practices.[10]

Nebeker was at his best, and most passionate, when he finally tied the evidence to the conspiracy charges, however briefly, through the issue of violence. "Talk about violence. They don't believe in violence. Oh, no. All they believe in and all they do is to throw boys off railroad trains when they are in motion. That is not violence. All they believe in is putting lye in the shoes of honest, sincere, good workingmen. That is not violence, of course not. Put acid on the clothing of workingmen. Subject them to all sorts of petty and sometimes violent oppression. Oh, no, that is not violence."[11]

His clincher, if the unpatriotic attitude and actions of the defendants and the IWW as a whole were not enough, was the concept of the general strike that the organization advocated. That sort of strike would have "prevent[ed] this government from getting materials" from basic industries, would "have struck the final blow" against the government in the war effort.[12]

In all, though, Nebeker was conventional in his approach and did little to incite the jury to more than the common loyalty to country, especially in wartime, for which the jurors probably needed little encouragement anyway. The defense could expect a much greater eruption of pumice and lava from Porter in rebuttal.

But that was not to be. As Nebeker thanked the jury calmly and returned to his chair at 10:33 a.m., Vanderveer awaited not even a word from Landis. "Your Honor," he said, rising, "I am going to submit the justice of our cause, to this jury without argument. I want to thank you for your patient consideration, and ask your honest, Christian judgment."

Then Vanderveer sat.

Porter would have no rebuttal. There was nothing to rebut. The defense had waived argument, so it was over. The *Chicago Herald & Examiner* reported that Vanderveer was "in high glee" over his "sabotage."[13]

Landis recovered his wits first. He spoke tersely. "You may go to your room, gentlemen," he prompted the jury, "and it will be some few minutes before I can give you the instructions in this case. I am taken a little bit by surprise here. You go to your room."[14]

They did. Once again according to Harrison George, a stricken Porter fled the courtroom to wire the Iowa newspapers not to print his momentous speech. He did it in time. The rebuttal that never was never ran.[15]

19

The First Final Chapter

Vanderveer seems never to have explained his gambit in waiving closing argument altogether. Whether it was more than spiteful gamesmanship remains a mystery. Remarkably, of his clients who left a written record of the trial—Haywood, Harrison George, Ralph Chaplin, and Ed Doree—not one questioned his decision. The leftist press did not take him to task for it, either, or even wonder aloud.

Whatever the wisdom of Vanderveer's choice, Landis now tidied his final jury instructions in chambers. Today, federal judges (and almost all state judges) rely heavily on "pattern jury instructions," the work of committees composed of judges, prosecutors, defense lawyers, and academics. Patterns make uniform the suggested instructions on common crimes and on recurrent general issues, such as burdens of proof, the presumption of innocence, and weighing witness credibility. In 1918, though, no judge had pattern instructions. A judge well might keep copies of instructions he had given in past cases, for reuse and refinement in a future case; Landis did this. But he was on his own, aided only by the lawyers for each side and by such reported precedent as he might find, in writing jury instructions.[1]

Nebeker had been focused on one particularly important point of law for a jury instruction since early in the defense case: "a comprehensive instruction . . . with respect to the liability and responsibility of each member of the conspiracy for each and every act committed by any member of the conspiracy in furtherance of its purposes." He was relying on a top Justice Department lawyer, Oliver E. Pagan, who had played a role behind the scenes from the outset of the case, to draft such an instruction, and wrote to Fitts asking that Pagan be assigned to that task. Nebeker wanted such an instruction "placed in the hands of Judge Landis before the case closes, in order to give him an opportunity to become familiar with the different propositions of law the Government expects to rely upon in this case." In short, the government wanted to convict on a theory of vicarious liability: Person B may be convicted for Person A's act, provided only that they both had joined the unlawful agreement and that A's act was foreseeable and in pursuit of the agreement's ends.[2]

Vanderveer and his team submitted fifty-eight pages of proposed instructions to Landis. Many of those may have been the work of Caroline Lowe or Otto Christensen, whose work out of court went unnoticed but was as important as the work in court. Defense submissions like these confirm the lawyerly, participatory approach that Vanderveer and the others took to the case. They had an eye on the appellate record, which meant they acknowledged the possibility of losing, but they clearly were not just trying a protest case or one devoted to political theater. Hours and hours spent researching and typing proposed jury instructions would have been wasted if protest or theater had been the defense team's purpose.

Landis kept the defense instructions in his private papers, for some reason, but he gave none of them as drafted. He did incorporate the thrust of some instructions proposed by the defense into his final instructions. Landis's files include no proposed instructions from the government in the IWW case.[3]

By 2:30 that afternoon, Landis had called the jurors back into the courtroom. His instructions would be lengthy, covering forty-two pages of transcript and, by that gauge, consuming probably an hour or so of time to read from the bench.

At the outset, Landis explained that "in the discharge of my duty," he had decided to withdraw the fifth conspiracy count, alleging a conspiracy to violate the postal laws that excluded from the mails anything in pursuit of a scheme to defraud. It appeared to him "to be the just thing" to submit the first four conspiracy counts only.[4]

The jurors would have a copy of the indictment so that they could read it closely themselves, he promised, but Landis trudged through the remaining four conspiracies, condensing the lengthy indictment. His summary alone consumed thirteen pages of transcript. He went on to explain what a conspiracy is, and what the government need and need not show to prove one, in terms that a twenty-first-century federal judge still might use very nearly. Two or more people agreeing to do an unlawful act, or a lawful act by unlawful means, formed a conspiracy; completion of some act named in the indictment by at least one of them in furtherance of the conspiracy's purposes completed the crime. The conspiracy need not succeed; not even one person need have refused to register for the draft, for example. The defendant's own words or actions, not the say-so of others, were necessary to show that he joined the conspiracy. But once in, all that every other conspirator did or said in furtherance of it was proof against him, too. In other words, in for a penny, in for a pound.

Landis did tell the jury that "mere passive knowledge" of a conspiracy was not enough: a defendant had to participate actively in some way, and intentionally with the common purpose in mind. At the same time, though, conspiracies are secret by nature, and "guilt can generally be proved only by circumstantial evidence."[5]

His explanations of the presumption of innocence and the government's burden of proof beyond a reasonable doubt in a criminal case were standard fare, too, and delivered with adequate gusto. Landis told the jury that, while he was free to offer an opinion on the facts (which they, as the sole finders of fact, also were free to disregard), he would not give an opinion. He kept his word, in the sense that he made no express comment at all on guilt or innocence.[6]

Not that Landis kept a hidden thumb entirely off the scales. His explanation of how jurors should use the mass of evidence of speeches, pamphlets, and letters before the period charged in the indictment was opaque, and obviously so. "All the evidence that has gone to you of acts and doings and sayings prior to the period mentioned in the indictment in the case was admitted by the court to enable the jury to come to an understanding of the frame of mind of the men accused here as conspirators; of going to enable the jury to correctly determine the fact of the intent of these defendants charged here as conspirators," Landis droned. "All that evidence came in here to enable you men to intelligently form a judgment of these men, to enable you gentlemen to accurately determine the question as to the intent of these defendants. All the evidence, all the acts and doings before the period covered by this indictment, you will consider with all the other evidence that has come in here; the things said and done by the defendants during the period covered by the indictment, to enable you to determine the question whether or not there was a common design; whether they entered into an agreement; whether they came together for the purpose specified in the first four counts of the indictment, or one of them."[7]

Landis warned the jurors that "our industrial society is not on trial here" but that neither was organized labor. "Men belonging to what is referred to here as the laboring class have a perfect right to organize. They have got a perfect right by the force of their members in organization, to strive to improve their condition in dealing with the employers of labor." But there was one important caveat. "The only limitation upon the right being that they must not use their organization to accomplish an unlawful purpose; a purpose prohibited by law."[8]

Then came an instruction that invited conviction. It was the very concept that Nebeker had flagged to Fitts in early July, and on which he had asked Pagan to draft a proposed jury instruction. The government's key jury instruction in fact was a union of common concepts at the time, vicarious liability joined with the principle that Person A's offending act need only have been a natural and probable consequence of the overall agreement, even if Person B did not intend it. Indeed, it would be another sixty years, almost exactly, before the U.S. Supreme Court would restrict sharply part of that jury instruction, the "natural and probable consequences" aspect, because it relieved the prosecution's burden of proof on an essential fact, intent. And in 1946, the Supreme Court would make clear that vicarious liability of one conspirator for another's act in pursuit of the conspiracy's goals is acceptable.

In this case, the instruction as a whole potentially was devastating to defense hopes for an acquittal.

> Now there is a principle of law that men are chargeable with the natural, responsible and necessary consequences of their acts, and in this case, having reference to the appropriate count or counts, if it appears that these defendants by the processes charged in the indictment, set about solely to better labor conditions as to environment, wages, compensation, and that what they did not contemplate anything except the bettering of labor conditions as to environment or compensation, then your verdict should be "not guilty"; with this qualification: that men are chargeable, as I indicated before, with the reasonable, natural and necessary consequences of their acts, and they may not join together with a common purpose to intend to accomplish one object, if, in the accomplishment of that one object which may be lawful, they naturally, reasonably and rationally will accomplish another object which the law prohibits. So in this case, having reference to the count or counts that I am now dealing with, if you find the defendants did come together—that they had a common purpose,—a common

160

understanding to accomplish an object, and that that object was lawful, but that also there was in the situation obviously apparent to persons of intelligence, another object which would be accomplished, it being forbidden by law, while they were accomplishing the object itself permitted by law, they should go on with that common understanding of those conditions, doing a thing to give effect to that common understanding, it would be a conspiracy denounced by the statutes of the United States.[9]

In so many words, then, there was a war on; and if a strike for lawful ends, like higher wages or shorter hours, foreseeably would cause interruption of the government's war effort, it could be a violation of the conspiracy statutes in the indictment—not because the defendants intended disruption of the government's efforts but because they should have foreseen that disruption would be a natural consequence.

And with that, Landis was done, other than asking the lawyers if he had missed anything or if they had any objections to his instructions. Vanderveer did object to several instructions, including that last one. Landis was utterly gracious about allowing the defense its appellate record, and giving an exception to every defense proposal that he did not accept. But he held to his views. No, he would not direct verdicts of not guilty on the four counts, for all or for anyone. Then, as an afterthought before excusing the jury to deliberate, he noted that their verdicts must be unanimous. It was 4:15 p.m.[10]

Landis then shooed the defendants out of the courtroom, sending them to the chuckhouse down the hall where they had taken their meals for months. He wanted the jury to have the courtroom for its use in examining the many hundreds of trial exhibits. A reporter who wandered into the chuckhouse to see what the defendants might say as they waited got Haywood's assessment of Landis's jury instructions. "Fair enough charge," Haywood commented diplomatically.[11]

Of the 112 who began trial at jury selection, 97 men now remained after the attrition through dismissals and illness. Each faced four separate conspiracy charges. In addition to plowing through the indictment and hundreds of exhibits, and recollecting a solid three and a half months of testimony, the jury had 388 separate determinations of guilt or its absence to make: each defendant had to be considered separately on any given count, times four. The task was massive, and Landis had told them pointedly, "Now, in determining whether there is a reasonable doubt, determining on the facts existing, you have got to go over the evidence in the case."[12]

Nebeker, Porter, and the government team could wait it out in the Justice Department offices on the floor below in the courthouse. They sent a telegram immediately to the attorney general, telling him that the jury had the case. "We are feeling confident of result," they added.

Vanderveer and the defense team had only their hotel as refuge while the jury deliberated. At least Vanderveer retreated there, knowing that the jury had a long siege ahead of it.

Or so he reasonably thought.

Not an hour passed. In as few as twenty-five minutes, and in no more than fifty or fifty-five minutes, the jury told a bailiff that it had verdicts.

Landis reassembled in Courtroom No. 627 about one hour and thirty-five minutes after the jury had retired. It was not just that he had to summon the lawyers with news that the jury had a verdict. Landis also beckoned two hundred "hefty" police officers to the courtroom, in addition to the usual complement of deputy U.S. marshals and Bureau of Investigation agents. Among the defense lawyers, only Otto Christensen had arrived back in court by the time Landis convened to hear the verdicts.

Guilty. Everyone, on every count. Notably, there was only one form verdict, typed and submitted to the jury in advance (along with, presumably, "not guilty" form verdicts). The single guilty verdict listed every name and said simply, "guilty as charged in the indictment." Jurors theoretically could have crossed out names of any they wished to acquit. But the verdict form did not give them a way to convict anyone, or all, on one or another count without convicting on all counts. It was an all-or-nothing verdict form as to everyone, contrary to basic notions of individual justice on each charge in an indictment.[13]

Mathematically, using a fifty-five-minute estimate for deliberations, if jurors took just two or three minutes to elect a foreman without debate, this meant that they had spent about thirty seconds per defendant on all four counts. That broke down further to roughly eight seconds per count for each individual defendant. Had the foreman done nothing more than read the forty-three-page indictment aloud to the other eleven (even minus the dismissed charge, Count 5), he would have consumed maybe half or even most of the total time the jury gave to deliberating the fate of nearly one hundred men. But juries, of course, do not work mathematically.

Landis thanked the twelve men and sent them home. They had done what he subtly had steered them to do over the course of months, by evidentiary rulings big and small. The men on trial, after all, had disobeyed the commander-in-chief during wartime.

Now, too, the ninety-seven men on trial no longer could claim a presumption of innocence. However hastily, a jury had found them guilty of four separate conspiracies, beyond a reasonable doubt. Landis revoked their bonds on the spot. They would return as a group to the Cook County Jail to await sentencing. There would be no more chuckhouse on the sixth floor with edible food, no more shiny new cuspidors. Caroline Lowe cried as her clients left in handcuffs.[14]

20

Have You Anything to Say?

Before sentencing, there was the dreary formality of motions in arrest of judgment and for a new trial, just to preserve arguments for appeal. Court reconvened ten days after the guilty verdicts, on Tuesday, August 27, to set scheduling on those motions. George Vanderveer dutifully soldiered through timing of the written motions and their supporting brief. Affirming tacitly that this was pure formality, Landis scheduled the hearing on the motions at the same time as the sentencings. The actual writing almost surely fell to Caroline Lowe and Otto Christensen.

If Landis dropped any hint that he would give the arguments actual consideration, it came in his request for a defense memorandum naming specific defendants as to whom Vanderveer claimed the evidence insufficient. This request was different. And Landis wanted that memorandum the next day, by 1 p.m. Insufficient evidence would mean that a given defendant was entitled to acquittal by the judge, in spite of the jury's verdict.[1]

If that request for an extra memorandum raised any hope at all at that late stage, Landis banished it immediately as sentencing began on Thursday morning, August 29. He denied the motions for arrest of judgment and a new trial summarily, without explanation. He acquitted no one for insufficient evidence.[2]

What followed after that first five or ten minutes is a tradition dating back to early English courts. A defendant facing sentence is entitled, as a matter of unwritten right, to speak directly to the judge before the court imposes sentence. If a defendant has not testified at trial, it may be the first and only time either the judge or the public hears him speak. A judge will inquire, ritually, of the prisoner if he wishes to be heard before sentence is imposed, or if he has any reason why sentence ought not be imposed.

At English common law for centuries, a person facing a felony indictment neither was allowed a lawyer—except on points of law—nor allowed to testify or to call witnesses. Queen Mary I began to open the witness box to defense witnesses in criminal cases in the mid-sixteenth century, but she made only a recommendation to judges. A right to call defense witnesses did not emerge until the late seventeenth century, and then slowly. And the prohibition of defense counsel (again, other than on pure points of law) in serious criminal cases slackened only in the late seventeenth and eighteenth centuries, and most defendants still had no counsel. This ritual after a guilty verdict, then, was the convict's last chance—and practically his first as well—to urge a flaw in the indictment, the existence of a parliamentary pardon, a right to benefit of clergy (which, for present purposes, eased punishment), or a mistake in the proceedings that would bar imposition of sentence.

Allocution, as it is known in the United States, has produced some of the most memorable moments in the legal history of English-speaking peoples. In 1803, after a grotesque trial at the Green Street courthouse in Dublin, the young Irish insurgent who led a brief, futile uprising against British rule, Robert Emmet, faced a certain death sentence. Famously, he closed his allocution to the King's judges, "Let no man write my epitaph: for as no man who knows my motives dare now vindicate them, let not prejudice or ignorance asperse them. Let them and me repose in obscurity and peace, and my tomb remain uninscribed, until other times, and other men, can do justice to my character. When my country takes her place among the nations of the earth, then, and not till then, let my epitaph be written. I have done."[3]

Not many have gone to the scaffold as eloquently.

Closer to home and much closer to that day, Eugene Debs's ringing declaration ("While there is a lower class I am in it; while there is a criminal element I am of it; while there is a soul in prison I am not free") would come in his allocution in a Cleveland federal court just two weeks later.[4]

Landis told the ninety-five Wobblies in court that he would hear from them in alphabetical order. (At the moment, no longer were there ninety-seven: Pete Dailey was seriously ill and seemed unable to appear in court that day; Pietro Nigra was in the hospital again, too.) Their statements, although individually brief in the main, ran fully three hours. As he called each man up, by his last name only, Landis asked, "Have you anything you want to tell me before this case is disposed of?" or something close. The transcript reads as if he were impatient but trying not to sound that way.[5]

Some of the men did not speak at all, declining the chance. Ray Fanning, the nineteen-year-old Harvard student, was one. But Vanderveer intervened for him, saying, "This boy, Your Honor, has been working in my office. I have come to feel rather a personal interest in him. He was taken from Harvard where he was trying to earn an education, he was working in a munitions plant making shells." As to another man, Dave Ingar, who had not testified, Vanderveer took the blame for court and jury not hearing Ingar's story.[6]

Haywood was comparatively restrained. Although he said, "I feel that the verdict in this case is one of the greatest mistakes, one of the greatest blunders ever committed in a court of justice," his entire statement was but one short paragraph of transcript.[7]

James P. Thompson spoke the longest and gave a prepared speech about the war that covered almost five pages of transcript. None of the others seem to have written out their remarks.[8]

Some were moving. In response to Landis's peremptory, "Anything you want to say?" Anson E. Soper, no longer young, explained that he was an American citizen, as was his father and his grandfather before him; that he had been taught that the best government was a democracy or republic, that "monarchies are wrong." He believed that still. He was proud of the Wobblies who registered for the draft. Then, "Your Honor, I have received one very stunning blow in this trial, and only one. I am a man fifty-one years of age, and your court is the first court I was ever into in my life with a charge against me, but the prosecuting attorney stepped in front of that jury and said that I was a man with a hard face and soft hands. I wish to deny that, Your Honor. Perhaps I cannot in the face, but I do in the hands. I am a man, Your Honor, that worked thirty-eight years in essential industry, and provided a home for my family, for my wife and my babies, and perhaps provided luxuries for some others who were hiring me. I venture to say that the prosecuting attorney today cannot boast of ever putting in thirty-eight days in essential industry."

Soper had more. "If it would be possible that you can find a place in any of those laws that will permit me," Soper implored Landis, "in addition to the sentence you are going to impose upon me, to serve that of fellow-worker N. G. Marlatt, my fellow-worker, and allow him to go back to his family, to his wife and his babies where I know he is needed . . . I am willing to serve his time if it can possibly be arranged. That is all."[9]

Some of the men were bitter, some sarcastic, some resigned, some even contrite. A few were philosophical. Harry Lloyd spoke briefly, beginning, "All I have got to say is that there are causes why we are all here today. If society would only dig down into the root of these causes perhaps they would be able to eliminate a great lot of the misery and poverty that is in the world today."[10]

As to most of the men, Landis simply listened without comment. But some he engaged, usually with questions that were probing but not obviously hostile. He assured Benjamin Schraeger that "the exhibition of one or two of these men here is not going to hurt you or any of the rest of these defendants—except the man who makes the exhibition. I may have to take it into consideration in connection with his case." Ominously, Landis referred to Ralph Chaplin by name in his exchange with Schraeger.[11]

The allocutions went longer than Landis anticipated. When they ended, he adjourned abruptly until 2 p.m. the next day, which he had not planned. With bail revoked since the guilty verdicts, all the defendants were trooped back to jail under guard. All but two, that is. Before adjourning, Landis released Norval Marlatt until November, which in practical terms meant that he would not be sentenced at all. But, Landis barked, it had nothing to do with Soper's plea for Marlatt. Earlier, he had addressed Pete Dailey. Somehow, Dailey had made it to court that day, late and unannounced. When his time had come to speak, Landis stopped him. "The case as to you is continued generally. You may go without any bond." In other words, he was free. The *Chicago Tribune* reported that Dailey was dying.[12]

On Friday afternoon, Landis was ready for the remaining men. Opening court, Landis gave a long recitation of the evidence; he read aloud from some of the pamphlets and letters in evidence. "I am obliged to say," Landis began to sum up, "that the jury were left, in my judgment, no avenue of escape from that verdict on this evidence." He repeated again minutes later, "The jury could not have done anything else on this evidence but find a verdict of guilty."

Why? Landis explained immediately. "When the country is at peace, it is a legal right of free speech to oppose going to war and to oppose even preparation for war; but when once war is declared, this right ceases."[13]

Now he called the defendants forward in ranks. The first two, Meyer Friedkin and Glen Roberts, got just ten days in the Cook County Jail on all counts, to run concurrently. Today was Friday; they would be done the Monday after next.

Then came twelve, including the generous Soper. One year and one day in prison. The extra day had meaning then, unchanged now. To earn good-time credit toward an early release date, an inmate must be sentenced to more than one year. So, in the world of American criminal law, a sentence of 366 days is significantly shorter in administration than a sentence of 364 days.

Next Landis commanded twenty-six to stand and approach. These men got five-year sentences in the penitentiary. The stakes were increasing sharply.

But then Landis released Benjamin Schraeger, whose allocution he had coaxed, without any sentence at all. Like Marlatt the day before, Schraeger was free until November. He never would be sentenced.

The largest group followed: thirty-two men. Landis had been toying with the men, slipping in a moment of lenity as to Schraeger. These thirty-two got ten years each. Ed Doree was in this group.

Again, though, Landis manipulated the proceedings for dramatic tension. The next group of seven dropped back down to five years.

The final fifteen remained, Haywood and other prominent Wobblies among them. Doree's brother-in-law, Walter Nef, stood in this last group. They would go to prison for twenty years—the maximum term on Count 4—with all shorter sentences to run concurrently. Fines for everyone would run as high as $30,000. Sentencing was over.[14]

No, Landis would not grant bail pending appeal. He was done with the dead Frank Little's coconspirators, every last one. But he did order the men held in Chicago until at least the following Friday evening, to permit them to seek bail in the U.S. Circuit Court of Appeals, upstairs in the same building.[15]

The courtroom was silent as Landis left the bench. Soon the deputy marshals were leading the men out. Ben Fletcher, who just had received a sentence of ten years but avoided twenty, found his wits first. "Judge Landis is using poor English today," he remarked to reporters as he passed them. "His sentences are too long."[16]

Fletcher offered a good quip, no doubt. Looking at the spoken words of these working men, though, one allocution most stands out. With nearly eight dozen men speaking, none of the Wobblies had the attention of the court the way an Emmet or a Debs did. But some found power in brevity, and one in particular. Ralph Chaplin was a poet, a dreamer, and a writer. Landis had no use for him especially, as he had let slip while encouraging Schraeger. Chaplin stood to say his piece at sentencing. "I have been convicted of an imaginary crime," Chaplin launched, "by a stupid jury—." Landis cut him off.

"Well, then, I will say this, Your Honor," Chaplin resumed. "That I am proud that I have climbed high enough for the lightning to strike me."[17]

He got twenty years.

Top right: Sixteen of the Chicago defendants pose shortly after the U.S. Supreme Court refused their case in April 1921. They and several others had been free on bail pending appeal. None of these fled. Ed Doree is in the back row, second from right. The man in the front row, far right, was not a defendant. (University of Michigan Library, Special Collections Research Center, Joseph A. Labadie Collection)

Bottom right: During their time in the Cook County Jail awaiting trial, IWW members published a newsletter in pencil. Dry humor is evident in the masthead: the "Can" is a slang reference to the jail, and the cost of the newsletter is "priceless." (University of Michigan Library, Special Collections Research Center, Joseph A. Labadie Collection)

I.W.W. PRISONERS

This is how we looked returning from defense
activities on bail to Leavenworth prison, 1921.

The Can Opener

PRICELESS

Office
Publication
CELL 456
C.C.C.

SPECIAL
—DETROIT EDITION—

VOL I. NO V. — COOK CO. CAN-CHICAGO. — NOV. 15-1917

WUXTRA !! I.W.W. PLOT

JAIL DELIVERY NIPPED IN THE BUD

H.I.I — WHEN THE CAT GETS LOOSE

MAKING THE WORLD
SAFE FOR PLUTOCRACY
AND THE FREEDOM OF THE
SIEZE.

BELIEVED TO BE NATION-
WIDE CONSPIRACY
(special assigned suppress)

(CHICAGO NOV. 12-17 - WHAT IS BELIEVED
TO BE NATION WIDE PLOT WAS UNCOVERED
WHEN A BEAN WAS FOUND IN THE CELL
OF A WOBBLY ALLEGED I.W.W. IT IS
DARKLY HINTED THAT THE COOK IS IN-
VOLVED FOR ALLOWING SAID BEAN TO
GET AWAY WHILE DISHING UP SOUP
ANOTHER I.W.W. WAS FOUND WEARING
A PAIR OF 39¢ SUSPENDERS AND
CAN OFFICIALS BELIEVED THEY
INTENDED TO COOPERATE AND MAKE
SLING-SHOTS OF SAID GALLUSES AND
SHOOT BEANS AT THE JAIL SCREWS
AND THUS EFFECT A WHOLESALE JAIL
DELIVERY. A WOBBLY WAS HELD
FOR THE FIRING SQUAD. TO BE SHOT
AT SUNRISE ON JULY 4TH THE NEXT
ANNIVERSARY OF OUR INDEPENDENCE
WERE LITTLE DANDIE WORKER

Ten of the Chicago defendants in an undated photograph. The colorful John T. "Red" Doran is in the front row on the right. James "Big Jim" Thompson is in the back row on the left. (University of Michigan Library, Special Collections Research Center, Joseph A. Labadie Collection)

A deputy U.S. marshal signals for a street car to yield as other marshals and plainclothes police officers lead the Chicago defendants, handcuffed two by two, on the walk between the Cook County Jail and the Chicago federal courthouse. (University of Michigan Library, Special Collections Research Center, Joseph A. Labadie Collection)

Judge Kenesaw Mountain Landis of the United States District Court for the Northern District of Illinois, at about the time of the IWW trial. Throughout, he steered the trial subtly. (University of Michigan Library, Special Collections Research Center, Joseph A. Labadie Collection)

Two studio photographs of Ed Doree, before his mustache. He signed the photograph above with the inscription, "Yours for Industrial Freedom." On the right, he poses with Frank H. Little behind him. Little was the most uncompromising opponent of World War I on the IWW General Executive Board. In death, Little would be a constant presence in the government's case at trial. (University of Michigan Library, Special Collections Research Center, E. F. Doree Papers, Joseph A. Labadie Collection)

Pals.

J. H. Little
and
Ed. Doree

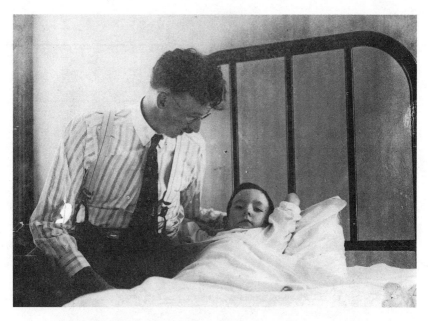

Ed Doree at the hospital bedside of his five-year-old son, Bucky, during a furlough from prison. (University of Michigan Library, Special Collections Research Center, E. F. Doree Papers, Joseph A. Labadie Collection)

Ed and Ida "Chiky" Doree (*on the left*), with their son, Frederick Lee Doree, known always as "Bucky." To the right is Ida's sister Feige, who was married to Walter T. Nef (*at far right*), Doree's colleague in the IWW and at trial. The photograph is from 1921, shortly before Doree and Nef returned to prison following the loss of their appeal. (University of Michigan Library, Special Collections Research Center, E. F. Doree Papers, Joseph A. Labadie Collection)

Big Bill Haywood (*lower right*) and other staff in the headquarters of the IWW in 1917. (Wayne State University, Walter P. Reuther Library, Archives)

Arturo Giovannitti (*left*) and Joseph J. Ettor. Both had played important roles in eastern textile strikes, and both were named in the Chicago indictment. With Carlo Tresca and Elizabeth Gurley Flynn, they avoided trial through the work of Flynn's separate lawyer. (Wayne State University, Walter P. Reuther Library, Archives)

Elizabeth Gurley Flynn in 1913, during the Paterson, New Jersey, silk strike. She was the so-called Rebel Girl and briefly a defendant in the Chicago indictment. Flynn split from the others, though, in seeking a separate trial with her own lawyer. (Wayne State University, Walter P. Reuther Library, Archives)

Top left: Charles L. Lambert in his mugshot for the Chicago trial. Lambert was a member of the IWW General Executive Board. (Wayne State University, Walter P. Reuther Library, Archives)

Bottom left: Frank H. Little, IWW General Executive Board member. His murder on August 1, 1917, spurred the Justice Department's new strategy to destroy the IWW. (Wayne State University, Walter P. Reuther Library, Archives)

George Francis Vanderveer (1875–1942) of Seattle, lead lawyer for the Chicago IWW defendants. Vanderveer wrestled demons, including during the trial. He was a brawler outside the courtroom but skilled and controlled in court. (Wayne State University, Walter P. Reuther Library, Archives)

Ben Fletcher, an IWW organizer of eastern dock workers, head of Local 8 in Philadelphia, and the only black defendant in the Chicago trial, holding an unidentified boy. Fletcher had a quick wit and was popular among his IWW colleagues. (Wayne State University, Walter P. Reuther Library, Archives)

Deputized gunmen and mining company hirelings directing suspected IWW members and others onto freight cars on July 12, 1917, in the Bisbee, Arizona, "deportation." (Wayne State University, Walter P. Reuther Library, Archives)

Claude R. Porter of Iowa, the primary assistant prosecutor in the Chicago case, in November 1910. Porter's hope that the trial would boost him to the Iowa governor's office failed. He had more luck with presidential appointments after the Chicago trial, first as an assistant attorney general and later as a member of the Interstate Commerce Commission for many years. (George Grantham Bain Collection, Library of Congress)

Top left: A rare photograph of Bill Haywood with his family, outside the Ada County Jail in 1907 while awaiting trial for the Steunenberg murder. His first wife, Nevada Jane (née Minor), is in the wheelchair at left; a difficult childbirth apparently left her disabled. His eldest daughter, Vern Florence, is at the right, and his younger daughter, Henrietta Ruth, stands next to Haywood with her arm around him. The other woman is unidentified. The marriage was unhappy and foundered in fewer than ten years. As usual, Haywood hides his blind right eye from the camera. (Wayne State University, Walter P. Reuther Library, Archives)

Bottom left: Otto Christensen, the Chicago lawyer who joined the defense team at trial and played a significant role on appeal. He proved skillful and steady. (Wayne State University, Walter P. Reuther Library, Archives)

FRANK K. NEBEKER
Son of Ira Nebeker and Delia Lane. Born
May 15, 1870, Laketown, Utah. Instruc-
tor of Mathematics at B. Y. C. of Logan.

Frank K. Nebeker of Salt Lake City, the lead prosecutor in the Chicago
case. Nebeker had represented western business interests and brought
zeal to the task of breaking the IWW. Rewarded with high Justice
Department posts after the trial, he lived comfortably in Washington,
DC, for the rest of his long life. ("Utah, Pioneers and Prominent Men
of Utah, 1847–1868," Digital File Number 100094571, Image Number
00426, www.familysearch.org, database with images excerpted from
Frank Esshom, *Pioneers and Prominent Men of Utah: Comprising
Photographs, Genealogies, Biographies* [Salt Lake City: Utah Pioneers
Books, 1913])

Part III

This train carries saints and sinners
This train carries losers and winners
This train carries whores and gamblers
This train carries lost souls.
I said, this train carries broken-hearted
This train, thieves and sweet souls departed
This train carries fools and kings
This train, all aboard.

Bruce Springsteen,
"Land of Hope and Dreams"

21

The Train

———————————◆———————————

Summer was waning now, and in the upper Midwest most of the harvest
was in. On Saturday, August 31, the morning after sentencing, the
men in the Cook County Jail waited to learn where and when they would
go. Two relatively lucky ones, and only two, would be free in nine days.
For the rest, the court of appeals was not going to move quickly enough to
consider bail pending appeal in the coming week.[1]

Some ninety-one men faced a trip somewhere. On balance, that was a
good prospect, not a bad one. Wherever they went, they would be free of
the miseries of the Cook County Jail. Then and now, jails mean harder
confinement than almost all prisons: they restrict movement more sharply,
usually allow no outside recreation, offer little inside employment to make
the hours pass more quickly, and have harsher living conditions than all
but the most secure prisons. At a minimum, there would be a change of
scenery after nearly a year in Chicago, much of that spent in jail for most
of the men.

As September came, so did a vengeful act that may have sped their
departure. On the afternoon of Wednesday, September 4, as Chicago was
preparing to host the Boston Red Sox for game one of the World Series the
next day, two men—one short and squat with a black fedora pulled down
low over his eyes—walked into the Adams Street entrance of the federal
courthouse and post office. A few moments later, they walked out and
broke into a run. They were not half a block away when the bomb went off.

It killed and injured a midweek assortment of people who might be in
a downtown post office. Ella Miehlke, nineteen and from the south side,
lost an entire side of her head; she died as passersby tried to drag her to

187

safety. Her sister was injured but lived. J. B. Ladd, a twenty-two-year-old sailor down from the Great Lakes Naval Station in Waukegan, just north of Chicago, died. So did Edward Kolkow, who lived so close to Weeghman Park (renamed Wrigley Field in 1927) on Waveland Avenue that he might have heard the crowd had he lived another day. He was sixty-five and still working as a postal clerk. A forty-five-year-old mailman, William Wheeler, died, too. Around thirty more were injured, some badly and many by flying glass. A nearby eighteen-inch-thick wall came down, plate glass windows across the street up to the third floor disappeared, and the entire north side of the courthouse itself was "havoc."[2]

The inference that the IWW had planted the bomb in the building that housed Judge Landis and his courtroom was obvious. Like many other mainstream newspapers, the *New York Times* flatly and immediately called it an "I.W.W. Bomb." The local head of the federal Justice Department's Bureau of Investigation declared the bomb "an act of reprisal" by the IWW and set about rounding up IWW members on the double. His men were questioning new prisoners "as fast as we can get to them."

Foreknowledge of the event among the remaining defendants was less obvious. No less than Bill Haywood was in the federal courthouse at the time, after all. The marshals had moved him from the jail to their lock-up—the "cage room," in the parlance of the day—on the eighth floor, apparently so that he could dictate letters to his private secretary before leaving for prison. That raises interesting questions, relating in some way to why the federal marshals afforded him the privilege. But had Haywood known that the building would be the target of a powerful bomb that day, making the trip there would have been a strange, even suicidal, decision. As it was, the two deputy marshals sitting with him claimed colorfully that the explosion "nearly lifted us out of our chairs." By contrast, Haywood sat placidly, tapping his pencil on the table. Tap . . . tap . . . tap, as the sounds of frenzy on the street below rose in rapid crescendo.

"What do you think of the affair?" marshals soon demanded of Haywood.

"Well, what do you think?" he answered coolly.

With suspicions focused on the IWW, they prodded further.

"It might have been a German outrage," Haywood deflected. "It is a terrible thing. No I.W.W. would be so foolish as to do such a thing. It must have been German fear propaganda." But, Haywood conceded, "I suppose the I.W.W. will be blamed. We have been blamed for many things."[3]

Yes. Whoever was to blame, though, the bombing of the Chicago federal courthouse would remain unsolved. Dynamite bombings—on Wall Street in September 1920, in the Milwaukee police station in November 1917, and elsewhere—were common then, and often the known or suspected work of anarchists. In early June 1919, an Italian immigrant and anarchist, Carlo Valdinoci, blew himself up while setting a bomb at the home of Attorney General A. Mitchell Palmer. That bomb was one of several in coordinated attacks across eight cities that day. Some years later, in late September 1932, the judge who presided over the convictions of famed anarchists Nicola Sacco and Bartolomeo Vanzetti saw his home destroyed by a bomb.[4]

Ed Doree wrote his last letter from the Cook County Jail to his parents on the day after the Chicago bombing. "Some fool or crank placed a bomb in the Federal Building here, killing four persons and wounding several more. It was a miserable affair, a thing which makes the heart revolt at the thought." He understood the practical effect on him and the other IWW defendants, too. "There are some suspects found by the Naval Intelligence Bureau. If the man they seek proves to be the man, then we will be vindicated. Should it prove that the real criminal is caught before long, then I will try again for bail."[5]

Not quite everyone blamed the IWW instantly. Among the few showing restraint and waiting for facts was none other than Judge Landis. He had been at his northern Michigan lake cottage that day, not in the courthouse. When a reporter reached him at Burt Lake, near Alanson, Landis was measured. "No threats of any kind, either written or verbal, have been made," he said. "I have no reason to suspect an I.W.W. plot or to blame the organization or any of its members for the outrage."[6]

Whatever the role of the defendants or their supporters, if any, the train from Chicago now would leave sooner rather than later. At 9:30 p.m. on Friday, September 6, ten police vans and fifty-two uniformed and plainclothes officers pulled up in the dark outside the Cook County Jail. They herded the defendants bound for prison into the vans. The trip to the LaSalle Street station was short. There, a special train waited. Sixty city police detectives and federal agents waited on board, with three cars for the prisoners. The U.S. marshal in Chicago himself, John J. Bradley, was in charge. Handcuffed in pairs as usual, the prisoners shuffled aboard under guard. Ed Doree was half of the last duo. Guards and prisoners alike were silent. Within minutes, the short train was off, chugging west on the Rock Island route, for the federal prison in Fort Leavenworth, Kansas. In secret and under cover of night, they were gone.[7]

The men were in a good mood. "I did not know anything about the place I was going to," Bill Haywood remembered later. "But together with the others I was glad to be leaving the gloomy, dank surroundings of the Cook County Jail." In darkness, they chugged west through the brick, stone, and steel canyons of Chicago into neighborhoods of wooden frame homes and row houses and then on through ripe or already harvested fields and scattered towns and villages. The train groaned and screeched through small stations without slowing.

Sleeping would have been hard, handcuffed to the man next to him and sitting up, and the men were alert. To pass time that night, Ben Fletcher convened a mock court. He burlesqued Judge Landis amusingly (and convincingly, Haywood thought). After swearing in the IWW men as a jury, Fletcher called the guards and detectives up one at a time, sentencing each "without further ado to be hanged and shot and imprisoned for life."[8]

By Saturday morning, still awake as they rolled west-southwest through the plains, Ed Doree was writing to his wife, Chiky. Was it forced cheerfulness to encourage an anxious wife? Or maybe relief to be out of the jail and on to the prison term that would mark the beginning of the end of the ordeal? Was it a bit of both? Whatever the reason, Doree sounded chipper. "We are having a fine trip. Everybody happy," he assured her. "Edwards and I are hand-cuffed together. We were the last two aboard the train, but we got the best seats. Well, love and kisses to you and Bucky. . . . Bye, bye, baby. Hope you are as happy as I am. Your loving Ed."[9]

Just west of the Missouri River that separates Kansas from Missouri to the east, and a few miles northwest of Kansas City, stood Fort Leavenworth. The fort dated back to 1827, when it became a western outpost against plains Indians and took its name from Colonel Henry Leavenworth, its first commander. In 1901, after the Spanish-American War, Secretary of War Elihu Root and others convinced Congress that the army needed a general staff to fix shortcomings laid bare in that recent war. Fort Leavenworth became the home of the Command & General Staff College. There the college remains. For one year, too, Fort Leavenworth hosted the Army War College, although that moved permanently to the Carlisle Barracks in Pennsylvania's Susquehanna Valley in 1951. Men like Dwight Eisenhower, Omar Bradley, George Patton, and many others all graduated from the Command & General Staff College at Leavenworth. Brigadier General Lesley J. McNair, namesake of today's Fort McNair in Washington, DC, served as commandant for eighteen months in 1939–40.[10]

The fort maintained a military prison—the disciplinary barracks—from the late 1870s. In 1895, though, Congress decreed a civilian maximum-security prison on the same vast tract of federal land, four miles south of the fort. A massive stone structure built with prison labor, the U.S. Penitentiary at Leavenworth opened in 1903. From the outside, the main building looks now as it did in 1918: handsome in a governmental way. Outwardly, it might be at home as a cabinet department headquarters off the National Mall in Washington. From the inside, of course, the prison was and is something else.

The ninety-one men arriving there had crossed more than five hundred miles of American heartland, through Illinois, Iowa, and Missouri, then over the trestle to the bluff above the Missouri River on the Kansas side. Westbound, dawn had been behind them, not before them; the train raced toward lingering darkness, not light. Manacled to their comrades throughout the night, after sunrise caught up they could see, though, as wheat fields and small towns whisked past. There, in years previous, some of them had organized agricultural workers, slept in hobo "jungles" around fires in metal barrels, operated threshers themselves, enveloped in the smell of cut crops, grease, and hot soil under an unblinking sun, and beat their way in freight cars on the same rails. Now they had seats at last in a passenger car, unfree but maybe less uncomfortable.

At about 4 p.m. Saturday, the special train hissed and squealed to a stop within the walls of the penitentiary, then just fifteen years old. Uncuffing them at last, guards led the men into the auditorium. There, despite sore wrists, the warden impressed them: as Doree reported, he gave them "a short talk and a real human one. He met us on the 'man to man' ground," and showed "an attitude admired by everybody." Supper and the cells followed.

The next two days saw a bath, a shave removing all facial hair, prison clothes swapped for their own, photographs, weighing, physical examinations, and vaccinations. Fingerprints and Bertillon measurements of their skulls, feet, middle fingers, and forearms would come later. Most of the men were assigned to the "D" cell house, with its narrow cells in at least five tiers. Ben Fletcher's assignment is uncertain: the penitentiary generally kept the IWW prisoners together, but it also was a racially segregated prison. Black prisoners went to the "C" cell house.[11]

Work assignments came Monday afternoon. Doree drew the kitchen, waiting tables for a time. Leavenworth's vast dining hall seated perhaps

1,500, and the prisoner band often played from the time the inmates marched in until they marched out. Walter Nef worked in the tin shop. Haywood was assigned to the clothing department as assistant bookkeeper. Asked what trade he plied, Haywood had told the deputy warden that for the last seventeen years, "I had been most of the time in an office or on the lecture platform."[12]

They could write a letter once a week. Ed Doree's first letter home from Leavenworth, in his neat handwriting on prison stationery, went out the following Sunday, September 15. "My dearest little Chiky," he began. His second sentence asked about "little Bucky boy." "I guess he has forgotten his papa altogether. Well, so much the better for him for the time being." But that moment of self-indulgence in fear and loneliness gave way quickly to the pragmatic. The prison gave him "a frightful pen": would she please send two fountain pens? He joked that inmates there liked the place, "home," so much that they "settle down here for long periods."

Turning serious again, he wanted to assure Chiky, "I am feeling *fine*. Got to be a regular fiend for food." The food was "wholesome and there is more than plenty," and the "cells are clean and airy. Plenty of sunlight." They were a remarkable "contrast to the filthy cells at Cook Co. Jail." Tobacco at the prison canteen was cheap—about what it cost on the outside, a clever morale-booster by administrators. Days featured an hour outside at the ballpark in the large penitentiary yard. All in all, it was a welcome change from life constantly indoors in jail. Doree, the former semi-pro player, enjoyed "the ball game between the white and colored teams," and resolved to get on the team the next year.

That is, if he still was there. In the only cryptic part of his letter, Doree told Chiky, "Miss Inglis was here to see me. We had quite a visit together." Agnes Inglis was a Detroit social worker and settlement house veteran who became a friend and ally of the famous anarchist Emma Goldman as the years after 1900 bent her politics in a radical direction. Inglis would use her influence and family money to help arrange bail pending appeal for several of the IWW defendants. She also would become the principal curator and self-taught archivist of the University of Michigan's Joseph A. Labadie Collection of materials on social protest movements.

Meanwhile, like every federal inmate then and since, Doree already knew his maximum release date, good behavior assumed. That date was and is an important goal. "I'll be out in May, 1925, if not sooner. We'll only be kids yet, Chiky, just kids." At most, six and a half years to go.

"Say, Chiky, send me one of the last pictures we had taken of Bucky."[13]

22

Doing Time

That same month, September 1918, Eugene Debs went to federal prison for making the socialist case against the war and the draft. The Justice Department had tried him alone in Cleveland, Ohio, that summer, also under the Espionage Act. By the time that the old IWW cofounder Debs became federal Inmate No. 9653 in the U.S. Penitentiary in Atlanta, Ed Doree and the others who had remained active in the IWW were settling in to Leavenworth.

Debs would make his last run for president of the United States from the Atlanta penitentiary in 1920. He would get almost 898,000 of the 26.7 million votes cast, coming in third in a field of seven with Republican Warren G. Harding winning in a landslide. Ed Doree and the other Wobblies, though, would pass their time more typically.[1]

On the eve of leaving the Cook County Jail, Doree had written a pensive letter home—not without a tinge of self-pity. "Well, mamma dear, I am in a peculiar position. Guilty of no crime, in prison. I, who thought of love, think the thoughts peculiar to criminals. I, who have all my life fought against violence, am now told that my life theme was violence." But then the train had carried him and the others away from the gray misery of the jail.[2]

That trip brought the initial giddiness, if not elation, of leaving the Cook County Jail. In Leavenworth, the men found fresh air, work that was menial but helped make time go quickly, and an hour a day for outdoor recreation in the yard or on the ball field. Still, the men eventually stooped in part to the tedium of prison life and to the recognition that they remained prisoners and might for years. Life was regimented. And even men

193

with low expectations could remain enthusiastic about prison food only for so long. For those who missed wives, lovers, children, parents, lives spent wandering, or just Saturdays blowing their wages in a beer hall, loneliness and boredom were foes. "The monotony of prison life was bearing down heavily upon me," Haywood reminisced some years later. "I was beginning to realize what was meant by 'prison blues.'"[3]

Yet Doree sounded chipper in his letters. Back in October 1917, not long after his arrest, he had been frantic and demanding in the Cook County Jail. He had implored Ida, always "Chiky" to him, to work harder on raising bail money and had complained anxiously that there had been no tobacco "since Wednesday." Now, a year later, his early letters from Leavenworth displayed a good sense of humor. He made frequent and fond references to "Big Bill" and the other "boys." "On Oct. 7th, school starts," he told Chiky. "I am going to take a course in stenography. When I have completed that, I'll take up something else. I'm determined to come out of here better physical and mentally than when I came in."

Not long after, Doree reported "a cramp in the stomach" but noted cheerily that with one visit to the prison hospital, he "got fixed up in fine shape. Feel great now." And then, too earnestly, "Believe me, girlie, this is some place for a prison. Didn't think they could be so human. If it were not for being away from you and Bucky, I wouldn't care if Landis had said three times ten years. To tell the truth, this place affords me the first real rest in years." Still, he could not mask entirely the loneliness and boredom. "There is really too little to think and plan about. It will be better when school starts. More action. But of all things here, it's letters from home."[4]

Doree's days followed an unvarying schedule. "We 'crawl out' at 6:30. Think of me getting up at 6:30 with no strike on. But it is true." They would dress and make their beds. At 7:15 a.m., it was off to the kitchen to dress in white jackets and aprons. Mush and muffins were served first in the "big mess," holding 1,250 men, and then in the "small mess," for 250 to 300 men. After all the other inmates had eaten, the waiters ate. They then cleared and washed the tables. At 10:30 a.m., the waiters set the tables and this time ate before the other inmates. At lunch, the order was the small mess first, then the big mess hall. Afterward they would clean the tables again. One hour of recreation outside followed at 2 p.m. Then it was back to the kitchen, again for meal set-up and service. But at 5 p.m., Doree's shift went back to its cells; a late crew did the dinner clean-up. At 9:30 p.m., it was lights out. "This is our day—rain or shine." Saturdays brought one variation: outdoor recreation on the ball field for ninety minutes, rather than the single hour during the week. For Chiky's sake, presumably, Doree omitted the "silent system" enforced in the dining mess: at pain of solitary confinement or loss of good time, the men could not talk while in the mess, and used a system of hand signals that the penitentiary imposed when they wanted bread, salt, or pepper. The white-coated waiters also faced the greatest suspicion of acting as snitches—another little item that Doree left out of letters home.[5]

Dulling routine and inhumanities aside, in the early months Doree remained eager to affirm his camaraderie and zeal. In words meant for his mother but mailed to Chiky, he wrote of the recent sentencing hearing. "Gee, mamma, I never hope to see a finer picture of real rebel spirit in action than I saw the day we were found guilty and the day we were sentenced. No faltering, no whimpering, no begging for mercy; neither was there the slightest show of braggadocio on the part of anyone, man or woman. All seemed reconciled to the fact that the class war required victims and that sooner or later we must pay the penalty for our agitation for human freedom. A real class-conscious rebel becomes hardened to persecution. He looks upon it as a part of life, a part preferable to that of an abject, submissive slave, and fortunately or unfortunately you must be one or the other unless, of course, if you are a clever thief."

He continued to admire Haywood. "Today I sat and looked at Big Bill with numbers on each knee and on his back—in jail," he told Chiky. "Tomorrow he may be the [Karl] Liebknecht or Trotsky of America, who can tell?? Bill has that quality in him. When the workers ask for Haywood's release, the powers that be had better get busy. Once the workers want him out, he'll get out, even if they have made him the 'first' man of the nation. We live in the days of revolt! Gee, I'm glad I'm alive today, yes, even in jail. This is the decade when labor is coming into its own—the world."[6]

As Doree wrote from prison that first autumn, world events were unfolding dramatically. The Bolshevik revolution had toppled the tsar the previous November. Communists were trying to rule Russia. And now the war in Europe, although not yet over, plainly was coming to an end. There were rumors that the government would relent and release political prisoners once the war ended. Doree and the others shared Clarence Darrow's view that President Wilson would free socialists and the IWW prisoners when peace came; Darrow supposedly had met with Wilson himself. But Doree took a hard line. "Some of the boys figure that they would be able to secure a pardon as soon as the war is over," he mused to Chiky. "As for me, I prefer to stay here to taking a pardon from anyone. I have done nothing I must be pardoned for. If released today I would go on just as I did when arrested." And, as to rumors that those who renounced the IWW and radical politics would win release first, Doree was emphatic. "Let me surprise you, baby. Many of us can get out of here in less than three months, war or no war. We would have to pay the price, namely, traitorship to our class. I do not think there is one here would buy liberty at that price. I would not, you would hate me if I were to do so. The war may soon be over and then we will walk out of here like men."[7]

Some events Doree omitted from his letters home. In December 1918, for example, more than twenty of the IWW prisoners went on strike, refusing to work at their prison jobs. The warden had an answer. The striking men went to isolation cells. There, they found a hammer and a pile of rocks in the corner of each small cell. Until they had broken the rocks, they got no food. The strike lasted less than a week.[8]

But the mundane reality of prison life did leak into Doree's letters between the brave words. His teeth needed work, which meant constant nudging for money: the prison would pull teeth for free, but for dental work to save them, like a crown, the prisoner had to pay. Doree wanted to save his last upper molar and asked Chiky for $5. Tired of the tobacco in the prison commissary, he requested cigarettes and packages of pipe tobacco—*Bull Durham*, *Dukes Mixture*, *Sweet Caporal*, and *Old Judge*. Acquiring the preoccupation with physical condition and ailments common among prisoners, Doree bragged about his handball prowess and reported his weight (162 lb.). His teeth remained a frequent topic. One week, he would assure Chiky bravely, "This is *not* a spirit-breaking institution. Men can improve here." Another week, he would admit in passing, "Understand, I'm not cracking this place up as a summer resort."[9]

Other than solicitude for Chiky's well-being and constant encouragement, this young father's letters most consistently included longing and fond imagining of Bucky, their little boy. Bucky Doree spoke his first words before Ed had been in Leavenworth for a month; dad missed those, of course. He fretted that Bucky would not know him but soothed himself that the child was happier for that. He asked after Bucky's health. He promised time and again to bring candy with him for Bucky when he finally could take a train home. He was encouraged that Bucky was gaining weight. He wanted more photographs, with a Kodak camera if possible. He doted. He pined. Almost every letter other than the hastiest and shortest ended with Bucky.[10]

On February 18, 1919, the little boy turned two years old. A single page of paper arrived for him in the mail. It had a carefully drawn, ornamental heading, noting his birthdate and the year, with the largest letters reading, "To Bucky." A poem, in neatly printed, fancy penmanship suggesting the emerging *style moderne*, followed:

> When to this sun-kissed world you came,
> Two years ago,
> You knew not what you meant to me,
> Nor do you know,
> Nor will you know, nor will you ever care
> That ev'ry year you pass still leaves me there.
> But when at last—you are a man;
> Remember me,
> For when I'm old and near the death
> I'll think of thee—
> Not as the man, full-grown; but as the child,
> The new-born babe, the pure, the undefiled.

Bucky's father signed the homemade birthday card only with his prison identity, No. 13125.[11]

23

Reaching for the Rich

From their first days at Leavenworth, when not reassuring their families, Ed Doree, Bill Haywood, and most of the other Wobblies were thinking and writing about one urgent possibility: release on bail while their anticipated appeal inched through the appellate process. But bail prospects were complicated in several ways. First, bail raised issues about appearances and commitment to the cause: would not the zealous class warrior rather remain heroically in prison, a martyr in the making, than beg capitalist judges for freedom, perhaps with odious conditions? Second, the very decision to seek bail also might test the tensile strength of the One Big Union, whose creed held that there were only two classes, those who worked and those who employed others to work, and that men and women in the first class all were equal in the IWW. Financial practicalities might stretch the organization far enough to open fissures along subtle class lines within the union. After all, bail money was likely to be tight. Who should have it first? And if bail amounts predictably proved higher for Haywood and more notorious top leaders like him than for less visible members in the Chicago case, should scarce money rise to the top both quickly and disproportionately? Third and perhaps most vexing, how would the IWW raise sufficient bail money at all, with ninety-plus Chicago defendants in prison, scattered others already there, and the Sacramento and Wichita mass trial defendants foreseeably headed to prison in large numbers, too?

All of those complications were visible at Leavenworth. Doree's letters to Chiky revealed his ambivalence about bail, or at least his wish to project ambivalence. His first direct mention of bail came about three weeks after the men arrived. "About bail. Baby, I will do nothing at all. I will not try to get it. If Miss Inglis or Wm. Bross Lloyd wants to go my bail, all right." This was Agnes Inglis again, who had visited him within a week of his arrival at Leavenworth. Lloyd was the wealthy Chicago son of Henry Demarest Lloyd, and a Communist. Doree allowed himself a distinction between a pardon and bail. He insisted that he would not take a pardon because he had done nothing wrong and refused to accept the likely conditions the president would attach to one; whether he would accept bail pending appeal was a harder call.[1]

The possibility was tantalizing. He wanted to see Bucky and Chiky, of course. His early letters, then, often touched on bail prospects. "Miss Inglis wrote me that she has seen Mrs. [Kathleen McGraw] Hendrie and they will go bond for John Pancner and me. They expect that the bond will be about the same as it was before, however, I am sure that they will go more if necessary." But bail was not a central theme of his letters those first weeks.[2]

That changed with time. By mid-October, Doree—and surely others— appreciated that the appeal would "drag a couple of years or more," as the lawyers began to visit the IWW men in Leavenworth and explain the process. Two years or more would be a long time to sit. Increasingly, Doree's letters home reported the surges and stalls in efforts to get the appellate court in Chicago to set bond, to find people to post property to secure the bonds, and to prepare the paperwork. "Vanderveer was here yesterday and today," Doree reported just after the new year. "He left for Chicago at noon today. While he had not been to Chicago before coming here—he came directly from the coast—he knew fairly well how far preparation had been made in the appeal. He stated that he could not now set a definite date, but said that we can expect bond to be set anywhere from the 14th of this month to the 1st of February—everything depending upon the action of the court."

Similar letters, some excited and some discouraged, followed for weeks. Then the weeks became months. On April 2, 1919, as bond again looked imminent, he wrote, "Tell Bucky papa is coming home. And he'll bring some candy." Eleven days later, after another delay, he remained optimistic: "Tell Bucky papa hasn't forgot about his candy. Will sure have some for him. And tell him we'll have a long talk before very long."[3]

As time went on, Doree's letters began to hint at the first fissures among the Chicago group. As early as his first letter of 1919, Doree warned Chiky, "During the past week things have happened which lead me to think that we may not get bail as soon as we had expected." Doree's source was Vincent St. John. The previously stalwart ex-Wobbly was seeking new representation—alone—with his old acquaintance, Clarence Darrow.

After the war, Darrow was working to mend relations with his more radical friends and associates who had resented his support for America's role in the war. Once America joined it, Darrow had traveled the country, and even England and France, stumping for Liberty Bonds and victory. If labor and political radicals had not renounced Darrow over his war stance (many in labor had rejected him earlier, after he pled the McNamara brothers guilty in Los Angeles in 1911 and plunged from his pedestal), at least they had kept their distance. For his part, although he had supported American troops once the country entered the war, Darrow also disagreed with the government's excesses in muffling dissent.

He explained himself to Woodrow Wilson in a dexterous July 29, 1919, letter on behalf of another old friend and client, Eugene Debs. "When the United States entered the war, I gave my time and energy without reserve to support the Allies' cause. I was sorry for many men and women who were sent to jail for speaking what they believe to be the truth in opposition to the act of Congress in declaring war," Darrow wrote. "I believe that many of these were guilty of no moral wrong, but I likewise know that self-preservation is the first law of nations as well as of men and that while the war was on we could not weigh individual motives, but were bound to take all necessary measures to protect ourselves, even from those who committed no moral wrong. . . . But the war is over and it is right to examine the motives of men; and to keep in prison one who felt it his duty to disagree, after the need has passed, would not be self-defense but a punishment undeserved."[4]

Now St. John had solicited Darrow's aid and Darrow had been quick to give it; whether to atone for his perceived sins or just to restore old friendships and trust, Darrow took up the cause of several like St. John and Debs in the months and years after the war. Doree's news to Chiky on Darrow's progress in these efforts was not good, though: "Clarence Darrow went before the Appellate Court and asked for bail for St. John. He did not enter all the papers necessary, that is, he wanted to reserve the right to add some matters which will come into the general appeal. Judge Evans refused to set bail and went on to say that he did not have to set bail at all *after* conviction but went on to say that the setting of bail *after* conviction was so common that most members of the bar looked upon it as a matter of common law. This is the first time I knew that they could refuse to set bail."[5]

Doree packed much into those few sentences—perhaps more than he knew. Both St. John and Doree were fair reporters of legal information: they understood what they were told sufficiently to relay it well. Darrow had relayed faithfully to St. John his encounter with Judge Evans, it seems, including the possibly embarrassing bit about not having his bail application entirely in order. Darrow was candid with St. John, too, in explaining that bail on appeal is a matter of grace, not of right: the presumption of innocence no longer applies after conviction, so liberty while an appeal proceeds was not, and need not be, the norm. In effect, Darrow seems to have warned St. John not to expect too much. Lastly, the fact that all this was news to Doree says something about what Vanderveer, Fred Moore, Otto Christensen, and other IWW lawyers had *not* told their clients. They had left their clients with high expectations that may have been unrealistic, as the lawyers should have known. Whether that was condescension, cowardice, or lack of competence, we cannot know; we do know that it was not kind to nearly eight dozen men in prison who had expected bail pending appeal as a near certainty.

However, the IWW lawyers were able to deliver in the end, with a significant qualification. On April 2, 1919, Vanderveer and Christensen sent a telegram from Chicago announcing that bail had been granted. But those first allowed bail numbered only thirty-six, fewer than half of the Chicago defendants in prison. Those thirty-six included the big names: Ralph Chaplin, Vladimir Lossieff, Ben Fletcher, St. John, leaders and organizers of locals, and editors. Both Doree and Walter Nef made the list. Of course, it included Bill Haywood, too. But nearly sixty would be left behind, to serve out their time while the appeal went forward.

Among those granted bail, there was an important gradation. For a few, only $1,000 would be required. For others, the amount was $5,000. Doree and Nef were in the $10,000 group, which was the largest. Big Bill Haywood was apart and alone: $15,000.[6]

Now the question was how to raise the money. The IWW's General Defense Committee, of which Doree had been secretary before the trial, was already working on that task. But the task was an impossible one. The IWW had ninety-plus prisoners from the Chicago case. At that point, about five dozen were on trial in Sacramento; thirty-four faced a trial in late 1919 in Wichita; and twenty-eight awaited trial in Omaha. Those were just the federal mass indictments. Other Wobblies were in jail or facing jail all over the country in state courts, individually, or in small groups. Plus, the General Defense Committee was charged with more than just raising bail. It also had to pay the costs of defense, including fees for lawyers, investigators, and witnesses. On top of that, it was supposed to provide stipends to the wives and families of those imprisoned for more than ten weeks. Nickels and dimes from miners, longshoremen, lumberjacks, and farmhands the country over just could not meet those financial demands, especially with the union itself in understandable disarray after the government seized its leaders and most of its records.[7]

Tough decisions loomed. For the $15,000 it would take to free Haywood, all four of the $1,000 group could go home plus two in the group of eleven with $5,000 bail. Was Haywood's liberty worth more than the liberty of six? What about that of three, or two? To make matters worse, the dollar figures were cash amounts. If prisoners sought to post real property instead, the Justice Department could demand much more by dithering over market value, assurances of clear title, and location of the property. The government did all of that, in the end. And just the increased value necessary if real estate, rather than cash, was to secure the men's release meant that the General Defense Committee and individual prisoners had to find dozens of wealthy patrons with land holdings to stand as sureties. How many generous benefactors would risk their land for men whose organization proclaimed class warfare against them?

This is where women like Agnes Inglis and Kathleen McGraw Hendrie became so important to the IWW. Inglis was a sincere radical burning through a sizable inheritance at the time. She later would live on an allowance from her businessman brother. Hendrie was a wealthy socialite and suffragist, also from Detroit, who had family money and married a man with his own wealth. Men such as William Bross Lloyd, the Chicago communist living on inherited wealth and about to stand trial himself in the summer of 1920, also were very important. Maybe under the pressure of the moment, the IWW prisoners could imagine these benefactors as belonging to an acceptable third class. Neither wage earners nor employers, their patrons were liberals or radicals who had either inherited or married into their money; they were one degree removed from the exploitation by which that money was acquired. Whatever the IWW prisoners told themselves, they now were willing—eager—to accept the charity of the sympathetic wealthy. Doree wrote respectfully and even gratefully of his two sponsors, Inglis and Hendrie, to Chiky. They always were "Miss Inglis" and "Mrs. Hendrie" in his letters home, and he both expressed written thanks to them and urged Chiky to do the same.[8]

Haywood, though, does not appear to have considered the irony or possible contradiction of asking the wealthy to bail him out. His autobiography also betrays no egalitarian impulse when it came to his own post-trial release in place of other IWW members. Haywood demanded bail, for which he offered no apologies or hand-wringing, and he acknowledged only in passing the efforts of others to obtain bond for him on appeal. "The General Defense Committee was endeavoring to raise bail and many personal friends were exerting their efforts to get bond for me," he mentioned.[9]

The process of securing bail bonds and gaining release became arduous. In part, that was just the necessary shuffle of papers: surety bonds from the people posting property around the country had to be prepared and signed, probably with some proof of fair market value and a title report. Those had to go to Chicago for approval by the prosecutors before submission to the clerk of the appellate court. The government lawyers engaged in foot-dragging, too. But it was clear who was first in line to get out. "As you see, I'm still here and don't know how much longer I'll have to stay here," Doree wrote home on April 13. "No one has been released as yet but I expect to see Haywood and [Joseph J.] Gordon and possibly some more out in the next two or three days." That did not happen, in part because the bond amounts went up once the government understood that the prisoners intended to post real property, not cash. For Doree, an additional $15,000 in property would be required as of May 11.

On June 9, Doree reported again: the amounts and sureties were settled. But the papers had to be revised and resubmitted. One of his sureties had signed and dated her undertaking after Doree had signed, and either the court or the prosecutors were insisting that the prisoner sign the form last. The papers had to circulate anew from Detroit to Leavenworth to Chicago, there to be examined closely again. Two weeks later, Doree wrote Chiky that all was in order, and he thought he would be out in a week, on June 30. "Tell Bucky that papa is coming home this time. Bye, bye, for my last letter is written."[10]

And so it was. On or shortly after June 30, 1919, Doree left Leavenworth. He rejoined Chiky and Bucky, now staying with family in Oregon. Nef walked out through the gates at about the same time. Haywood's delay was greater in the end. He left on July 28.

In all, about one-third of the Chicago defendants enjoyed release on bond during the appeal. Those with the shortest sentences finished their time that summer. But some just stayed while the appeal proceeded at a crawl. For practical purposes, the IWW prisoners had divided into tiers, with the top tier favored. Within that group, money and property had gone disproportionately to serve Haywood at the very top and those just below him. In the end, too, the key had been property from the rich, not pennies from the ranks.

Yet a final distinction matters. Of the "many personal friends" who "finally secured" Haywood's release on property bonds that totaled much more than the $15,000 cash figure, not all were wealthy. Some had only modest means and posted property worth $5,000 or less only because they believed in Haywood's cause. A year and a half later, that would become a very sobering fact.

24

The Other Three

Meanwhile, the Chicago case had been only the first and largest of the Justice Department's conspiracy indictments against the IWW. The other three cases remained, in Sacramento, Wichita, and Omaha. After his success in Chicago, the Justice Department asked Frank Nebeker to lead the prosecution in those cases, too. He was coy initially and agreed to do it only "if his private practice [permitted]." In fact, Nebeker eventually declined a role in the three other cases, and indeed, seems to have left the prosecution team abruptly. Claude Porter cabled Attorney General Gregory, perhaps self-servingly, on September 3, 1918: "Am surprised at Nebeker's resignation he assured me Saturday before leaving Chicago that he would look after appeal of Chicago case but in any event I will see that the government's interests are fully protected there and elsewhere in IWW cases."[1]

The sudden departure did not diminish Nebeker's fortunes, though. By mid-July 1919 Nebeker had accepted a position as assistant attorney general in charge of the Public Lands Division of the U.S. Department of Justice. He left Salt Lake City for Washington after a dinner in his honor at the Hotel Utah, during which the governor, the mayor of Salt Lake City, and other dignitaries paid him tribute.[2]

Of the three lesser indictments, the Sacramento case was second in size and timing to Chicago: in February 1918, an additional fifty-five people were indicted on conspiracy counts copied from Chicago. In Wichita, another thirty-four were charged in four conspiracies also essentially identical to the Chicago charges, and one entirely new charge concerning distribution of food and fuel. The Omaha group was last but not smallest, with fifty-one alleged conspirators (although not all were arrested).[3]

The additional Sacramento defendants were fifty-four men and one woman, Theodora Pollok. She had been arrested when she appeared at the Sacramento police station to arrange bail for some of the others. Pollok was from a prominent Baltimore family but had gone west to ease her asthma and tuberculosis. She had become engaged in the defense of Tom Mooney and Warren Billings, charged and convicted for a Preparedness Day bombing in San Francisco in 1916. Pollok was well educated and well connected. Although her family convinced President Wilson, Labor Secretary William Wilson, and Attorney General Thomas Gregory, among other government officials, that she should not have faced charges, they did not secure her release. In a show of the practical autonomy that local federal prosecutors still retained then, U.S. District Attorney John W. Preston reasoned that, because the evidence against her was no worse than against the other fifty-four, dismissing Pollok's charges would undermine the entire case. "Better," Preston's reasoning went, "[to] try and convict an innocent woman than weaken the case against fifty-four dangerous Wobblies." Sir William Blackstone's famous ratio—"The law holds that it is better that ten guilty persons escape than that one innocent suffer"—evidently left Preston unmoved.[4]

Unlike Pollok, most of the Sacramento defendants had been scooped up in the September and November IWW office searches. But they had not been targets of those raids: those who had been targets were transferred to Chicago for the first case. In a sense, those held in Sacramento were defendants of convenience. Once they had been arrested, the government had the opportunity to hold them before eventually deciding on charges. This was not a process of identifying, investigating, indicting, and then arresting. It was mostly the opposite: the accused had been arrested, then identified, investigated, and indicted. In the case of some, they had been indicted and only then investigated. Pollok was only the most extreme example. She simply had walked into a police station, hoping to arrange bail for others, and had been arrested for that and nothing else. Once in custody, she became easy to include in loose conspiracy charges because of her radical sympathies. After all, who but a fellow believer would have sought to post bail for the others?[5]

By the time the Sacramento case came to trial in December 1918, after a calculated delay to accommodate the Chicago trial in the hope of securing more evidence against the Sacramento group, only forty-six defendants remained. The jail conditions had been miserable. Four had died there of influenza. A fifth may have died before trial. At least three were released on bail before trial for other reasons and their trials postponed indefinitely.

The Justice Department's case mimicked the Chicago trial, both in its charges and in the manner of proof. The federal judge, Frank H. Rudkin, allowed letters, pamphlets, and testimony dating back to the IWW's founding in 1905 as proof of conspiracies that could not have been illegal until June 1917. Acknowledging the obvious—that this evidence was "rather remote"—still Judge Rudkin allowed the jury to hear it "for what it was worth." The government had no more direct evidence of the actual conspiracies charged in the indictment than it had mustered in Chicago.

But, in addition to the distinction between defendants by design (Chicago) and defendants by convenience (Sacramento), there was one other stark difference between the Chicago and Sacramento trials. In Chicago, the defendants had believed that evidence, or its absence, would matter. They had shown considerable faith in the institutions of the very government and class structure they opposed. They had been full and earnest participants in the trial, cooperating with their lawyers and contesting the government's case, contending all the while that the government did not make out the case it alleged under the rules that federal courts were to apply. They gave the system the benefit of the doubt that it was proceeding on the presumption of innocence, or at least proceeding in good faith. After the bitter experience in Chicago, the Sacramento defendants had no such illusions. Vanderveer had been on hand early in Sacramento, but in the end he had no active role.[6]

The Sacramento group opted in the main for a silent defense rather than a lawyerly one. Indeed, almost all refused to defend themselves: they sought and accepted no lawyer, cross-examined no witnesses, objected to no evidence, made no arguments, and declined to testify themselves. They thought a fair trial impossible. Only Theodora Pollok and two little-known IWW members, A. L. Fox and Basil Safores, took a different view. They engaged counsel and sought a severance from the silent others. When Judge Rudkin denied them a separate trial, they contested the government case. They and their lawyers played their parts.

Not that it moved the jury. After more than one month of trial, the Sacramento jurors did as their Chicago peers had done: in under one hour of deliberations, they convicted all forty-six of everything. Only then did the Wobblies break their silence. After the jurors declared them guilty, they burst defiantly into "Solidarity Forever," the anthem that Ralph

Chaplin had written and set to the tune of "The Battle Hymn of the Republic" (which also had been the tune of "John Brown's Body").

Although the jury convicted Pollok and the pair, too, at sentencing those three gained something by having participated cooperatively in the theater of justice. The day after the verdicts, Rudkin sentenced the other forty-three to prison terms of one to ten years. Those sentences came after several of them, silent no more, "made impassioned speeches to the Court." For five months, he postponed sentencing the remaining three who had defended themselves. When he finally sentenced Pollok and the two men in June 1919, Rudkin imposed a $100 fine on Pollok, considering her poor health, and two-month jail terms on the other two. Her class and probably her sex helped some, but only at sentencing; they had not spared her the ordeal of trial.

The forty-three men with prison sentences arrived in Leavenworth on January 25 after their own train ride. Ed Doree wrote his wife, "They looked bad, most of them." For his part, no longer a believer in cooperating with the court system after his conviction, Bill Haywood wrote, "The Silent Defense of the Sacramento group stands as a record, a scathing denunciation not to be expressed by words, of judicial procedure."[7]

The Wichita case was next up. This group, also defendants of convenience, sought defense counsel from the usual IWW roster. There, the IWW lawyers—Fred Moore and Caroline Lowe, both Chicago trial veterans—had achieved some success in pretrial motions. Twice the judge had quashed the indictments. But each time the government returned to the grand jury. In Leavenworth, the imprisoned Wobblies passed along persistent rumors that the government would drop the case.[8]

The government did not. Its third indictment, repeating the four conspiracies from the Chicago case and adding a fifth count concerning food and fuel, stood. Trial began in Kansas City, not in Wichita, on December 1, 1919. A local lawyer and Democratic Party loyalist, Samuel Barker Amidon (1863–1926), served as special prosecutor. On December 18, the jury convicted all twenty-seven defendants who remained. One was spared prison; the other twenty-six got terms spanning from one to nine years. Amidon received a nice letter from the new attorney general, A. Mitchell Palmer, for his efforts. "The verdict was not only a great victory for law and order, which will have a splendid effect upon the country," Palmer assured him, "but was a great victory for you personally."[9]

That left only Omaha. The fifty-one indicted there were the least significant group, mere members of the IWW. Many had been arrested as a group in November 1917, when they arrived in Omaha for a special convention of the Agricultural Workers branch of the IWW. These indisputably were mere defendants of convenience: arrivals in town on IWW business, they immediately were assumed no good and worthy of arrest. An indictment eventually would parrot what had worked in Chicago and Sacramento. But even before the war ended, the government began to lose interest in this last case. The U.S. district attorney for Nebraska, Thomas Stinson Allen (1865–1945), married to William Jennings Bryan's sister, particularly had little appetite for a trial. In June 1918, he offered the jailed defendants a deal: plead guilty in exchange for a sentence of time served. They refused. Finally, in April 1919, after holding the men almost a year and a half in jail, the government dismissed the indictment with no fanfare. The men went free. With that, the federal legal campaign against the IWW was over—in the trial courts.[10]

And it really was over there. The government made no attempt to resurrect the Chicago case against Elizabeth Gurley Flynn, Carlo Tresca, Joseph Ettor, or Arturo Giovannitti. By splitting from the other defendants and seeking a separate trial successfully, they won altogether. Procedural maneuvering prevailed.

The imprecision of the government's handling of the three cases after Chicago, and to some extent its handling of Chicago itself, is interesting. The drop-off from arrest to indictment to trial was not trivial: more were arrested than indicted; more indicted than ever tried. Indeed, some of the Chicago defendants, like Doree, were indicted again in one or more of the other three cases. Doree, for example, was named in the Wichita indictment. Yet, even though he was in Kansas in prison already, the government made no effort to procure him for trial. Deaths in jail and poor health, again related to jail conditions, explained some of the drop-off, but not all of it. The government seemed content to indict 166 in Chicago but try only 112 at the outset, or to indict 55 in Sacramento but try only 46. This suggests that the goal was bigger than punishing crimes committed. The goal was suppressing the IWW itself: an organization that the government perceived as a threat to the entire social order.[11]

Two appeals remained, Chicago and Wichita. Because most of the Sacramento defendants had chosen a silent defense, they had preserved no arguments for appellate review; they appealed, but with only the indictment for the appellate court to review, the appeal was pointless. It failed entirely.

Even with a good appellate record, the Wichita appeal succeeded only in part. In 1920, the U.S. Circuit Court of Appeals for the Eighth Circuit reversed the convictions on Count 1 but left the other counts of conviction in place. This was not a hollow victory for many, as removal of the longer sentence on Count 1 meant that twenty of the men in prison went free immediately.[12]

In all, though, well more than twelve dozen IWW men had gone to prison for a year or more in the three federal conspiracy trials. Many in Omaha had languished in jail awaiting a trial that never happened. The intellectual, emotional, and practical leaders of the One Big Union were imprisoned or free on bond pending appeal, one and all. This new federal strategy, legal rather than quasi-military, national and coordinated rather than local and accidental, mostly had worked. The IWW leaders and thousands of lesser-known men and women had made the union strong, arguably. The union in turn had made them stronger than they could have been individually. But the coordinated efforts of the federal government—with the Justice Department in the lead—had proven stronger still.

25

The Seventh Circuit

At the time, though, the Chicago appeal remained. That case towered over the others, both in the number of convicted defendants and in potential consequences to the government and to the future of the IWW. With most of the top IWW leaders out on bail at the end of July 1919, the defense lawyers could turn their attention exclusively to the appeal briefs.

The appeal would go to the federal court of appeals that also sat in Chicago, upstairs from Landis's courtroom. Then and now, federal courts of appeals covered regions of the country, numbered roughly from east to west (with some doubling back, as large circuits later split because of caseload growth). The U.S. Circuit Court of Appeals for the Seventh Circuit covered Indiana, Illinois, and Chicago. In 1948, Congress dropped the word "Circuit" from the appellate courts' names, so each became simply the U.S. Court of Appeals for the such-and-such circuit. Each federal court of appeals had at least three judgeships, and they heard appeals in panels of three. Because dissents were and are possible, although not common, a majority of 2–1 could decide a case.[1]

An appeal began with the losing party giving notice of plans to appeal. After the clerk of the trial court had assembled the record and mailed it to the Circuit Court of Appeals, the losing party would file a written argument, or brief. The appellant's brief would include a statement of relevant facts, a list of errors alleged, and an argument explaining how the trial court erred, citing prior cases the appellant thought important.

The winning party below then would file a responsive brief. That brief might agree or disagree with the appellants' factual statement, and might

211

add omitted facts that the respondent thought important. It would include an argument on the alleged errors, not necessarily framed or ordered in the same way as in the appellant's brief. That counterargument usually would defend the rulings of the trial court below, although in rare instances the respondent (or appellee) might concede some error.

The appellant then could reply, although he need not. Because it bears the burden of persuasion in the trial court, the government gets the first and last word in a criminal trial. For the same reason, with the burden of persuasion flipped on most issues, the appellant—typically, the criminal defendant—gets the first and last word on appeal. In other words, on appeal the presumption of innocence is gone and the defendant now is presumed guilty, or at least the trial court's judgment is presumed correct. American law favors the *status quo ante* in almost every setting, and certainly on appeal.

Finally, after briefing was completed, a Circuit Court of Appeals then typically scheduled oral argument. At oral argument, the panel of three appellate judges allowed the contending sides their say, often asking questions to clarify the record or to sharpen an issue appealed. Again, the appellant's lawyer argued first and last in rebuttal, with argument by the respondent or appellee's lawyer sandwiched in between. The appellate court then might rule from the bench or, more commonly, take the case "under advisement" for a written decision weeks or months later. That was the ordinary appellate process then. In broad strokes, it remains largely unchanged now.

Little about this appeal would be ordinary, though. There were, after all, more than ninety defendants seeking appellate review on writ of error, the specific mode at that time. Only the defendants who had avoided prison and no longer were serving a sentence did not appeal.

The filings were massive. A commercially printed and bound Assignment of Errors, just a list of alleged errors available for review, ran more than 1,008 pages. The opening defense brief was printed and bound in three volumes that together came to 650 pages, without indexes. By comparison, the government's opening brief was concise: printed and bound, it came in at 275 pages, again before appendices and indexes.

For the defense, Otto Christensen now took the lead role on appeal, with George Vanderveer the only other lawyer appearing officially in the Seventh Circuit. Here, the government outdid the defense, as it often does. Six lawyers appeared for the government. Charles F. Clyne, the hapless local U.S. district attorney in Chicago, got the place of honor at the top of the list. Frank Nebeker, now an assistant attorney general in

Washington, DC, appeared third in the list. Claude Porter was listed fourth as a "special assistant attorney general"; his was an appointment of convenience so that he could carry on with the case. Two more special assistants attorney general rounded out the roster. Probably the bottom man, Oliver Pagan, actually did most of the work drafting the brief. A valued lawyer at the main office of the Justice Department, he had been a principal researcher and drafter throughout the Chicago case.

The usual three briefs would not suffice here. After the reply brief from the plaintiffs in error that would have closed usual briefing, the government filed a surreply brief, seemingly without seeking leave of the court of appeals. We "are taking the liberty of presenting a further analysis of the decisions applicable to the facts now before this court," the government lawyers huffed. They did that in 121 pages. Predictably, this drew a supplemental reply brief from Christensen and Vanderveer. "The following pages have been very hastily thrown together," they explained with excessive candor, "in an effort to place our reply to counsel's new brief in the court's hands before the argument is concluded." This brief, the fifth altogether and the third for the defense, was 45 pages. Apparently unwilling to give the IWW defendants the final word that was their right on appeal, the government filed a sixth brief *after* the oral argument. That one came in at 206 pages, printed and bound again.[2]

Of course, this was only the beginning of the reading material for the three judges on the Seventh Circuit who would hear the appeal. In theory, the court also had to review 693 government exhibits (most of them multipage letters), more than 12,375 pages of trial transcript, and 181 pages of sentencing transcript.[3]

Christensen and Vanderveer distilled—if that is the right word—the 1,008 pages of assigned errors into twenty-eight principal issues for review, many with multiple subparts. Today, conventional wisdom holds, with good reason, that this is too many: cluttering a brief with many weak arguments obscures one or two good ones and invites judicial suspicion that all is bluster. Appellate judges, who may consider themselves very busy, prefer that winning arguments come to them by special delivery and unwrapped, rather than in a buried package at the end of a long scavenger hunt.

Indeed, some of the IWW arguments were tedious and unimportant. For example, hearsay testimony that one hundred unnamed men in a crowd of two hundred had IWW cards, or that unnamed people were prosecuted in Duluth, Minnesota, for failing to register for the draft, hardly could have contributed seriously to mistaken convictions here. That sort of error also did not suggest much risk to the judicial system's reliable operation in future cases. It was very unlikely to be the reason for setting aside a four-month trial, even if it was one more in a list of cumulative errors: this straw probably would not have broken any camel's back. A complaint that the judge refused a jury instruction telling the jury to disregard any letter or newspaper article in evidence unless a defendant's signature on it was proven independently also was, in context, lighter than fluff.[4]

But other claimed errors were serious. The stronger arguments near the top of the list addressed the government's use (both in the grand jury and at trial) of the documents seized on September 5, 1917, without probable cause, and also the indictment's failure in the four remaining conspiracy counts to make out a crime, or at least to allege separate crimes. In other words, how could the government charge and convict the defendants with documents it obtained and held only by violating the Fourth Amendment? And what had the defendants done wrong? Specifically, what crimes against the federal government had they agreed to commit, simply by opposing a war vociferously and crudely? Had they not a right under the First Amendment to speak their minds in public, even if intemperately? Even if this sort of inflammatory talk was a crime, did the proof establish that four separate criminal agreements really were involved, or was the government instead violating the Fifth Amendment's double jeopardy clause by charging the same criminal agreement four times over? All of these were fair and important questions. Vanderveer had done lawyerly work, too, in preserving them for appellate consideration by making, and never dropping, these arguments to Judge Landis in the first trial. He had waived nothing here.

What the defense appeal omitted starkly, however, was the most basic consideration in a criminal appeal: whether the evidence at trial was inadequate to support any reasonable jury's conclusion that the government had proven its charges beyond a reasonable doubt. This argument, called insufficiency of the evidence, usually is a weak one. Whatever the other reasons to question a conviction, more often than not the government offers enough evidence to warrant conviction if a jury chooses to believe it. But at the same time, it is an appellate lawyer's first consideration because if the government's evidence was too scant, the defendant goes free altogether. The government took its shot and missed; the guaranty against double jeopardy bars a second trial. Most other errors, like testimony that a jury should not have heard because of some rule of evidence or an improper jury instruction, do not bar retrial: they are flaws in the process, not fundamental failures of the government's case. The defendant may be due a new trial (one not skewed by the unfair mistake) but not necessarily freedom.

Here, to a fair eye, the evidence was sufficient to support a jury's decision to convict some of the nearly eight dozen men who appealed (assuming that the indictment charged crimes at all). But it was insufficient to allow any reasonable group of jurors to conclude beyond a reasonable doubt that many of the defendants had committed the charged crimes. As to a number of them, there had been no damning letters or speeches—not after Congress had declared war, and not even after Congress had passed the very law, the Espionage Act, that they allegedly violated. At most, some of the men had opposed a war that the United States had not yet entered, or had made statements that might offend only a law not yet enacted. Some did even less than that. As to some, the government's evidence proved no more than their membership in the IWW—an organization that, the government had contended repeatedly, was not on trial.

Where, then, was the defense's argument that the evidence against John M. Foss was insufficient to support a conviction? He had written one letter in August 1917 "regretting Frank Little's death" and added, "Hope we can prevent repetition and protect I.W.W. members." He also had favored "a general strike, if such a thing is possible, against [the] employing class." Or where was the defense's argument for Joe McCarty, who had written nothing on the war or conscription and had said nothing, and whom the government's evidence had not connected to any strike? What about V. V. O'Hare, Charles McWhirt, James Phillips, and many more whom the government's case had left similarly untouched? How about Clyde Hough? He had gone to jail on unrelated charges before the Espionage Act passed, had remained there continuously, and had done nothing in jail. Yet he, too, had been convicted and sentenced.[5]

What the defense offered instead was a closing summary in broadest terms. It was lofty rhetoric but wholly unspecific; the court could not have known for whom it was a winning argument, and for whom not. "There are many of the defendants against whom this evidence of membership, or rather the stipulation entered into at the beginning of the trial, was the only evidence which the Government could produce," the defense wrote. "In many of their cases, there is not a syllable of evidence to show that they said or wrote a word or committed a single act of any kind after the 6th of April, 1917. There is no evidence even to show where they were after that date. The only proof that they were even alive after that date is that they were present in court and on trial."6

But who were these men specifically? The defense lawyers did not say.

Answers as to why Vanderveer and Christensen failed to proceed man by man, arguing that the evidence was insufficient at least as to some—and why they never tendered their clients as individuals to the Seventh Circuit at all—must remain speculative. Still, the realities of a mass trial, and then a mass appeal of ninety-plus men, guide that speculation. The briefs and trial record already were very long. The number of issues on appeal exceeded two dozen. A discussion of the specific evidence against each of the men would have added significantly to the whole. With that many defendants, it might have appeared to mire the appeal in minutiae. From the perspective of the man against whom the evidence was nil, though, the failure to argue his case individually risked disastrous injustice.

The tension between group interests and individual interests was inherent in the mass representation that the defense lawyers undertook. Only two lawyers represented all ninety-plus men and owed the same moral duty to each: undivided loyalty. Yet both lawyers were hired by, and had a history with, the IWW as an organization. Vanderveer's commitment to the organization seemed mercenary at moments, but less so over time. Christensen was committed not just to the organization but also to its causes, as a matter of principle. Both attorneys might have worried that arguing insufficiency of the case specifically against Defendant A or B tacitly would concede sufficiency against Defendant C or D. Then again, making the opposite tactical choice would mean favoring the group as an undivided whole, thereby sacrificing the individual interests of A and B. Vanderveer and Christensen unavoidably had divided loyalties on appeal, as at trial.

But the practical choice for these pauper workmen, the forgotten farmhands, lumberjacks, and factory laborers swept up in the Chicago indictment, was to accept these two lawyers or have no lawyer at all. Ethical niceties aside, they had no other option.

For its part, the government made the same defense as to the seized documents that it had in the trial court. The wrong people had gone to the wrong court to complain at the wrong time: too bad, the Fourth Amendment violations by the government did not matter. The organization, not the individuals who wrote the letters, owned the seized correspondence. And the organization should have gone to the federal courts in the dozens of districts in which the searches occurred (and the search warrants were issued), not waited to object in the court in which the government actually made use of its unconstitutional booty. With dripping disdain, the government closed that argument, "We could feel more sympathy for the position of the plaintiffs in error if it concerned the merits of their case. Their claim, however, amounts simply to an attempt to escape the legal consequences of criminal activities because some of the evidence which admittedly showed their guilt was obtained by means which they resent. No question of the competency or probative force of the evidence is here raised." Then, in an argument that the Justice Department has repeated many times since, the prosecutors moaned, "The plaintiffs in error are relying on a *further* extension of a much criticized extension of the application of the Fourth Amendment, in a case where justice both to the people and to those charged with crime demands no further extension."[7]

The government did not defend the search warrants, in other words. Instead, it played offense, attacking the defendants as the greater evil. Government violations of the nation's fundamental law, its basic limits on the federal government's powers, the Constitution, were but a cause of misplaced resentment.

As to the challenges to the indictment, the government countered that the indictment did sketch out crimes, by the loose notice requirements to which federal courts hold a charging document. And words preceding the declaration of war or passage of the Espionage Act were admissible to show ongoing intentions after that act took effect; the jury properly could infer continuing intention to agree on criminal objectives. The government's principal brief also outlined basic evidence against the defendants.

There is no record of the oral argument. Judges Francis E. Baker, Samuel Alschuler, and George T. Page heard the case. At least one of the three judges must have expressed concern about the adequacy of the evidence against individual defendants, in spite of the defense omission. Quite possibly that judicial concern caught both sides off guard, and perhaps the government lawyers left worried. The government's final written word, its second supplemental brief, again came after oral argument and devoted itself almost entirely to addressing the adequacy of the case against specific defendants by name. Only a discussion at oral argument reasonably explains that post-argument submission.

By that time, the government was tiring of the suggestion that it should prove everyone guilty individually, rather than in gross. There were so many, after all. It bridled, "We have undertaken to set forth briefly an outline of the activities of the individual plaintiffs in error and the participation of each in the criminal conspiracies which menaced the country in the early months of the war. To have accomplished this in an exhaustive manner would have meant a task beyond the limitations of time under which the writers of this supplemental brief are laboring."[8]

The defense, incidentally, did not rebut that final government brief. Possibly Vanderveer and Christensen saw no need. The government could not, after all, point to more than it had offered at trial. As to many of the convicted, the trial evidence consisted of little or nothing more than IWW membership, if not in summer 1917 then earlier.

On October 5, 1920, the Seventh Circuit issued its written decision. Judge Baker, the longest tenured on the panel, wrote for the court. His decision was dry, even desiccated, and dispassionate in tone, as was the judicial style of the day. But by the second paragraph of the decision, Baker was offering a limp renunciation of responsibility. "Before proceeding further, we think it right to emphasize the fact that a review by an appellate tribunal is not a requirement in affording a defendant the due process of law that is secured to him by the Constitution," he warned. "In England writs of error in criminal cases are of comparatively recent origin. In our country, though writs of error with certain limitations have been allowed from the beginning, the grant has been of grace or expediency, not of constitutional demand." This all was true, in the abstract. Yet if these working-class malcontents had no claim to justice or even to law, if they had a claim only to governmental grace, it was over. In law, rhetoric both forecasts and casts reality.

But rhetorically again, the court of appeals would make no other show of shirking. Substantively, the court began by striking down the convictions on Count 1. It was a more general charge under an older statute of conspiring to use force in hindering execution of the newer Selective Service and Espionage Acts. Counts 3 and 4 alleged conspiracies specifically to violate those new acts. Congress could not have meant double punishment under both the older and the newer provisions, the court concluded. Moreover, interfering with private manufacturers might have violated local laws, but it was not interference with government officials, and only that was a federal concern. For both reasons, Count 1 would be set aside.

Count 2 would fall for similar reasons. Strikes or sabotage against private producers, who could have been anyone and included people and companies outside the United States, were not within compass of a statute that punished conspiracies to injure American citizens in exercise of rights or privileges that United States law secured. All three "industrial counts" of the indictment now were gone. Landis had dismissed Count 5 before giving the case to the jury, and the court of appeals had dispatched Counts 1 and 2.

The Seventh Circuit's decision striking down the convictions on the first two counts was no clearer and no more persuasive than was the indictment that laid those counts in the first place. Still, the court appeared to the casual or unschooled observer to extend some grace to the defendants.

That left the "war counts," Counts 3 and 4. With any reasonable plea for mere grace now answered, the court could turn to those. That meant confronting the seized documents, for they supplied the basis of both the indictment on those counts and the convictions. The court conceded squarely, that "The affidavits, on which the search warrants issued, failed to describe the property to be taken except by reference to its general character, and failed to state any facts from which the magistrates could determine the existence of probable cause." In other words, the seizures under those warrants violated the Fourth Amendment.

But the court then went on to accept entirely the government's argument. "If the proper parties had made prompt application, it may be assumed that they would have obtained orders quashing the writs and restoring the property." The "proper parties" did not do that, though. "Nothing of the sort occurred. Government attorneys, without objection or hindrance, used the property as evidence before the grand jury." By the time of the motion to return the property and quash the indictment, "there was sufficient basis of facts to justify the trial judge in finding that there was probable cause to believe that the property . . . had been used in the commission of the felonies described in counts 3 and 4." Besides, the individual defendants did not own or possess the documents at that point: the IWW did. "Each defendant moved for the return of property that had never been in his possession and was not taken from his person or home or place of business." In other words, the government had not violated the defendants' Fourth Amendment rights; it had violated the organization's. Moreover, "[the] Defendants were indicted as individuals, not as members of the I.W.W. That organization was not on trial."[9]

This was a fine example of a judicial tradition: a form of dishonesty by fantasy. In general, that describes an abuse of hindsight, by which judges intent upon a preconceived outcome either omit facts or conjure up actions that litigants theoretically could have or should have taken that might have produced a better outcome—while in truth, circumstances of poverty, unawareness, lack of education, geography, or some other limitation made those actions improbable or impossible at the time. Dishonesty by fantasy is a deliberate form of counterfactual make-believe in service of justifying a preferred judicial outcome.

Here, by remaining silent on the facts of who the convicted men were, what their lives had been, and what the objective situation was in the summer and early autumn of 1917, the court opened space to imagine something very different about these men and the immediate past, and then to erect that construct in place of truth. The omission of facts, the silence, was itself a bit of judicial casuistry that could be presented as parsimony of factual statement. Judicial writing often distills complicated facts to the essentials, so that the application of legal principles might be clear and compelling to the discerning reader. To the lazy reader, this silence could be palmed off as that.

But honest parsimony is very different from the omission of pertinent fact and substitution of a false fantasy of the past in its place. The Seventh Circuit retrospectively drew up imaginary men who, after four dozen raids across the country, would have had the mental, physical, and financial resources to determine whose letters had been in which office's correspondence files, to hire counsel in dozens of cities, and to seek immediate redress of unlawful searches. It fantasized that every federal judge who issued a groundless warrant would have appreciated, recanted, and remedied his legal mistake. It conjured that these defendants could have taken action to hinder the grand jury's use of their correspondence—and been viewed by a Chicago federal judge as engaging righteously in that "objection and hindrance." And it engaged in a fantasy that this group, some of whom were in jail already on September 5, could have accomplished all that in the twenty-three days between the raids and the grand jury's return of the indictment. It posited, in short, not the actual eight dozen scruffy and impoverished miners and day laborers now languishing in Leavenworth. It fantasized instead an assemblage of faceless Rockefellers, Fords, and Morgans with their freedom, money, and lines of lawyers and subordinates at their beckoning. The unstated premise of that fantasy was that the rich might vindicate their constitutional rights, but others might not. Of course, the moneyed were unlikely ever to find themselves in a situation like the IWW members faced in September 1917.

The Seventh Circuit did not invent dishonesty by fantasy in the IWW case and could not claim a monopoly on it. It was common before and is common now. For example, courts frequently encounter cases in which the criminal accused claims that the police wrongly ignored his request for counsel before questioning, or in fact restarted questioning after a short lapse. In such cases, the accused almost invariably has made a halting request for a lawyer, in some unpolished vernacular, and the police usually have calculated that they could carry on undeterred, thanks to the accused's poor word choice or grammar; or they have paused, but soon slyly provoked the accused to start talking about the allegations anew. Courts often omit the full context of the accused's circumstances—they are at least silent on the hard reality—and then offer a fantasy of what an articulate, self-possessed, and poised person might have said, or pretend that police officers did not understand full well what the accused actually meant. Courts not uncommonly posit winning facts or legal arguments that an untutored jailhouse litigant, acting without a lawyer, could have or should have discovered earlier—without physical liberty, without money, without legal training—but now are unavailable to him. In civil cases challenging a consumer contract, courts may omit the reality in which the contract was struck and substitute instead a fantastic pair of thoughtful bargaining parties, each with about equal social position, money, and negotiating leverage.

The IWW decision was not judicial imagination of a better present or future, inspired by the best of the nation's values or the most convincing reasoning found in prior cases. Dishonesty of the Seventh Circuit's sort was retrospective imagination, substituting without constraint the unreal for the real in service of a predetermined outcome—the reasons for which must remain unstated if the people the judges serve are to believe in the legitimacy of the judgment. A judge who decides a case well relies upon the decency and discernment, the integrity, of his or her fellow citizens. The judge who engages in dishonesty by fantasy counts upon their credulity or complicity.[10]

If this kind of dishonesty by fantasy has an analog in the literary aspect of judging, the closest example may be the view of Justice Benjamin N. Cardozo (1870–1938) that as a judge, one can "permit oneself, and that quite advisedly and deliberately, a certain margin of misstatement" of the facts in a case. But Cardozo did not endorse wholesale, fanciful reconstitution of the past and substitution of a spun unreality into a large void left by silence on fact. Cardozo worked, however imperfectly, for a principled pragmatism in law. Dishonesty by fantasy instead works for subjection of principle to preference—and typically for subjection of the weak to the strong.[11]

Through factual silence, then, and an ensuing act of dishonesty by fantasy, the Seventh Circuit blinked away the unconstitutional seizure, retention, and use of truckloads of words, thoughts, and musings of men resisting the power of government and capital. As to the war counts, the government would have the benefit of the very material the court conceded the government had no right to seize.

The Seventh Circuit was not just silent about facts. It also was silent about law. More than five years earlier, in *Weeks v. United States*, the U.S. Supreme Court had reversed a federal conviction in which the trial judge had refused a defendant's motion for return of property taken from his house without a warrant, in violation of the Fourth Amendment. The trial court had allowed that property to be used at trial against him, again over his objection. The Supreme Court reversed the conviction, holding that property seized in violation of the Fourth Amendment rights of the defendant could not be used as evidence over his objection.

In *Weeks*, the disputed evidence clearly belonged to the man on trial: it had come from his house. The U.S. marshal had seized it without any warrant at all, not just with invalid warrants, as the government had used here. And the seizure had occurred in the same judicial district as the trial.

But the Supreme Court's opinion clearly rested not just on the trial court's refusal to order return of all property before trial: it rested also on the decision to allow the district attorney to use that property at trial. This was an explicit basis for the Supreme Court's holding. It was not just that the seizure and retention were unconstitutional but also that use at trial was unlawful.[12]

The only possibly meaningful legal distinction between *Weeks* and the IWW case, then, was the government's claim that the owner of the disputed property, the IWW itself, was not on trial in Chicago. In *Weeks*, the owner was on trial. Then again, the government itself claimed at trial that various defendants had signed or written the very letters that the government had seized unlawfully and now used at trial: in other words, on the government's own contention these documents *were* or had been a given defendant's. And Bill Haywood, from whose files and office many of the letters came, probably could—and did—claim a right to ownership of the correspondence he had retained.

Maybe there were other factual distinctions between *Weeks* and the IWW case that swayed the court of appeals, however subtly. *Weeks* concerned one man, employed by an express company in Kansas City, whom the government suspected of selling lottery tickets. To all appearances, the accused was an employed, middle-class clerical worker. The items actually seized were stock certificates, a bond, $75 in cash, and heirlooms. Illegal lottery ticket sales on the scale suggested by the evidence are unlikely to have agitated many federal judges of that era in comparison to the activities of the IWW. While these factual distinctions in theory should not have borne on the constitutional question, possibly they did. Judges, of course, are imperfect and human.

Whatever its actual motivations, the Seventh Circuit cited *Weeks* just once and discussed at length only the refusal to return the seized property. Because the documents belonged to the IWW, not to its individual members, "there was no error in impounding the property, overruling the motion for the return thereof, and refusing to quash the indictment." Even accepting that reasoning, the court never addressed the separate issue of use at trial. If membership in the IWW alone was enough to support conviction, as the government now insisted, and if a letter or article could prove guilt because this man, and no other, authored and signed it, the notion that this man then could object to its use against him is no great stretch.[13]

None of that mattered to the Seventh Circuit. For these IWW men, the papers were theirs for the purpose of convicting them of sprawling, vague conspiracies, but not theirs for the purpose of challenging government illegality.

When it moved on to the substance of Counts 3 and 4, the court considered some of the technical points that the defense raised, but little more. Count 3 did not impermissibly charge two crimes in one count: one conspiracy may embrace several illegal ends. A conspiracy to impede the draft could precede the act creating the draft and could persist after men registered and reported. A person could anticipate the chance to commit a crime and agree in advance to do it. And once set in motion, an agreement persists unless one withdraws from and renounces it affirmatively. The indictment gave adequate notice of the crimes charged; details were to be left for trial. While earlier words and deeds might not prove conspiratorial intent, any error was harmless because they did prove "possession and knowledge of the use of the means by which these felonies could be committed," whatever that meant. Other claims of error concerning admission of evidence or the propriety of jury instructions "have disappeared," in the court's words, because the Seventh Circuit had eliminated Counts 1 and 2. Counts 3 and 4 would stand.[14]

Unfortunately for the defendants, their longest sentences were on Count 4. All sentences were concurrent. So, the reversal of the convictions on Counts 1 and 2 would shave not a day off of their prison sentences.

Only their total fines would be reduced, by the amounts linked to the first two counts. Of course, those fines had been symbolic and practically un-collectable all along. Not one of these men had $5,000, let alone $10,000 or $20,000. They never would.

Apart from factual and legal dishonesty on the Fourth Amendment issue and *Weeks*, the Seventh Circuit's opinion included two notable areas of legal silence. The first of those two remaining legal omissions was free-dom of speech and press, the First Amendment's promises. The second was sufficiency of evidence as to individual defendants.

The court never mentioned the First Amendment. Yet this was a case in which the essence, very nearly the entirety, of the government's case was proof of speeches, editorials and other published articles, and letters that did no more than express unpopular opinions and views. Certainly with the industrial counts gone, on the war counts the appellants stood con-victed as conspiring dissenters and nothing more. Today, Americans would expect the First Amendment to bar those convictions, or at least to require explanation.

However, through World War I and for years after, the legal rules on speech and the press were different. It would be unfair to accuse the Seventh Circuit of intellectual dishonesty as to the First Amendment. Although the text of the First Amendment never has changed since 1791, for most of two centuries, American courts did not understand First Amendment free-doms as they do today. IWW members were not the only ones sent to prison in those years for opposing the draft publicly; for denouncing the war; or for condemning the president, the army, or the government. That governments could punish "utterances inimical to the public welfare, tend-ing to corrupt public morals, incite to crime, or disturb the public peace," the Supreme Court wrote as late as 1925, "is not open to question." In war-time, even less was this an open question.[15]

In a sense, the IWW case got to the federal court of appeals too early. Eventually, in the years following, the appeals of other war dissenters, radi-cals, and rabble-rousers would change the U.S. Supreme Court's view of the limits of free speech. The case of Jacob Abrams, a radical convicted of tossing revolutionary leaflets from a window, began the loosening of those limits. There, Justice Oliver Wendell Holmes reconsidered his long intoler-ance of risky speech in a famous dissent, arguing that the government had not proved the necessary "clear and present danger" of actual and serious lawbreaking. Abrams lost his 1919 appeal, but Holmes's dissent foretold the future. The words of the legal test did not change, but how the court applied it did; the court began to consider the seriousness of the risk more tolerantly. In 1931, the Supreme Court overturned its first criminal conviction on First Amendment grounds.

But that was too late for the socialists, anarchists, and antiwar activists of the Great War era—for Eugene Debs, Emma Goldman, Alexander Berkman, Benjamin Gitlow, Charlotte Whitney, Charles Schenck, Jacob Frohwerk, Jacob Abrams, Molly Steimer, and the IWW defendants. They all came before the Supreme Court began to tolerate distasteful speech at some remove from immediate incitement to crime. The law still stood in 1920 just about where Landis said it did. The right to oppose war vocally and publicly ended when the nation went to war.[16]

As to sufficiency of the evidence, whatever doubts the judges aired at oral argument evaporated before the Seventh Circuit issued its opinion. The court's will to consider individual justice flagged as the government's and the defense lawyers' had. Relying again on silence, the court gave exactly this individuality of consideration to the adequacy of the government's case: "Some of the defendants claim that there was no evidence connecting them with the conspiracy, except the fact that they were members of the I.W.W. And several, who were not members at the time, insist that there is no evidence against them at all. In each such case our finding is that there was sufficient evidence on which to submit to the jury the question whether the particular defendant was a member of the established conspiracy."[17]

That was it. After more than 1,000 pages of briefing and four months of trial, the Seventh Circuit's entire opinion filled just under 14 pages in the Federal Reporter, the main compilation of the opinions of federal courts of appeal.

In the end, then, two of the four thought-crimes stood, and all of the prison time. The Seventh Circuit had peered into the minds of more than ninety men, often with nothing but mere membership in the IWW or presence in court from which to divine the dark contours of these men's agreements. The court's final opinion hardly was more edifying or explanatory than the jury's quick, terse verdicts of guilt.

Still, the effect of the Seventh Circuit's decision was clear. Many, maybe most, of the convicted men stood thrice-removed from substantive or completed criminal conduct: first, because courts then understood the First Amendment to allow criminal convictions for speech that tended merely to disturb the peace or incite crime; second, because even if intemperate words were not intended to lead to crime, the law then presumed that a person also intended "natural and probable consequences" of his words or actions, whatever a jury might think those consequences could be; and third, because every conspirator becomes responsible for all acts of any other conspirator that further some goal of the conspiracy. They may have done and even said nothing criminal, but as conspirators they were guilty just the same. An IWW member here need not have spoken or written at all; those who did need not have intended to incite crime so long as they might have foreseen it as "natural and probable"; and the words themselves need only have tended to disturb public peace or incite crime—they did not have to present a clear and present danger of crime.

Vanderveer and Christensen dutifully would ask the U.S. Supreme Court to hear the case. But that court would duck. It need not hear any criminal case, and it decided not to hear this one. By April 11, 1921, the appeal was over.

Grace aside, law and justice had failed in larger part. Some, perhaps many, of the IWW men may not have been innocent in conscience. But the United States never proved them guilty of a crime. Their convictions stood all the same.[18]

26

Consequences

W hether guilty or innocent, perhaps the whole world could be divided into just two groups of people: those who would seek bail pending appeal and enjoy freedom while hoping that an appeal would succeed, and those who would stay in prison, advancing daily toward completion of the sentence and avoiding the heartbreak of return to prison if the appeal failed. Some think tomorrow will be better. Some figure it could be worse.

Of course, many of the Chicago defendants had no real choice. After a modest start, eventually the Seventh Circuit had set terms of release for seventy-four of the Chicago defendants. But terms of bond are one thing; raising the money or property for the cash terms is another. No one had offered to post bail for many of the seventy-four during the appeal, so they sat. The IWW's priority, and that of its lawyers, had been to secure release pending appeal for Haywood and other top leaders. People who had led locals or organized nationally, like Ed Doree and Walter Nef, just made the cut. Not everyone at their level did. About twenty-six of the defendants, maybe more, actually obtained release on appeal. The others had to sit and hope.[1]

The Seventh Circuit ruled two years, one month, and a day after the men had left the Cook County Jail for Leavenworth. Another six months had passed before the U.S. Supreme Court put an end to all hope for appellate relief, denying review on April 11, 1921. By then, the luckiest men had been free on bail for almost two years.

When an appeal ends, bail on appeal ends with it. Losing appellants must surrender again and return to finish sentences that release on bail suspended. Tearful good-byes would be followed quickly by boarding a train back to Leavenworth or, for the poorest, surrendering to the nearest U.S. marshal.

The men knew the score. Doree, Nef, and others did what they had to do. During his release, Doree mostly had been living in Philadelphia, as had Nef and Ben Fletcher. They were among the first to return to Leavenworth, reporting in on April 24 or 25 with several others who had been at liberty during the appeal. "Others came straggling in from day to day for two weeks thereafter," the *New York Times* sneered. Most were back, though, less than two weeks after the Supreme Court refused to hear their petition. Doree put up a good front for Chiky again when he wrote on April 27. He now was focused on "news of amnesty, pardons, applications for pardons, etc." Four days later, he elaborated, "I will do any honorable or decent thing to get out, sign anything necessary except a petition for pardon. I have done nothing to ask anyone's pardon for."[2]

Like Doree, all wanted to return home again, but some were unwilling to beg. Others had different views.

A new president now lived in the White House. After eight years of Democratic administration under Woodrow Wilson, the war was over and many citizens were eager to look ahead. In the November 1920 presidential election, voters could choose, on the Republican ticket, an Ohio newspaper editor and U.S. senator, Warren G. Harding, whose running mate was the taciturn governor of Massachusetts, Calvin Coolidge. Or they could pick, on the Democratic ticket, another Ohio newspaper editor and the governor of that state, James M. Cox; his running mate was a thirty-seven-year-old who had spent seven years as Wilson's assistant secretary of the navy, Franklin D. Roosevelt. They also had the option of voting for a familiar federal prisoner, Eugene Debs, who was running again on the Socialist ticket from his cell in Atlanta.

Harding promised a return to normalcy and won in a popular and electoral college landslide. Now, as Harding and others sought to put World War I behind them, members of Congress and other prominent people were murmuring, or even saying aloud in so many words, that the Wobblies were political prisoners. At a minimum, there was a growing view that, while the severe measures of 1917–18 may have been justified in wartime, they should be relaxed now that peace had returned. Congress repealed the 1918 Sedition Act in March 1921. As early as April 1919, a lawyer in the Military Intelligence Division of the Army, Captain Alexander Sidney Lanier, had published an open letter to President Wilson in *The New Republic*, urging amnesty. In 1921, more than two dozen prominent Philadelphia citizens issued a public appeal to President Harding to pardon Doree, Nef, Fletcher, and a fourth Philadelphian, John J. Walsh. A joint resolution in Congress seeking "Amnesty for Political Prisoners" had a hearing in the full House Committee on the Judiciary on March 16, 1922.[3]

Quietly, the Wilson administration had signaled as early as 1919 that it might commute the sentences of IWW prisoners who would renounce publicly the organization. Harding's administration, with his crony Harry M. Daugherty now the attorney general, continued that policy. It was a clever one. The offer of clemency would vent public pressure to moderate the harshness of wartime prosecutions. It also might create friction or out-right division within the IWW, further weakening it.

Gradually, the policy began to work. Public fissures among the IWW prisoners began to appear as a few of the men began to buy their freedom with a renunciation. Among the first to go: the nineteen-year-old Harvard student, Ray Fanning, whose separation from the others by social class was greatest. By 1919 he had seen enough. He repudiated the IWW and accepted a commutation from Wilson.

Olin B. Anderson, Charles Plahn, and C. H. Rice took parole in ex-change for a renunciation in autumn 1921. Several more got Christmas commutations from Harding in 1921, on generally similar terms. For non-citizens, the deal had a twist. They had to agree to deportation. Charles Ashleigh and John Baldazzi did that. Baldazzi agreed to "immediate" de-portation to Italy, "never to return to this country," and his commutation also rested "on the further condition that if he did return the commutation should become null and void." If he returned, "he should be immediately apprehended and returned to the penitentiary to serve the unexpired por-tion of the sentence."

In total, eighteen of twenty-eight men subject to deportation accepted the same terms. By rejecting their past in the IWW, Albert Prashner and Jack A. Law also obtained commutations on Christmas Day 1921. One month later, in January 1922, William Tanner, Frank Westerlund, and Luigi Parenti followed them. Clyde Hough, against whom there had been no evidence because he had been in jail for the duration of the charged con-spiracies, refused to purchase freedom by renouncing the One Big Union, so he remained in prison for the time.[4]

The cracks and gaps in the Chicago IWW group now were plain. A few in the working class did have something new in common with the employing class, after all: physical freedom.

Not all of the Chicago defendants who obtained a commutation paid the price of renunciation or deportation, though. President Harding released two just because the evidence that they conspired was weak—here doing by grace, at least for two men, what both Judge Landis and the Seventh Circuit had a duty under law to do, but did not. Vincent St. John, the former leader who had left the IWW to become a mine owner and employer, went home on June 23, 1922, after the attorney general acknowledged that "there appeared to be very meager evidence to sustain" the charge of conspiring to violate the Espionage Act. Three days later, Clyde Hough finally walked out of prison after the attorney general belatedly admitted that his jail stay had meant he "had no opportunity to violate" the Espionage Act.[5]

Then there were some who had a different strategy altogether for pursuing freedom. When April 25, 1921, came and the others reported back to Leavenworth as the conditions of the appeal bonds required, these did not. These nine fled the country.

Bill Haywood was first among that group, and the eight others disproportionately were from the upper echelon with the longest sentences. Five of the nine had gotten twenty-year sentences. Three more were in the ten-year group. Only one was in the five-year group. On April 29, Haywood sent May Day greetings from Moscow to the "fellow workers" he had abandoned. "I hope that hereafter when any person addresses me as comrade, he will be ready to fight for the establishment of the Soviet in America," he wrote stiffly. "I shall return to America when I have finished the work assigned to me by the International Council of Trade and Industrial Unions and when the interests of the workers demand my return." The other eight fugitives were George Andreytchine, J. H. Beyers, Fred Jaakola, Leo Laukki, Vladimir Lossieff, Herbert McCosham, Grover H. Perry, and Charles Rothfisher.[6]

The Communist Party took credit for Haywood's escape to Russia and also tried to deflect anticipated anger. "Comrade Haywood did not leave the United States of his own accord, but at the direct command of the communist Internationale, of which he is a disciplined member and whose authority he recognizes as the highest in the world," huffed the secretary of the Pan-American Agency of the Communist Internationale.[7]

The deflection did not work entirely. By May 2, the government had moved to forfeit the bonds of the eight fugitives other than Haywood. For some reason, Charles Clyne entertained the notion that Haywood might return voluntarily, so he did not at the moment seek to forfeit Big Bill's bond. But he did later, when Haywood remained in Russia.

That left the IWW with an enormous and unexpected moral obligation to repay the wealthy friends and other supporters who had posted cash and real estate to secure the bonds. The federal government now had claimed their cash and property; it was gone. The secretary of the IWW's strapped General Defense Committee estimated that it would take a year to raise the necessary $65,000 from the diminished union's remaining 25,000 members, by assessment and donation.[8]

Behind the scenes, the IWW turned to the Communist Party to make good the loss. After all, the Communists had claimed credit for Haywood's flight. Although the Communists may have promised to shoulder the loss—they did, according to the IWW General Defense Committee—by early 1922, the Communists had disclaimed the obligation. The IWW was stuck as a moral matter. The sureties, of course, were the ones who actually bore the loss for the time.

In January 1922, some within the IWW ranks spewed anger publicly. "The personalities of the few individuals who ran away amount to nothing," the New York members of the General Defense Committee fumed. "Their flight as members of the I.W.W. was a blow to the organization and the working class of the world. No purpose other than that of petty self-preservation was served and the I.W.W. is not built on that principle."[9]

Fissures now were fractures. Leaders, starting at the very top, had left the loyalists in Leavenworth. When they skipped, they cheated their benefactors and saddled working men and women across the country with debts those workers did not owe but sought to repay as a matter of conscience. Having drawn down the resources of the union, and of its members and friends, to secure the privilege of release that others did not enjoy, now to keep their own freedom these leaders in effect gave others' money and property to the very government that had persecuted the union. Haywood and the other eight did this without apology.

Writing a few years later, Haywood offered a partial explanation but no concession or contrition. He acknowledged that the IWW had raised $400,000 in total for all the trials and the appeals, and another half-million dollars for bail. This had come from working men and women in small donations, in dues assessments, and in contributions from others who either supported the IWW's work or felt sympathy for its imprisoned members. While out on appeal bond, Haywood had crisscrossed the country, given lectures, and hustled to raise defense funds. He also had found time to relax at a "summer resort" where he "enjoyed the hospitality of the caretaker of a summer home belonging to one of the Chicago capitalists."[10]

In 1920, he joined the fledgling Communist Party of the United States. Then, after the Seventh Circuit had denied the appeal but while the U.S. Supreme Court was considering whether to accept the case, Haywood recounted gauzily, "The suggestion had been made to me that I should go to Russia." He held out little hope that the Supreme Court would act favorably. "My friends thought it would be an unnecessary sacrifice for me to spend the rest of my life in prison," he wrote.

Before the Supreme Court even refused to hear the appeal, someone booked Haywood and "friends" on the SS *Oscar II*, bound for Riga, Latvia. From there, they would pass by railroad box car to the Soviet border. Haywood boarded with a false passport. His last sight of America was the Statue of Liberty as the ship steamed outbound. "Saluting the old hag with her uplifted torch, I said: 'Good-by, you've had your back turned on me too long. I am now going to the land of freedom.'" He had not a word to say about those who had posted cash, property, and homes to gain his release on appeal.[11]

Again, several of Haywood's supporters who had secured his appeal bond were moneyed. If necessary, they could take the hit if the IWW in the end could not reimburse them.

Not all of Haywood's sureties were wealthy, though. Some had stood their modest houses, all they had, for him simply because they believed that he was a hero pursuing a noble cause, a better world for all working people. Mary Marcy, an editor for the *International Socialist Review*, was one of those.

When Haywood forfeited bond, neither the Communist Party nor the IWW covered her loss. The IWW might have reimbursed her in time, but it could not do that immediately. Meanwhile, the U.S. government took Mary's home.

Mary took her life.[12]

27

Bucky

After Haywood and the eight others had exercised the privilege of fleeing and causing losses to sureties while fellow workers returned to prison, Leavenworth began to look different to Ed Doree. Departures of those who repudiated the IWW and abandonment by those who led it were taking a toll.

As Doree's daughter would explain years later, already by early summer 1921, "A bitter split developed and festered among the ranks of the Wobblies in Leavenworth. Some of the prisoners, with the support of Roger Baldwin of the [National] Civil Liberties Bureau (later, the American Civil Liberties Union), felt that release should be sought on an individual basis, since the administration was unlikely to issue a general amnesty. They felt that the success of each prisoner paved the way for another. . . . Other prisoners, by and large those under shorter sentence, were resolved that everyone should remain in prison until all were free."

Once more, some in the lowest ranks of the IWW were the great stalwarts. Doree was among those who favored pursuing individual relief without admission of wrong. But IWW headquarters favored the unified approach, and in June, headquarters cut off the weekly relief check that the IWW had been sending Chiky.[1]

Still, Doree continued to do what he could for the whole. In August 1921, for example, he contributed a lengthy affidavit that detailed the government's interference before and during trial. This aided efforts of the IWW General Defense Committee to raise funds for legal fees and expenses related not just to the Chicago trial but to all legal entanglements. Doree's affidavit explained the history of government harassment of defense efforts. First, the government denied second-class mailing privileges to GDC circulars. Next, when the IWW paid third-class postage, the Post Office simply confiscated the mailings and kept the postage. Then the government raided IWW headquarters in Chicago again in December 1917, occupying it and preventing any printing or mailing at all. Finally, in February 1918, the government began to intercept all outgoing mail from the defendants and IWW headquarters. The Post Office held it until late July 1918, when it was too late to raise significant money for the Chicago defense and too late to secure some of the defense witnesses whom letters asked to appear voluntarily.[2]

Doree went on for months, soldiering for the group while also encouraging those who sought clemency for him individually. His letters became sarcastic. "News, news, where's the news. I might say that we had a fine dinner today, that is, fine for prison fare, bacon, new potatoes and onions with cream gravy. . . . In order to keep the place full, the various federal judges donated the institution 20 new men today. In the year 1921 we now have 1921 prisoners."

Sarcasm aside, in January 1922, his resolve to repent nothing still remained. "We have some lessons on the futility of promises here," he mused. "Phin Eastman has quit the I.W.W., renounced his fellow prisoners, is willing and has promised everything, his wife is an invalid with no hope to live, Eastman is in bad health himself. He applied for executive clemency. . . . He, you might say, wore the buttons off of his vest crawling up for mercy, and, today, he got a flat turn-down. Why? Can you imagine? Because it was feared that he would be a menace to society!!! He is done with all revolution, all movements, everything, he wants only to be left to go into the restaurant business, care for his wife whom he loves very dearly. But no! he's dangerous. His promises were not worth a damn. Moral, don't promise too much."[3]

Always, his letters included wishes for Bucky and, as the boy was nearing five years old, often a few lines for him in block print. Ed was not happy, but he was getting by. The IWW even restored weekly relief to Chiky and others in early 1922. Doree did not know immediately that both Chiky and Bucky were in the hospital with influenza in early March, but he was relieved to hear that they were home by March 12. Ten days later, though, Bucky still was too sick to join in the Children's Crusade for Amnesty march in Washington, DC, with other children of imprisoned men.[4]

Then came word in early April that Bucky was desperately ill. He had developed endocarditis, an inflammation of the inner membrane and often the valves of the heart, as a sequel to the flu. Antibiotics now treat that condition, although it still can be serious. But in 1922, penicillin was six years away. Bucky was failing.

Within a day or two, the warden of Leavenworth, William I. Biddle, approved a furlough. Doree would travel 1,270 miles by train to Philadelphia to see Bucky at the hospital, accompanied by the warden's brother but not in handcuffs and afforded "every courtesy that could be shown anyone."

It was an act of humanity that would not happen today. Furloughs have disappeared almost entirely from American prisons. But in 1922, they were possible. Ed Doree was home for a few days and gone from Leavenworth for more than a week.[5]

At least one newspaper, the socialist *New York Call*, reported on April 11, 1922, that Bucky had died after Ed's return to Leavenworth. He had not. The boy recovered—for the time.[6]

But his improved health did not last. In late August, Bucky again was in the hospital. Chiky had wired that the boy was gravely ill but seemed a little better.

Ed was frantic. He wrote to the attorney general himself, begging for another furlough.

Now, his refusal to seek a pardon or commutation on terms or to separate himself from the IWW at last was over. "You or our friends [prominent Philadelphians who had been pressing for clemency for Doree, Nef, Fletcher and others] are at perfect liberty to promise, on my behalf, any actions on my part that could reasonably be ask [sic] of any honorable man," he wrote hastily to Chiky. "As for the I.W.W. I'm done!"

There was more. "I do not want to take a cowardly position, but I feel it cowardly to stand loyal to those who have turned traitor to me, and still more cowardly if I failed to stay loyal to those who have been so loyal to me. The I.W.W. crowd have turned their backs on you and me. Bucky suffering means nothing to them. Why the devil, then, should I say I'm with them when in my heart I hate them for their brutality or at best, their indifference?" He pledged himself to Chiky's judgment and that of the wealthy Philadelphians who had taken up his cause. Employers they might be, but they now stood with him.

"What wouldn't I give to be home tonight? Half my life."[7]

Perhaps he would not have to give that much. On September 1, the Joint Amnesty Committee of the American Civil Liberties Union wrote that doctors' certificates of Bucky's condition were in the hands of President

Harding's secretary, to support a pardon. Meanwhile, Warden Biddle approved a second furlough, so that Ed Doree once more could race home to Bucky's hospital bed.

The next day, September 2, some fifty-two IWW prisoners at Leavenworth wrote an open letter to the president, explaining why they had not filed individual petitions for clemency and would not. "We know we are now in prison solely for exercising the constitutional right of free speech at a time when discretion might have been the better part of altruism," they explained. "We must decline to make individual applications for clemency because . . . we were convicted, as a group, of a conspiracy of which we are all equally innocent or all equally guilty. We believe it would be a base act for us to sign individual applications and leave the Attorney General's Office to select which of our numbers should remain in prison and which should go free." Doree did not join the letter.[8]

No, that same day, beside another escort who again saw no reason to embarrass him with handcuffs on a public train, Doree rushed from the penitentiary by grace of the second furlough. He could spend the trip wondering whether a five-year-old boy, who had lived more than half his life separated from an imprisoned father, was alive or dead.[9]

28

All Rise

Doree made it back to Philadelphia in time. The little boy lay alive in his hospital bed. Indeed, he soon rallied. If not cured, still Bucky recovered enough to go home.

While Ed Doree was on the train home, another process was at work in the White House and the Department of Justice. Whatever the inside political calculations of that process, from the outside it looked very much like mercy.

On September 8, 1922, Warren G. Harding commuted Doree's sentence to end immediately. The next day brought a telegram from Leavenworth, Kansas, to Edwin F. Doree and his escort officer in Philadelphia, Pennsylvania:

PRESIDENT HAS COMMUTED YOUR SENTENCE TO TERM ALREADY
SERVED YOU NEED NOT RETURN HERE STOP MR HILL IS TO RETURN
HOME STOP ACKNOWLEDGE RECEIPT OF TELEGRAM

BIDDLE WARDEN.[1]

For Doree and his family, it was over.

As a necessary concomitant of the power to kill, imprison, fine, or otherwise punish, sovereignty always has carried the power to remit; to desist from punishment, to relent, to forgive. None but the powerful can offer clemency or bring the benefits that come with its possibility. In this sense, clemency is power.

More, clemency is unique among modern manifestations of sovereign power in one way. It remains, almost invariably, the prerogative of one

237

actor on behalf of the whole sovereign entity. In the United States, one president or one governor has the power to decree clemency. The populace sees a sovereign power—the power of grace or mercy—personified, made solitary and human. In most modern democracies, no other sovereign act is so personal: not even declaring war. Seneca never has been alone in appreciating that one person with the sovereign power to withhold punishment, or to mitigate it, can inspire as much awe in a governed people as one person with the power to inflict it.[2]

Here, the U.S. government did not commute Ed Doree's sentence. Neither did the Justice Department. The President of the United States did, in the person of Warren Gamaliel Harding.

Commutation is one of four basic acts in the category of clemency, always committed to executive branch discretion and usually to one person, the executive. The least is a reprieve, which is just a temporary delay in implementation of a sentence—often, but not always, a death sentence. A furlough from prison also can be viewed as a reprieve. Commutation of a sentence is an intermediate act. It shortens or reduces a sentence, substituting a life sentence for a death sentence or setting a prisoner free at a date earlier than the sentencing court contemplated, but leaves the conviction itself in place to cast whatever permanent shadow it will. The greatest acts of clemency are amnesty, which spares someone a trial in the first instance, and pardons, which typically expunge the conviction itself, not just freeing the prisoner but also restoring all civil rights and clearing the prisoner's reputation to the extent any sovereign act can. Harding granted Doree the intermediate grace, a commutation.

Parole is different categorically from clemency. While it also results in a prisoner's release from a judicial sentence of indeterminate length, and the process itself may be committed to the executive branch, the decision to allow paroles at all and the creation of a system for administering parole are legislative. Moreover, a prisoner paroled remains under judicial or executive supervision, on conditional liberty, until his or her full judicial sentence has lapsed. Often, a commutation and a pardon both restore unconditional liberty. But executives can impose conditions on pardon, amnesty, or commutation as they wish: consider President Harding's condition that IWW members like Baldazzi accept deportation and never return to the United States.[3]

Presidential clemency has fluctuated through most of the nation's history, with few if any discernible longterm trends. A president's own disposition and the times themselves seem to explain much about a particular administration's use of the power of pardon and commutation. For example, President Lincoln and Andrew Johnson, his successor, were prolific granters of pardons and commutations: but they governed during the Civil War and its aftermath, when the nation was in need of clemency not just to bind it back together but also to amend the excesses of wartime actions of courts and courts-martial. Some presidents have been slow or reluctant to pardon or commute; others, relatively quick. Some have been systematic in their process of considering clemency; others, quirky and individual. All presidents have used clemency (or withheld it) in part for political reasons, although not always or even usually for partisan or petty reasons. Some presidents have been quick to spare supporters or cronies; others have avoided exactly that. The main constant has been inconstancy. Because the power is so personal to the office the president holds, the use of clemency reflects the personality of the president.

However, by raw numbers, the story of executive clemency is not a tale of presidents. It is a tale of governors. Most American criminal cases arise in state courts, not in federal courts, and always have—in the range of 99 percent. Presidents can pardon or commute only those facing federal charges or already convicted of federal crimes. Governors are left to consider the vast majority of prisoners, who are convicted of state crimes.

There, a long-term trend is discernible, dimly. No single source of information for state grants of executive clemency exists, and states have different and fragmented systems of reporting clemency statistics. So assembling an accurate national picture is hard. But since the late 1970s or early 1980s, executive clemency in the states seems to have fallen off dramatically. The timing of this drop in gubernatorial willingness to grant clemency is hard, maybe impossible, to explain with confidence. All the same, it coincided roughly with widespread public disapproval of President Ford's 1975 pardon of former President Nixon and with the broad public approval of reinstatement of the death penalty in 1976 after a 1972 U.S. Supreme Court decision functionally imposed a moratorium on executions for four years. And it occurred after the 1968 presidential campaign introduced a new and successful theme into executive, legislative, and judicial branch races that has become a standard ever since: the idea of being "tough on crime" and with it, the rising political utility of demagoguery on criminal justice. Later controversial pardons, like President George H. W. Bush's Christmas 1992 clemency for Caspar Weinberger and others linked to the Iran-Contra affair and President Clinton's last-minute clemency for Marc Rich and 139 others, some also donors like Rich, eroded public confidence in the high-mindedness of executive clemency.[4]

Maybe most interesting, the sharp decline in acts of clemency by the nation's governors followed shortly after the 1976 presidential election. Historically, before 1976, only nine men had risen to the presidency from a governor's office. And even they had come from the most populous or in-fluential states of their day: for example, Virginia of the late eighteenth century or Ohio and New York of the late nineteenth and early twentieth centuries. Then came Jimmy Carter, former governor of Georgia—hardly an especially large or important state at the three-quarter mark of the twentieth century. Across the country, in governors' mansions, the occupants may have concluded that they might not be in a terminal political office after all. There might be one higher office to seek. They also could have concluded in the late twentieth and early twenty-first centuries, accurately as a matter of political instinct, that acts of mercy and grace in criminal justice would not improve odds for the White House.[5]

Of course, Warren Harding already occupied the White House in 1922. He had ascended to the top. For whatever reasons, Harding was willing often to use his power of executive clemency. He commuted not just Doree's sentence but, in an uneven trickle, many IWW prisoners' terms. On Christmas Day 1921, after just nine months in office, he also freed Eugene Debs. Woodrow Wilson twice had refused to grant Debs clemency, calling him a "traitor." Harding seems to have overruled the strong objections of his own attorney general in releasing Debs. Indeed, Harding did more: the president invited Debs to the White House on his way home from the penitentiary in Atlanta. Debs accepted. But he did not credit Harding with the commutation in his memoirs.[6]

Harding pardoned others about the same time, too, like a wealthy Cincinnati banker who had not spent a day in jail. The pardon power has remained a tempting and mostly unchecked means to reward allies; it can display venality as easily as it can display grace.

As to the World War I–era radicals, though, venality was no explanation. As of April 1, 1922, ninety-six IWW prisoners still remained in Leavenworth. Harding may have thought his pardons and commutations consistent with his campaign promise to return the nation to normalcy. Whatever his reasons for considering clemency, these eight dozen men were not his cronies. They were not businessmen from his home state. They certainly were not political allies. He could not cover up his subordinates' own wrongdoing—

and there was plenty of that in and around his administration—by pardoning IWW members or commuting their sentences.[7]

In the end, he did not require these men even to ask for clemency: by late October 1922, the Justice Department was weighing commutations or pardons for about fifty World War I prisoners who had not applied. Not two weeks earlier, Harding had granted conditional commutations to six IWW prisoners, including Doree's brother-in-law, Walter Nef, and Ben Fletcher. The nebulous condition was only that they must "observe the laws" or return to prison. In June 1923, Harding commuted the sentences of twenty-two more Chicago IWW prisoners.[8]

President Harding obviously did not wait to act until near the end of a second term, when clemency would carry no political risk (as at that time it was a matter of custom for a president to serve no more than two terms). For Harding, indeed, there would be no second term; there would not even be the end of a first term. One week exactly after falling ill in San Francisco, he died there on August 2, 1923.[9]

During his two and a half years in office, Harding followed a moderately generous course on clemency for wartime prisoners. Many Americans opposed any clemency for this group. That faction included prominent people. But another faction viewed most or all of the wartime convicts as political prisoners and sought a full general amnesty for them. This faction included people such as Helen Keller, Indiana author Booth Tarkington, the governor of South Carolina, and Senator Robert M. La Follette of Wisconsin. Harding found a middle position, but it leaned toward grace.[10]

Among those who opposed clemency for the IWW prisoners, implacably, was Kenesaw Mountain Landis. He had no sympathy for the Chicago men even after war's end. In a January 1920 speech to the American Protective League in Minneapolis, Landis—still a sitting federal judge—had endorsed publicly the guilty verdicts in the Chicago IWW case and condemned socialism as an idea.

After he left the bench, in one of his several speeches over the years to the national conventions of the American Legion, Landis lashed out at those who suggested that Wobblies or socialists (whom he lumped together) were "political prisoners."

> There is a lot of talk now about getting some of these men out of the penitentiary. . . . [N]ow there is a society in operation throughout the country, sobbing about the terrible fix these poor fellows are in. They are called "Political Prisoners." Now, why not tell the truth? They are not political

prisoners. They are just guilty of fighting their own country in time of war. They are just guilty of adding to the burdens and perils of the soldier in the front line trench. They are just guilty of those things which caused probably 10,000 additional soldiers of the United States to lie in graves in France by their activities. And there is an organized whine throughout the country that these gentlemen ought to be turned loose.

Let me tell you something. In actual military operations, if a private soldier after a long day's march, is put on guard and he stands as a lone sentry at midnight and falls asleep, the penalty is death. So, I say to you, that I think twenty years in the penitentiary for men of influence and power among a certain class of people, whose aid and support of the government would be of some additional help in giving force and power to the blow being struck by the men in the front line trench,—when that man turns against his own country and insists upon the right in time of war to fight his own country and to discourage enlistments, I regard twenty years in the penitentiary,—when I think of the death penalty for the private soldier for going to sleep on guard duty,—I regard twenty years in the penitentiary for these other gentlemen as a mere inconsequential triviality.

The American Legionnaires interrupted Landis twice in that passage with applause.[11]

Still, Landis and other dissenters proved unable to stop what Harding started. After Vice President Calvin Coolidge became president at Harding's death, Alice Roosevelt Longworth, Teddy Roosevelt's daughter, famously quipped that Coolidge looked as if he had been "weaned on a pickle." Maybe so. But sour countenance or no, he continued calmly with the clemency that Harding began.

On December 15, 1923, President Coolidge ordered the release of the last thirty-one IWW prisoners still in Leavenworth, including seven from the Chicago case. C. J. Bourg, Alexander Cournos, Harry Lloyd, Burt Lorton, Charles H. McKinnon, James Rowan, and James P. Thompson were the last to go. They would be somewhere of their choosing by Christmas. Only Thompson fairly could have been described as an upper tier member. The others were simple loyalists, men left behind.

Woodrow Wilson's former secretary of war, Newton D. Baker, and Senator William E. Borah, progressive Republican of Idaho, cheered Coolidge's act. These last IWW prisoners had offered no apology; they had not begged. However obscure the reasons and however long the wait, by grace they went home.[12]

29

A Justice Department Emerges

Recall that in February 1918, as he grasped for a way to avert a trial, George Vanderveer had approached that same secretary of war who more than five years later approved of clemency, Newton Baker. But in 1918, that approach had been futile. In a long letter to the president of the United States at about the same time, Vanderveer also had expressed confusion about why the Department of Justice was addressing a labor problem generally, or the IWW specifically, at all. In part, Vanderveer may have been posturing: he may have been shut out of the Justice Department and instead met with the highest government official he could find; he may have been blustering or engaging in tactical misdirection, bluffing, with his claim of confusion.

But possibly, too, there was at least some element of sincerity in his actions and words. In 1918, Vanderveer really would not have known a template for federal prosecution of labor radicals on a scale this broad. He would have known isolated contempt of court prosecutions for violating an injunction not to restrain trade in a given strike but never would have seen a nationwide, federal preemptive action such as the IWW indictments his clients then faced. There was no such template or precedent then. And because local, state, and federal responses to labor unrest generally had been quasi-military in the past, perhaps the cabinet official in charge of the nation's army seemed in early 1918 a logical person to whom to turn. In other words, Vanderveer's observed actions and words may be revealing. A genuine change was in the offing and he did not comprehend it at the time.[1]

In all events, as the last of the freed Wobblies found again the fields, factories, or forests in the years that followed, the Department of Justice that had prosecuted them was growing up. The Department turned fifty in 1920. It was beginning to come into its own.

In Chicago, as in Sacramento, it had relied greatly not just on lawyers from within but on private lawyers from industry as special prosecutors. The Justice Department had been unable to take on these prosecutions alone. It also had relied very heavily, indeed essentially, on illegally seized evidence, which only the contortions of Judge Landis and the federal court of appeals in Chicago had allowed. In a real sense, it was the government—not the accused criminal—that won on a Fourth Amendment technicality. The government also had the benefit of judicial disregard of Supreme Court precedent, particularly the 1914 *Weeks* decision, and the dishonest discard of reality in favor of a factual fantasy that furthered the government's ends.

Still, a shift had begun. From Washington, DC, the DOJ had looked westward and planned a coordinated legal attack on hundreds of radical dissenters. It had played the largest role in implementing that attack in four matched indictments from Chicago all the way west to Sacramento, and in two cities in between. Its legal theory was new and very aggressive—as well as chancy—but also coherent, in the sense of creative, replicable, and internally consistent. The legal theory was calculated to wipe out a union with membership approaching 100,000, in part by decapitating the organization with an overwhelming, unexpected, and untested tactic. Of five different conspiracy theories, three had missed or failed in Chicago. But two had stuck when the case was over, and one really was all the Justice Department needed to land a fatal blow.

The department did this in a courtroom, without immediate assistance of vigilantes, thuggish deputy sheriffs, strikebreakers running riot under official cover, unaccountable private detectives, or state militia troops with bayonets fixed. Yes, it did this with the help of outside lawyers: but these were outsiders with pens, not pistols. Local law enforcement officers also had been conscripted to supplement the few federal agents in the Bureau of Investigation. Yet the unprecedented federal strategy had not depended upon the happenstance of the sympathies of local sheriffs, mayors, or governors to labor or capital. Legalism got a trial run as a possible alternative to quasi-militarism. An orchestrated federal strategy nationwide arose as an alternative to spotty, local efforts.

The results had not been justice, of course, at least in any fine-grain sense. Mail had been intercepted, read, censored, and stolen by government employees. Private couriers had done the same at the government's bidding. When not intercepted, mass mailings of the IWW—newspapers, bulletins, fundraising appeals—simply had been rejected by the U.S. Post Office, for political and tactical reasons. Dozens or hundreds of the innocent or probably innocent had been convicted, lost in the mass of defendants. Men had gone to prison for arbitrary lengths of time, and for arbitrary reasons. The space between speech and opinion, on one side, and criminal action on the other had collapsed, even been erased. Conscience had been punished.

But in a very practical way, prisons had been substituted for morgues and hospitals. Frank Little's fate represented an old way; Bill Haywood's and Ed Doree's and more than two hundred others' fates, an emerging new way. That new way was through the federal Justice Department.

The DOJ had not attempted any legal action on this national scale before. But it soon would again. In a period of three months from November 1919 through January 1920, Thomas Gregory's successor as President Wilson's attorney general, A. Mitchell Palmer, approved a series of raids in about thirty cities that swept up thousands, including communists, socialists, and anarchists. Several hundred were deported quickly before public support for the mass arrests waned.[2]

There soon were other signs of a changing role for the Justice Department, too. Although establishing an exact relationship with the IWW indictments and trials is impossible, the IWW cases came as the Justice Department first began to use conspiracy charges regularly. By 1925, a famed federal judge, Learned Hand, fairly could describe conspiracy as the "darling of the modern prosecutor's nursery." Today, federal prosecutions still stand apart from state prosecutions in the frequency of the Justice Department's reliance on one or more conspiracy counts to lead an indictment.[3]

The years after World War II brought renewed fear of socialists and communists in the United States. By then, ad hoc harassment by local officials was a tactic mostly of the past. The Justice Department was the main antagonist of actual and suspected communists. Legal tools—surveillance, infiltration, and prosecution—had replaced quasi-military tools, even if those legal tools were not always used lawfully. What had started as a small Bureau of Investigation within the Justice Department had become the semi-autonomous Federal Bureau of Investigation in 1935. No longer were Pinkerton or Burns detectives, hired by employers' associations or state and local law enforcement agencies, much involved in covert operations against radical organizations. The FBI, theoretically more or less within the control of the DOJ, now was the nearly exclusive sponsor of such efforts.

In court, the Alien Registration Act of 1940, known popularly as the Smith Act, was the principal basis for these prosecutions for roughly twenty years, until use of the act tapered off in the early and mid-1960s. While the Justice Department first prosecuted suspected Nazis under it, the department mostly invoked the Smith Act against communists.[4]

In the 1950s and 1960s, the FBI began to monitor and harass civil rights activists and organizations, as well as those on the far right. The Justice Department often proved more effective than state and local officials in prosecuting racially motivated crimes in the South and in shepherding the process of integration of public universities and schools. While integration required the president to call out the National Guard on occasion, often it was deputy U.S. marshals—agents within the DOJ—who were at the center of efforts to assure that black students could study alongside white ones, in spite of violent racist responses. A federal role, usually under the auspices of the DOJ, had become the norm.

As the Vietnam War led to campus unrest and new radical organizations, the DOJ again played a critical role. National Guard troops still supplemented local police during tense marches or protests on campuses: Kent State University in May 1970 is an especially notable and tragic example. But when prosecutions followed, they often were federal. In Boston, Dr. Benjamin Spock, Yale chaplain William Sloane Coffin Jr., and others were indicted in federal court for resistance to the draft.

In Chicago, in March 1969, another flashy federal indictment of radicals sounded faint echoes of the IWW trial just over fifty years earlier. This time, though, there were not 166 defendants: there were eight originally, facing charges stemming from protests during the 1968 Democratic Party convention there. Seven eventually went to trial, in a new federal courthouse that Ludwig Mies van der Rohe designed, just east of a plaza on which the old courthouse sat when the Wobblies faced trial. This time, a jury acquitted the defendants of conspiracy—although it convicted five on a substantive count. The seven served time in a newer version of the Cook County Jail.[5]

The 1990s brought new radicals, often immigrant Islamic fundamentalists or homegrown opponents of the federal government. With them came a new spike in fear of terror. Whether the first bombing of the World Trade Center in 1993; the 1995 bombing of the Oklahoma City federal building; the prosecution of "twentieth hijacker" Zacarias Moussaoui after the September 11, 2001, attacks; or other late twentieth- and early twenty-first-century terror cases, the Justice Department consistently has been the vanguard of governmental response. Domestically, that response has been legalist in the main.[6]

To be sure, the legalist response remains imperfect; legal form has not always meant lawful substance. Civil rights abuses, small and large, noticed and unnoticed, have recurred time and again. The 1950s brought COINTELPRO and its domestic surveillance and harassment of dissidents and activists from the far right to the left for at least fifteen years. The 1960s saw the FBI's overt effort to drive Martin Luther King Jr. to suicide, for example. Questions about how the FBI wields power, and its motivations, are not new.

And not all of the abuses have been investigative. Many have come in the courtroom. The DOJ often has engaged in general prosecutorial overreach. Overcharging, usually in the number of counts and sometimes in the number of defendants, remains a systemic problem. The department today commonly extorts guilty pleas by threat of mandatory minimum sentences, superfluous charges, or despotic civil forfeitures. Specific prosecutorial misconduct (hiding evidence that suggests innocence, doubt, or mitigation; improper arguments to juries; intimidating defense witnesses), although typically situational, not systematic, continues. More than sixty years ago, the department's lawyers likely sought the execution of Ethel Rosenberg not because her conduct warranted it but because they thought her a useful instrument to put pressure on her husband, Julius. When he did not buckle, she went to her death in the electric chair. Closer to our day, Justice Department lawyers compelled an unwilling sibling to testify against Timothy McVeigh in a specific effort to obtain a capital sentence, not life in prison. In short, they forced a sister to serve as an instrument to procure her brother's death.[7]

It also is a department, though, that sometimes dismisses a case or confesses error on appeal rather than risk diminishing the dignity of the United States. It is a department that employs thousands of lawyers, as assistant U.S. attorneys or trial attorneys from "main Justice," who feel honored and humbled to stand up in court and say that they speak on behalf of that same United States. Over time, thousands more lawyers who have left the Justice Department for other jobs, often more visible or better paid, have reflected on their days in the department as the time when they did the most meaningful work of their lives.

All of this, though, concerns how the Department of Justice uses the position it occupies. That question rightly deserves constant attention.

But there is an antecedent: the predicate question of how DOJ came to occupy its position at all. The fact that it grew into what Americans know it as today gets very little attention.

This ascendancy was not foreordained. For more than eighty years, federal prosecutors in patronage posts operated with no executive branch oversight, living off a share of the fees and fines that flowed into federal courts from the people they prosecuted and from civil litigants. U.S. district attorneys, such as Charles Clyne in Chicago during the Wobbly trial, did not receive a regular salary to replace this bounty system until 1896. For longer than that after 1870, the DOJ was thinly funded and staffed as it faced the daunting proposition of reining in and assisting more than ninety U.S. district attorneys spread across the nation's breadth. Today, the ninety-plus U.S. attorneys retain considerable discretion. But importantly, much of it now is discretion that the attorney general has delegated back to them, in part through a multivolume U.S. attorney's manual of encyclopedic length and in part by regular directives that also cabin decision-making at the local level of U.S. attorneys' offices.

While U.S. attorneys remain presidential appointees, today many are skilled lawyers and administrators. Not a few come to the job only after a long career in civil service. For better or worse, the twenty-first-century DOJ is a regimented, hierarchical, and vast federal agency, employing well over 115,000 people, with a professional ethos. It is the governmental body that Americans now almost unthinkingly expect to address the most significant or visible domestic threats of the day, whether those are the rise of organized crime that Prohibition produced, communist infiltration, civil unrest during an unpopular war, violent racist groups, or al-Qaeda and ISIS operatives at home. George Vanderveer and many in his day looked to other federal departments when they wondered how the government would respond to possible or actual threats that radicals posed: Labor, Interior, War. Today, one hundred years later, Americans look instead to the Justice Department.

A critical point in that history, the moment at which the slope of the Justice Department's growth and role arguably changed, came in the campaign against the IWW in the summer of 1917 and the year that followed, after events like the Bisbee deportation and Frank Little's lynching. Grim excesses in America's biggest mass trial were undeniable. Indeed, one tacit if overlooked indication that the Chicago IWW trial seemed an excess even within the DOJ is the fact that in the century since, the department never has attempted such a trial again. Only once, during the next world war, did the department indict more than half the number tried in Chicago.

And only on very rare occasions has it attempted to try even one-sixth as many. The IWW trials became a general model of a new legalist approach to domestic radical threats. They did not become a specific model for later trials themselves.[8]

Obviously, too, other events and trends during the twentieth century contributed to the rise of legalist approaches to radical threats or violence, just as the growth of government and the spread of legalist approaches have become more common in many areas of social life in the hundred years since the Chicago IWW trial. But some causal role of the IWW prosecutions in the emergence of the modern U.S. Department of Justice also seems clear; what is debatable is the relative causal effects of those cases among the other changes of the twentieth century. At the very least, though, Chicago had a role in changing how the country confronts perceived domestic threats by radicals and dissenters and how it acts on domestic fear. This country's biggest mass trial in civilian courts marked a turning point.

30

Endings

For the direct participants in that trial, Chicago changed much, too. Those defendants who sought separate counsel and then maneuvered at the outset to delay their trial by severance from the others—Elizabeth Gurley Flynn, Carlo Tresca, Arturo Giovannitti, and Joseph Ettor—fared the best. They stayed free. But their connections with the IWW, what remained of it, were strained permanently. That had begun earlier, with the 1916 expulsion of Tresca and Gurley Flynn from the IWW after the internal dispute over the Mesabi Range strike. The separation lasted.

Tresca, Gurley Flynn's lover at one time, became a vocal anti-fascist and opposed Stalin's excesses. He also campaigned against the Mafia, which probably was behind his assassination on a New York City street in 1943.[1]

Giovannitti, the poet and translator into English of Emile Pouget's *Sabotage* (which played a recurrent role in the Chicago trial), had been tried and acquitted after the 1912 Lawrence, Massachusetts, textile mills strike, along with Tresca and Ettor. He remained a leftist, and a drinker, all his life. Giovannitti died quietly, a poor man residing in the Bronx in early 1959.

Ettor eventually ran a fruit orchard in California. He died in San Clemente in 1948.

Gurley Flynn was an activist to the end. She spoke well of the IWW all her life. A devoted Communist, she was active in the American branch of the party. She died at age seventy-four in Moscow, in September 1964. Her remains came home to be buried in Chicago—but not at Waldheim Cemetery, a favored final resting place of radicals since the Haymarket Square defendants were buried there.

The prosecution's "main man" who granted the severance motion at the government's invitation, Kenesaw Mountain Landis, became much more visible some years after the trial than he had been during it. Landis had developed close ties to Chicago's Charles Comiskey and other major league baseball club owners over the years. In the wake of the gambling scandal that enveloped professional baseball in 1919 with the "Black Sox" episode of rigging the World Series, the owners decided that they had a serious problem, both substantively and as a matter of public image. They turned to Landis. Soon, he was supplementing his federal judicial salary of $7,500 with $42,500 a year from the baseball owners to operate first informally and then formally on the side as an arbitrator with final authority over all of baseball.

That dual role sat poorly with some members of Congress, who in 1921 introduced articles of impeachment in the House of Representatives. Although inclined to fight back, Landis instead resigned his judgeship in 1922 to serve exclusively as the first commissioner of major league baseball.

He ruled baseball as an autocrat for the next twenty-two years, becoming an iconic—if often controversial—figure in the game and a fixture of American culture. Landis remained for many years a frequent speaker at American Legion conventions and, although a political progressive on some issues, a fierce defender of the crackdown on wartime dissent.

Still the baseball commissioner, Landis died at age seventy-eight on November 25, 1944. His death came just a few days after the principal author of the next world war, Adolf Hitler, abandoned his wartime headquarters and retreated to Berlin. Landis's son, Reed, served in and survived both world wars.

Major league baseball finally admitted its first black player of the twentieth century, Jackie Robinson, a little more than two years after Landis's death. Landis (like the team owners) had done nothing to end the segregation of the sport during his more than two-decade reign.

There is room for another biography of Kenesaw Mountain Landis. He was if nothing else a man who had a knack for winding his way into visible roles at cultural pivot points. That was true from the Standard Oil case during heady antitrust days in the first few years of the 1900s, to the nation's biggest mass trial during the surge of fear and nationalist sentiment of World War I, to presiding over the most visible, and entirely white, leagues that made up a large part of the nation's pastime when baseball plausibly was exactly that.[2]

By comparison to baseball, the IWW integrated from the outset. But Ben Fletcher was the only defendant of African ancestry, and a rare black man in the leadership ranks. His Local 8 of dockworkers in Philadelphia set a lasting standard for interracial labor organizing. After prison, he remained popular, personally and as a speaker. Eventually, he moved to New York City from Philadelphia. There, his health failed early. He died at age fifty-nine in 1949 and is buried in Brooklyn.

Of the other Chicago defendants, maybe Ray Fanning and Big Bill Haywood stood figuratively at either end of the long rank of men between them, as opposing ends of a spectrum. For the stray nineteen-year-old Harvard student, his conviction and time in prison marked the end of his youthful experiment with radical politics and unions. He eventually went to Harvard Law School, served as a colonel in the Army Air Corps in World War II, and practiced corporate law in New York City until 1968. At least in the early 1940s, he was active in New York Republican Party politics. He lived a quiet, conventional life in New Milford, Connecticut. Fanning died in November 1975 at age seventy-seven. His obituary mentioned nothing about his early flirtation with the IWW or the trial.[3]

The self-taught, lifelong radical unionist Haywood, aged beyond his years, never returned from the Soviet Union. In declining health, he wrote an autobiography of no more than ordinary honesty and self-examination—which is to say, not much. It appeared after he died. Haywood died in a Moscow hospital on May 18, 1928, at age fifty-nine, after months of failing health with complications from diabetes. He was, supposedly, lonely. A little more than a year before he died, Haywood married a younger Russian woman. Perhaps the marriage was a metaphor for his isolation: she reportedly spoke no English and he no Russian. Or, conceivably, it was an example of the human ability to overcome isolation and loneliness.[4]

Haywood's later years of his exile as a fugitive were dotted, too, with occasional wild stories in the U.S. press that almost surely were fiction, whether intended or not. He supposedly appeared at an orphanage in Armenia in 1925, "a starving, ragged tramp" begging for "food, clothes and shelter overnight." "I'm hungry and homesick," this account quoted him telling the unnamed orphanage director, "and if I cannot find work in Constantinople, I am going back to the United States. I had rather live in Leavenworth than Bolshevist Russia. It ain't a white man's country."

Also in early 1925, about the same time he supposedly would have been in Armenia, another story had Haywood in Chicago, homesick, ready to give himself up. The story was untrue.[5]

After Haywood's death, Clarence Darrow, who had defended him successfully in the 1907 Idaho murder trial, commented, "I'm glad to hear he is dead. Haywood had been unhappy for a good many years." Explaining, Darrow said, "'Big Bill' was an able man, not much of a philosopher, but a good propagandist. Like all men who have big ideas he was unhappy."[6]

Haywood had sounded it. In remarks quoted at his death, but not ascribed to a particular date or interview, he talked about his flight from the twenty-year sentence. "It was a death sentence for me. I am an open country man. I couldn't live even five years cooped up in prison. Landis could have better hung me. When the chance came to get out as a stoker I went. I know how some of the boys feel about me—those who stuck and took the rap. But they were younger than me."[7]

Part of Haywood's cremated remains are buried at a Kremlin wall, in a place of honor. Part of them came home in an urn, laid to rest in Chicago's Waldheim Cemetery. In death, he was a man asunder: one part of him isolated from the other.[8]

One of the writers who covered the last month of the Chicago trial, John Reed, was buried at the same Kremlin wall more than seven years earlier. He died young, at age thirty-three, in 1920. His book *Ten Days That Shook the World* remains in the canon. In 1981, it and Reed inspired the film *Reds*, with Warren Beatty playing Reed.

Carl Sandburg, by contrast to Reed, lived a long life after covering the Chicago trial. By the time he died in 1967 at age eighty-nine, he had won three Pulitzer Prizes. The first was for a volume of poetry, *Cornhuskers*, published the same year he covered the IWW trial for the *Chicago Daily News*. The second was for his four-volume 1939 biography of Abraham Lincoln, subtitled *The War Years*. That set of books still shapes in part the nation's relationship with Abraham Lincoln. A final Pulitzer followed later for a collection of verse.

The lawyers in the case mostly remained true to form. Claude Porter never did win office in Iowa again. Not three months after the IWW trial ended, he lost the race for Iowa governor on November 5. But he had a future in federal political appointments. His performance in Chicago earned him an immediate appointment in the Justice Department, as assistant attorney general in charge of the Criminal Division from 1918 to 1919. President Wilson named him chief counsel for the Federal Trade Commission in the summer of 1919. Then, in 1928, President Coolidge reached across party lines to appoint the Democrat Claude Porter to the Interstate Commerce Commission. President Roosevelt later reappointed him, and for several years Porter presided as chairman of the ICC. He served on the ICC for eighteen years in all and was at midterm when he died suddenly in August 1946 at the age of seventy-four.[9]

Unlike Porter, Frank Nebeker never ran for office. But he, too, remained in Washington, DC, for the rest of his life. The Chicago prosecution brought him a succession of posts within the Justice Department. He first served as assistant attorney general in charge of the Public Lands Division. That was a potentially attractive post for a westerner if he had a selfish mindset, especially one who had long represented western mining interests. But research discloses no reason to doubt that Nebeker acted honorably in office. In 1920, President Wilson moved him within the department, making him a special assistant to the attorney general with responsibility for antitrust work and other significant litigation. He handled a number of antitrust and other complex cases for the government over the years. In 1935, Nebeker earned $10,000 from the Justice Department, which then was $1,000 more than the annual salary of an assistant attorney general or the director of the FBI, J. Edgar Hoover.[10]

Nearly twenty years after the Chicago IWW trial, Nebeker rejoined forces with a colleague from that trial, and together they became a footnote to the U.S. Supreme Court's most famed footnote. George Murdock, the Bureau of Investigation's lead agent at the Chicago trial, eventually left the Justice Department and opened a law practice in Chicago. He came to represent the Carolene Products Company in Litchfield, Illinois. The company made a product called "Carolene" (later "Milnut"), which it promoted as useful in recipes calling for whole milk, cream, or whipped cream. It was especially good for whipping, the manufacturer claimed. And it was more affordable than cream, with a longer shelf-life.

The problem, according to the U.S. government, was that "Carolene" was a powdered milk product that contained coconut or vegetable fats that were not from milk. In other words, it was considered "filled milk," and a statute forbade its interstate shipment.

When his successors in the Justice Department's Chicago offices charged the company, Murdock convinced the federal district court to quash the indictment on the ground that the Filled Milk Act exceeded Congress's power to regulate interstate commerce and also denied the equal protection implicit in the due process clause of the Fifth Amendment. The government appealed directly to the U.S. Supreme Court.

Murdock now turned to his old acquaintance Nebeker, who had experience in the Supreme Court. Nebeker joined the Carolene Products defense team as cocounsel.

In a 1938 decision, the government won. The Commerce Clause allowed the regulation unless it denied due process. And there, the company could not overcome the presumption of constitutionality that courts apply to acts of Congress. Besides, Congress had some evidence that filled milk threatened public health.

But in the course of Justice Harlan Fiske Stone's otherwise pedestrian opinion, he and the Court dropped Footnote 4, arguably the most enigmatic and portentous footnote in the Court's history. The Court had no cause to consider in this case, it noted, whether more exacting scrutiny of a congressional act might apply (1) when legislation impinges on some explicit right under the first ten amendments to the Constitution; (2) when legislation restricts the very political processes on which Americans rely to identify and repeal bad laws; or (3) when legislation seems directed at "discrete and insular minorities," whether religious, racial, or other. That footnote became the foundation for later cases giving some legislation "strict scrutiny" or, if not that, an intermediate level of scrutiny above mere rational-basis review, in an equal protection challenge.

So, Nebeker, Murdock, and "Milnut" lost. But the footnote led to something. An Oklahoma man won when he challenged forced sterilization because only some odd felonies constituted habitual criminality. So did a black man and a white woman forbidden to marry in Virginia because of race, and Amish parents in Wisconsin wishing to withhold their children from public school after eighth grade for religious reasons. These later litigants all won in part because of Footnote 4.[11]

Nebeker lived a long life and eventually faded from public view and memory. His last quarter century was quiet. He died on September 5, 1962, at age ninety-two, the last of the principal lawyers from the Chicago case to go. Outside of his family, the world hardly noticed. But it was the forty-fifth anniversary of the illegal searches that began the IWW cases.[12]

Caroline Lowe, a rare example of a female lawyer in 1918—and an even rarer example of a woman doing criminal defense work—continued on with the Wobblies, participating in the appeal of the Chicago case and also in the defense in Sacramento and Wichita. Her public visibility, though, traveling and giving speeches, was greatest between 1908 and 1919. During those years, she appeared frequently in newspaper reports, especially before the war in the socialist *Call to Reason* in Girard, Kansas. She died in 1933 at about age fifty-nine.

Fred H. Moore, whose role in the Chicago trial was not often visible but who played a major role in Wichita, later led the defense of Nicola Sacco and Bartolomeo Vanzetti in 1921 and welcomed a political trial.

Tresca had recommended him. At least in hindsight, some have thought Moore's defense disastrous. Sacco and Vanzetti went to the electric chair in 1927. Although sometimes a deft trial lawyer, Moore was a drinker and also may have developed a drug addiction during the time he represented Sacco and Vanzetti.[13]

George Vanderveer devoted his later practice, with precipitous financial peaks and valleys, increasingly to representing the IWW and, eventually, mainstream unions. He also took personal injury cases for the money. In 1920, he defended ten Wobblies and their local lawyer on murder charges for the Armistice Day 1919 shooting of an American Legion commander in Centralia, Washington. He won acquittals for four, including the lawyer. The remaining seven were convicted.

During this time Van also lost his home and all its furniture, finally, to creditors while Ellinor was escaping him on a free cruise with friends. He took up residence in a hotel, living on the tab of an old friend. And he sent for Kitty Beck, who joined him.

Ellinor came home to Seattle to find her husband drinking more, living with another woman, and casually ignoring her return. He offered her neither himself nor a divorce. When after two years she summoned the courage to meet Vanderveer's anger and demanded the divorce, he acceded, so long as he could avoid publicity by filing in another county. On a drizzly May 22, 1922, their fifteenth wedding anniversary, George and Gus traveled together to court for their final divorce hearing.

Now free to cohabit openly with Kitty, Vanderveer began to refuse free or underpaid legal work. With his new business plan of getting paid to work, he amassed a small fortune quickly as even in the worst of times he never was short of offers for personal injury, labor, and criminal cases. George and Kitty moved into a grand home on Lake Burien. He also quickly set about cheating on her with other women, back at the hotel where he and Kitty had carried on in secret. When exactly Kitty discovered this is unclear. What is clear is that she killed herself in the master bedroom of the Lake Burien mansion in 1924, shortly after her last, frantic effort to win Van back.

Vanderveer was trying a case in neighboring Tacoma right then. He discovered Kitty's body when he returned home that night. He was in court again the next morning.

Eventually, George would marry another woman, Ethel Hoover, make and lose enormous amounts of money, chase risky investments and get-rich-quick schemes, drink still more, and lose most of his frequent brawls as age slowed him. He was cynical, defiant, drunk, and most of all, lonely, according to his mostly sympathetic biographers.

But he was not drunk in court. Those who despised his politics, loathed his personal life, and detested his personality acknowledged his skills in court as among the best they knew. His biographers write, too, that even disapproving colleagues never doubted his word and his handshake, as Nebeker had.[14]

In addition to the Chicago case and the Centralia defense, Vanderveer also defended a Seattle bootlegging case against gang members, in which the government made extensive use of wiretapped conversations. The federal judge admitted the tapes over Vanderveer's strong objections. That decision assured conviction, but Vanderveer led an appeal to the U.S. Court of Appeals in San Francisco. He lost there and next served as co-counsel on consolidated appeals to the U.S. Supreme Court. Although the defense lost again, by a 5–4 vote, the dissents in that case, *Olmstead v. United States*, spurred federal wiretapping legislation. Justice Louis D. Brandeis's dissent especially, urging a "right to be let alone," remains a classic and stirring defense of privacy.[15]

Dissolute and damaged, Vanderveer died after surgery in October 1942. He was sixty-seven. His biographers recount a moment of grace worth repeating. Some years before he died, Vanderveer took the appeal of a young man, a member of one of the Northwest tribes, who had worked as a deckhand on a Puget Sound steamer. The young man was convicted of raping a white woman and sentenced to death. Vanderveer's eventual federal appeal focused on the inadequacy of the young man's trial lawyer. When one of the appellate judges pointed out that an argument was waived because the trial lawyer had failed to object, Vanderveer roared, "Would you hang a man because his lawyer failed to except to a ruling?"

No, at least that court would not. The young man got a retrial, and Vanderveer represented him there. A new jury acquitted.[16]

At a casual glance, the IWW itself looks like the first to die after the Chicago trial. Following the federal government's coordinated campaign against it in Chicago, Sacramento, Wichita, and Omaha, it indeed collapsed. Membership slid sharply and never again came close to the breadth and sheer numbers during the years just before the United States joined World War I. Internal rifts over whether to embrace the Soviet Union specifically, and communism generally, also contributed to its splintering and decline in the 1920s. The One Big Union never could be described fairly as "big" again after the Chicago trial.

A heartbeat continues, though, and in Chicago at that. There and in small clusters elsewhere, a cadre of believers keeps alive the idea of organization of labor by industry or sector rather than by trade or skill. In Butte, Montana, Frank Little's grave remains an active pilgrimage site, fresh mementos scattered within the low, iron fence that surrounds the plot. The headstone proclaims that he was "slain by capitalist interests for organizing and inspiring his fellow men." Pines stand sentinel behind it; mountains behind them.

Mostly, though, the singing union sings no more. It does not play a major role in organizing labor against capital. The core idea of "one" survives, and the songbooks remain if ever a chorus of tens or hundreds of thousands should assemble to sing them again.

By contrast, today capital continues to organize against labor as effectively as ever. Through chambers of commerce, trade associations too numerous to count, political action committees, and captured government agencies, large corporations and wealthy shareholders enjoy the advantages of their comparatively small numbers, closely aligned interests, and vast sums at stake. All these factors help in overcoming natural barriers to collective action on the side of capital. Whether in right-to-work legislation, in measures to hobble public sector unions, in opposition to minimum-wage laws, in bars to mandatory dues deductions from paychecks, or in fostering political divisions among workers, organized capital has succeeded often in exploiting and increasing the free-rider problems and other natural barriers to effective organization that large numbers of working people, with only generally or loosely aligned interests and relatively small sums of money at stake individually, face in collective action.[17]

In fostering political divisions among workers, corporate organizations and their allies have copied, probably unknowingly, Nebeker's ploy of portraying union officers and organizers as effete impostors and elitists; as men and women with "soft hands and hard faces." In Chicago in 1918, that argument lacked authenticity. It has not always.

With collective action hampered, and hard even in the best of circumstances, individual workers are tempted, no matter how poorly paid, to throw in their lot with employers and the wealthy. If they choose that, perhaps they can hope to climb into moneyed ranks one day or at least to avoid scorn and the scars of battle.

Ed Doree, for one, went that way. Out of prison at last, he chose a life of quiet and safe service to capitalism. He took a position as a field accountant for a construction company. The man who had so missed Chiky in jail and prison now traveled for weeks and months at a time for his job. Sometimes his family came with him; sometimes not.[18]

His little boy never had to make this hard, adult choice. Although Bucky left the hospital and went home after his father returned to Philadelphia the second time in September 1922, his heart was damaged. Bucky died on March 27, 1923.[19]

Ed and Chiky still had each other. Indeed, they remained devoted spouses for life. They also had another child, Ellen, in 1924, and then a boy in 1927. But they both mourned a loss.[20]

Whether in time Ed Doree could have overcome Bucky's death with the help of younger children's hands to hold, who knows. A gall bladder surgery led to complications. He died on September 7, 1927, one day short of the fifth anniversary of his commutation. Ellen was not yet three years old; the baby boy was just five months.[21]

After he left Leavenworth and mostly before, Edwin Doree saw not five years of freedom: not five years' freedom from anything; not five years' freedom to do or be something. He saw not five years of peace.

Chiky survived for years. Decades later, though, Ellen would recall of her mother that "she was truly alive only during the thirteen years of her marriage."

Their children fared better. Chiky and Ed Doree's second boy grew up to be a commercial artist. Ellen Doree Rosen became a professor, interested in public sector productivity and public administration.[22]

She dedicated her book about Edwin F. Doree's peaceless time with the IWW to Ed and Chiky's grandchildren and great-grandchildren. In the book's closing words, this only daughter wrote of her father, "I want them to know their progenitor was in prison and they should be proud of him." Here was a daughter reflecting on her father for the benefit of his descendants—an act in the present, careful reflection on the past, to bring an offering to the future.[23]

A broader, less personal lesson from the story of the IWW and America's biggest mass trial can come from that process, too. The rule of law is essential, yes. But law without justice is only rule, and oppression waits there also.

Notes

Foreword

1. Attorney General Gregory, referring to war dissenters, declared in November 1917, "May God have mercy on them, for they need expect none from an outraged people and an avenging government." Geoffrey R. Stone, *Perilous Times: Free Speech in Wartime: From the Sedition Act of 1798 to the War on Terrorism* (New York: Norton, 2004), 153.

2. *Dassey v. Dittmann*, 897 F.3d 297, 319 (7th Cir. 2017) (en banc) (Wood, C.J., dissenting).

Chapter 1. The Railroad Trestle

1. As to the cause of Little's broken ankle and his recent beatings, see *United States v. Haywood et al.*, No. 17-26916 (N.D. Ill.), Trial Transcript at 1374 (May 23, 1918) (hereafter "Chicago Trial Tr."), IWW Records Collection, Boxes 103–12, Walter P. Reuther Library, Wayne State University, Detroit. For general information on Frank Little, see the book by his great-grandniece Jane Little Botkin, which includes more family history and details than any previous work that touches on Little. Jane Little Botkin, *Frank Little and the IWW: The Blood That Stained an American Family* (Norman: University of Oklahoma Press, 2017); as to the accident, see 257–58.

2. The indictment later that year in *United States v. William D. Haywood et al.* included the figure 200,000. But the lead prosecutor admitted in his opening statement that the real number probably was closer to 40,000–60,000. Chicago Trial Tr. 12–13 (May 2, 1918).

3. As to Frank Little's parentage, see Will Roscoe, "The Murder of Frank Little: 'An Injury to One Is an Injury to All'" (unpublished manuscript, July 1, 1973), 9, http://www .willsworld.org/butte/franklittle.pdf. Roscoe writes that Little explained he was Cherokee

on his mother's side. But Botkin (*Frank Little and the IWW*, 9–64) gives a more detailed and convincing family history and an account of Frank's personal history. For general details and background, see Melvyn Dubofsky, *We Shall Be All*, abridged ed. (Urbana: University of Illinois Press, 2000), 223–24; David Montgomery, *The Fall of the House of Labor* (Cambridge University Press, 1987), 370–99; Roscoe, "The Murder of Frank Little." Little's departure from Bisbee for Butte the day before the deportation is detailed in Botkin, *Frank Little and the IWW*, 277. On machine guns at Bisbee, see Harrison George, *The I.W.W. Trial* (New York: Arno Press & New York Times, 1969), 199–201, and the Chicago Trial Transcript. Additional details of Bisbee and Little's role at the December 1916 annual convention and the army's complicity are from the Chicago Trial Tr. 1191–96, 1373.

4. For a detailed description of the disaster, see Eric Thomas Chester, *The Wobblies in Their Heyday* (Amherst, MA: Levellers Press 2014), 83–85.

5. Frank Little's July 19, 1917, speech, Chicago Trial Tr. 1341–83, 1384–91, 1418–19, 1438; "I.W.W. Strike Chief Lynched at Butte," *New York Times*, August 2, 1917, 20. On the rift with Haywood, see Botkin, *Frank Little and the IWW*, 290–91. Later trial testimony and letters introduced as trial exhibits bore out the tension between the two men.

6. Joyce Kornbluh, ed., *Rebel Voices: An IWW Anthology* (Oakland, CA: PM Press, 2011), 295. For a detailed account of the lynching, see Botkin, *Frank Little and the IWW*, 295–304.

7. William D. Haywood, *Bill Haywood's Book* (New York: International Publishers, 1929), 301. Eric Thomas Chester makes the case for murder by a combination or overlap of Anaconda company gunmen and law enforcement officers in some detail, and with documentary support. *The Wobblies in Their Heyday*, 98–104. See also Botkin, *Frank Little and the IWW*, 295–311.

8. Even the kidnapping would not have violated federal law in 1917. Only after Charles Lindbergh's baby son was kidnapped in 1932 did Congress make that a federal crime, and then only if the kidnapping had some connection to interstate commerce or the mails. 18 U.S.C. § 1201. Congress refused repeatedly between 1917 and 1952 to enact an anti-lynching law.

9. "I.W.W. Strike Chief Lynched at Butte," *New York Times*, August 2, 1917, 20, gives the basic details of the lynching and statements by public officials. As to details of torture, see Helen Keller, "In Behalf of the I.W.W.," *The Liberator* 1, no. 1 (March 1918): 13. Keller describes the kidnappers and killers as "masked citizens." See also Chicago Trial Tr. 1377–79 for details of the lynching. On the unclaimed reward money, see Chicago Trial Tr. 1440.

10. As to the coordinated efforts of mine owners and western government officials, both state and local, see generally Dubofsky, *We Shall Be All* (abridged ed.), 215–27. For Butte's population, see United States Census Bureau, *Estimate of Population, 1917*, 14. In a rough quadrant running from Denver north through Cheyenne, Wyoming, to the Canadian border, west to the Puget Sound, south along the coast to Sacramento, California, and then east through Salt Lake City to Denver again, only Denver itself, Portland, Salt Lake City, and Seattle were larger than Butte. Mining was the reason. In 1917, Butte was significantly

more populous than Spokane or Sacramento, and Boise was a speck in comparison. As to Vice President Marshall, see *Mother Earth Bulletin* 1, no. 3 (December 1917): 4.

11. Eric Thomas Chester, *The Wobblies in Their Heyday*, 105.

12. Botkin, *Frank Little and the IWW*, 306–9; Dubofsky, *We Shall Be All* (abridged ed.), 392–93.

13. See Montgomery, *The Fall of the House of Labor*, 370–410; Dubofsky, *We Shall Be All* (abridged ed.), 168–242.

14. See *United States v. Carolene Products Co.*, 304 U.S. 144, 152n4 (1938); Ralph Chaplin, *Wobbly: The Rough-and-Tumble Story of an American Radical* (Chicago: University of Chicago Press, 1948), 244 (John Reed's role at trial).

15. As to Little's burial site, see Botkin, *Frank Little and the IWW*, 308–9.

Chapter 2. One Big, and Different, Union

1. Elizabeth Gurley Flynn, *Memories of the Industrial Workers of the World*, American Institute for Marxist Studies, Occasional Paper No. 24 (1977) (a transcript of Flynn's November 8, 1962, appearance at Northern Illinois University), 33.

2. Details of the founding events of the IWW come from Patrick Renshaw, *The Wobblies: The Story of the IWW and Syndicalism in the United States* (1968; repr., Chicago: Ivan R. Dee, 1999), 33–41; Philip S. Foner, *History of the Labor Movement in the United States*, vol. 4, *The Industrial Workers of the World 1905–1917* (New York: International Publishers, 1965), 14–39; Melvyn Dubofsky, *We Shall Be All*, abridged ed. (Urbana: University of Illinois Press, 2000), 43–49; Gurley Flynn, *Memories of the Industrial Workers of the World*, 13. The term "wage slave" was common parlance among socialists, labor activists, syndicalists, and anarchists of the day, who themselves were distinct if loose groups with overlapping and shifting areas of agreement and discord.

3. *Preamble to the Industrial Workers of the World Constitution*, 1905 (first and last sentences).

4. As to the possible deliberate opaqueness of "industrial democracy," see Foner, *History of the Labor Movement in the United States*, vol. 4, 141–42.

5. Foner, *History of the Labor Movement in the United States*, vol. 4, 98, 147, 462; Renshaw, *The Wobblies*, 71–73; Dubofsky, *We Shall Be All* (abridged ed.), 43–45.

6. The 200,000 number was in the September 1917 indictment of IWW members in Chicago. *United States v. William D. Haywood et al.*, No. 6125 (N.D. Ill. September 28, 1917), Indictment at 7 (obtainable online from the National Archives Catalog, Records Group 21, National Archives Identifier 7372720). As to the government conceding that the actual number was lower, see *United States v. Haywood et al.*, Transcript 12–13 (May 2, 1918), at Walter P. Reuther Library of Labor and Urban Affairs, Wayne State University, IWW Collection, Accession No. 130, Boxes 103–121 (hereafter Chicago Trial Tr.). Renshaw estimates that, because membership turnover was so great (he asserts an average rate of 133 percent between 1905 and 1915), something like 1 million workers may have held IWW cards at a time in their lives. Renshaw, *The Wobblies*, 2, citing Paul F. Brissenden, *The*

IWW: A Study of American Syndicalism (New York: Russell & Russell, 1920), 351–52; John S. Gambs, *The Decline of the IWW* (New York: Columbia University Press, 1932), 164–69. As to the 100,000 estimate in 1917, see Dubofsky, *We Shall Be All* (abridged ed.), 200. Leading an itinerant life, as many Wobblies did by necessity, was treated as illegal. This meant that police harassment was frequent. Decades would pass before the Supreme Court looked at the effect and constitutionality of vagrancy laws. See Risa L. Goluboff, *Vagrant Nation: Police Power, Constitutional Change, and the Making of the 1960s* (Oxford University Press, 2016).

7. Renshaw, *The Wobblies*, 170 (the period 1914–17 saw the IWW's greatest growth); Dubofsky, *We Shall Be All* (abridged ed.), 200.

8. Dubofsky, *We Shall Be All* (abridged ed.), 200–227.

9. Melvyn Dubofsky, *We Shall Be All: A History of the IWW* (Chicago: Quadrangle Books, 1969), ix, 485n1.

10. As to readings and views on IWW, see Chicago Trial Tr. 5946, 5948, 5960. As to the forms of sabotage, the trial transcript makes repeated reference to these and similar acts of sabotage throughout, disputably attributing them to IWW members or to the organization.

11. As to the loss of eyesight, see Richard Brazier, "The Mass I.W.W. Trial of 1918: A Retrospect," *Labor History* 7, no. 2 (1966): 178.

12. Foner, *History of the Labor Movement in the United States*, vol. 4, 151–57; Renshaw, *The Wobblies*, 144–60.

Chapter 3. Big Bill

1. William D. Haywood, *Big Bill Haywood's Book* (New York: International Publishers, 1929), 8–13. Haywood's early life largely defies objective study or corroboration. This autobiography and his testimony in his 1907 Idaho murder trial provide most of the details that biographers and other students must rely upon. Melvyn Dubofsky, *"Big Bill" Haywood* (New York: St. Martin's, 1987); Peter Carlson, *Roughneck: The Life and Times of Big Bill Haywood* (New York: W. W. Norton, 1983); see also Joseph R. Conlin, *Big Bill Haywood and the Radical Union Movement* (Syracuse: Syracuse University Press, 1969). As Dubofsky notes, some persons unnamed insist that the autobiography, produced during the last year of Haywood's life when his health was failing in Moscow, was ghostwritten by Communist Party members in part for their own purposes. Dubofsky, *"Big Bill" Haywood*, vi, 3, 150. Carlson, though, squarely rejects that suspicion—possibly on the nonresponsive claim that "his account of his adventures is generally accurate and sometimes excellently rendered." Carlson, *Roughneck*, 332. And even Carlson acknowledges that Haywood's autobiography has other "glaring faults." Ibid. Dubofsky is a respected academic historian with strong credentials and a career-long serious interest in the IWW. He praises Carlson's book highly, although by Carlson's own admission he is not an academic and did not set out to write a "scholarly" biography. Dubofsky, *"Big Bill" Haywood*, 150; Carlson, *Roughneck*, 331. As this book aspires to present a legal history of the IWW Chicago trial, not anything like a complete biography of any participant, I leave it at that.

2. Haywood, *Bill Haywood's Book*, 12–19.

3. Dubofsky, *"Big Bill" Haywood*, 11–12.

4. Haywood, *Bill Haywood's Book*, 30–31; Dubofsky, *"Big Bill" Haywood*, 12–13; Emma Goldman, *Living My Life*, 2 vols. (1931 New York: Da Capo Press, 1970 reprint), vol. 1, 10; see also James Green, *Death in the Haymarket* (New York: Pantheon, 2006), 267–77.

5. Haywood, *Bill Haywood's Book*, 32–33, 62–64; Dubofsky, *"Big Bill" Haywood*, 14–16; Carlson, *Roughneck*, 43–53.

6. Dubofsky, *"Big Bill" Haywood*, 22–23.

7. Haywood, *Bill Haywood's Book*, 71–173; Carlson, *Roughneck*, 43–77; Dubofsky, *"Big Bill" Haywood*, 21–33.

8. Carlson, *Roughneck*, 23, 293; Dubofsky, *"Big Bill" Haywood*, 4.

9. Melvyn Dubofsky, *We Shall Be All* (Chicago: Quadrangle Books, 1969), 91–119.

10. Haywood, *Bill Haywood's Book*, 220, 223. For a magisterial account of the Steunenberg murder trials (and much else in that era), see J. Anthony Lukas, *Big Trouble* (New York: Simon & Schuster, 1997).

11. Haywood, *Bill Haywood's Book*, 216–17, 229, 230; Carlson, *Roughneck*, 149.

12. Dubofsky, *"Big Bill" Haywood*, 58–59.

13. Elizabeth Gurley Flynn, *Memories of the Industrial Workers of the World (IWW)*, American Institute for Marxist Studies, Occasional Paper No. 24 (1977), 10–11; Carlson, *Roughneck*, 160–86; Dubofsky, *We Shall Be All* (abridged ed.), 139–51.

14. *Speech of Wm. D. Haywood on the Case of Ettor and Giovannitti* (Lawrence, MA: Ettor-Giovannitti Defense Committee, 1912), 16. In autumn 1912, a Salem, Massachusetts, jury acquitted Ettor and Giovannitti of the very weak murder charge they faced. Carlson, *Roughneck*, 190–91.

15. Gurley Flynn, *Memories of the Industrial Workers of the World (IWW)*, 11; Dubofsky, *"Big Bill" Haywood*, 141.

16. Dubofsky, *"Big Bill" Haywood*, 73; Carlson, *Roughneck*, 197–99; Haywood, *Bill Haywood's Book*, 257–60, 276; Patrick Renshaw, *The Wobblies: The Story of the IWW and Syndicalism in the United States* (1968; repr., Chicago: Ivan R. Dee, 1999), 138.

Chapter 4. Ed

1. Joe Hill was then and is now another important face of the IWW in the public mind. But Hill was a poet and songwriter, an important messenger to both the membership and the public, not a leader in the formal hierarchy. He also was dead by 1916. Again, the State of Utah had executed him by firing squad in 1915 after a controversial trial of doubtful reliability. See, e.g., William M. Adler, *The Man Who Never Died* (New York: Bloomsbury USA, 2011).

2. Much of Edwin F. Doree's biography I draw from his daughter's memoir. Ellen Doree Rosen, *A Wobbly Life* (Detroit: Wayne State University Press, 2004). Other sources include Doree's own letters home to his wife, Ida Doree née Salinger, whom he invariably called "Chiky"; the Chicago trial transcript; and secondary sources, all cited below.

3. Rosen, *A Wobbly Life*, xi (on Maria Doree's pronunciation of her son's name) and 2–3 (on Ed Doree's early history). As to his night school studies, see Doree's testimony, Chicago Trial Tr. 5904.

4. Rosen, *A Wobbly Life*, 3, 200–201.

5. As to the absence of the rule of law, see Chicago Trial Tr. 5931. As to details of the gun-barrel shacks and the wage differentials between white and black workers, see Chicago Trial Tr. 5908, 5913–15. As to the danger of arguing over wages or debt and the cost of murdering a black worker, see Chicago Trial Tr. 5914. For other details, see Chicago Trial Tr. 5902–68. Incidentally, the problem of wage theft that Doree described, in its 1912 particulars, remains with modern variations more than one hundred years later. The Economic Policy Institute in May 2017 released a study of ten large states, from which it extrapolated that wage theft—through methods such as denial of legally mandated overtime pay, illegal deductions, refusal to pay for all hours worked, misclassification of employees to avoid minimum wage laws, and simple withholding of pay—may cost American workers $15 billion a year. If so, that number exceeds FBI estimates of all other forms of property crime (robbery, burglary, larceny, and car theft) combined. David Cooper & Teresa Kroeger, *Employers Steal Billions from Workers' Paychecks Each Year* (Washington, DC: Economic Policy Institute, May 10, 2017), 28.

6. Chicago Trial Tr. 5927–30.

7. Rosen, *A Wobbly Life*, 12.

8. Rosen, *A Wobbly Life*, 23.

9. Rosen, *A Wobbly Life*, 24.

10. Their daughter, Ellen Doree Rosen, describes the marriage that way throughout her book. And the letters that Ed and Chiky exchanged at least weekly during his years in prison unmistakably reflect mutual reliance, affection, and intimacy. They suggest strongly a mature and solid marriage. As to Chiky's sadness, see Rosen, *A Wobbly Life*, 6. On his nickname for her, see ibid., 5.

11. Rosen, *A Wobbly Life*, 24, 26.

12. Chicago Trial Tr. 5960.

13. To a striking extent, the brief autobiographies that IWW defendants offered in the opening pages of their testimony at the Chicago trial in 1918 reflected a "culture of poverty" that the sociologist Oscar Lewis noted almost fifty years later. Their life histories reflected "family disruption, violence, brutality, cheapness of life, lack of love, lack of education, lack of medical facilities," and so on. Oscar Lewis, *La Vida* (New York: Random House, 1966), xlv. Although Lewis's book later was the subject of thoughtful criticism for racist assumptions and attitudes, in part because his case studies focused on Puerto Ricans, I am not aware of any fair criticism leveled specifically at that general, prefatory insight. The great historian of the IWW, Melvyn Dubofsky, noted this culture within the IWW, too, although not in direct connection with the Chicago defendants. Melvyn Dubofsky, *We Shall Be All* (Chicago: Quadrangle Books, 1969), 149.

14. Rosen, *A Wobbly Life*, 7, 26. Rosen notes that letters between her father and mother refer to unspecified ailments in 1915, and she writes as if the young couple were unsure that pregnancy would be possible.

Chapter 5. Qui Pro Domina Justitia Sequitur?

1. Act of June 22, 1870, 41st Cong., 2d Sess., ch. 150, 16 Stat. 162.

2. U.S. Const., Art. I, § 8; see also U.S. Const., Amend. X (powers not delegated to the federal government, or prohibited to the states, remain reserved to the states).

3. For example, in FY2014 (the most recent year that the U.S. Department of Justice, Bureau of Justice Statistics, reports as of this writing), just over 80,000 criminal defendants were charged in the nation's federal courts. In calendar year 2014, which both started and ended three months after the federal fiscal year, the correlative number of state criminal defendants in the nation's state courts was over 15 million. U.S. Department of Justice, Office of Justice Programs, Bureau of Justice Statistics, *Federal Justice Statistics, 2014 Statistical Tables*, Table 4.1, at p. 15; National Center for State Courts, Court Statistics Project, *2014 Incoming Caseloads (by Tier) and Case Category*, www.courtstatistics.org (last visited April 23, 2017) (14,762,238 criminal defendants reported by 40 states and the District of Columbia, with 10 states not reporting). Note that these numbers refer to the total of persons charged, not to the total of distinct individuals. Many people are charged more than once in a given year. These numbers also reflect only persons charged, not persons convicted.

The stark disproportion of federal prisoners (which includes only those in state or federal prisons, not persons in local jails) is due to the fact that federal prosecutors tend to prosecute only serious federal crimes in the main. The misdemeanor caseload in federal courts is minimal. However, misdemeanors and relatively minor traffic crimes make up the vast majority of all state criminal prosecutions, and defendants typically do not go to prison for those offenses.

4. Judiciary Act, § 35, ch. 20, 1 Stat. 73, 92–93 (September 24, 1789). See generally Susan Low Bloch, *The Early Role of the Attorney General in Our Constitutional Scheme: In the Beginning There Was Pragmatism*, 1989 DUKE L. J. 561, 566–90 (June 1989). As to 1831, see Luther A. Huston, *The Department of Justice* (New York: Praeger Library of U.S. Government Departments and Agencies, 1967), 9.

5. Judiciary Act, § 35; *Historical Register of the United States* (Philadelphia: G. Palmer, 1814), vol. 1, § 28 at page 44. In 1896, Congress finally replaced a patchwork of compensation for district attorneys of "salaries, fees, per centums, and other compensations now allowed by law" with fixed annual salaries. Even those varied by judicial district, though. 54th Cong., 1st Sess., ch. 252, § 7, 29 Stat. 180–81 (May 28, 1896). The initial salaries were generous in 1896 dollars, ranging from $2,000 to $5,000, depending on the district.

6. Militia Act of 1792, 2d Cong., 1st Sess., ch. 28, 1 Stat. 264 (May 2, 1792) (also called the Calling Forth Act, to distinguish it from a second Militia Act passed six days later, on May 8, 1792).

7. For more on the early KKK prosecutions, see, e.g., Ron Chernow, *Grant* (New York: Penguin Press, 2017), 701–11.

8. Lincoln's assassination and its aftermath have been the subjects of any number of books and articles, of course. Just a sampling includes Michael W. Kauffman, *American Brutus: John Wilkes Booth and the Lincoln Conspiracies* (New York: Random House, 2004); James L. Swanson, *Manhunt: The 12-Day Chase for Lincoln's Killer* (New York: William

Morrow, 2006); Harold Holzer, compiler, *President Lincoln Assassinated!! The Firsthand Story of the Murder, Manhunt, Trial, and Mourning* (New York: Library of America, 2014).

9. As to the history of the Molly Maguires and the official response to them, see, e.g., Kevin Kenny, *Making Sense of the Molly Maguires* (New York: Oxford University Press, 1998). As to Bisbee, see chapter 1 and notes there.

10. The Oshkosh woodworkers' case, in which the lead defendant was Thomas I. Kidd, was one of Clarence Darrow's first victories for the labor movement. An edited version of his closing argument appears in Arthur & Lila Weinberg, eds., *Attorney for the Damned* (Chicago: University of Chicago Press, 1957), 269–326. See also Virginia Glenn Crane, *The Great Oshkosh Woodworker Strike of 1898: A Wisconsin Community in Crisis* (privately printed, 1998).

11. For one example only, consider the federal prosecution of Eugene Debs following the American Railway Union's Pullman strike. Although the U.S. district attorney for the Northern District of Illinois, initially Thomas Milchrist and later John C. Black, participated, the lead prosecutor was in fact Edwin Walker, counsel for the Chicago, Milwaukee & St. Paul Railroad Co. and for the General Managers Association, the railroad owners' association. The attorney general of the United States, Richard Olney, approved the appointment of his friend Walker as special prosecutor. Olney himself was a wealthy railroad lawyer before and after serving as President Grover Cleveland's attorney general (1893–95). John W. Johnson, ed., *Historic U.S. Court Cases: An Encyclopedia*, 2nd ed. vol. 1 (New York: Routledge, 2001), 457–59. Walker's role continued on appeal in the U.S. Supreme Court. See *In re Debs*, 158 U.S. 564 (1895).

As to the frequency of labor disputes and their relationship to changes in law generally, like the growing use of the injunction to stop strikes, economists Janet Currie and Joseph Ferrie assembled a data set of almost 13,000 labor disputes between 1881 and 1894 for their analysis. They did not address the use of private corporate lawyers as special prosecutors, in either state or federal court. Janet Currie & Joseph Ferrie, "The Law and Labor Strife in the U.S., 1881–1894," *Journal of Labor History* 60, no. 1 (March 2000): 42–66.

12. The Posse Comitatus Act, which translates from Latin into "power of the county," has been amended several times, including in recent decades in response to shifting congressional ideas about how best to respond to the international drug trade. The current codification is 18 U.S.C. § 1385. Among many other statutory exceptions, the president may call out federal troops when mass obstruction or rebellion makes it "impracticable to enforce the laws of the United States in any state or territory by the ordinary course of judicial proceedings." 10 U.S.C. § 332. See also Eric V. Larson & John E. Peters, *Preparing the U.S. Army for Homeland Security: Concepts, Issues, and Options*, Monograph MR-1251-A (Santa Monica, CA: RAND, 2001), Appendix D.

13. As to statutory terms, see the act of June 22, 1870, 41st Cong., 2d Sess., ch. 150, § 17, 16 Stat. 162. As to the final quote, it is the U.S. Supreme Court's construction of that provision in *United States v. Crosthwaite*, 168 U.S. 375, 381 (1897).

14. Robert H. Jackson reprints a speech given on April 1, 1940, in "The Federal Prosecutor," *Journal of the American Judicature Society* 24 (1940): 18–22.

Chapter 6. Something Must Be Done

1. My list is nowhere near exhaustive. See, e.g., Philip Taft, "The Federal Trials of the IWW," *Labor History* 3, no. 1 (1962): 57–91 (his is the most general article; it gives only an overview and focuses mostly on the trials themselves); Patrick Renshaw, "The IWW and the Red Scare, 1917–24," *Journal of Contemporary History* 3, no. 4 (October 1968): 63–72; William Preston Jr., *Aliens and Dissenters* (Cambridge, MA: Harvard University Press, 1963), 85–117; Melvyn Dubofsky, *We Shall Be All* (Chicago: Quadrangle Books, 1969), 398–422 (detailed recounting of the efforts leading up to indictment); Peter Carlson, *Roughneck: The Life and Times of Big Bill Haywood* (New York: W. W. Norton, 1983), 240–54; Melvyn Dubofsky, *"Big Bill" Haywood* (New York: St. Martin's, 1987); Eric Thomas Chester, *The Wobblies in Their Heyday* (Amherst, MA: Levellers Press, 2014), 133–58. Of the historians and economists who have covered the campaign against the IWW in the period 1916–17, Carlson is an accomplished lifelong journalist and book author, while Chester has the thinnest academic background. Chester is critical of several of the academics as too conservative in their assessments of the IWW and the popularity of radical ideology among workers of the era. See Chester, *The Wobblies in Their Heyday*, 297–301. But he also had access to newly declassified government documents that earlier writers never saw.

2. National Archives II, Record Group 60, Straight Numerical Case No. 186701, Entry A1 112 B, Boxes 2181–86. For W. G. Miller's telegram in specific, see Straight Numerical Case No. 186701-5.

3. The opposition to war on Canadian farms and in rural communities led, in part, to the "khaki election" of 1917, which temporarily extended the vote to widows, wives, and mothers of soldiers as a gambit to gain support for the new draft there. The Unionist coalition government of Prime Minister Borden calculated, correctly, that women would support the draft as a way to spread the burden of sending young men abroad and shorten their tours of duty. See generally Tim Cook, "'Our First Duty Is to Win, at Any Cost:' Sir Robert Borden during the Great War," *Journal of Military and Strategic Studies* 13, no. 3 (2011): 1–24. For American soldiers' deaths, see https://encyclopedia.1914-1918-online.net/article /war_losses.

4. "Report of the President's Mediation Commission," reprinted in *Monthly Review of the U.S. Bureau of Labor Statistics* 6, no. 3 (March 1918): 60. The records of the President's Mediation Commission are located in the National Archives, U.S. Department of Labor Records Group No. 174, and elsewhere on microfilm.

5. Dubofsky, *We Shall Be All* (1969), 5–16, 349–75. Specific quotations are from pages 10 and 373.

6. Chester, *The Wobblies in Their Heyday*, 134, 154–56.

7. Dubofsky, *We Shall Be All* (1969), 294–98, 393–94; Chester, *The Wobblies in Their Heyday*, 133–34, 151–56; Preston, *Aliens and Dissenters*, 126–27. Ford was pardoned in 1925; Suhr, in 1926. Philip S. Foner, *History of the Labor Movement in the United States*, vol. 4, *The Industrial Workers of the World 1905–1917* (New York: International Publishers, 1965), 278.

8. John Lind Telegram to Thomas W. Gregory (July 26, 1917), and Gregory reply to Lind (July 27, 1917), National Archives II, Record Group 60, Entry A1 112 B, Straight Numerical Case Nos. 186701-24-1 & 186701-24-2, Boxes 2181–86; Carlson, *Roughneck*, 250; Dubofsky, *We Shall Be All* (1969), 382, 394–95. Cargill remains a privately held company today, and its own recounting of corporate history reports in 1917, "Cargill posts record profits and grain exchanges are criticized for the high price of wheat arising from wartime demand." *Cargill Timeline, 1865–Present*, www.cargill.com/doc/1432078093613/pdf-cargill -timeline.pdf (accessed July 29, 2017).

9. Chester, *The Wobblies in Their Heyday*, 133, 152–53; Dubofsky, *We Shall Be All* (1969), 393–94; Carlson, *Roughneck*, 249–50.

10. President Wilson blanched at internment and refused to carry it out. Lest the idea seem fanciful, though, consider President Franklin Delano Roosevelt's treatment of Japanese Americans in the West twenty-five years later. Under Executive Order 9066, the army interned some 117,000 citizens and lawful residents of Japanese ancestry. Western business organizations and politicians played a role in that policy, too.

11. Dubofsky, *We Shall Be All* (1969), 394. As to Ashurst's nickname for the IWW, see ibid., 376. As to Bell and the California Commission more generally, see Chester, *The Wobblies in Their Heyday*, 133, 153–54. As to the untruth of the rumor that the Germans were financing the IWW, at the Chicago trial the government called an accountant whom the Justice Department had retained, F. M. Bailey. He admitted on cross-examination that he concluded, after examining all the IWW's financial records, that it had not received money from Germany or Austria. Chicago Trial Tr. 614–18 (May 8, 1918); see also Philip Taft, "The Federal Trials of the IWW," *Labor History* 3, no. 1 (1962): 57, 60.

12. Preston, *Aliens and Dissenters*, 103–10; Dubofsky, *We Shall Be All* (1969), 401–3; Chester, *The Wobblies in Their Heyday*, 143–45; Carlson, *Roughneck*, 259–60; Paul F. Brissenden, "The Butte Miners and the Rustling Card," *American Economic Review* 10, no. 4 (December 1920): 755, 757–58; Robert Justin Goldstein, *Political Repression in Modern America from 1870 to the Present* (Boston: G. K. Hall, 1978), 116; Steven Parfitt, "The Justice Department Campaign Against the IWW, 1917–1920," *IWW History Project*, University of Washington, http://depts.washington.edu/iww/justice_dept.shtml (accessed August 4, 2017).

13. U.S. Const., Art. IV, § 4.

14. William C. Fitts Letter to Sen. Miles Poindexter (August 30, 1917), National Archives II, Record Group 60, Entry A1 112 B, Straight Numerical Case No. 186701-211, Boxes 2181–86.

15. As to the western campaign to influence local U.S. district attorneys, and the Justice Department through them, see Dubofsky, *We Shall Be All* (1969), 378–82.

Chapter 7. The Color of Law

1. *United States ex rel. Milwaukee Social Democratic Pub. Co. v. Burleson*, 255 U.S. 407 (1921). Victor L. Berger and his wife, Meta Berger, are interesting and important figures. In

addition to publishing the newspaper *Milwaukee Leader* and others, he was a leading figure in the Socialist Party of America and a U.S. congressman from 1911 to 1913 (originally in the Socialist Party wave of 1910 in Milwaukee) and again in the period 1923–29. Following denial of second-class mailing privileges to the *Milwaukee Leader*, Berger himself was indicted under the Espionage Act. Defiant voters re-elected him to Congress while he was under indictment in 1918, and again after his conviction in 1919, when the refusal of Congress to seat him required a special election for his open seat. Congress once more refused to seat him. By 1922, voters re-elected him yet again and he served three more terms. The judge who presided over his 1919 trial, the year after the trial at the heart of this book, was the same Kenesaw Mountain Landis in Chicago federal court. Landis sentenced Berger to 20 years in prison. In early 1921, over three dissents, the Supreme Court reversed that conviction because Landis wrongly declined the defendant's request that he recuse himself for actual bias. *Berger v. United States*, 255 U.S. 22 (1921). The government did not retry Berger, who had been free on bond pending appeal. See Victor L. Berger, American National Biography Online, www.anb.org (article by Sally M. Miller); Dean A. Strang, *Worse than the Devil: Anarchist, Clarence Darrow, and Justice in a Time of Terror* (Madison: University of Wisconsin Press, 2013), 6, 69, 215n19.

2. I leave outside the scope of this book the role of the American Protective League and its origins in a February 1917 agreement with the attorney general. I also do not explore the interdepartmental rivalry, and personal tussling, between Attorney General Thomas Watt Gregory's Justice Department and Treasury Secretary William Gibbs McAdoo's Secret Service. That ongoing and often spirited struggle for budgetary and departmental advantage continued in the background of the federal government's efforts to form a coherent strategy for responding to the IWW throughout the summer of 1917. In the end, with both President Wilson and Congress, the Justice Department and its Bureau of Investigation won the leading role in enforcing wartime legislation. For treatments of the Bureau of Investigation in its early years, see Tim Weiner, *Enemies: A History of the FBI* (New York: Random House, 2012); Beverly Gage, *The Day Wall Street Exploded: A Story of America in its First Age of Terror* (Oxford: Oxford University Press, 2009); and William H. Thomas Jr., *Unsafe for Democracy: World War I and the U.S. Justice Department's Covert Campaign to Suppress Dissent* (Madison: University of Wisconsin Press, 2008). The legal historian Michal R. Belknap also has written extensively on the FBI, focusing on the time since WWII. But he covers this era in his article "The Mechanics of Repression: J. Edgar Hoover, the Bureau of Investigation and the Radicals, 1917–1925," *Crime and Social Justice* 7 (1977): 50. For the story of the APL, which still is a lightly explored topic, see, e.g., Joan M. Jensen, *The Price of Vigilance* (Chicago: Rand McNally, 1968); and Bill Mills, *The League: The True Story of Average Americans on the Hunt for WWI Spies* (New York: Skyhorse, 2013). For a short history of the rivalry between the Secret Service and the Bureau of Investigation, see John F. Fox Jr., "Bureaucratic Wrangling over Counterintelligence, 1917–18," www.cia .gov/library/center-for-the-study-of-intelligence/csi-publications/csi-studies/vol49no1 /html_files/bureaucratic_wragling_2.html. The misspelling of "wrangling" in the URL is the CIA's mistake, not mine.

3. His contributions to the University of Texas were real and lasting. Still today, the main campus in Austin retains a Gregory Gymnasium named for him, now expanded to include an Aquatic Complex.

4. Thomas W. Gregory, "Reconstruction and the Ku Klux Klan," originally published in the *Dallas News* and reprinted in *Confederate Veteran* 29, no. 8 (August 1921): 292–96.

5. Melvyn Dubofsky, *We Shall Be All* (Chicago: Quadrangle Books, 1969), 404; Preston, *Aliens and Dissenters* (Cambridge, MA: Harvard University Press, 1963), 123–24.

6. *Official Register of the United States, 1918* (Washington, DC: Government Printing Office), 73. In 2018 dollars, that $7,500 salary would be roughly $148,175. Attorney General J. Howard McGrath appointed the first deputy attorney general, to serve as second in command, in 1950. Congress authorized the position permanently in 1966. Pub. L. 89-554, § 4(c), 80 Stat. 612 (September 6, 1966).

7. Michael Allan Wolf, "Charles Warren," *American National Biography Online*, www.anb.org (accessed November 28, 2018). Note that Warren fit within the general contours of the Progressive movement of his day, advocating pragmatic government goals, centrist and middle-class values, and a robust role for legislation in curing perceived social ills. Many, but not all, progressives in public life were Republicans or western Democrats. Progressives shared something, too, with "good government" or "goo goo" politicians in the northeast.

8. "William C. Fitts, U.S. Ex-Aide, Dies," *New York Times*, February 28, 1954; "Alabama Attorneys General, William C. Fitts," Alabama Department of Archives and History, www.archives.alabama.gov/conoff/fittswc.html (accessed August 5, 2017). As to the fear quotation, see Dubofsky, *We Shall Be All* (1969), 410.

9. Dubofsky, *We Shall Be All* (1969), 404–5; Wolf, "Charles Warren."

10. It is hard to determine the exact number of Bureau of Investigation agents because the bureau grew very rapidly in and after 1917. But the 425 number when the United States declared war in April 1917 comes from Jamie Bisher, *The Intelligence War in Latin America, 1914–22* (Jefferson, NC: McFarland, 2016), 110. Incidentally, 1917 also was the year that a twenty-two-year-old lawyer, John Edgar Hoover, joined the Bureau of Investigation at an entry level. Luther A. Huston, *The Department of Justice* (New York: Frederick A. Praeger, 1967), 223.

11. Dubofsky, *We Shall Be All* (1969), 394–95.

12. William C. Fitts to Sen. Albert B. Fall (August 30, 1917), National Archives II, Record Group 60, Entry A1 112 B, Boxes 2181–86, Straight Numerical Case No. 186701-27-16; see also Dubofsky, *We Shall Be All* (1969), 397, quoting same letter, cited at 519n44.

Chapter 8. Five Tons

1. Melvyn Dubofsky, *We Shall Be All* (Chicago: Quadrangle Books, 1969), 396, 405–6; Peter Carlson, *Roughneck: The Life and Times of Big Bill Haywood* (New York: W. W. Norton, 1983), 251–52. Covington served as chief justice of the Supreme Court of the District of Columbia from 1914 to 1918. In 1919, leaving the bench, he would cofound the law firm of Covington & Burling. That remains an eminent DC firm, now known as Covington & Burling, LLP, with offices around the world.

2. Carlson, *Roughneck*, 251–52; Melvyn Dubofsky, *"Big Bill" Haywood* (New York: St. Martin's, 1987), 108–9. As to Toledo, see Bulletin of August 28, 1914, IWW Records Collection, Accession No. 130, Box 121.

3. Chicago Trial Tr. 137–59 (May 3, 1918); Chicago Trial Tr. 161–203 (May 3, 1918); Carlson, *Roughneck*, 253–54; William D. Haywood, *Bill Haywood's Book* (New York: International Publishers, 1929), 302.

4. IWW Records Collection, Accession No. 130, Box 119, File 9 for quotes of Haywood and Little exchanges; Dubofsky, *We Shall Be All* (1969), 354–58; Eric Thomas Chester, *The Wobblies in Their Heyday* (Amherst, MA: Levellers Press 2014), 123–31; Carlson, *Roughneck*, 242–44.

5. National Archives II, Record Group 60, Straight Numerical Case No. 186701-14 (all seven telegrams and draft telegrams in this file), Entry A1 112 B, Boxes 2181–86.

6. Thomas W. Gregory Telegram to United States Attorney (August 30, 1917), National Archives II, Record Group 60, Entry A1 112 B, Straight Numerical Case No. 186701-14-28, Boxes 2181–86.

7. Although probable cause and particularity remain active topics of judicial discussion and definitional refinement, at this level of generality, both assertions were true in 1917 in spite of the scant attention the Supreme Court had paid to the Fourth Amendment at that point. Indeed, both are rooted in the express terms of the Fourth Amendment. See, e.g., *Entick v. Carrington*, 19 Howell's State Trials 1029, 2 Wils. K.B. 275, 95 Eng. Rep. 807 (C.P. 1765) (direct antecedent of the Fourth Amendment); *Boyd v. United States*, 116 U.S. 616 (1886) (unreasonableness of a law permitting seizure of private papers without a proper warrant); *Weeks v. United States*, 232 U.S. 383 (1914) (need for proper warrant and particular description of items to be seized). At the time, at least some federal courts construed "probable cause" more narrowly, and more naturally from the viewpoint of the ordinary meaning of its words, than I have defined it here: the term required not just a reasonable possibility but a "probability" that the target of the warrant had committed a crime. See, e.g., *United States v. Baumert*, 179 F. 735 (D.C. Cir. 1910). I use a more modern description here because the exact meaning of the term "probable cause" was then, and is now, unsettled and slippery. Note that my qualification of a *federal* search warrant was important then, for the Supreme Court did not hold until 1949 that the Fourth Amendment applied to the states as well, through the Due Process Clause of the Fourteenth Amendment. *Wolf v. Colorado*, 338 U.S. 25 (1949).

8. *Boyd*, 116 U.S. at 630.

9. See, generally, *Boyd*, 116 U.S. 616, which in turn relied heavily on *Entick v. Carrington* on this point. The quoted reference to a "man's private papers" is at page 622 and elsewhere in the Court's opinion in *Boyd*. For a history of the mere evidence rule, see also William T. Rintala, *The Mere Evidence Rule: Limitations on Seizure under the Fourth Amendment*, 54 Cal. L. Rev. 2099, 2103–13 (Dec. 1966). The mere evidence rule would reach its peak four years after the IWW searches, in *Gouled v. United States*, 255 U.S. 298 (1921). Federal courts, and most or all state courts, since have abandoned it. A subpoena requiring the production of documents, rather than just a personal appearance, usually is called a subpoena *duces tecum*, the latter two words Latin for "you shall bring with you."

The word "subpoena" itself is Latin, meaning "under penalty." In the text, I omit *duces tecum* as unnecessary.

10. Espionage Act of 1917, 65th Cong., Sess. I, Ch. 30, Title XI, §§ 2(3), 22, 40 Stat. 228, 230. The government later made exactly this argument on appeal. Brief of United States, pages 1–16, *Haywood v. United States*, IWW Records Collection, Accession No. 130, Box 122, File 3.

11. As to the government's theory in using the Espionage Act's search warrant provisions, and its tacit admission that the warrants lacked probable cause, see Brief of United States on appeal in *Haywood v. United States*, pages 1–6, IWW Records Collection, Accession No. 130, Box 122, File 3; Brief for Plaintiffs in Error in *Haywood v. United States*, pages 67–69, 73, IWW Records Collection, Accession No. 130, Box 122, File 2. At the time, when federal appeals from criminal convictions still were by writ of error, the defendants were called "plaintiffs-in-error" on appeal; the government either was the "defendant-in-error" or just the United States. As to the language of the search warrants on the crimes supposedly committed, see, e.g., the warrants for the search of the Pittsburgh, Pennsylvania, IWW office, IWW Records Collection, Accession No. 130, Box 99, File, 13, and for the Tacoma, Washington, IWW office, IWW Records Collection, Accession No. 130, Box 99, File 22.

12. IWW office search warrant, page 2, Pittsburgh, Pennsylvania, IWW Records Collection, Accession No. 130, Box 99, File 13; *Haywood v. United States*, 268 F. 795, 801 (7th Cir. 1920).

13. Charles Clyne Telegram to William C. Fitts (August 30, 1917), National Archives II, Record Group 60, Entry A1 112 B, Straight Numerical Case No. 186701-14, Boxes 2181–86.

14. *Haywood v. United States*, 268 F. 795, 801 (7th Cir. 1920); Steven Parfitt, "The Justice Department Campaign Against the IWW, 1917–1920," *IWW History Project*, University of Washington, 2016, www.depts.washington.edu/iww/justice_dept.shtml.

15. All inventory information on the September 5 and subsequent raids comes from IWW Records Collection, Accession No. 130, Box 99. I cite the following cities: Philadelphia (File 12), Tacoma (File 22), Pittsburgh (File 13), Omaha (File 11), Minneapolis (Files 8 and 10), Great Falls (File 7), Butte (File 24), and Chicago (File 3). Some of the information comes from search warrant inventories and returns prepared by the government, the filing of which with the issuing court is a requirement of a search warrant (and was under the Espionage Act's statutory provisions). The Reuther Library's IWW Records Collection does not have those official inventories and returns for all warrants. Other information comes from reports and informal inventories that local IWW officials sent back to Chicago headquarters. As to the greatest bulk of seized materials coming from Chicago headquarters, see *Haywood v. United States*, 268 F. 795, 801 (7th Cir. 1920).

16. Again, Box 99 of the IWW Records Collection contains references to searches in various cities on all of these dates. The government searched all 48 offices on September 5. Subsequent searches targeted only subsets of those offices, sometimes as few as one. The figure of more than five tons comes from Brief of Plaintiffs in Error in *Haywood v. United States*, page 71, quoting February 1, 1918, Petition for Return of Papers and Articles, IWW Records Accession No. 130, Box 122, File 2. The government never disputed that figure.

17. The 15,000-page number comes from the Brief of Plaintiffs in Error in *Haywood v. United States*, page 4, IWW Records Collection, Accession No. 130, Box 122, File 2. The roles of Clabaugh and Murdock and the storage location of the seized materials in the Chicago federal courthouse come from briefs of both sides on appeal, in various mentions, and from the Chicago Trial Transcript itself. The use of paperclips and blue pencil annotations also appears repeatedly in the trial transcript.

Chapter 9. The Copper Trust Lawyer

1. "Class Notes, Law '02," *The Michigan Alumnus* 25 (August 1919); "Illness of One Again Delays Case of 113 I.W.W.'s," *Chicago Daily Tribune*, April 25, 1918, sec. 2, 1; Charles Francis Clyne obituary, *Chicago Tribune*, December 16, 1965.

2. National Archives II, Record Group 60, Straight Numerical Case No. 186701-14-6, 186701-14-17, 186701-14-24, 186701-14-26, 186701-14-27, Entry A1 112 B, Boxes 2181–86.

3. "Moving to Indict Socialist Leaders," *New York Times*, September 8, 1917, 1, 7.

4. On Aquila Nebeker, see "The Utah Senatorship," *New York Times*, November 25, 1898; Aquila Nebeker, Utah Department of Heritage & Arts, https://collections.lib.utah .edu. As to John Nebeker, see Hal Schindler, "Crime and Punishment: Settlers Relied on Ostracism, Whipping to Curb Lawlessness," *Salt Lake Tribune*, May 28, 1995, sec. J, 1. As to the relationship between Aquila and Frank K. Nebeker and professions in the family, see Oral History Project, The Historical Society of the District of Columbia, "The Honorable Frank Q. Nebeker" (interviews conducted by David W. Allen between August 12, 2003, and July 9, 2008), 1–2.

5. "Franklin Knowlton Nebeker," in *History of the Bench and Bar of Utah* (Salt Lake City: Interstate Press, 1913), 180; "Frank K. Nebeker," www.justice.gov/enrd/frank-k-nebeker (accessed November 25, 2018).

6. "Mack Names Committees," *New York Times*, August 7, 1908.

7. Nebeker's first two U.S. Supreme Court cases were *Cherokee Nation v. United States*, 270 U.S. 476 (1926), and *Independent Coal Coke Co. v. United States*, 274 U.S. 640 (1927). His last case in the Supreme Court was *United States v. Carolene Products Co.*, 304 U.S. 144 (1938): for more about that, see chapter 30.

8. As to successive jobs in the Justice Department, "Frank K. Nebeker," www.justice .gov/enrd/frank-k-nebeker; "Palmer Recasts Force of Helpers," *New York Times*, July 17, 1919, 5; "Wilson Makes Two Appointments," *New York Times*, November 20, 1920. As to salary in 1935, see "989 in New Deal Top $10,000 in Pay," *New York Times*, May 5, 1935, 5. As to the home on Woodley Road and wedding announcements, see "Delia Nebeker a Bride," *New York Times*, October 26, 1926; "Nuptials Are Held for Joyce N. Moyle," *New York Times*, June 23, 1946; "Miss Janet Young to Become a Bride," *New York Times*, November 3, 1946. As to role as counsel for the Cherokee Nation, see "Picked for Weirton Case," *New York Times*, April 3, 1934. As to the title "judge," see "Thorough Building Search," *New York Times*, January 11, 1921; "Weirton Counsel Lose Move in Suit," *New York Times*, October 9, 1934. The latter describes Nebeker as a "former Judge." The honorific was

uncommon at best for men who never had served as a judge (it was not like "Colonel" for prominent southern men at one time, by comparison), and here the *Times* asserts that he in fact once held such an office. Why the *New York Times* thought Nebeker a former judge remains unclear.

9. The name "Copper Trust lawyer," or some version of that, was a frequent epithet for Nebeker in the *Daily Bulletin* and *Trial Bulletin* that the IWW published before and during the trial. The quoted example is from the April 16, 1918, *Daily Bulletin* ("the legal luminary of the Copper Trust, attorney Nebeker"). Both the Justice Department website and the contemporary *History of the Bench and Bar of Utah* (1913) refer only to the Oregon short line railroad, although it is clear that Nebeker had a thriving corporate practice.

10. National Archives II, Record Group 60, Straight Numerical Case No. 186701-14-44, 186701-14-45, Entry A1 112 B, Boxes 2181–86.

11. Henry C. Evans, "Claude R. Porter: Character Sketch," *The Midwestern* 1, no. 3 (November 1906): 18.

12. "Claude R. Porter," *The Annals of Iowa*, vol. 28 (1946), 161–62; "Claude R. Porter, Candidate for Governor," *Adams County Free Press*, October 29, 1910, 1.

Chapter 10. True Bill

1. "Blow at I.W.W., 168 Are Indicted; Scores Arrested," *New York Times*, September 29, 1917, 1. The *Times* was wrong: the number indicted was 166.

2. As to the drafting of the indictment, which began in August 1917 at the latest, see Frank Dailey Letter to Attorney General (August 21, 1917) & Charles Clyne Letter to Attorney General (September 8, 1917), National Archives II, Record Group 60, Entry A1 112 B, Straight Numerical Case Nos. 186701-14-26 & 186701-14-38, Boxes 2181–86.

3. See William Blackstone, *Commentaries on the Laws of England*, 4 vols. (Oxford: Clarendon Press, 1769), vol. 4, 301; *Hale v. Henkel*, 201 U.S. 43, 60 (1906).

4. On occasion, a prosecutor does not try to obtain an indictment—or more rarely, affirmatively tries not to obtain one. In the latter group, the paradigmatic situation is when a possible crime occurs and either the prosecutor or a significant share of the general public, or both, sees the case from the prospective defendant's point of view and doubts his guilt. Examples may be cases of probably justified self-defense, or police shootings. In such cases, a prosecutor may encourage the grand jury not to indict, use the grand jury as a buffer by assigning it responsibility for the decision not to charge, and then rely on grand jury secrecy to deflect any criticism for the failure to file charges. After the grand jury refuses to indict, at the prosecutor's suggestion, the prosecutor can report to the media and public that the grand jury declined to indict and that the reasons are secret and known only to the grand jurors, redirecting anger. Less affirmatively and a bit more commonly, a scrupulous prosecutor may concede to a grand jury that an investigation just did not pan out in the end and that the evidence is weak or insufficient.

5. For one indication of the confusion that an indictment this large can cause, Philip Taft counted only 165 defendants, asserting that one had been named twice. Philip Taft, "The Federal Trials of the IWW," *Labor History* 3, no. 1 (1962): 61n16. I still count 166, as

have others, including one of the Chicago defendants himself. Harrison George, *The I.W.W. Trial* (New York: Arno Press & New York Times, 1969), 12. As to the Sioux trials, see Douglas O. Linder, "The Dakota Conflict Trials," 1999, http://famous-trials.com/da kotaconflict; Kenneth Carley, *The Sioux Uprising of 1862* (Minneapolis: Minnesota Historical Society Press, 1976). For the Houston riot courts-martial, see C. Calvin Smith, "The Houston Riot of 1917, Revisited," *The Houston Review* 13 (1991): 85–102.

6. As to this largest group of Heart Mountain resisters and other groups of *Nisei* prosecuted for refusing the draft, see Eric L. Muller, *Free to Die For Their Country: The Story of the Japanese American Draft Resisters in World War II* (Chicago: University of Chicago Press, 2001). On appeal, the convictions stood because although the men had been relocated and held unlawfully, they failed to seek relief earlier, by writ of habeas corpus in federal court, rather than later, by resisting the draft. According to the court, they sought justice at the wrong time and by the wrong legal procedure, so now they could not get relief at all. *Fujii v. United States*, 148 F.2d 298 (10th Cir. 1945). Given the U.S. Supreme Court's earlier rejection of a claim that the military internment of Japanese Americans was unconstitutional (see *Korematsu v. United States*, 323 U.S. 214 [1944]), the *Fujii* court's claimed certainty that federal habeas corpus would have provided a sure remedy seems, at best, a bit of convenient fantasy. As to such acts of dishonest fantasy by courts, see chapter 25.

7. "I.W.W. Leaders Get 20-Year Terms," *New York Times*, August 31, 1918, 1, 7. For the numbers in the Sacramento and Wichita cases, see Philip Taft, "The Federal Trials of the IWW," *Labor History* 3, no. 1 (1962): 57–91. As to Omaha, see David G. Wagaman, "The Industrial Workers of the World in Nebraska, 1914–1920," *Nebraska History* 56 (1975): 295–337. For an overview of all three of these other cases, see Melvyn Dubofsky, *We Shall Be All* (Chicago: Quadrangle Books, 1969), 438–44.

8. "17 Found Guilty in 'Pizza' Trial of a Drug Ring," *New York Times*, March 3, 1987, A1, B3. Prosecutor Louis J. Freeh served as director of the FBI from 1993 to 2001, after a two-year stint as a federal district judge. His colleague, Andrew C. McCarthy III, in 1995 led the terrorism prosecution of Sheikh Omar Abdel Rahman and today is a columnist for the *National Review*. Giuliani's political career after his time as U.S. attorney for the Southern District of New York is well known.

9. Two significant spiritual and intellectual leaders were omitted: Frank Little, organizer and G.E.B. member, had been lynched in Butte, Montana, on August 1, 1917; and Joseph Hillstrom, or "Joe Hill," the bard of the IWW, had been executed by a Utah firing squad in 1915 after a murder conviction in a trial of very doubtful integrity, reliability, or accuracy. As I note, though, Little's name was prominent in the indictment as a named but necessarily unindicted coconspirator. As to Ray Fanning, see "Bad Company for a Youth: Raymond Fanning Caught in I.W.W. Net," *Chattanooga Daily Times*, September 30, 1917, 1; Defendants' Brief of Evidence, Box 119, File 9, IWW Records Collection (Accession No. 130), Walter P. Reuther Library, Wayne State University.

10. *Haywood v. United States*, 268 F. 795, 798–806 (7th Cir. 1920); Indictment, *United States v. Haywood*, Case No. 6125, Labadie Collection, University of Michigan, H_8055.I5 H43 v.1; Patrick Renshaw, *The Wobblies: The Story of the IWW and Syndicalism in the United States* (1968; repr., Chicago: Ivan R. Dee, 1999), 174–75; Otto Christensen, *Statement*

Submitted to the Attorney General of the United States Concerning the Present Legal Status of the I.W.W. Cases (Washington, DC: Joint Amnesty Committee, undated in 1921), 6–7 (Christensen was one of the defense lawyers at trial and on appeal). People went to prison during and right after America's time in WWI for simply opposing the draft publicly. Emma Goldman and Alexander Berkman were two of the most prominent examples: they were prosecuted in the U.S. District Court in Manhattan after organizing the No Conscription League and giving speeches advocating that view. The Supreme Court let stand their convictions and two-year prison sentences, as did federal courts generally in such cases.

11. Indictment, *United States v. Haywood*, Case No. 6125, Labadie Collection, University of Michigan, H_8055.I5 H43 v.1.

12. Indictment, *United States v. Haywood*, Case No. 6125, Labadie Collection, University of Michigan, H_8055.I5 H43 v.1.

13. Indictment, *United States v. Haywood*, Case No. 6125, Labadie Collection, University of Michigan, H_8055.I5 H43 v.1.

14. "Haywood and 8 Others Held for Conspiracy," *New York Call*, September 29, 1917, 2.

15. *Daily Bulletin*, December 1, 1917; Renshaw, *The Wobblies*, 175.

16. "Shaven I.W.W.'s Kiss as Trial Is Postponed," *Chicago Tribune*, April 2, 1918, 7.

17. National Archives II, Record Group 60, Entry A1 112 B, Straight Numerical Case No. 188032-90, Boxes 2219–20.

18. See Elizabeth Gurley Flynn, *The Rebel Girl: An Autobiography, My First Life (1906–1926)*, rev. ed. (New York: International Publishers, 1973), 215–16, 226–27.

19. Frank K. Nebeker Letter to Thomas W. Gregory (October 25, 1917), National Archives II, Record Group 60, Entry A1 112 B, Straight Numerical Case No. 188032-45, Boxes 2219–20.

20. National Archives II, Record Group 60, Entry A1 112 B, Straight Numerical Case No. 188032-88, 188032-146, 188032-161, 188032-203, Boxes 2219–20.

21. Renshaw, *The Wobblies*, 175–76; Melvyn Dubofsky, *"Big Bill" Haywood* (New York: St. Martin's, 1987), 115–16; William D. Haywood, *Bill Haywood's Book* (New York: International Publishers, 1929), 313; Elizabeth Gurley Flynn, *Memories of the Industrial Workers of the World (IWW)* (San Jose, CA: American Institute for Marxist Studies, Occasional Papers Series No. 24, 1977), 14–15 (transcription of a November 8, 1962, talk at Northern Illinois University). As to Flynn's letter to President Wilson, see Philip Dray, *There Is Power in a Union: The Epic Story of Labor in America* (New York: Anchor Books, Random House, 2011), 362. As to her lawyer's promise, see Dubofsky, *We Shall Be All* (1969), 428. Possibly, too, the government did not relish the public appearance of trying just one woman among one-hundred-plus men. But that is entirely speculative: I have found nothing to support that possibility.

22. Principal Brief and Argument for Plaintiffs in Error (that is, the defendants) 18–19 IWW Records Collection, Box 122, File 2; Harrison George, *The I.W.W. Trial* (New York: Arno Press & New York Times, 1969) 12; Haywood, *Big Bill Haywood's Book*, 313; Dubofsky, *"Big Bill" Haywood*, 117. As to demurrers, see generally *Black's Law Dictionary*, 9th ed. (St.

Paul, MN: Thompson Reuters, 2009), 498. In almost all U.S. jurisdictions today, a pretrial motion to dismiss has replaced the demurrer and most other so-called special pleas. As to Vanderveer's gun, see "103 I.W.W. Leaders Face Judge Landis," *New York Times*, December 16, 1917, 6; "Find Revolver on Counsel for I.W.W.," *Milwaukee Sentinel*, December 16, 1917, 2.

23. Transcripts of the pretrial proceedings on the search and seizure issues apparently no longer exist. But I can reconstruct confidently the parties' arguments and the rulings in the trial court from the appellate briefs, which do exist. They are in various files within Boxes 119, 120, 122, and 123 of the IWW Records Collection, Accession No. 130, in the Walter P. Reuther Labor & Urban Affairs Library at Wayne State University. Here, I rely specifically on the principal Brief and Argument for Plaintiffs in Error (that is, the defendants) 3–6, 17, IWW Records Collection, Box 122, File 2; and the principal Brief of United States 1–16, IWW Records Collection, Box 122, File 3, both in *United States v. Haywood et al.*, No. 2721 (7th Cir. October Term 1920). As to the Espionage Act, see 65th Cong., Sess. I, Ch. 30, Title XI, §§ 2, 15, 16, 40 Stat. 228 (June 15, 1917). As to the mere-evidence rule, see chapter 8, notes 7 and 9.

24. For centuries by that time, April 1 had been known as April Fool's Day. In his memoir thirty years later, Ralph Chaplin noted the irony of the trial starting on April Fool's Day. Ralph Chaplin, *Wobbly: The Rough-and-Tumble Story of an American Radical* (Chicago: University of Chicago Press, 1948), 237.

Chapter 11. Twelve Good Men and True

1. Details of the Cook County Jail are taken from William D. Haywood, "On the Inside," *The Liberator* 1, no. 3 (May 1918): 15–16. As to the Easter weather, see "Billy Sunday Rained Out; Storm Checks Billy's Tirade Against Satan; Preacher Does His Best but Rain Seems on Devil's Side," *Chicago Daily Tribune*, April 1, 1918, 6.

2. Haywood, "On the Inside," 15–16. The reasons why some defendants were housed in DuPage County Jail have never been clear. *Jail Bulletin*, February 9, 1918, IWW Records Collection, Accession No. 130, Box 123, File 6.

3. "100 I.W.W. Found Guilty," *Chicago Herald & Examiner*, August 18, 1918 (Extra), 1–2; as to the defendant who died, see Haywood, "On the Inside," 15–16.

4. Harrison George reported that 113 defendants were arraigned on December 15, 1917. Harrison George, *The I.W.W. Trial* (New York: Arno Press & New York Times, 1969), 12. With the one death in jail that Haywood described, that would make accurate the contemporary newspapers' counts of 112 defendants as the trial began. See, e.g., "I.W.W. Trial Drags as Jury Is Still Sought," *Chicago Tribune*, April 30, 1918, 3. But other articles early in the trial also referred to 113 defendants—e.g., "Illness Again Postpones Trial of 113 I.W.W.'s," *Chicago Tribune*, April 3, 1918, sec. I, 10.

5. George F. Vanderveer Letter to J. P. Tumulty & Woodrow Wilson (February 11, 1918), National Archives II, Record Group 60, Straight Numerical Case No. 188032-164, Entry AI 112 B, Boxes 2219–20.

6. As to the courtroom scene, A. C. Christ, and defendants' grooming, see "Shaven I.W.W.'s Kiss as Trial Is Postponed," *Chicago Tribune*, April 2, 1918, sec. 1, 7. As to tobacco chewing, see "Illness Again Postpones Trial of 113 I.W.W.'s," sec. 1, 10. On the number of deputy U.S. marshals, see "I.W.W. Jury Ready; Trial Begins To-Day," *Chicago Herald & Examiner*, May 2, 1918, 6.

7. George, *The I.W.W. Trial*, 12.

8. Arturo Giovannitti, "Selecting a Perfect Jury," *The Liberator* 1, no. 5 (July 1918): 8–10; John Reed & Art Young, "The Social Revolution in Court," *The Liberator* 1, no. 7 (September 1918): 20–28.

9. Giovannitti, "Selecting a Perfect Jury," 8.

10. "Shaven I.W.W.'s Kiss," sec. 1, 7; "Illness Again Postpones Trial of 113 I.W.W.'s," sec. 1, 10.

11. *Daily Bulletin*, April 11, 1918, IWW Records Collection, Accession No. 130, Box 123, File 20.

12. "Two Jurymen Are Accepted for I.W.W. Trial," *Chicago Tribune*, April 4, 1918, 9. As a member of the U.S. Circuit Court of Appeals for the Seventh Circuit, based in Chicago, since President Wilson appointed him in May 1916, Judge Evans only rarely would have had need of a courtroom. His primary duty was hearing appeals on a panel of three judges. As to Evans's judicial career, see "Evan Alfred Evans: Senior Circuit Judge: Seventh Circuit," *American Bar Association Journal* 33, no. 6 (June 1947): 554–57.

13. The final provision of the often-overlooked Civil Rights Act of 1957, Pub. L. 85-315 (September 9, 1957), amended 28 U.S.C. § 1861 to open jury service to women in every federal court. See also *Glasser v. United States*, 315 U.S. 60 (1942) (upholding an indictment, where women were excluded from the federal grand jury that returned the indictment). As to removing wage earners from federal jury pools, see *Thiel v. Southern Pacific Co.*, 328 U.S. 217 (1946).

14. See Giovannitti's report on jury selection, "Selecting a Perfect Jury," 9. With reference to loyalty, see "Loyalty Issue Bars Jurors at Trial of I.W.W.," *Chicago Tribune*, April 6, 1918, 6. On the pace of jury selection, see "Two Jurymen Are Accepted for I.W.W. Trial," 9. On the Collinsville lynching, see "Illinoisan Lynched for Disloyalty," *Chicago Tribune*, April 5, 1918, 1. On the Oklahoma near-lynching, see "Disloyalist Nearly Killed in Oklahoma," *Chicago Tribune*, April 20, 1918, 1. As to the tarring of Metzen and the IWW member, see *Jail Bulletin*, February 14, 1918, IWW Records Collection, Accession No. 130, Box 123, File 7.

15. *Daily Bulletin*, April 8, 1918, IWW Records Collection, Accession No. 130, Box 123, File 17.

16. As to striking the panel, see "Jury Tampering in I.W.W. Case Charged by U.S.," *Chicago Tribune*, April 7, 1918, sec. 1, 7. Noting the scant reason for dismissing the panel, see Giovannitti, "Selecting a Perfect Jury," 9. On resumption of jury selection, see "Socialists Are Kept off Jury in I.W.W. Case," *Chicago Tribune*, April 16, 1918, 5.

17. "Socialists Are Kept off Jury in I.W.W. Case," *Chicago Tribune*, April 16, 1918, 5.

18. "Hendricks Given Four Year Term by Judge Landis," *Chicago Daily Tribune*, April 16, 1918, 5.

19. "I.W.W. Attorneys Tender 12 Jurors to Government," *Chicago Tribune*, April 21, 1918, sec. 1, 12; "Illness Halts Completion of I.W.W. Jury," *Chicago Tribune*, April 23, 1918, 9; "Illness of One Again Delays Case of 113 I.W.W.'s," *Chicago Tribune*, April 25, 1918, 6; "I.W.W. Venire Exhausted and Trial Is Halted," *Chicago Tribune*, April 27, 1918, sec. 2, 12.

20. "11 Jurors Agreed Upon in Trial of I.W.W.," *Chicago Tribune*, May 1, 1918, 8; "One Indicted as Jury Fixer in I.W.W. Trial," *Chicago Tribune*, May 2, 1918, 7. I found no record that the indicted supposed jury fixer ever was tried. That indictment well may have been dismissed quietly after the main trial ended. As to the composition of the jury, see *Trial Bulletin*, May 1, 1918, IWW Records Collection, Accession No. 130, Box 123, File 31.

21. Giovannitti, "Selecting a Perfect Jury," 9–10. As to Pietro Nigra, see *Jail Bulletin*, February 14, 1918, IWW Records Collection, Accession No. 130, Box 123, File 7.

Chapter 12. Van and the Squire

1. Lowell S. Hawley & Ralph Bushnell Potts, *Counsel for the Damned* (Philadelphia: J. B. Lippincott, 1953), 16.

2. Again, Anthony Lukas's remarkable book remains the definitive account of the trials of Haywood, Moyer, and Pettibone for Steunenberg's murder by a bomb rigged to the front gate of his house. J. Anthony Lukas, *Big Trouble: A Murder in a Small Western Town Sets Off a Struggle for the Soul of America* (New York: Simon & Schuster, 1997).

3. As to Darrow's absence, see, e.g., Peter Carlson, *Roughneck: The Life and Times of Big Bill Haywood* (New York: W. W. Norton, 1983), 21; Ellen Doree Rosen, *A Wobbly Life* (Detroit: Wayne State University Press, 2004), 79; Patrick Renshaw, *The Wobblies: The Story of the IWW and Syndicalism in the United States* (1968; repr., Chicago: Ivan R. Dee, 1999), 179; Hawley & Potts, *Counsel for the Damned*, 227; Ralph Chaplin, *Wobbly: The Rough-and-Tumble Story of an American Radical* (Chicago: University of Chicago Press, 1948), 225–26. Melvyn Dubofsky does not comment on any approach to Darrow; he presents Vanderveer as close at hand, a champion of the Wobblies, and willingly accepting the offer to defend them in Chicago. Melvyn Dubofsky, *We Shall Be All* (Chicago: Quadrangle Books, 1969), 429.

4. As to the arc of Darrow's life and career beginning with the McNamara case and continuing through the Armistice in 1918, see Geoffrey Cowan, *The People v. Clarence Darrow: The Bribery Trial of America's Greatest Lawyer* (New York: Times Books, 1993). More generally, see any of the capable biographies of Darrow. Among them are Arthur & Lila Weinberg, *Clarence Darrow: A Sentimental Rebel* (New York: G. P. Putnam's Sons, 1980); John A. Farrell, *Clarence Darrow: Attorney for the Damned* (New York: Doubleday, 2011); Andrew E. Kersten, *Clarence Darrow: American Iconoclast* (New York: Hill & Wang, 2011); Kevin Tierney, *Darrow: A Biography* (New York: Book Sales, 1981); and the venerable but

adulatory Irving Stone, *Clarence Darrow for the Defense* (Garden City, NY: Doubleday, 1941). There also is Darrow's autobiography, *The Story of My Life* (New York: Charles Scribner's Sons, 1932), which is useful but has the self-interested recalcitrance and other flaws of many autobiographies. As ever, Randall Tietjen's collection of Darrow's correspondence is an invaluable reference for those interested in Darrow's own voice and his times. Randall Tietjen, ed., *In the Clutches of the Law: Clarence Darrow's Letters* (Berkeley: University of California Press, 2013). As to Darrow posting money for Haywood's appeal bond, see Carlson, *Roughneck*, 317. Patrick Renshaw notes that Darrow offered "staff assistance," to which Ellen Doree Rosen also refers. Renshaw, *The Wobblies*, 179; Rosen, *A Wobbly Life*, 79n26; see also Hawley & Potts, *Counsel for the Damned*, 227, on Darrow's offer of staff assistance.

5. Hawley and Potts's *Counsel for the Damned* is the only biography of Vanderveer. It has no notes, no list of sources, and no index. Especially as to Vanderveer's early background, before his legal practice, it may be quite unreliable. For example, while it asserts that David Vanderveer was over fifty when George was born and that Mary died when George was fourteen, online genealogical records have it that David was forty-five at George's birth and that Mary died in 1883, when George was eight. I tread lightly on the biographical details for this reason, and lean toward ancestry.com on disputed issues. But I also note that the Hawley and Potts book got nice, if not glowing, reviews in both the *New York Times Book Review* and the *Los Angeles Times* in late 1953.

6. As to football and life lessons, see Hawley & Potts, *Counsel for the Damned*, 29, 31–32.

7. Hawley & Potts, *Counsel for the Damned*, 87–88.

8. Hawley & Potts, *Counsel for the Damned*, 126.

9. Hawley & Potts, *Counsel for the Damned*, 136.

10. Hawley & Potts, *Counsel for the Damned*, 158–70.

11. Hawley & Potts, *Counsel for the Damned*, 131–34, 234.

12. As to the Everett shooting, see Hawley & Potts, *Counsel for the Damned*, 184–87. On all the following topics, see the corresponding pages in Hawley & Potts, *Counsel for the Damned*: the judge's recommendation, 189; Sunday School teachers, 190; a political trial, 191; the Everett trial, 193–209; Vanderveer's bender after the trial, 213; his failed attempt to enlist in the army, 215–17; Barbara, 133; gifts to Ellinor, 120; doubts about Vanderveer's commitment to the IWW and his doubts about their financial sense, 212–13. Of course, Vanderveer hardly was one to complain about others' loose finances. Indeed, the combination of the IWW and Vanderveer would prove financially disastrous to him during the Chicago trial.

13. As to the 121 slackers, see "One Hundred and Twenty-One Men," *International Socialist Review* 27, no. 2 (August 1917): 96–97. As to Hendricks, see "Hendricks Given Four Year Term by Judge Landis," *Chicago Daily Tribune*, April 16, 1917, 5. As to Berger, see David Pietrusza, *Judge and Jury: The Life and Times of Judge Kenesaw Mountain Landis* (South Bend, IN: Diamond Communications, 1998), 149.

14. I draw biographical details on Landis from two principal sources: John Henderson, "'The Most Interesting Man in America': Folk Logic and First Principles in the Early

Career of Judge Kenesaw Mountain Landis" (PhD diss., University of Florida, 1995); and Pietrusza, *Judge and Jury*. Both Henderson (29) and Pietrusza (3) agree on Landis's wariness of religion.

15. Pietrusza, *Judge and Jury*, 9–10; Henderson, "The Most Interesting Man in America," 45.

16. Pietrusza, *Judge and Jury*, 3, 8; Henderson, "The Most Interesting Man in America," 40.

17. Pietrusza, *Judge and Jury*, 11; Henderson, "The Most Interesting Man in America," 59–60. Note that Henderson makes no claim that Indiana law gave an advantage to a state employee in Landis's position in admittance to the bar. He describes the qualifications for anyone wishing to be a lawyer as only (1) registering to vote, and (2) proving good moral character.

18. Pietrusza, *Judge and Jury*, 14–27; Henderson, "The Most Interesting Man in America," 65–115. As to the "best friend" comment about Gresham, see Henderson, 75.

19. Henderson, "The Most Interesting Man in America," 149–175 (as to collecting gavels, see 149); Pietrusza, *Judge and Jury*, 32–41.

20. Mary Landis's telegram, cited in Pietrusza, *Judge and Jury*, 40.

21. Henderson, "The Most Interesting Man in America," 193–243; *Standard Oil Co. of Indiana v. United States*, 164 F. 376 (7th Cir. 1908), *cert. denied*, 212 U.S. 579 (1909). See also Pietrusza, *Judge and Jury*, 47–93.

22. Pietrusza, *Judge and Jury*, 42–43.

23. Henderson, "The Most Interesting Man in America," 72. I paraphrase Henderson closely here and use the same quotations from Landis's speech that he uses.

Chapter 13. A Gathering

1. As to the courtroom number, see David Pietrusza, *Judge and Jury: The Life and Times of Judge Kenesaw Mountain Landis* (South Bend, IN: Diamond Communications, 1998), 40–41; Art Young & John Reed, "The Social Revolution in Court," *The Liberator* 1, no. 7 (September 1918): 20–28.

2. As to spittoons, see "Two Jurymen Are Accepted for I.W.W. Trial," *Chicago Daily Tribune*, April 4, 1918, 9. As to the defendants' posture and activities during trial, see Young & Reed, "The Social Revolution in Court," 21–22; Ralph Chaplin, *Wobbly: The Rough-and-Tumble Story of an American Radical* (Chicago: University of Chicago Press, 1948), 243 (noting that he read both Carl Sandburg and Mark Twain during the long trial). As to defendants standing to be identified, see the Chicago trial transcript throughout.

3. As to the right to counsel at public expense, see *Gideon v. Wainwright*, 372 U.S. 335 (1963). The Chicago trial transcript reflects the roles of defense counsel and the prosecutors throughout. As to Cleary's speech, see "I.W.W.'s Sing, But Not to Star Spangled Strain," *Chicago Daily Tribune*, April 22, 1918, sec. 2, 1.

4. Frank K. Nebeker Letter to Thomas W. Gregory (December 3, 1917), National

Archives II, Record Group 60, Straight Numerical Case No. 188032-80, Entry A1 112 B, Boxes 2219-20.

5. "100 I.W.W. Are Found Guilty by Jury," *Chicago Herald & Examiner*, August 18, 1918, 1, 2; Pietrusza, *Judge and Jury*, 120.

6. See, e.g., William D. Haywood, *Bill Haywood's Book* (New York: International Publishers, 1929), 328 (although Haywood's assessment of Landis was colored, surely, by being written well after the trial); Arturo Giovannitti, "Selecting a Perfect Jury," *The Liberator* 1, no. 5 (July 1918): 8–10; Young & Reed, "The Social Revolution in Court," 20; "I.W.W. in Jail Admit They Got a Square Deal," *Chicago Daily Tribune*, August 19, 1918.

7. Pietrusza, *Judge and Jury*, 123.

8. "I.W.W. Jury Ready; Trial Begins To-Day," *Chicago Herald & Examiner*, May 2, 1918, 6.

9. "Haywood Longs for 'Other Boys' in Jail," *Chicago Daily News*, October 2, 1917; Peter Carlson, *Roughneck: The Life and Times of Big Bill Haywood* (New York: W. W. Norton, 1983), 24–25. The Sandburg interview of Haywood was reprinted in the November 1917 issue of *International Socialist Review*.

10. Young & Reed, "The Social Revolution in Court," 20; Pietrusza, *Judge and Jury*, 122. The August 1918 issue of *The Liberator* 1, no. 6, carried Reed's last dispatch from Russia and noted that he now had gone to Chicago. *The Liberator* was a successor to Max and Crystal Eastman's *The Masses*, which had lost its second-class postage permit. Max Eastman and several others were indicted, too, but not convicted.

11. Helen Keller, "In Behalf of the I.W.W.," *The Liberator* 1, no. 1 (March 1918): 13. Note the striking similarity of Eugene Debs's sentencing allocution six months later, after his federal trial in Cleveland, Ohio.

12. As to history of women on juries, see Holly J. McCammon, *The U.S. Women's Jury Movement and Strategic Adaptation: A More Just Verdict* (New York: Cambridge University Press, 2012). Note, too, that the U.S. Supreme Court commented in passing in 1880 that states, while not free to exclude black Americans from juries, could exclude all women. *Strauder v. West Virginia*, 100 U.S. 303 (1880). As to women supporters of the defendants, see, for example, "I.W.W. Beauties to Dazzle Jury from Front Row," *Chicago Daily Tribune*, April 5, 1918, 5; "Illness Halts Completion of I.W.W. Jury," *Chicago Daily Tribune*, April 23, 1918, 9 (commenting on Theodora Pollok's arrival in court); "Trial End Comes after 138 Days," *Chicago Journal*, August 17, 1918, 1, 2. As to Pettigrew's visit, see "I.W.W. Witness Flees Court on Call to Stand," *Chicago Daily Tribune*, May 4, 1918, 5. Descriptions of the placement of counsel tables and the press table, and other courtroom details, come from Haywood, *Bill Haywood's Book*, 313–14.

13. Thomas W. Gregory Telegram to A. B. Bielaski (December 21, 1917), A. B. Bielaski Memorandum to Attorney General (November 29, 1917), & William C. Fitts Letter to Rep. Carl Hayden (January 31, 1918), National Archives II, Record Group 60, Entry A1 112 B, Straight Numerical Case Nos. 186701-40 & 186701-not recorded, Boxes 2181–86; Frank K. Nebeker Letter to Attorney General (November 12, 1917), Straight Numerical Case No. 188032-69, Boxes 2219-20.

Chapter 14. This Un-American Institution

1. Chicago Trial Tr. 2–3, 5 (May 2, 1918).

2. Chicago Trial Tr. 41–43 (May 2, 1918).

3. Chicago Trial Tr. 22 (May 2, 1918).

4. As to salaries, see Chicago Trial Tr. 190 (May 3, 1918). At $90 a month, Haywood's annual pay in 1917 was $1,080. That same year, the Commissioner of Internal Revenue reported that 47.25 percent of American households earned between $1,000 and $2,000 in income, with another 13.84 percent earning between $2,000 and $2,500. Haywood's pay, then, was well within the lower half of American households. Treasury Department, U.S. Internal Revenue, *Statistics of Income: Compiled from the Returns for 1917* (GPO 1919), Table 3 at page 28. As to swivel-chair soldiers, see, e.g., "I.W.W Jury Ready; Trial Begins To-Day," *Chicago Herald & Examiner*, May 2, 1918, 6.

5. Chicago Trial Tr. 63 (May 2, 1918).

6. Chicago Trial Tr. 44–52 (May 2, 1918).

7. Chicago Trial Tr. 5 (May 2, 1918). Selective Service Act, Pub. L. 65-12, 40 Stat. 76 (May 18, 1917); Espionage Act, Pub. L. 65-24, 40 Stat. 217 (May 16, 1917). Note that the effective dates of the Acts were later than that, in June.

8. Chicago Trial Tr. 5 (May 2, 1918).

9. See the following references in the indicated trial records: large caliber cannon, Chicago Trial Tr. 73; membership figures, Chicago Trial Tr. 12–13; criminal organization from inception and antiwar appeal, Chicago Trial Tr. 55 (May 2, 1918).

10. On the evidence of sabotage but not armed force, see Chicago Trial Tr. 23–24; examples of sabotage, Chicago Trial Tr. 76–79; the black cat and the wooden shoe, Chicago Trial Tr. 74 (May 2, 1918). Note that in French, a simple wooden clog or shoe is a *sabot*. The term sabotage derives from that, and from the notion of disabling machinery by tossing a wooden shoe into it.

11. Chicago Trial Tr. 69 (May 2, 1918).

12. As to the IWW's attack on the wage system and all employers, see Chicago Trial Tr. 60–62. For the comparison with AFL and other unions, see Chicago Trial Tr. 80 (May 2, 1918).

13. Chicago Trial Tr. 88–89 (May 2, 1918).

14. William D. Haywood, *Bill Haywood's Book* (New York: International Publishers, 1929), 322.

15. Chicago Trial Tr., Box 108, File 5 (June 19, 1918), IWW Records Collection, Accession No. 130, Walter P. Reuther Library, Wayne State University.

16. Depot Quartermaster Memorandum to Adjutant General of the Army (January 21, 1918), and William C. Fitts Memorandum to Frank Nebeker and Claude Porter (January 25, 1918), National Archives II, Record Group 60, Entry A1 112 B, Straight Numerical Case No. 186701-36, Boxes 2181–86.

17. Chicago Trial Tr. 90–136, 152–54 (May 3, 1918).

18. As to witnesses, see Chicago Trial Tr. 137–301. As to Landis's distraction, see Chicago

Trial Tr. 140. As to the defendants' inability to hear, see Chicago Trial Tr. 161–62. As to Porter's concern that the newspaper reporters hear, see Chicago Trial Tr. 236. As to Porter's tough track record at the polls, see Iowa State Historical Society, *The Annals of Iowa: Claude R. Porter* 28, no. 2 (Fall 1946): 161–62.

Chapter 15. Polly-Foxing

1. The change to an earlier starting time came on Monday, May 27. Chicago Trial Tr. 1813.
2. As just one example, see Chicago Trial Tr. 606–11 (May 8, 1918).
3. Chicago Trial Tr. 728–29 (May 10, 1918).
4. As to blocking Vanderveer's cross-examination, see Chicago Trial Tr. 797. As to the red-ink letter and Landis's ruling, see Chicago Trial Tr. 804–13 (May 13, 1918). John Avilla's name probably should be spelled Avila, one could assume. However, I have retained the spellings of names that the trial transcript adopts, right or wrong.
5. Chicago Trial Tr. 817, 823 (May 13, 1918).
6. Chicago Trial Tr. 1007–8 (May 15, 1918).
7. Lowell S. Hawley & Ralph Bushnell Potts, *Counsel for the Damned* (Philadelphia: J. B. Lippincott, 1953), 231.
8. Chicago Trial Tr. 468, 551 (May 7, 1918).
9. For example, Chicago Trial Tr. 566 (May 7, 1918).
10. Chicago Trial Tr. 674 (May 9, 1918).
11. Chicago Trial Tr. 877 (May 15, 1918); as to Landis's admonishment of Vanderveer and Nebeker, see Chicago Trial Tr. 667–68 (May 9, 1918).
12. Chicago Trial Tr. 466 (May 7, 1918).
13. Chicago Trial Tr. 476 (May 7, 1918).
14. Chicago Trial Tr. 663–65 (May 9, 1918).
15. Kenesaw Mountain Landis Papers, Chicago History Museum, Series I, Box 9, File 2.
16. Kenesaw Mountain Landis Papers, Chicago History Museum, Series I, Box 6, Files 1–7; Box 7, Files 1A, 2A; Box 9, File 2 contains a July 27, 1917, letter from a U.S. senator's office, giving Landis advance notice that his son soon would ship out to France.
17. Chicago Trial Tr. 902 (May 15, 1918).
18. As to jurors wanting full versions, see Chicago Trial Tr. 751–52 (May 11, 1918).
19. Chicago Trial Tr. 879 (May 15, 1918).
20. As to ill defendants, on May 16, 1918, for example, doctors were examining one defendant and two or three of the jurors. Chicago Trial Tr. 1029. As to bail during trial, see, e.g., Chicago Trial Tr. 5514 (June 29, 1918) (Charles Ashleigh describing release on bail one month earlier; he later would have bail revoked, incidentally, when he came to court late); and Pietrusza, *Judge and Jury*, 124–25.
21. Chicago Trial Tr. 885–86 (May 15, 1918).
22. Chicago Trial Tr. 1028–29 (May 16, 1918).
23. Prosecutors did not recognize the men on trial. Chicago Trial Tr. 487–88 (May 7,

1918), 1284–85 (May 22, 1918). As to Landis's difficulty recognizing witnesses, see, among several examples, Chicago Trial Tr. 339, 366 (May 6, 1918). As to Landis enforcing the bill of particulars, see Chicago Trial Tr. 1870–72, 1947 (May 28, 1918).

24. Chicago Trial Tr. 1313–14, 1318–19 (May 22, 1918).

25. Chicago Trial Tr. 1552, 1554 (May 25, 1918).

26. As to the government's concession that its case failed on nine men, see Chicago Trial Tr. 4727, 4737, 4742, 4744. As to Nebeker's assertion about active participation after June 15, see Chicago Trial Tr. 4728–29. As to Landis's denial of all other defense motions for directed verdict (dismissal, in other words) and to strike evidence, see Chicago Trial Tr. 4697–98, 4700–14, 4725, 4730–36 (June 20, 1918).

27. Chicago Trial Tr. 4713 (June 20, 1918).

28. Vanderveer and the defense team were staying at the Hotel Washington. See Chicago Trial Tr. 11,922 (August 15, 1918). On Washington Boulevard, it was just about three blocks north of the courthouse. But it was not among the city's elegant hotels, and it certainly was not the Palmer House, the finest hotel near the federal courthouse.

Chapter 16. If Christ Came to Chicago

1. As to Cleary's bumbling, see Chicago Trial Tr. 1900–33 (May 28, 1918). He favors open-ended questions, is unfocused, and explores new and risky areas, with answers unknown, for no discernible purpose.

2. As to the promised fee, see Lowell S. Hawley & Ralph Bushnell Potts, *Counsel for the Damned* (Philadelphia: J. B. Lippincott, 1953), 221, 229, 242. As to the phone call and Ellinor selling her diamond ring, see Hawley & Potts, *Counsel for the Damned*, 234–35.

3. As to Kitty Beck, see Hawley & Potts, *Counsel for the Damned*, 237–38. As to drinking, smoking, and shabby clothing, see 244–45, 249.

4. Chicago Trial Tr. 4745–46 (June 24, 1918).

5. Chicago Trial Tr. 4750–51 (June 24, 1918).

6. Chicago Trial Tr. 4751 (June 24, 1918).

7. On discussion of defendants' actual intentions, see Chicago Trial Tr. 4761, 4778–82. On the inadmissibility of the Industrial Relations Commission report and the general industrial condition, see Chicago Trial Tr. 4828 4837, 4839. As to Nebeker's argument about war making a lawful strike now unlawful and Vanderveer's response, see Chicago Trial Tr. 4814–25 (June 24, 1918).

8. As to the chronology of miseries generally, see Chicago Trial Tr. 4830–70. As to Liberty Bonds and draft registration specifically, see Chicago Trial Tr. 4869 (June 24, 1918).

9. Chicago Trial Tr. 4875–76 (June 24, 1918).

10. Chicago Trial Tr. 4890–91 (June 24, 1918).

11. As to Ashleigh, see Chicago Trial Tr. 5531 (June 29, 1918). The prosecution's opening questions about alien status recurred with every, or nearly every, defense witness who was not a U.S. citizen. At least one more witness, whose surname was not obviously Jewish, was asked to admit on cross-examination that he was Jewish. Chicago Trial Tr. 6530.

12. Chicago Trial Tr. 4892–93 (June 24, 1918).

13. Chicago Trial Tr. 4897, 4923–45 (June 24, 1918).

14. Chicago Trial Tr. 4921.

15. Chicago Trial Tr. 4904 (June 25, 1918).

16. Chicago Trial Tr. 4900–4901 (June 25, 1918).

17. Chicago Trial Tr. 5285 (born in New York City), 5403 (Doran's wife "a cripple"), 5452 (support for war and two brothers serving), 5460–89 (Nebeker implies that Doran speaks Irish, and Doran does not contradict him) (June 27–28, 1918).

18. Chicago Trial Tr. 5294–5413 (June 27–28, 1918).

19. As to Landis wandering, see Chicago Trial Tr. 5491. As to scolding the late prosecutor, see Chicago Trial Tr. 5465 (June 29, 1918).

20. Chicago Trial Tr. 5413 (June 28, 1918). For two of several accounts of Doran's quip, see Patrick Renshaw, *The Wobblies: The Story of the IWW and Syndicalism in the United States* (1968; repr., Chicago: Ivan R. Dee, 1999), 229–30; Hawley & Potts, *Counsel for the Damned*, 235. The accounts are consistent, although there is some question about Landis joining in the laughter.

21. Chicago Trial Tr. 5488 (June 29, 1918).

22. *Evidence and Cross-Examination of J. T. (Red) Doran in the Case of United States vs. Wm. D. Haywood et al.* (Chicago: IWW General Defense Comm., 1918).

Chapter 17. Lives

1. Chicago Trial Tr. 5498–99, 5503 (June 29, 1918). First names or even nicknames reappeared in direct examination several times again. For example, Chicago Trial Tr. 6671, 7667, 8132, 9501.

2. As to the exchange between Vanderveer and Nebeker, see Chicago Trial Tr. 5525–26. On the colloquy between Vanderveer and Landis, see Chicago Trial Tr. 5559.

3. Chicago Trial Tr. 7842–43 (July 20, 1918), 7897–98 (July 22, 1918). Mostly, though, Landis appears a distracted presence throughout the trial transcript.

4. Chicago Trial Tr. 6396; 7870–71; 7928, 7901–6; 7950–54; 6719; 8269, 8270; 8330–31; 8545, 8563, various dates.

5. Chicago Trial Tr. 7240 (July 15, 1918).

6. As to Trotter, see Chicago Trial Tr. 10,541–47 (August 6, 1918). Relying on one New York newspaper, David Pietrusza, Landis's biographer, put Trotter's age at eighty and noted that he had difficulty answering questions. David Pietrusza, *Judge and Jury: The Life and Times of Judge Kenesaw Mountain Landis* (South Bend, IN: Diamond Communications, 1998), 124. As to Kirkanen, see Chicago Trial Tr. 11,693–94 (August 13, 1918). As to revocation of Ashleigh's bond, see Chicago Trial Tr. 12,036 (August 16, 1918).

7. As to defendants of German ancestry, see Chicago Trial Tr. 7870–71. As to noncitizens, see Chicago Trial Tr. 7998–99, 8238–39, 8405, 8609–14, 8738, 9439, 9913–14. As to defendants' divorced or unmarried status or homelessness, see Chicago Trial Tr. 8738, 8777, 8819, 9031, 10,376, 10,913–14 (various dates).

8. As to Porter's gaffe on Spanish, see Chicago Trial Tr. 8884 (July 26, 1918). As to the

exchange with Rice, see Chicago Trial Tr. 8451 (July 24, 1918). As to Walsh, see Chicago Trial Tr. 9335, 9345 (July 30, 1918).

9. Harrison George, *The I.W.W. Trial* (Chicago: IWW General Defense Committee, 1918), 164.

10. Frank K. Nebeker Letter to Attorney General (October 22, 1917), Straight Numerical Case No. 186701-14-62; Frank K. Nebeker Letter to William C. Fitts (October 30, 1917), Straight Numerical Case No. 188032-63; Report of Inspectors V. E. Albertie & F. N. Davis re Alleged Violation of the Espionage Act by the Industrial Workers of the World (July 1, 1918) under cover of W. H. Lamar Letter to Charles F. Clyne (July 23, 1918), Straight Numerical Case No. 188032-230; William C. Fitts Letters to Solicitor, Post Office Department (February 14, 1918, and July 25, 1918), Straight Numerical Case No. 188032-45, 188032-262. All in National Archives II, Records Group 60, Entry A1 112 B, Boxes 2181–86 & 2219–20. Wells Fargo & Co. Letter to Committee on Express Transportation (February 18, 1918), Record Group 60, Entry A1 112 B, Straight Numerical Case No. 186701 (no file or subfile noted), Boxes 2181–86. As to the intercepted Haywood letter to Liga de Trabajadores, see Record Group 60, Entry A1 112 B, Straight Numerical Case No. 186701-57. Further, as to intercepting mail and American Express deliveries, see Chicago Trial Tr. 6115–17 (Doree); 11,201–10 (Haywood); 10,685–90 (Caroline A. Lowe, defense lawyer); 11,933–34 (William B. Cleary, defense lawyer).

11. As to arrests of soldier witnesses, see Chicago Trial Tr. 9,241–49. As to arrests of citizen witnesses, see Chicago Trial Tr. 11,761–63, 11,764–82 (August 14, 1918); 11,911–21, 11,926–34.

12. Chicago Trial Tr. 10,377 (August 6, 1918).

13. Haywood's testimony ran from August 9 into August 13, 1918, and included a Saturday session. Chicago Trial Tr. 11,075–530. As to his work history starting at age nine, see Chicago Trial Tr. 11,076. As to the inflammatory racial claim, see Chicago Trial Tr. 11,080–81. As to jurors' difficulties hearing Haywood, see Chicago Trial Tr. 11,100, 11,246. As to Haywood's direct action comparison, see Chicago Trial Tr. 11,497–98.

14. For Porter's testimony, see Chicago Trial Tr. 12,162–63 (August 16, 1918).

15. For the defense resting, see Chicago Trial Tr. 12,235. For the government's rebuttal case, see Chicago Trial Tr. 12,237–42 (August 17, 1918).

16. As to mutual accusations of lying and Landis's comment, see Chicago Trial Tr. 6466. For Nebeker's warning to Vanderveer to keep his distance, see Chicago Trial Tr. 6480 (July 6, 1918).

17. Chicago Trial Tr. 11,956 (August 15, 1918).

Chapter 18. Argument

1. As to Vanderveer urging Nebeker to waive all closing arguments, see Chicago Trial Tr. 12,215 (August 16, 1918).

2. Harrison George, *The I.W.W. Trial* (Chicago: IWW General Defense Committee, 1918), 203.

3. Chicago Trial Tr. 12,220 (August 17, 1918).

4. Chicago Trial Tr. 12,243 (August 17, 1918).

5. Chicago Trial Tr. 12,245 (August 17, 1918).

6. Chicago Trial Tr. 12,269 (August 17, 1918).

7. Chicago Trial Tr. 12,248 (August 17, 1918).

8. Chicago Trial Tr. 12,252 (August 17, 1918).

9. Chicago Trial Tr. 12,254, 12,262, 12,264–66 (August 17, 1918). Of all the ninety-seven men remaining on trial then, perhaps the nineteen-year-old college student, Ray Fanning, alone had soft hands. But he certainly did not have a "hard face," and no one would have thought that he did.

10. Chicago Trial Tr. 12,253–61 (August 17, 1918).

11. Chicago Trial Tr. 12,265–66 (August 17, 1918).

12. Chicago Trial Tr. 12,269–70 (August 17, 1918).

13. "100 I.W.W.'s Found Guilty," *Chicago Herald & Examiner*, August 18, 1918, 1–2. As to the time when Nebeker ended, see George, *The I.W.W. Trial*, 203.

14. Chicago Trial Tr. 12,271 (August 17, 1918).

15. George, *The I.W.W. Trial*, 203.

Chapter 19. The First Final Chapter

1. See Kenesaw Mountain Landis Papers, Series III, Box 49, File 5 (Standard Oil case jury instructions); Box 51, File 3 (various jury instructions); and Boxes 52, 53, 55, 56, 57, each with various files containing proposed or final jury instructions, Chicago History Museum.

2. Frank K. Nebeker Letter to William C. Fitts (July 10, 1918), National Archives II, Record Group 60, Entry A1 112 B, Straight Numerical Case No. 188032-250, Boxes 2219–20.

3. Kenesaw Mountain Landis Papers, Series III, Box 52, File 6.

4. Chicago Trial Tr. 12,272–73. The entire jury charge runs from page 12,272 through 12,313 (August 17, 1918).

5. Chicago Trial Tr. 12,288–93, 12,298 (August 17, 1918).

6. As to reasonable doubt and presumption of innocence, see Chicago Trial Tr. 12,301–3. As to not offering a factual opinion, see Chicago Trial Tr. 12,287 (August 17, 1918).

7. Chicago Trial Tr. 12,295–97 (August 17, 1918).

8. Chicago Trial Tr. 12,305–6 (August 17, 1918).

9. Chicago Trial Tr. 12,306–7 (August 17, 1918). Instructions of this nature, that a defendant was responsible for unintended but natural and probable consequences, became constitutionally precarious at best with *Sandstrom v. Montana*, 442 U.S. 510 (1979), at least in cases requiring intent as the state of mind. But the Supreme Court approved vicarious liability for conspirators more generally in *Pinkerton v. United States*, 328 U.S. 640 (1946). As to Nebeker's early focus on this instruction and his request for Pagan's help, see note 2.

10. Chicago Trial Tr. 12,312, 12, 310, 12,313 (August 17, 1918).

11. Chicago Trial Tr. 12,313 (August 17, 1918). As to Haywood's assessment, see "100 I.W.W.'s Found Guilty," *Chicago Herald & Examiner*, August 18, 1918, 1.

12. Chicago Trial Tr. 12,303 (August 17, 1918). As to time, see Frank Nebeker & Claude

Porter Telegram to Attorney General (August 17, 1918), National Archives II, Record Group 60, Entry A1 112 B, Straight Numerical Case No. 188032-277, Boxes 2219-20.

13. As to the guilty verdict form, see *United States v. Haywood et al.*, No. 6125, Verdict (National Archives Catalog, Records Group 21, National Archives Identifier 7372723). There are different accounts of the length of jury deliberations, but all agree that the jury signaled a verdict in less than one hour. The defense briefs put the length of actual deliberations at twenty-five minutes. Brief and Argument for Plaintiffs in Error at 14, IWW Records, Accession No. 130, Box 122, File 2, Walter P. Reuther Library, Wayne State University. Vanderveer's version during his argument on the motions for a new trial and arrest of judgment put the deliberations at fifty minutes in total, but with only fifteen minutes of actual discussion. Chicago Trial Tr. 12,347-48 (August 27, 1918), Box 118, File 4. Haywood recalled several years later that "the jury's verdict was given within an hour." William D. Haywood, *Bill Haywood's Book* (New York: International Publishers, 1929), 324. The *Chicago Tribune* reported inconsistently in the same story that the jury was out just fifty-five minutes, but also that it retired shortly after 4 p.m. and announced that it had reached a verdict at 5:10 p.m. "Convict 100 I.W.W. Chiefs," *Chicago Sunday Tribune*, August 18, 1918, 1, 7. The ACLU's April 1922 pamphlet on the case, which mostly but not entirely gave accurate details, put the deliberations at fifty-five minutes. American Civil Liberties Union, *The Truth about the I.W.W. Prisoners* (New York: ACLU, 1922), 21. Charles Clyne, the U.S. district attorney, told Assistant Attorney General Fitts that the jury "deliberated only fifty-five minutes." Charles F. Clyne Letter to William C. Fitts (August 22, 1918), National Archives II, Record Group 60, Entry A1 112 B, Straight Numerical Case No. 188032-289. See also Ralph Chaplin, *Wobbly: The Rough-and-Tumble Story of an American Radical* (Chicago: University of Chicago Press, 1948), 246 (describing the deliberations as less than an hour). As to the court reconvening after one hour and thirty-five minutes, and the security complement in court, see "100 I.W.W.'s Found Guilty," *Chicago Herald & Examiner*, August 18, 1918, 1-2. As to only Otto Christensen being at the defense table when the verdicts were read, see "100 I.W.W.'s Guilty of War Plotting," *New York Times*, August 18, 1918, 1; "Guilty Verdict in I.W.W. Case," *Sunday State Journal* (Lincoln, Nebraska), August 18, 1918, 1.

14. As to Lowe sobbing, see "Convict 100 I.W.W. Chiefs," *Chicago Sunday Tribune*, August 18, 1918, 1.

Chapter 20. Have You Anything to Say?

1. Chicago Trial Tr. 12,314-77, especially 12,358-59, 12,375 (August 27, 1918), Box 118, File 4, IWW Records Collection (Accession No. 130), Walter P. Reuther Library, Wayne State University.

2. Chicago Sentencing Tr. 1-3 (August 30, 1918), Box 118, File 6, IWW Records Collection (Accession No. 130), Walter P. Reuther Library, Wayne State University.

3. As to the right of allocution generally, see Paul W. Barrett, *Allocution*, 9 Mo. L. Rev. 115 (1944); Kimberly A. Thomas, *Beyond Mitigation: Towards a Theory of Allocution*,

75 FORDHAM L. REV. 2641 (2007); *Green v. United States*, 365 U.S. 301, 304 (1965) (noting that a judge's failure to ask a defendant if he wished to speak before sentencing was a reversible error as early as 1689); see also William Blackstone, *Commentaries on the Laws of England*, vol. 4 (Oxford: Clarendon Press, 1769), 348–49 (describing as "a settled rule at common law" the denial of counsel "upon the general issue, in any capital crime, unless some point of law shall arise proper to be debated," but objecting to the rule). As to the movement toward allowing defense witnesses, Blackstone credits Queen Mary I with the impetus for change, at pages 352–53 of the same volume. Note that Blackstone was not always accurate historically and never was complete. The actual course of the roles of defense counsel and defense witnesses in English trials is more complicated and less linear than casual or summary studies suggest. See, e.g., Marvin Becker & George Heidelbaugh, *Right to Counsel in Criminal Cases: An Inquiry into the History and Practice in England and America*, 28 NOTRE DAME L. REV. 351 (1953). As to Emmet's allocution, see Patrick M. Geoghegan, *Robert Emmet: A Life* (Montreal: McGill-Queen's University Press, 2002), 253–54. That allocution appears, in full or in part, in many other places, too.

4. See the epigraph to Eugene V. Debs, *Walls & Bars: Prisons and Prison Life in the "Land of the Free"* (1927; repr., Chicago: Charles H. Kerr, 2000).

5. "100 I.W.W., Denied Retrial, Face Sentence Today," *Chicago Daily Tribune*, August 30, 1918, sec. 2, 1. The allocutions fill 134 pages of the sentencing transcript. As to Dailey and Nigra, see "100 I.W.W., Denied Retrial, Face Sentence Today," *Chicago Daily Tribune*, August 30, 1918, sec. 2, 1; Chicago Sentencing Tr. 89. As to Landis's inquiries, see, for example, Chicago Sentencing Tr. 116.

6. Chicago Sentencing Tr. 24–25 (Fanning), 39–41 (Ingar).

7. Chicago Sentencing Tr. 37–38.

8. Thompson's speech is at Chicago Sentencing Tr. 126–30.

9. Chicago Sentencing Tr. 116–19.

10. Chicago Sentencing Tr. 51.

11. Chicago Sentencing Tr. 109.

12. Chicago Sentencing Tr. 19 (Dailey), 131–34 (Marlatt). "100 I.W.W., Denied Retrial, Face Sentence Today," *Chicago Daily Tribune*, August 30, 1918, sec. 2, 1 (Dailey fatally ill).

13. Chicago Sentencing Tr. 173, 174, 175.

14. Chicago Sentencing Tr. 175 (10 days; one year and a day), 176–77 (5 years), 177 (Schraeger released), 178–79 (ten years), 179 (back to five years), 179–80 (twenty years). As to fines, which were an afterthought by Landis, see Brief and Argument for Plaintiffs in Error pp. 15–16, Box 122, File 2, IWW Records Collection (Accession No. 130), Walter P. Reuther Library, Wayne State University.

15. Chicago Sentencing Tr. 181.

16. "I.W.W. Leaders Get 20-Year Terms," *New York Times*, August 31, 1918, 1, 7.

17. Chicago Sentencing Tr. 17; Ralph Chaplin, *Wobbly: The Rough-and-Tumble Story of an American Radical* (Chicago: University of Chicago Press, 1948), 247 (Chaplin's recollections thirty years later were not always accurate, but this rejoinder he remembered exactly).

Chapter 21. The Train

1. "Haywood and 14 Other I.W.W. Given 20 Years," *Chicago Herald & Examiner*, August 31, 1918, sec, 2, 1.

2. "I.W.W. Bomb Kills Four in Chicago," *New York Times*, September 5, 1918, 1, 9; "Bomb Kills 4; Wounds 30," *Chicago Daily Tribune*, September 5, 1918, 1; "Victims of Bomb at Post Office," *Chicago Daily Tribune*, September 5, 1918, 1. One person not injured was a young substitute mail carrier walking through the lobby that day, Walt Disney. "Chicago Bombs," Smithsonian National Postal Museum, https://postalmuseum.si.edu /behindthebadge/chicago-bombs.html (accessed April 24, 2018).

3. "I.W.W. Bomb Kills Four in Chicago," *New York Times*, September 5, 1918, 1, 9. Two days later, police and federal agents surmised that the bomb had contained dynamite— perhaps three sticks—and as much as twelve pounds of black powder. "Bomb Suspect Held; Described by 2 Witnesses," *Chicago Daily Tribune*, September 6, 1918, 1, 4. This would not be the last bomb directed at IWW enemies. The following spring, on May Day, postal authorities discovered thirty-six bombs in parcels addressed to nemeses of the IWW, including Judge Landis, Attorney General A. Mitchell Palmer, Justice Oliver Wendell Holmes, immigration authorities, the mayors of Seattle and New York, and prominent capitalists John D. Rockefeller and J. P. Morgan. The discovery came after the post office delivered one bomb to the home of former Senator Thomas W. Hardwick in Atlanta. It exploded there and seriously injured his maid. "36 Were Marked as Victims by Bomb Con- spirers," *New York Times*, May 1, 1919, 1, 3. The next day, the government discovered five more bombs in post offices, including one addressed to Frank K. Nebeker, chief prosecutor in the Chicago IWW trial. "Find More Bombs Sent in the Mails; One to Overman," *New York Times*, May 2, 1919, 1, 3.

4. For an excellent account of the September 16, 1920, bombing on Wall Street near the J. P. Morgan Bank, see Beverly Gage, *The Day Wall Street Exploded: A Story of America in its First Age of Terror* (Oxford: Oxford University Press, 2009). As to the Milwaukee police station bombing, see Dean A. Strang, *Worse than the Devil: Anarchists, Clarence Darrow, and Justice in a Time of Terror* (Madison: University of Wisconsin Press, 2013). Both books describe the history of dynamite bombings in that era. As to the bombing of Judge Webster Thayer's home in 1932, see, e.g., "Home of Judge in Sacco-Vanzetti Trial Is Blown Up," *St. Louis Post-Dispatch*, September 27, 1932, 1.

5. Ed Doree Letter to parents and wife, September 5, 1917, from Cook County Jail, Labadie Collection, University of Michigan.

6. "Latest News of Hunt for Bomb Placer," *Chicago Daily Tribune*, September 5, 1918, 1. Alanson, Michigan, is less than a half hour from the present-day Mackinac Bridge. As to Landis's cottage on Burt Lake, which he had for about forty years, see David Pietrusza, *Judge and Jury: The Life and Times of Judge Kenesaw Mountain Landis* (South Bend, IN: Diamond Communications, 1998), 89, 396.

7. "Haywood and His 92 Pals Are Off to Prison," *Chicago Daily Tribune*, September 7, 1918, 1; Edward F. Doree Letter to Ida Doree, September 7, 1918, E. F. Doree Collection

(Accession 1658), File 2, Walter P. Reuther Library, Wayne State University; Ralph Chaplin, *Wobbly: The Rough-and-Tumble Story of an American Radical* (Chicago: University of Chicago Press, 1948), 248–50 (describing the departure and the first sight of the penitentiary at Leavenworth the next afternoon).

8. William D. Haywood, *Bill Haywood's Book* (New York: International Publishers, 1929), 327–28, 329.

9. Edward F. Doree Letter to Ida Doree, September 7, 1918, E. F. Doree Collection (Accession 1658), Walter P. Reuther Library, Wayne State University.

10. Colonel Orville Z. Tyler Jr., *The History of Fort Leavenworth, 1937–1951* (Fort Leavenworth: Command and General Staff College, 1952), ix, x, 56–57, 66.

11. Haywood, *Bill Haywood's Book*, 329–32; Ed Doree Letter to Ida Doree, October 13, 1918, E. F. Doree Collection, File 2. The Bertillon System was a crude method of identification developed in the 1890s, resting on the belief that no two people would share the exact same anthropometric qualities. It blended with the eugenics of the day, a form of quackery that posited in part that criminal tendencies could be deduced from physical characteristics.

12. Haywood, *Bill Haywood's Book*, 330. Doree's September 7, 1918, letter to Chiky explained his own work assignment and Nef's, and confirmed Haywood's.

13. Edward F. Doree Letters to Ida Doree, September 7 and 15, 1918, E. F. Doree Collection (Accession 1658), File 2, Walter P. Reuther Library, Wayne State University. His exact maximum parole date was May 25, 1925. Edward F. Doree Letter to Ida Doree, September 29, 1918, E. F. Doree Collection, File 2. For a brief biography of Agnes Inglis, see Agnes Inglis Papers (1909–1952), University of Michigan Library, Special Collections Finding Aids, https://quod.lib.umich.edu/s/sclead/umich-scl-inglisa?view=text.

Chapter 22. Doing Time

1. The case against Debs was *United States v. Eugene Victor Debs* (N.D. Ohio, 1918), arising out of a June 1918 speech in Canton, Ohio, in which he praised draft resisters. The case file is Record No. 2765897, Series: Criminal Case Files, 1912-1986, Record Group 21, National Archives at Chicago; see also *Debs v. United States*, 249 U.S. 211 (1919) (affirming conviction in an opinion by Justice Oliver Wendell Holmes for a unanimous court). The most famous lines from his allocution before sentencing are the epigraph to Debs's memoir, *Walls & Bars: Prisons and Prison Life in the "Land of the Free"* (Chicago: Charles H. Kerr, 2000) (originally published in 1927, just after Debs died). Vote totals are from the Office of the Clerk, U.S. House of Representatives, http://history.house.gov/Institution/Election-Statistics/Election-Statistics/, and *Congressional Quarterly's Guide to U.S. Elections*, 6th ed. (Washington, DC: CQ Press, 2009).

2. Ed Doree Letter to parents and wife, September 5, 1917, from Cook County Jail, Labadie Collection, University of Michigan.

3. William D. Haywood, *Bill Haywood's Book* (New York: International Publishers, 1929), 339.

4. Ed Doree Letter to Ida Doree, October 7, 1917, E. F. Doree Collection (Accession 1658), Box 1, File 2, Walter P. Reuther Library, Wayne State University; Ed Doree Letter to

Ida Doree, September 15, 1917, E. F. Doree Collection, File 2; Ed Doree Letter to Ida Doree, September 22, 1917, E. F. Doree Collection, File 2.

5. Ed Doree Letter to Ida Doree, September 29, 1918, E. F. Doree Collection, File 2. As to the "silent system" and the inmates' suspicion about men assigned as kitchen help, see Haywood, *Bill Haywood's Book*, 334–35. Haywood added that "by no means" all of the waiters were informers or snitches. There is no reason to think that Doree was.

6. Ed Doree Letter to Ida Doree, October 10, 1918, E. F. Doree Collection, File 2. Note that, while Doree's handwriting was excellent and his spelling generally good, his punctuation was less reliable. So, I have taken small liberties in correcting his punctuation and, less frequently, his spelling. This letter refers to the German Communist and founder of the Spartacus League, Karl Liebknecht. Liebknecht was in a German prison as Doree wrote, but would be freed after the Bolsheviks came to power and the German government felt pressure from revolutionaries closer to home. However, there was no happy ending. Three months later, on January 15, 1919, Liebknecht was arrested again with Rosa Luxemburg, now by a provisional government less radical than Liebknecht and Luxemburg. Both were executed summarily the same day.

7. Ed Doree Letter to Ida Doree, October 13, 1918, E. F. Doree Collection, File 2 (as to Darrow and Wilson); Ed Doree Letter to Ida Doree, October 6, 1918, E. F. Doree Collection, File 2 (as to class treason).

8. "Loaded Pistols Found in Federal Prison Laundry," *Leavenworth (Kansas) Times*, December 15, 1918, 1.

9. His teeth were a regular complaint. For one example, see Ed Doree Letter to Ida Doree, October 6, 1918. See also Ed Doree Letter to Ida Doree, September 29, 1918 (on the institution not breaking men's spirits); March 20, 1919 (on comparison to a summer resort and his weight); September 22, 1918, and October 10, 1922 (on tobacco). All from the E. F. Doree Collection, File 2.

10. See, generally, E. F. Doree Collection, File 2.

11. Birthday Greeting to Bucky, February 18, 1919, E. F. Doree Collection, File 2. Here, I have not altered Doree's punctuation and occasionally stilted grammar. The quotation is full and verbatim.

Chapter 23. Reaching for the Rich

1. Ed Doree Letter to Ida Doree, September 29, 1918, E. F. Doree Collection, File 2. The letter referring to Inglis's visit was dated September 15, 1918. As to rejecting a pardon, see Ed Doree Letters to Ida Doree, September 29 and October 6, 1918.

2. Ed Doree Letter to Ida Doree, October 10, 1918, E. F. Doree Collection, File 2. "Mrs. Hendrie" is a reference to Kathleen McGraw Hendrie (1880–1968), who like Agnes Inglis was a wealthy liberal in Detroit. Kathleen McGraw was well-to-do, one of four children of William A. McGraw, a boot and shoe wholesaler, whose own father also was a wealthy businessman. John William Leonard, *The Industries of Detroit* (Detroit: J. M Elstner, 1887), 101–2. She was from high society: circumstantial evidence of that is her appearance in three separate society notices the same day in the *Detroit Free Press*, February 8, 1903, part 2,

page 2 (including a description of a trip from Detroit to Florida by automobile, usually a rich man's toy in 1903). She married George Trowbridge Hendrie in 1906. He was the son of a Scottish immigrant who made a fortune in banking and real estate. The younger Hendrie expanded that fortune, including by developing land in the wealthy communities on Grosse Pointe, just over the mouth of the Detroit River on Lake St. Clair. Albert Nelson Marquis, *The Book of Detroiters* (Chicago: A. N. Marquis, 1908), 221–22. Kathleen McGraw Hendrie is remembered best as an active suffragist. Eventually, she posted $60,000 in real estate to secure Doree's appeal bond, in part. Ellen Doree Rosen, *A Wobbly Life* (Detroit: Wayne State University Press, 2004), 64.

3. Ed Doree Letters to Ida Doree, October 13, 1918, January 9, 1919, April 2, 1919, and April 13, 1919, E. F. Doree Collection, File 2.

4. Clarence Darrow Letter to Woodrow Wilson, July 29, 1919, set out in full in Randall Tietjen, ed., *In the Clutches of the Law: Clarence Darrow's Letters* (Berkeley: University of California Press, 2013), 233–34. Darrow likely knew Vincent St. John from Western Federation of Miners days, and specifically from the time of the Frank Steunenberg murder case in Idaho in 1907, in which Darrow had represented Bill Haywood, Charles Moyer, and George Pettibone. Darrow plainly was fond of St. John. See, e.g., Clarence Darrow Letter to Negley D. Cochran, October 14, 1921, set out in full in Tietjen, *In the Clutches of the Law*, 259–60. Tietjen's book is magnificently researched, edited, and annotated. For these reasons, it is indispensable to those interested in Darrow and his day.

5. Ed Doree Letter to Ida Doree, January 5, 1919, E. F. Doree Collection, File 2. The judge Doree mentions was Evan A. Evans (1876–1948), who sat on the U.S. Circuit Court of Appeals for the Seventh Circuit, in Chicago, from 1916 to his death.

6. Ed Doree Letter to Ida Doree, April 2, 1919, quoting the Vanderveer-Christensen telegram verbatim. E. F. Doree Collection, File 2.

7. As to Doree's role on the General Defense Committee and the role of that committee itself, see Edward F. Doree Affidavit, August 17, 1921, E. F. Doree Collection, File 2. As to the stipend to wives and families, see Ed Doree Letters to Ida Doree, October 6, 1918, E. F. Doree Collection, File 2. As to the number of defendants in Sacramento, Wichita, and Omaha, see IWW Records Collection, Accession No. 130, Box 128, File 4.

8. See note 2 for more on Agnes Inglis and Kathleen McGraw Hendrie.

9. Haywood, *Bill Haywood's Book*, 340.

10. Ed Doree Letters to Ida Doree, April 13, May 11, May 18, June 9, June 23, 1919, E. F. Doree Collection, File 2; Haywood, *Bill Haywood's Book*, 340. Incidentally, Doree's April 13 reference to Joseph J. Gordon with Haywood is puzzling, as Gordon was not an especially prominent Chicago defendant.

Chapter 24. The Other Three

1. Claude R. Porter Telegram to Thomas W. Gregory (September 3, 1918), National Archives II, Record Group 60, Entry A1 112 B, Straight Numerical Case No. 188032-300, Boxes 2219–20.

2. "Friends Give Dinner to Frank K. Nebeker," *Salt Lake Tribune*, July 10, 1919, 22.

3. "Want Nebeker for Other I.W.W. Cases," *Sacramento Union*, September 3, 1918, 2; "To Try Wichita I.W.W.'s," *Manhattan (Kansas) Nationalist*, September 4, 1918, 5. For an overview of the Sacramento and Wichita cases, see Philip Taft, "The Federal Trials of the IWW," *Labor History* 3, no. 1 (1962): 57–91. On the Omaha case, see David G. Wagaman, "The Industrial Workers of the World in Nebraska, 1914–1920," *Nebraska History* 56 (1975): 295–337. On all three cases, see Melvyn Dubofsky, *We Shall Be All* (Chicago: Quadrangle Books, 1969), 438–44.

4. Dubofsky, *We Shall Be All* (1969), 440, 524–25n37, citing letters from the government officials. As to deaths before trial, see Taft, "The Federal Trials of the IWW," 77–78. On Blackstone's ratio, see William Blackstone, *Commentaries on the Laws of England*, vol. 4 (Oxford: Clarendon Press, 1769), 358. Incidentally, some writers spell Theodora Pollok's surname "Pollak." But both Melvyn Dubofsky and most contemporaneous newspaper articles render it "Pollok," which I adopt.

5. As to the timing of arrests and the transfer of intended targets to Chicago, see Dubofsky, *We Shall Be All* (1969), 438.

6. As to Vanderveer's presence in Sacramento and initial involvement before trial, see Ed Doree Letter to Ida Doree, September 29, 1918, E. F. Doree Collection (Accession 1658), File 2, Walter P. Reuther Library, Wayne State University.

7. Dubofsky, *We Shall Be All* (1969), 440–41; Taft, "The Federal Trials of the IWW," 77–79. As to singing "Solidarity Forever" after the verdict, see "Sacramento Members Convicted," *Solidarity*, January 25, 1919. As to the Sacramento defendants' belief that a fair trial was impossible, see American Civil Liberties Union, *The Truth about the I.W.W. Prisoners* (New York: ACLU, 1922), 3. As to Doree's assessment of the newly arrived prisoners from Sacramento, see Ellen Doree Rosen, *A Wobbly Life* (Detroit: Wayne State University Press, 2004), 49–50 (quoting Doree's letter to Chiky, January 26, 1919). As to impassioned sentencing allocutions, see "Sacramento I.W.W. Sentenced Today," *Klamath Falls (Oregon) Evening Herald*, January 17, 1919, 1; "Sacramento I.W.W. Given Heavy Jolts," *Bisbee Daily Review*, January 18, 1919, 1. On Haywood's praise of the silent defense, see Haywood, *Bill Haywood's Book*, 311.

8. See, e.g., Rosen, *A Wobbly Life*, 48, 58–59, 62, quoting Ed Doree's letters home of January 12, March 16, and April 5, 1919. As to Fred Moore's lead role in Wichita, see Ed Doree Letter to Ida Doree, September 29, 1918, E. F. Doree Collection, File 2. As to Caroline Lowe's role, see Taft, "The Federal Trials of the IWW," 79.

9. Taft, "The Federal Trials of the IWW," 79–80; "Praise for Amidon," *Wichita (Kansas) Daily Eagle*, December 30, 1919, 5.

10. Dubofsky, *We Shall Be All* (1969), 442–43. As to Thomas S. Allen, see "Thomas Stinson Allen, 1865–1945 [RG3804.AM]," Nebraska State Historical Society, https://history.nebraska.gov/collections/thomas-stinson-allen-1865-1945-rg3804am.

11. As to Doree's inclusion in the Wichita indictment, see Ed Doree Letter to Ida Doree, September 29, 1918, E. F. Doree Collection, File 2.

12. The appeal in the Wichita case was reported as *Anderson v. United States*, 264 F. 75 (8th Cir.), *cert. denied*, 253 U.S. 495 (1920). The unsuccessful appeal in the Sacramento case was reported as *Anderson v. United States*, 269 F. 65 (9th Cir. 1920). For a description of the appellate outcomes, see Otto Christensen, *Statement Submitted to the Attorney General of the United States Concerning the Present Legal Status of the I.W.W. Cases* (February 1923), 17–22, IWW Records Collection (Accession No. 130), Box 125, File 1, Walter P. Reuther Library, Wayne State University; on the same subject, see also American Civil Liberties Union, *The Truth about the I.W.W. Prisoners*, 24, 28 (which had the date of the Eighth Circuit's decision in the Wichita appeal wrong by one year).

Chapter 25. The Seventh Circuit

1. See, generally, the Federal Judicial Center website, Courts, History of the Federal Judiciary page, www.fjc.gov/history/courts/u.s.-courts-appeals-and-federal-judiciary (accessed November 25, 2018).

2. The Assignment of Errors and all briefs are in Box 122, IWW Records Collection (Accession No. 130), Walter P. Reuther Library, Wayne State University.

3. As to the number of government exhibits, see Box 108, File 5, IWW Records Collection. As to the sentencing transcript, see Box 118, File 6.

4. Brief and Argument for Plaintiffs in Error, Specification of Errors XVI, XXII, pp. 40–44, 61–62, Box 122, File 2.

5. Typed notes, Defendants' Brief of Evidence, Box 119, File 9. Although these are defense summaries, the trial transcript supports them, and the government's brief (including its final supplemental brief after oral argument) does not disprove them. As to Clyde Hough, see Petition for Rehearing of Plaintiffs in Error, pp. 25–26, Box 123, File 2.

6. Brief and Argument for Plaintiffs in Error, p. 402, Box 122, File 2.

7. Brief and Argument of Defendant in Error, p. 67, Box 122, File 3.

8. Second Supplemental Brief of Defendant in Error, p. 204, Box 122, File 3. Incidentally, this second supplemental brief suggests strongly that the judges must have expressed real doubt about the future of Counts 1 and 2. The government defended the sufficiency of the evidence only as to Counts 3 and 4.

9. *Haywood v. United States*, 268 F. 795 (7th Cir. 1920). As to appeals being matters of grace, see *Haywood*, 268 F. at 798. See also 268 F. at 798–800 (Count 1,); 268 F. at 800–801 (Count 2,); 268 F. at 801–4 (Fourth Amendment challenge to seized documents). Quoted passages are from 268 F. at 801, 802, 804.

10. For thoughtful consideration of the proper role of legal imagination and creativity in judging, see, e.g., James Boyd White, *The Legal Imagination* (Boston: Little, Brown, 1973); and Ronald Dworkin, *Law's Empire* (Cambridge, MA: Harvard University Press, 1986). White takes up some of the same themes in his masterful *Living Speech: Resisting the Empire of Force* (Princeton, NJ: Princeton University Press, 2006), and throughout his other work.

11. Benjamin N. Cardozo, *Law and Literature* (New York: Harcourt, Brace, 1931). A

retired federal appellate judge, Richard Posner (coincidentally also from the Seventh Circuit), has considered Cardozo's pragmatic program and occasional misstatements of fact in judicial opinions. See Richard A. Posner, *Cardozo: A Study in Reputation* (Chicago: University of Chicago Press, 1990), 43, and more generally at pp. 16–17, 38–40, 61n8, 92–124, 137.

12. *Weeks v. United States*, 232 U.S. 383, 388–89, 393–98 (1914).

13. *Haywood*, 268 F. at 803–4. The citation to *Weeks* is at page 803; the quoted passage at page 804.

14. *Haywood*, 268 F. at 805–8. As to most evidentiary and instructional issues no longer mattering after reversal of the convictions on Counts 1 and 2, see 268 F. at 806.

15. *Gitlow v. New York*, 268 U.S. 652, 667 (1925).

16. See, e.g., *Abrams v. United States*, 250 U.S. 616 (1919); *Debs v. United States*, 249 U.S. 211 (1919); *Frohwerk v. United States*, 249 U.S. 204 (1919); *Schenck v. United States*, 249 U.S. 47 (1919); *Whitney v. California*, 274 U.S. 357 (1927); *Terminiello v. City of Chicago*, 337 U.S. 1 (1949); *Brandenburg v. Ohio*, 395 U.S. 444 (1969). The case that first reversed a conviction as contrary to the constitutional freedom of speech, here applied to the states through the Fourteenth Amendment, was *Stromberg v. California*, 283 U.S. 359 (1931). For the history of Holmes's change of heart and the course of the World War I dissidents' cases, see Thomas Healy, *The Great Dissent: How Oliver Wendell Holmes Changed His Mind— and Changed the History of Free Speech in America* (New York: Metropolitan Books, Henry Holt, 2013).

17. *Haywood*, 268 F. at 807–8.

18. The U.S. Supreme Court denied the petition for a writ of certiorari on April 11, 1921. *Haywood v. United States*, 256 U.S. 689 (1921). The defendants earlier made a futile motion for rehearing in the Seventh Circuit, which that court denied without comment on December 9, 1920. *Haywood*, 268 F. at 795.

Chapter 26. Consequences

1. "Free 47 I.W.W. on Bonds," *New York Times*, May 28, 1919, 15 (noting that the court of appeals had set an appeal bond for forty-seven of the Chicago defendants, in addition to thirty-seven who earlier had succeeded in getting appeal bonds set); "Upholds Conviction of I.W.W. Agitators," *New York Times*, October 6, 1920, 6 (noting that only twenty-six of the defendants actually had been released pending appeal). Note that the accuracy of mainstream newspaper reporting never was high on the IWW case, and it fell off further after sentencing. Many of the newspaper articles are rife with errors, especially on numbers—regarding fines and number of people convicted or admitted to bail. Another *New York Times* article, for example, refers to more than thirty defendants surrendering in April 1921, after the U.S. Supreme Court refused to hear the case: "Haywood to Return and Give Himself Up," *New York Times*, June 30, 1921, 8. Nine more men skipped bail at that point. That would put the number actually released on bail at thirty-five to forty. What is clear, though, is that many of the Chicago defendants were not released pending appeal. Some, of course, finished their sentences before or during the appeal.

2. "Haywood to Return and Give Himself Up," *New York Times*, June 30, 1921, 8; Ellen Doree Rosen, *A Wobbly Life* (Detroit: Wayne State University Press, 2004), 107–9, quoting E. F. Doree Letters to Ida Doree, April 27 and May 1, 1921.

3. As to repeal of the 1918 Sedition Act, see Pub. Res. 66-64, 41 Stat. 1359 (March 3, 1921). A. S. Lanier, "To the President," *The New Republic* 28, no. 233 (April 19, 1919): 383–84; see also Labadie Collection, University of Michigan, HD 8055.I5L36. As to the four Philadelphia defendants, see George Biddle et al., *An Appeal in the Name of Justice* (1921), Box 125, IWW Records (Accession No. 130), Walter P. Reuther Library, Wayne State University. As to the House Judiciary Committee hearing on the joint resolution, see *Amnesty for Political Prisoners*, Hearing before H.R. Committee on the Judiciary, 67th Cong., 2d Sess., Serial 31, March 16, 1922, copy in Box 129, File 1, IWW Records (Accession No. 130), Walter P. Reuther Library, Wayne State University.

4. Typed summary of sentences with marginalia (n.d., but after January 9, 1922), Box 131, File 2; *Amnesty for Political Prisoners*, Ex. 17 (Presidential pardons, commutations, and respites for fiscal year ended June 30, 1922), Box 129, File 1. The terms of Baldazzi's commutation are quoted from that Exhibit 17. See also "Harding Frees 8 I.W.W. Men for Deportation; Will Go Back to Prison if They Ever Return," *New York Times*, December 31, 1922.

5. *Amnesty for Political Prisoners*, Ex. 17 (Presidential pardons, commutations, and respites for fiscal year ending June 30, 1922), Box 129, File 1.

6. "Haywood from Russia Sends a May Day Note," *New York Times*, April 30, 1921, 3; "Eight I.W.W.'s Forfeit Bonds, But Word of Haywood is Sought," *New York Times*, May 3, 1921, 1. As to sentence length, see *Summary of Sentences Imposed on Members under the Chicago Indictment*, Box 128, File 4, IWW Records (Accession No. 130), Walter P. Reuther Library, Wayne State University.

7. "Haywood to Direct Lenin's Propaganda," *New York Times*, April 24, 1921, 1, 6.

8. "Eight I.W.W.'s Forfeit Bonds, but Word of Haywood Is Sought," *New York Times*, May 3, 1921, 1; "Haywood to Stay Abroad; I.W.W. Paying $65,000 Bonds," *New York Times*, October 27, 1921, 21.

9. "Say Haywood Fled on Communist Plea," *New York Times*, January 16, 1922, 5.

10. Haywood, *Bill Haywood's Book*, 344–45.

11. Haywood, *Bill Haywood's Book*, 360–62. The quote about the Statue of Liberty is on page 361. Years later, Charles Plunkett, a youthful anarchist and militant who became a professor of biology at NYU, said that Haywood spent his last night in America at Plunkett's house. He recalled Haywood as a great man. Paul Avrich, "Charles Plunkett," in *Anarchist Voices: An Oral History of Anarchism in America* (Oakland, CA: AK Press, 2005), 217.

12. Philip Taft, "The Federal Trials of the I.W.W.," *Labor History* 3, no. 1 (1962): 57, 76.

Chapter 27. Bucky

1. Ellen Doree Rosen, *A Wobbly Life* (Detroit: Wayne State University Press, 2004), 117. As to the IWW cutting off Chiky's relief check, see ibid., 116, quoting Ed Doree's June

19, 1921, letter home to Ida Doree. Actually, in January 1920, the National Civil Liberties Bureau had become the American Civil Liberties Union in name. Roger Baldwin carried over from one name to the other.

2. Edwin F. Doree Affidavit, August 17, 1921, E. F. Doree Collection (Accession No. 1658), Box 2, Walter P. Reuther Library, Wayne State University.

3. Rosen, *A Wobbly Life*, 167, quoting Ed Doree Letter to Ida Doree, January 27, 1922.

4. Rosen, *A Wobbly Life*, 121, quoting Ed Doree Letter to Ida Doree, July 8, 1921. See also ibid., 174 (on restoration of relief checks and influenza bouts) and 179 (on children's crusade).

5. Rosen, *A Wobbly Life*, 180–84. As to the details of the furlough and travel, see ibid. at 186, quoting Ed Doree letter to his parents, Frederick and Maria, April 16, 1922. As to total time away from Leavenworth, see ibid., 183–84.

6. "Little 'Bucky' Doree Dies after Father Is Brought Back to Political's Cell," *New York Call*, April 11, 1922.

7. Ed Doree Letter to Ida Doree, August 25, 1922, E. F. Doree Collection, Box 2, File 4.

8. "I.W.W. Convicts Write to Harding," *New York Times*, September 2, 1922, 5.

9. Rosen, *A Wobbly Life*, 219.

Chapter 28. All Rise

1. Both the commutation and the telegram are in Box 2, File 8, E. F. Doree Collection (Accession No. 1658), Walter P. Reuther Library, Wayne State University. See also "Harding Pardons Doree," *New York Times*, September 9, 1922, 11.

2. As to Seneca, for his classic case for clemency, intended to persuade Nero, see Lucius Annaeus Seneca, *De Clementia*, in Susanna Braund, trans., *Seneca, De Clementia* (Oxford: Oxford University Press, 2009), 94–152. For another classic oration on the virtue of clemency, intended to influence an earlier authoritarian, consider Cicero's speech in the senate after Caesar unexpectedly pardoned Marcus Claudius Marcellus, a republican and participant in Pompey's challenge to Caesar's rule. Marcus Tullius Cicero, *Pro Marcello*, in D. H. Berry, trans., *Cicero's Political Speeches* (Oxford: Oxford University Press, 2006), 204–21. Both Braund and Berry provide important commentary and annotations. Just as Seneca wrote for Nero, so Cicero spoke in Caesar's presence. Both men had reason to be cautious and deferential in choosing their words, but still their defenses of clemency are powerful. For a similarly thoughtful and moving contemplation on clemency, see also Portia's soliloquy on sovereign mercy in William Shakespeare, *The Merchant of Venice*, Act IV, Scene 1.

3. See *Black's Law Dictionary* (9th ed.) entries for pardon, amnesty, commutation, and reprieve; see also P. S. Ruckman Jr., "Executive Clemency in the United States: Origins, Development and Analysis (1900–1993)," *Presidential Studies Quarterly* 27, no. 2 (Spring 1997): 251, 261n25. For the president of the United States, the "Power to grant Reprieves and Pardons for Offenses against the United States, except in Cases of Impeachment," is found in the U.S. Constitution, Art. II, § 2, cl. 1.

4. As to the drop in state executive clemency, see, e.g., Hugo Adam Bedau, *The Decline*

of Executive Clemency in Capital Cases, 18 N.Y.U. REVIEW OF LAW & SOCIAL CHANGE 255 (1990–91); Jefferson E. Holcomb, "Executive Clemency in Ohio: A Historical Assessment," *Ohio Corrections Research Compendium* 2 (2004): 225–35. As to the Iran-Contra pardons, see "Bush Pardons 6 in Iran Affair, Aborting a Weinberger Trial; Prosecutor Assails 'Cover-Up,'" *New York Times*, December 25, 1992, 1. As to Clinton eleventh-hour pardons on January 20, 2001, see "Influential Backers Helped Commodities Trader Win Pardon," *New York Times*, January 24, 2001. Although a furlough is the least liberating of the typical forms of clemency, note that Vice President George H. W. Bush used Willie Horton's crimes while out of prison on a short furlough to devastating effect against Governor Michael Dukakis in a television advertisement during the weeks before the 1988 presidential election. The success of that advertisement may have been another contributing factor in the decline of clemency, as governors and presidential aspirants again possibly drew a lesson from it that the public disliked any form of clemency.

5. As to the history of former governors rising to the White House, see Dean A. Strang, *Humility in Criminal Justice: What It Might Invite Us to Reconsider*, 100 MARQUETTE LAW REVIEW 1433, 1441–43 (2017).

6. "Harding Frees Debs and 23 Others Held for War Violations," *New York Times*, December 24, 1921, 1, 4. As to Wilson's "traitor" label for Debs, see Eugene V. Debs, *Walls & Bars: Prisons and Prison Life in the "Land of the Free"* (1927; repr., Chicago: Charles H. Kerr, 2000), 119. As to the invitation to the White House, on which many have reported, see "Debs at White House; Not Asked, He Says, to Alter His Views," *New York Times*, December 27, 1921, 1, 4.

7. American Civil Liberties Union, *The Truth about the I.W.W. Prisoners* (New York, April 1922), 3.

8. As to fifty under consideration without application, see "Harding Pardoned 32," *New York Times*, October 27, 1922, 8. As to Nef and Fletcher, see "President Pardons Six War Offenders," *New York Times*, October 17, 1922, 7. As to the twenty-two freed in June 1923, see "Harding Sets Free Many Prisoners," *New York Times*, June 21, 1923, 3.

9. As to the Cincinnati banker's pardon, see "Harding Pardons Dierks," *New York Times*, December 31, 1921, 4. As to Debs's commutation and Harry Daugherty's opposition, see "Daugherty Fought Freedom for Debs," *Des Moines Register*, January 1, 1922, 7. On Harding's death, see "President Is Dead," *Chicago Daily Tribune*, August 3, 1923, 1.

10. "Harding to Receive Amnesty Committee," *New York Times*, April 1, 1921, 15.

11. Speech to American Protective League, Minneapolis, January 31, 1920, pp. 7–9, Kenesaw Mountain Landis Papers, Chicago Historical Museum, Box 58, File 1; Speech to American Legion convention, June 8, 1923, pp. 9–11, Kenesaw Mountain Landis Papers, Chicago Historical Museum, Box 58, File 13.

12. As to Alice Longworth's comment on Coolidge, see "Footnotes on a Week's Headliners," *New York Times*, December 20, 1931, 138. Late in life, incidentally, she gave credit to her dentist for the comment. William Safire, "Essay: 'Weaned on a Pickle,'" *New York Times*, February 25, 1980, 21. As to commutation of the last thirty-one Wobblies' sentences, see "Coolidge Releases All War Offenders as Christmas Gift," *New York Times*, December 16, 1923, 1.

Chapter 29. A Justice Department Emerges

1. George F. Vanderveer Letter to J. P. Tumulty and Woodrow Wilson (February 11, 1918), National Archives II, Record Group 60, Straight Numerical Case No. 188032-164, Entry A1 112 B, Boxes 2219-20.

2. As familiar as they are, the scholarly literature on the so-called Palmer Raids is not terribly deep. But see Stanley Coben, *A. Mitchell Palmer: A Politician* (New York: Columbia University Press, 1963); Roberta Strauss Feuerlicht, *America's Reign of Terror: World War I, the Red Scare, and the Palmer Raids* (New York: Random House, 1971); Christopher M. Finan, *From the Palmer Raids to the Patriot Act: A History of the Fight for Free Speech in America* (New York: Beacon Press, 2007).

3. *Harrison v. United States*, 7 F.2d 259, 263 (2d Cir. 1925).

4. 54 Stat. 670, 76th Cong., 3d Sess. (June 28, 1940). As amended several times, what remains of the Smith Act's sedition and violent overthrow provisions is 18 U.S.C. § 2385.

5. "The Law: Case Against Spock et al.," *New York Times*, January 14, 1968, 184; "16 Indicted by U.S. in Chicago Tumult," *New York Times*, March 21, 1969, 1, 32 (the other eight defendants described were Chicago Police officers, indicted separately; the seven officers who later went to trial all were acquitted); "Chicago 7 Cleared of Plot; 5 Guilty on Second Count," *New York Times*, February 19, 1970, 1, 16.

6. "'Mastermind' and Driver Found Guilty in 1993 Plot to Blow Up Trade Center," *New York Times*, November 13, 1997, 1; "At Sentencing, Moussaoui Is Defiant," *New York Times*, May 4, 2006, 1; "Jurors Reject Death Penalty for Moussaoui," *Washington Post*, May 4, 2006, 1. (A jury in Alexandria, Virginia, refused the Justice Department's argument to sentence Moussaoui to death. Jurors imposed life instead.)

7. As to COINTELPRO, see, e.g., Tim Weiner, *Enemies: A History of the FBI* (New York: Random House, 2012); see also "Excerpts from Senate Intelligence Report," *New York Times*, April 29, 1976, 31-33 (detailing FBI domestic abuses). As to the efforts to drive King to suicide, see Beverly Gage, "I Have a [Redacted]," *New York Times Sunday Magazine*, November 16, 2014, MM15. As to the Rosenbergs, see, e.g., "Brother's Secret Grand Jury Testimony Supporting Ethel Rosenberg Is Released," *New York Times*, July 16, 2015, A20; Sam Roberts, *The Brother: The Untold Story of the Rosenberg Case* (New York: Simon & Schuster, 2014). As to the McVeigh case, see "McVeigh's Sister Tells Why She Aided U.S. Case against Him," *New York Times*, May 7, 1997.

8. See the discussion of other large trials in chapter 10. See also *Fujii v. United States*, 148 F.2d 298 (10th Cir. 1945).

Chapter 30. Endings

1. See, generally, Dorothy Gallagher, *All the Right Enemies: The Life and Murder of Carlo Tresca* (New Brunswick, NJ: Rutgers University Press, 1988); Nunzio Pernicone, *Carlo Tresca: Portrait of a Rebel* (Oakland, CA: AK Press, 2010).

2. As to impeachment proceedings, see Kenesaw Mountain Landis Papers, Series III, Box 48, Chicago History Museum. As to Landis's opposition to integrating major league

baseball, in what may be generous assessments, see "Landis and Baseball before Jackie Robinson: Does Baseball Deserve This Black Eye?," *Baseball Research Journal* 38, no. 1 (2009): 1–14. The fullest biography of Landis to date is David Pietrusza's *Judge and Jury: The Life and Times of Judge Kenesaw Mountain Landis* (Lanham, MD: Diamond Press, 2001).

3. "Raymond S. Fanning," *Bridgeport (Conn.) Post*, November 16, 1975, 25. As to Republican Party activity, see "Jaeckle Attacked as 'Purge' Leader," *Ithaca (NY) Journal*, May 20, 1940, 11.

4. "'Big Bill' Haywood Weds," *New York Times*, January 14, 1927, 4.

5. As to the Armenian orphanage claim, see "'Big Bill' Haywood, Weary and Starving, Pleads to Come Back, Even to Prison," *Brooklyn Daily Eagle*, January 22, 1925, 18. The *Daily Eagle* attributed the story to the Constantinople (now Istanbul) bureau of the *Chicago Tribune*. The *New York Times* earlier ran a shorter version of the same wire story. "Haywood Is Coming Home," *New York Times*, January 3, 1925, 6. As to his ostensible return to Chicago, see "Hunt Haywood in Chicago," *New York Times*, February 15, 1925, 22.

6. As to basic details of Haywood's death and Darrow's comments, see "'Big Bill' Haywood Dies in Self-Imposed Exile," *Baltimore Evening Sun*, May 18, 1928, 1, 2. Haywood's autobiography is *Bill Haywood's Book* (New York: International Publishers, 1929).

7. "'Bill' Haywood, I.W.W. Founder, Dies a Fugitive," *St. Louis Star & Times*, May 18, 1928, 1.

8. "Russians Stay Away from Bier of I.W.W. Chief," *Chicago Tribune*, May 20, 1928, 12; "Body of Haywood Lies in State," *The Tribune (Coshocton, Ohio)*, May 20, 1918, 3.

9. As to losing the 1918 Iowa governor's race, see *State of Iowa Official Register, 1919–1920*, at 363–65. As to serving as assistant attorney general, as counsel for the FTC, and then with the Interstate Commerce Commission, as well as for unsuccessful political campaigns—and on date of death—see *The Annals of Iowa* 28 (1946): 161–62; "Trade Commission Counsel," *Washington Post*, July 10, 1919, 6. As to the immediacy of his appointment as assistant attorney general, succeeding William Fitts, see "Porter Will Not Resign Candidacy," *Des Moines Evening Tribune* (August 21, 1918), 1; "Porter to Get a Bigger Job," *The Daily Times* (Davenport, Iowa), August 26, 1918, 1.

10. "Wilson Makes Two Appointments," *New York Times*, November 20, 1920, 12; "Would Limit Judge in Weirton Case," *New York Times*, May 5, 1934, 23, 27. As to Nebeker's 1935 salary, see "989 In New Deal Top $10,000 in Pay," *New York Times*, May 5, 1935, 5.

11. *United States v. Carolene Products Co.*, 304 U.S. 144, 152n4 (1938); *Skinner v. Oklahoma*, 316 U.S. 535 (1942); *Loving v. Virginia*, 388 U.S. 1 (1967). Harlan Fiske Stone served as an Associate Justice from 1925 to 1941, and as Chief Justice of the U.S. Supreme Court from 1941 to his death in 1946. As to the footnote's significance, see Lewis F. Powell Jr., *Carolene Products Revisited*, 82 Colum. L. Rev. 1087 (1982).

12. The date of death is from ancestry.com. I could not locate an obituary for Nebeker. The local U.S. district attorney at the time, Charles F. Clyne, actually died last among the lawyers, at age eighty-eight on December 15, 1965. The *Chicago Tribune* carried a death notice and brief obituary the next day.

13. As to doubts about Moore and his defense of Sacco and Vanzetti, see, e.g., Susan Tejada, *Renegade Defense Attorney for Sacco and Vanzetti*, 12 THE DIGEST: NATIONAL ITALIAN AMERICAN BAR ASSOCIATION LAW JOURNAL 47 (2013); Susan Tejada, *In Search of Sacco and Vanzetti: Double Lives, Troubled Times, and the Massachusetts Murder Case that Shook the World* (Boston: Northeastern University Press, 2012). As to possible drug addiction, among other sources, see John F. Neville, *Twentieth-Century Cause Célèbre: Sacco, Vanzetti, and the Press, 1920–1927* (Westport, CT: Praeger, 2004).

14. See Lowell S. Hawley & Ralph Bushnell Potts, *Counsel for the Damned* (Philadelphia: J. B. Lippincott, 1953), 269–71. See ibid., 277–83 (for Ellinor's escape, George's adultery in the hotel), 277–83 (Centralia), 292–94 (divorce), 294–98 (Kitty, the Lake Burien home, her suicide, Vanderveer's response), 303–6, 315–17 (cynicism, defiance, greed, risky investment schemes), 307 (remarriage, to Ethel Hoover). As to Nebeker's suspicion about Vanderveer, see, again, National Archives II, Record Group 60, Straight Numerical Case No. 188032-80, Entry A1 112 B, Boxes 2219–20.

15. See *Olmstead v. United States*, 277 U.S. 438 (1928); Richard F. Hamm, Olmstead v. United States*: The Constitutional Challenges of Prohibition Enforcement* (Federal Judicial Center, 2010); Hawley & Potts, *Counsel for the Damned*, 299–302.

16. On Vanderveer's death and the earlier rape case appeal and retrial, see Hawley & Potts, *Counsel for the Damned*, 318–20; "George F. Vanderveer, Labor Attorney, Dies," *Baltimore Sun*, October 23, 1942, 15.

17. The free-rider problem bears brief explanation. A core tenet of American labor law is that a union must represent equally all members of the bargaining unit for which it is the certified representative; it may not discriminate against nonmembers of the union who are in the bargaining unit. This is the duty of fair representation. See, e.g., *Steele v. Louisville & Nashville Railway Co.*, 323 U.S. 192 (1944); *Vaca v. Sipes*, 386 U.S. 171 (1967). So, while collectively all workers in the bargaining unit benefit, in theory, from the union's work on their behalf, individually each worker has an incentive to shift the burden of union dues to other workers: the worker gets the benefits whether she contributes to the union's coffers or not. That is the free-rider problem. It is why barring unions from requiring fair-share contributions from nonmembers, or eliminating dues deductions from paychecks so that the union has to expend time and funds to collect dues, increases the difficulty of effective collective action with large numbers of people who have comparatively low financial stakes as individuals.

18. Ellen Doree Rosen, *A Wobbly Life* (Detroit: Wayne State University Press, 2004), 222–27.

19. As to Bucky's death, see Rosen, *A Wobbly Life*, 222–23.

20. Ibid., 223, 225–26.

21. Ibid., 227–29.

22. Ibid., 230–31.

23. Ibid., 231.

Index

Page references in italics indicate an illustration.

Trautmann, William E., 22
Tresca, Carlo, 82, 90, *177*, 209, 250, 255–56
trials, long, 76
Trotter, Harry, 145, 288n6
24th Infantry (Camp Logan), 74

unions: vs. capital, 258; companies' anti-union activities, 7; free-rider problem in, 258, 305n17; government/military intervention in activities of, 7–8; political vs. economic action by, 10–11; segregation in, 10; wartime growth of, 15–16; women in, 10. *See also specific unions*
United States v. Eugene Victor Debs, 193, 294n1
United States v. Standard Oil Co. of Indiana, 107
University of Texas, 51, 272n3

vagrancy laws, 264n6
Valdinoci, Carlo, 189
Vanderveer, David, 100, 282n5
Vanderveer, Elinor ("Gus"; *née* Hausman), 101–3, 134–35, 256
Vanderveer, Ethel (*née* Hoover), 256
Vanderveer, George Francis ("Van"), 92; affair with Kitty Beck, 134, 256; on bail on appeal, 199, 201; biography of, 282n5, 282n12, 305n14; childhood and family background of, 100, 282n5; commitment to the IWW, 216, 256; as controversial, 98–99; death of, 257; as a defense lawyer, 102–3; drinking by, 101, 103, 135, 256–57; education of, 100–101; finances of, 102, 134–35, 256, 282n12; guns carried by, 81, 98, 102; and the IWW, 102–3 (*see also under* IWW trial—VANDERVEER); at jury selection in the trial, 96; on the Justice Department, 91, 243; letter to the president about the trial, 90–91; marriage

to Elinor, 101–3, 134–35, 256; marriage to Ethel, 256; Nebeker on, 111; as a prosecutor, 101–2; rape case defense by, 257; on regrets, 100–101; stature of, 98, 257. *See also under* Seventh Circuit's review of IWW trial
Vanderveer, Mary Atwood (*née* Francis), 100, 282n5
Vanzetti, Bartolomeo, 189, 255–56
vicarious liability, 158, 160
La Vida (Lewis), 266n13
Vietnam War, 246
Villa, Pancho, 48

wages: vs. scrip, 29; theft of, 30, 266n5; wage slaves, 10, 263n2
Walker, Edwin, 268n11
Wall Street bombing (1920), 189
Walsh, Frank P., 25, 135
Walsh, John J., 146, 228–29
War Department, 8, 48–49
Warren, Charles, 52–54, 272n7; *The Supreme Court in United States History*, 52
Washington, George, 34
Weeks v. United States, 222–24, 244, 273n7
Weinberger, Caspar, 239–40
Wells Fargo, 50, 147
We Shall Be All (Dubofsky), xvii
Westerlund, Frank, 229
Western Federation of Miners. *See* WFM
Western Union, 53
WFM (Western Federation of Miners), 3, 10–11, 13, 21–23, 99
Wheeler, Burton K., 6
Wheeler, William, 188
Whiteside, George W., 82–83
Whitney, Charlotte, 225
Wilson, William B., 43, 50–51, 54, 206
Wilson, Woodrow: on amnesty for the IWW prisoners, 229; on Debs, 240; election of, 69; on internment of IWW members, 47, 270n10; IWW investigation